GLENCOE
INTRODUCTION TO
Desktop Publishing
With Digital Graphics

Real World Projects and Applications

- Microsoft® Word
- Microsoft® Publisher
- Adobe® Illustrator®
- Adobe® Photoshop®

Mc Graw Hill **Glencoe**

New York, New York   Columbus, Ohio   Chicago, Illinois   Woodland Hills, California

 **Glencoe**

The *McGraw·Hill* Companies

Send all inquiries to:
Glencoe/McGraw-Hill
21600 Oxnard Street, Suite 500
Woodland Hills, CA 91367

ISBN: 978-0-07-876045-7 (Teacher Resource Manual)
MHID: 0-07-876045-3 (Teacher Resource Manual)

ISBN: 978-0-07-872913-3 (Student Edition)
MHID: 0-07-872913-0 (Student Edition)

1 2 3 4 5 6 7 8 9   079   12 11 10 09 08 07

TABLE OF CONTENTS

PART 1: TEACHER RESOURCES

TABLE OF CONTENTS

TABLE OF CONTENTS

PART 3: REPRODUCIBLE WORKSHEETS

TABLE OF CONTENTS

Part 4: PowerPoint® PRESENTATIONS, *ExamView® Assessment Suite*, AND TechSIM™ INTERACTIVE TUTORIALS

PART 5: STANDARDS AND CORRELATIONS

PART

Teacher Resources

THE IMPORTANCE OF A DESKTOP PUBLISHING COURSE

The ability to use technology effectively, productively, and ethically has become an essential skill in almost every aspect of society, whether at home, at school, at work, or at play. *Introduction to Desktop Publishing With Digital Graphics* is a valuable teaching tool for helping students learn about fundamental desktop publishing, using Microsoft® Word®, Microsoft Publisher®, Adobe® Photoshop®, and Adobe Illustrator®. The course will also teach students important design concepts and ethical issues associated with desktop publishing.

COURSE PHILOSOPHY™

Introduction to Desktop Publishing With Digital Graphics addresses the real-world needs of students and teachers. The approach is student-centered with reliance upon teacher guidance and facilitation.

Standards-Based Learning The planning and structure of the course is designed to meet state and national standards while exploring a range of desktop publishing software applications.

Project-Based Learning The course promotes a project-based learning environment so that students learn concepts and practice skills in a real-world context.

Guided Step-by-Step Projects The text is written and designed to be used with the whole class and with individual students.

◆ Projects can be completed as a whole class (with the teacher guiding students through the steps). You may wish to walk students through project steps before they complete them on their own.

◆ Students can complete projects independently as self-guided exercises.

◆ Collaborative projects also provide students with the real-world experience of working with others.

Assessment and Evaluation The text includes traditional assessment strategies and also relies on evaluation techniques through competency-based projects.

◆ Assessments are provided at the end of every Workshop Foundations and Workshop Toolbox.

◆ Complete reviews and assessments are also provided at the end of every chapter and unit.

Reteaching and Enrichment Activities A variety of additional worksheets and activities are provided on the book Online Learning Center and in this Teacher Resource Manual. These are designed to extend learning opportunities for students who may need additional review and for those students who need enrichment.

COURSE OBJECTIVES

Introduction to Desktop Publishing With Digital Graphics sets the following objectives for students:

Key Concepts

◆ Understand the technology used for desktop publishing.

◆ Identify key steps of the design process.

◆ Evaluate the importance of client, audience, budget, and deadlines on design.

◆ Analyze effective design, particularly the PARC principles (**P**roximity, **A**lignment, **R**epetition, **C**ontrast), in print and Web publications.

◆ Determine which software to use for different elements of design.

◆ Compare vector and raster images.

◆ Evaluate the composition of different types of graphics.

◆ Identify design elements of desktop-published documents such as flyers, brochures, newsletters, booklets, business cards, posters, and banners.

◆ Evaluate resolution in images published in print and online.

◆ Compare file formats for different types of graphics.

◆ Discuss ethical issues associated with design.

◆ Identify the skills and tools necessary to work as a team.

Application Skills

◆ Identify the software tools used to create effective layout, text, and graphics.

◆ Apply effective design principles, including PARC.

◆ Select appropriate fonts and font styles for print and Web documents.

◆ Lay out text and graphics in documents using layout guides and grids.

◆ Create a variety of documents, including flyers, multi-fold brochures and cards, newsletters, booklets, business cards, stationery, posters, and banners.

◆ Choose appropriate software for desktop publishing projects.

◆ Create vector and raster images.

◆ Insert, edit, and resize graphics in documents.

◆ Identify tools and effects used to enhance and manipulate graphic images.

◆ Customize templates.

◆ Save documents in compatible formats for different applications.

◆ Design and tile print oversized publications.

◆ Create Web pages and add hyperlinks.

◆ Apply tools, like Microsoft Excel and PowerPoint, for team projects.

SCANS COMPETENCIES

In 1990 the Secretary of Labor appointed the Secretary's Commission on Achieving Necessary Skills (SCANS). It identified the competencies and skills necessary to achieve success in the workplace. As an educator, your task is to help your students connect school with job success. *Introduction to Desktop Publishing With Digital Graphics* echoes the message SCANS gave to educators.

SCANS identifies **Foundation Skills** essential for job success:

1. **Basic Skills** Reading, writing, arithmetic, mathematics, and listening and speaking skills.

2. **Thinking Skills** Creative thinking, critical thinking, and problem-solving skills.

3. **Personal Qualities** Responsibility, self-esteem, sociability, self-management, integrity, and honesty.

SCANS also identifies important **Workplace Skills:**

4. **Interpersonal Skills** The ability to work on teams, teach others, serve customers, exercise leadership, negotiate, and work with cultural diversity.

5. **Information** The ability to acquire, evaluate, organize, maintain, interpret, communicate, and use computers to process information.

6. **Systems** The ability to understand, monitor, correct, improve, and design systems.

7. **Resources** The ability to manage time, money, materials, facilities, and human resources.

8. **Technology** The ability to select, apply, maintain, and troubleshoot technology.

Connect Skills, School, and Careers

SCANS skills and competencies apply to various jobs in many different occupations. Becoming productive members of the work force demands that students acquire the appropriate skills and knowledge to compete in a technologically evolving economy.

Successful students are motivated students who know how to connect their school experiences with success in their careers. They realize that what they learn in school correlates directly with finding, keeping, and succeeding in their chosen career. Learning how to succeed in school will serve as a model for working effectively within a business organization. Connecting education and skills development to career pursuits helps students become employable decision-makers and problem-solvers.

21st CENTURY SKILLS

The SCANS workplace skills are as essential in the 21st century as they were in the 20th century. However, two major changes have occurred since 1991 when the U.S. Department of Labor released its report: a dramatic increase in the importance of computer technology and the passage of the No Child Left Behind Act (NCLB).

These two events prompted educational coalitions to revisit the concept of workplace skills. The most prominent of these the Partnership for 21st Century Skills, has created a framework integrating technology and the core academic subjects emphasized by the No Child Left Behind Act. These measures are meant to help students use the knowledge they have learned in school and apply it to all facets of their lives, including education, work, and community. Focusing on these skills, the Partnership for 21st Century Skills developed a framework integrating technology and core academic subjects.

Learning Skills	
Information and Communication Skills	**Information and Media Literacy Skills** Analyzing, accessing, managing, integrating, evaluating, and creating information in a variety of forms and media. Understanding the role of media in society **Communication Skills** Understanding, managing, and creating effective oral, written, and multimedia communication in a variety of forms and contexts
Thinking and Problem-Solving Skills	**Critical Thinking and Systems Thinking** Exercising sound reasoning in understanding and making complex choices; understanding the interconnections among systems **Problem Identification, Formulation, and Solution** Ability to frame, analyze, and solve problems **Creativity and Intellectual Curiosity** Developing, implementing, and communicating new ideas to others; staying open and responsive to new and diverse perspectives
Interpersonal and Self-Directional Skills	**Interpersonal and Collaborative Skills** Demonstrating teamwork and leadership; adapting to varied roles and responsibilities; working productively with others; exercising empathy; respecting diverse perspectives **Self-Direction** Monitoring one's own understanding and learning needs, locating appropriate resources, transferring learning from one domain to another **Accountability and Adaptability** Exercising personal responsibility and flexibility in personal, workplace, and community contexts; setting and meeting high standards and goals for oneself and others; tolerating ambiguity **Social Responsibility** Acting responsibly with the interests of the larger community in mind; demonstrating ethical behavior in personal, workplace, and community contexts

SOURCE: Partnership for 21st Century Skills

21st Century Skills Correlations

Easy-to-use 21st century skills correlations are provided for your convenience in the following locations:

◆ Each Unit Planning Guide in Part 2 of this manual includes at-a-glance 21st century skills correlations. Use the guide to quickly locate activities and projects that meet specific SCANS in the unit you are teaching.

◆ Complete 21st century skills correlations are also provided in Part 5 of this manual. **See pages 411–423 to find all the activities and projects throughout the student textbook that relate to 21st century skills.**

ISTE AND TECHNOLOGY STANDARDS

To live, learn, and work successfully in an increasingly complex and information-rich society, students must be able to use technology effectively. To provide guidelines for effective technology skills, the International Society for Technology in Education (ISTE) has developed National Education Technology Standards for Students (NETS·S).

National Educational Technology Standards for Students (NETS·S)

The ISTE National Educational Technology Standards for Students (NETS·S) describe what students should know about and be able to do with technology.

The technology foundation standards for students are divided into six broad categories. Standards within each category are to be introduced, reinforced, and mastered by students. These categories provide a framework for linking performance indicators to the standards.

Activities in the book are specifically designed to meet the standards within each category. Teachers can use these standards as guidelines for planning technology-based activities in which students can achieve success in learning, communication, and life skills.

1. **Basic operations and concepts**
   ◆ Students demonstrate a sound understanding of the nature and operation of technology systems.
   ◆ Students are proficient in the use of technology.

2. **Social, ethical, and human issues**
   ◆ Students understand the ethical, cultural, and societal issues related to technology.
   ◆ Students practice responsible use of technology systems, information, and software.

◆ Students develop positive attitudes toward technology uses that support lifelong learning, collaboration, personal pursuits, and productivity.

3. Technology productivity tools

◆ Students use technology tools to enhance learning, increase productivity, and promote creativity.

◆ Students use productivity tools to collaborate in constructing technology-enhanced models, prepare publications, and produce other creative works.

4. Technology communications tools

◆ Students use telecommunications to collaborate, publish, and interact with peers, experts, and other audiences.

◆ Students use a variety of media and formats to communicate information and ideas effectively to multiple audiences.

5. Technology research tools

◆ Students use technology to locate, evaluate, and collect information from a variety of sources.

◆ Students use technology tools to process data and report results.

◆ Students evaluate and select new information resources and technological innovations based on the appropriateness of specific tasks.

6. Technology problem-solving and decision-making tools

◆ Students use technology resources for solving problems and making informed decisions.

◆ Students employ technology in the development of strategies for solving problems in the real world.

NETS·S Performance Indicators for Technology-Literate Students

In this text, all students have opportunities to demonstrate the following performance indicators for technological literacy. Each performance indicator refers to the standards category or categories (listed on pages 6–7) to which the performance is linked.

Performance Indicators	NETS·S Standards
1. Identify capabilities and limitations of contemporary and emerging technology resources and assess the potential of these systems and services to address personal, lifelong learning, and workplace needs.	(2) Social, ethical, and human issues
2. Make informed choices among technology systems, resources, and services.	(1) Basic operations and concepts (2) Social, ethical, and human issues
3. Analyze advantages and disadvantages of widespread use and reliance on technology in the workplace and in society as a whole.	(2) Social, ethical, and human issues
4. Demonstrate and advocate for legal and ethical behaviors among peers, family, and community regarding the use of technology and information.	(2) Social, ethical, and human issues
5. Use technology tools and resources for managing and communicating personal/professional information (e.g., finances, schedules, addresses, purchases, correspondence).	(3) Technology productivity tools (4) Technology communications tools
6. Evaluate technology-based options, including distance and distributed education, for lifelong learning.	(5) Technology research tools

Performance Indicators	NETS-S Standards
7. Routinely and efficiently use online information resources to meet needs for collaboration, research, publications, communications, and productivity.	(4) Technology communications tools (5) Technology research tools (6) Technology problem-solving and decision-making tools
8. Select and apply technology tools for research, information analysis, problem-solving, and decision-making in content learning.	(4) Technology communications tools (5) Technology research tools
9. Investigate and apply expert systems, intelligent agents, and simulations in real-world situations.	(3) Technology productivity tools (5) Technology research tools (6) Technology problem-solving and decision-making tools
10. Collaborate with peers, experts, and others to contribute to content-related knowledge base by using technology to compile, synthesize, produce, and disseminate information, models, and other creative works.	(4) Technology communications tools (5) Technology research tools (6) Technology problem-solving and decision-making tools

Reprinted with permission from *National Educational Technology Standards for Students: Connecting Curriculum and Technology*, © 2000, ISTE® (International Society for Technology in Education). iste@iste.org. All rights reserved.

NETS·S Correlations

The student textbook has been written with the NETS·S in mind. Activities and projects are designed to follow the NETS foundation standards and performance indicators.

Easy-to-use NETS·S correlations are provided for your convenience in the following locations:

◆ Every Unit Planning Guide in Part 2 of this manual includes at-a-glance NETS·S correlations. Use the guide to quickly locate activities and projects that meet specific NETS·S in the unit you are teaching.

◆ Complete NETS·S Correlations are also provided in Part 5 of this manual. **See pages 394–404 to find all the activities and projects throughout the student textbook that relate to NETS·S.**

NETS·T Educational Technology Performance Profiles for Teachers

Building on the NETS for Students, the NETS for Teachers (NETS·T) define the fundamental concepts, knowledge, skills, and attitudes for applying technology in educational settings. The student textbook and this Teacher Resource Manual are written with these NETS for Teachers in mind. The six standards areas with performance indicators listed below are designed by ISTE to provide guidelines for teachers in the classroom.

1. Technology operations and concepts

◆ Teachers demonstrate introductory knowledge, skills, and understanding of concepts related to technology.

◆ Teachers demonstrate continual growth in technology knowledge and skills to stay abreast of current and emerging technologies.

2. Planning and designing learning environments and experiences

◆ Teachers design developmentally appropriate learning opportunities that apply technology-enhanced instructional strategies to support the diverse needs of learners.

◆ Teachers apply current research on teaching and learning with technology when planning learning environments and experiences.

◆ Teachers identify and locate technology resources and evaluate them for accuracy and suitability.

◆ Teachers plan for the management of technology resources within the context of learning activities.

◆ Teachers plan strategies to manage student learning in a technology-enhanced environment.

3. Teaching, learning, and the curriculum

◆ Teachers facilitate technology-enhanced experiences that address content standards and student technology standards.

◆ Teachers use technology to support learner-centered strategies that address the diverse needs of students.

◆ Teachers apply technology to develop students' higher order skills and creativity.

◆ Teachers manage student learning activities in a technology-enhanced environment.

4. **Assessment and evaluation**
   - ◆ Teachers apply technology in assessing student learning of subject matter using a variety of assessment techniques.
   - ◆ Teachers use technology resources to collect and analyze data, interpret results, and communicate findings to improve instructional practice and maximize student learning.
   - ◆ Teachers apply multiple methods of evaluation to determine students' appropriate use of technology resources for learning, communication, and productivity.

5. **Productivity and professional practice**
   - ◆ Teachers use technology resources to engage in ongoing professional development and lifelong learning.
   - ◆ Teachers continually evaluate and reflect on professional practice to make informed decisions regarding the use of technology in support of student learning.
   - ◆ Teachers apply technology to increase productivity.
   - ◆ Teachers use technology to communicate and collaborate with peers, parents, and the larger community in order to nurture student learning.

6. **Social, ethical, legal, and human issues**
   - ◆ Teachers model and teach legal and ethical practice related to technology use.
   - ◆ Teachers apply technology resources to enable and empower learners with diverse backgrounds, characteristics, and abilities.
   - ◆ Teachers identify and use technology resources that affirm diversity.
   - ◆ Teachers promote safe and healthy use of technology resources.
   - ◆ Teachers facilitate equitable access to technology resources for all students.

STUDENT TEXTBOOK

Introduction to Desktop Publishing With Digital Graphics is organized to help students learn fundamental desktop publishing concepts by first reading the Workshop Foundations and Toolbox, then applying this knowledge as they learn application skills in the chapter projects. The following textbook features have been designed to help students master desktop concepts and skills:

◆ **Unit Contents** give studetns an at-a-glance guide to the chapter topics covered in the unit.

◆ **Skills You Will Learn,** on the first page of a chapter, list the topics covered in each project within the chapter.

◆ **Design Process** tables, on the first page of the chapter, describe design elements for different types of documents at each stage of the design process.

◆ **Before You Read** features provide reading strategies for students.

◆ **Workshop Foundations** are at the beginning of each chapter to introduce students to key desktop publishing concepts.

◆ **Workshop Toolbox** is the companion feature to the Foundations and introduces tools that students will be using in the chapter projects.

◆ **Reading Checks** at the end of each Workshop article review the main ideas.

◆ **Eye on Ethics** features introduce important information about copyright concerns and other ethical issues affecting desktop publishing.

◆ **Sidebar** features present interesting facts and tips for students.

◆ **Go Online Preview** reminds students in the first project to visit **www.glencoe.com** so that they can find PowerPoint presentations and rubrics to help them preview and create their projects.

◆ **Spotlight on Skills** introduce the step-by-step projects, providing the basic concepts they will need, as well as key terms, objectives, and applications to other core subjects (Academic Focus).

◆ **Step-by-Steps** are illustrated, easy-to-follow instructions that allow students to practice their application skills. As students become more comfortable with software skills, the steps become less detailed and more self-guided.

◆ **Skills Studio** projects review skills that students have learned throughout the chapter, while sometimes introducing more advanced skills.

◆ **Instant Message** features provide software and other tips for students.

◆ **Review and Revise** features are provided at the completion of a publication so that students can check their work.

◆ **In the Workplace** shows students the different professions that use desktop publishing skills.

◆ **Reading Check and Critical Thinking** questions assess students' comprehension of the key terms and main ideas that they learned in the chapter.

◆ **Independent Practice Projects** let students work on their own or in groups to demonstrate their application skills. Students can go online to find rubrics for each project.

◆ **Go Online Activities** extend learning by directing students to more projects at **www.glencoe.com**.

◆ **Projects Across the Curriculum** integrate technology skills with a cross-curricular focus.

◆ **Technology Handbook** articles at the end of the textbook highlight important technology concepts in an easy-to-reference format.

◆ **Appendices** provide information on color theory and design, professional printing, and proofreaders' marks.

◆ **Glossary** terms provide definitions and pages where the words can be found in context.

TEACHER RESOURCE MANUAL

This Teacher Resource Manual (TRM) is designed to facilitate effective teaching. It is organized to help plan your lessons and curriculum and to give suggestions for presenting and teaching material. The TRM also suggests strategies for working with difficult students, special needs students, students who may need extra help, and those who may need additional enrichment. The TRM is divided into the following five parts:

◆ **Part 1: Teacher Resources** includes course planning resources and professional development tools for successful teaching and improved student learning. Pacing charts, course outlines, and reference charts are provided to help teachers plan, organize, and customize their course.

◆ **Part 2: Unit Lesson Plans and Answer Keys** are provided to help plan and prepare lessons, focus student attention, teach material, assess comprehension, and close each lesson. The following information is provided for each unit:

   ◆ Unit planning guides, including Internet and DVD resources

   ◆ NETS·S and 21st Century Skills correlations to unit content and activities

   ◆ Teaching strategies and troubleshooting tips

   ◆ Answers to all unit activities and projects

◆ **Part 3: Reproducibles and Visual Aids** includes **worksheets** for each unit along with **answer keys,** and blackline masters of customizable **graphic organizers**. Complete descriptions and instructions for use are also provided.

◆ **Part 4: Instructions for PowerPoint® Presentations, *ExamView*®** *Assessment Suite Software,* **and TechSIM™ Interactive Tutorials** *ExamView* software lets teachers easily print ready-made tests for each textbook unit or create their own tests. Instructions are given for integrating the **Unit PowerPoint Presentations** into the classroom curriculum. Suggestions are also provided for using the **TechSIM Interactive Tutorials** with the textbook.

◆ **Part 5: Correlations to Standards** are provided in one convenient place so teachers can easily note the location for each standard covered in the textbook, as well as on the DVD Web site. Correlations are provided for **NETS·S** and **21st Century Skills** standards.

INCLUSION IN THE COMPUTER TECHNOLOGY CLASSROOM BOOKLET

Practical information on how to help special needs students succeed in the computer applications classroom is presented in this booklet for the teacher. Case studies give a real-life look at how special needs students think and feel.

TEACHER RESOURCE DVD

A Teacher Resource DVD is also available that is packed with valuable tools for teachers and students:

◆ **PowerPoint Presentations** are provided for each unit in the textbook. Use these to introduce the units or as unit reviews. Students can also use the presentations on their own for independent study.

◆ **Student Data Files** allow students to quickly complete activities and projects. Whenever you see the Student Data File icon, be sure to locate the correct files to complete the activity.

◆ **Solution Files** are provided for Exercises and Guided Practice projects in the textbook. Before students begin the exercise, you may wish to display the corresponding solution file on a projection screen as a model for student work. If a student did not complete an exercise, then the solution file for that activity may be used as a starting point for the next activity.

◆ **Rubrics** for each Independent Practice and Unit Review Project are provided to help students create and evaluate their own work. Teachers can then add their own evaluation.

◆ **Worksheets** are provided as additional activities to accompany each Tech Talk and Project in the textbook. Complete answer keys are included.

◆ **Graphic Organizers** are provided to help students organize and comprehend material in the text. Simply reproduce the organizers you wish students to complete. Suggestions for use are provided.

ExamView® Assessment Suite CD

The optional *ExamView Assessment Suite* CD contains software and test-banks that allow teachers to print out ready-made tests for each unit, complete with answer keys. Each test includes the following types of questions: true/false, multiple choice, fill in the blank, and short answer. You can edit the provided tests or create your own tests on either Macintosh or Windows platforms.

TechSIM™ Interactive Tutorials CD

Interactive Tutorials are also available on a separate CD to help students master the selected topics listed below. The simulations let students follow guided step-by-steps to complete exercises similar to those in the student textbook, but through an interactive, hands-on interface.

◆ **TechSIM A: File Management**
◆ **TechSIM B: E-mail**
◆ **TechSIM C: System Settings and the Control Panel**

Simulations may be particularly useful if your lab uses computers with different operating systems and software, or if network settings prevent students from using Microsoft Outlook or from changing system settings.

ONLINE LEARNING CENTER WEB SITE

An accompanying Web site provides additional projects, assessments, and resources. Note that all the materials provided on the Teacher Resource DVD are also available on the Web site for easy student and teacher access.

> Visit the *Introduction to Desktop Publishing With Digital Graphics* Web site
> **www.glencoe.com**
> **Bookmark this site for easy reference!**

Student Online Learning Center Students can access the following materials:

◆ **PowerPoint Presentations** review the main ideas and skills for every textbook chapter, and provide visual examples of the publications that will be created in each project.

◆ **E-Review Self-Check Quizzes** assess students' understanding of all the main ideas and skills taught in each chapter.

◆ **Student Data Files** are available for easy access in or out of the classroom.

◆ **Rubrics** act as checklists that help students create and evaluate each project in the textbook, including assessment projects.

◆ **Reading Check and Critical Thinking Activities** allow students to complete chapter assessments online and e-mail their answers to their teachers.

◆ **Enrichment Activities** allow students to expand their knowledge of topics presented in the student textbook, and provide additional projects to reinforce students' desktop publishing skills.

◆ **Worksheets** for each chapter can be used to review material.

◆ **TechSIM™ Interactive Tutorials** provide hands-on simulations of skills that students might not have access to in the classroom such as managing files, adjusting system settings, using the Control Panel, and using e-mail.

◆ **Study-to-Go™** allows students to download practice quizzes and flash cards onto a Personal Digital Assistant (PDA).

◆ **Graphic Organizers** help students with reading and study skills, and they can also be used for brainstorming and organizing ideas for projects.

◆ **Web Links** provide other desktop-publishing resources on the Internet that students can access safely and easily.

Teacher Online Learning Center This portion of the site is password protected so that only teachers have access. Visit the Teacher Online Learning Center for username and password information (registration is *not* required).

◆ **Solution Files** are working files provided to teachers to use as models for each completed project in the textbook.

◆ **Assessment Answer Keys** are provided for Reading Checks and Critical Thinking Activities.

◆ **Key Terms Online** includes a list of key terms and an additional activity for each Workshop and project in the textbook.

◆ **Worksheet Answer Keys** have the answers for worksheets provided for each chapter of the textbook.

◆ **Teacher Planning Materials** include suggested course outlines, pacing charts, and lists of all data and solution files.

◆ **National Standards** correlate NETS·S and 21st Century Skills to pages in the textbook.

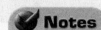

TEACHING WITH THE STUDENT TEXTBOOK

It has been shown that students who use their textbooks effectively learn the content more easily and more quickly than students who do not understand the author's design in writing the book. The student textbook has been specifically designed with a variety of features that can help students increase comprehension and recall information.

1. Use the following pages to acquaint yourself with the textbook features.

2. When you give students their textbooks, take a few minutes to introduce them to the textbook features so they can get the most out of their reading.

3. Have them complete the fun Scavenger Hunt activity at the front of their textbooks (on pages xvii–xix) to familiarize them with their textbook.

How to Use the Chapter Opener

The student textbook is divided into five units and ten chapters. The chapter opener prepares students to read the chapter and complete the projects.

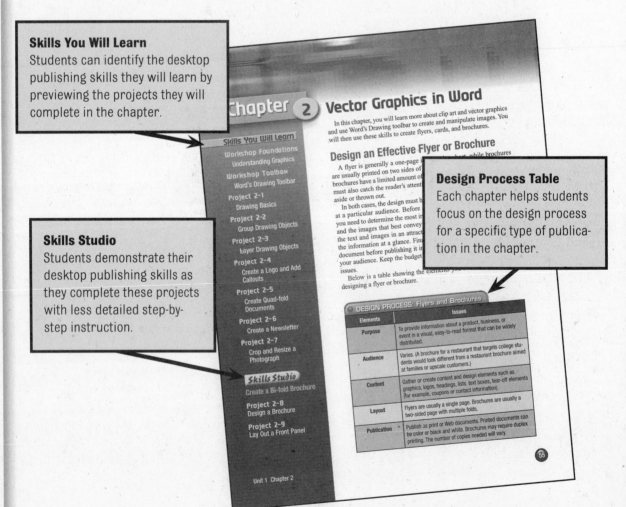

Skills You Will Learn
Students can identify the desktop publishing skills they will learn by previewing the projects they will complete in the chapter.

Skills Studio
Students demonstrate their desktop publishing skills as they complete these projects with less detailed step-by-step instruction.

Design Process Table
Each chapter helps students focus on the design process for a specific type of publication in the chapter.

How to Use the Workshop Foundations and Workshop Toolbox Articles

Every unit opens with two workshop articles: *Foundations* and *Toolbox*. These introduce students to new publishing and technology concepts. You may have students read all the articles before they begin the chapter projects, or assign a few pages of reading as students complete the projects. If your students share a limited number of computers, you may have some students read the articles while others use the computers to work on the projects.

You Will Learn To
Previewing the objectives helps students set a purpose for reading and make predictions as they read.

Key Terms
New vocabulary is highlighted. Students should look for the definition of the word nearby in the text.

Before You Read
The reading strategies outlined in this feature can help students increase comprehension in this course and in all subject areas.

Eye on Ethics
Ethical topics such as copyright laws are emphasized and reinforced.

Figures and Tables
Concepts are presented visually for quick comprehension and understanding.

Reading Check Assessment
Check students' understanding of the terms and topics covered in the Workshop articles.

How to Use the Projects

Each unit contains real-world projects to help students learn new application skills and reinforce desktop publishing topics.

Spotlight on Skills
Review and discuss the project introduction as a class to help student focus on the purpose of the project and why it matters.

Illustrations
Each illustration has been carefully selected to help students visualize chapter content more clearly.

Academic Focus Each project focuses on the integration of important academic requirements with the desktop publishing skill.

Sidebar
Ideas in the feature provide useful tips and information that enhance student learning and interest in desktop publishing.

In This Project
The students know exactly what type of publication they will design through this brief introduction to the project.

Project 2-4

Create a Logo and Add Callouts

A **logo** is a combination of text and graphics used to identify a business or product. An effective logo is very important to an organization because it must convey the company's message and must be instantly recognizable to customers.

Logos are almost always vector graphics. By using vector graphics, the same logo can be used whether the design is on a business card or a billboard. Vector graphics are **scalable**, retaining smooth and crisp images at any size. Vector graphics are typically created using illustration software, such as Adobe Illustrator (see Chapter 7), but simple ones can be created in Word.

Combine Text and Graphics in Logos

While logos tend to incorporate graphics, many logos simply use one or more fonts. Even in logos, you should apply the typeface rules you learned in Chapter 1:

- Use only typefaces from separate families.
- Do not use more than two fonts.
- Use fonts with dramatically different characteristics.

SewRight alterations and design

Also, be aware of the higher production costs when you use many colors in your logo. If your budget is limited, you need to limit the number of colors in the logo.

CapCo

Logos often have some sort of graphic element to go along with the font. Perhaps an image can be substituted for a letter, as in the CapCo logo. Sometimes the graphic element goes alongside the word, as in the Midnight Writer logo.

Midnight Writer
WRITE WHEN YOU NEED IT!

▶ In this project, you will create a logo for the pizza flyer you started in Project 2-3. You will also add callouts and a text box to the flyer. A **leader** is a type of text box that acts as a label for a graphic. A **callout** (a line or series of dots connecting information) points from the text box to a specific part of an image.

Spotlight on Skills
- Format WordArt
- Combine text and graphics
- Add callouts
- Add a background color

Key Terms
- logo
- scalable
- callout
- leader

Academic Focus
Language Arts
Communicate with clear visual messages

Sidebar

Logo Design
Organizations want people to instantly recognize their logos, whether it is an apple on an MP3 player or a red cross on an ambulance. A good logo has that power. Original logo design can be costly when designed by a graphic artist.

Analyze Describe two logos that you think are effective. Explain why.

Chapter 2 Project 2-4 Create a Logo and Add Callouts

Data Files
When you see this icon, locate the correct student data files to complete the project (see the lesson planning guides in this manual).

Step-by-Step Instructions
Easy-to-follow, illustrated instructions guide students through new application skills in each project.

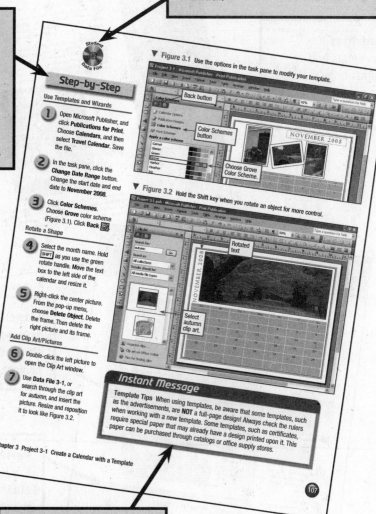

Instant Message
Software tips, keyboard shortcuts, and other important and useful information help keep students motivated.

Reinforce Skills
The Skills Studio projects reinforce desktop publishing skills and also present more advanced skills to allow students to showcase their design talents.

Go Online Activities
Enrichment projects and additional hands-on activities give students opportunities to enhance their design skills.

Large Project Illustrations
Accurate illustrations show students how their finished project might look.

Review and Revise
Students can easily evaluate their publications using the checklist provided at the end of each project.

How to Use the In the Workplace Feature

At the end of each chapter, students can learn about different careers that require desktop publishing and digital graphics skills.

Education, Salary, and Skills
Key topics help students focus on career awareness, how to research careers, and how to make career decisions.

Job Description
Students can learn how they can apply their skills in specific careers.

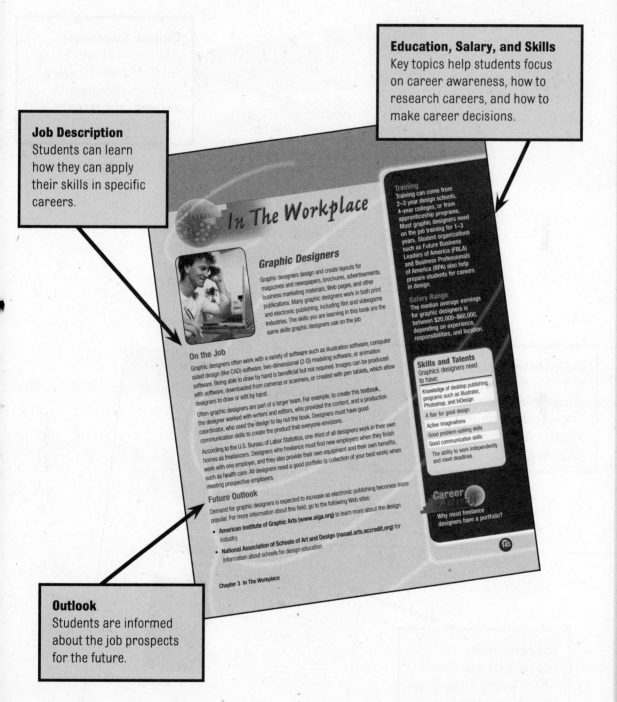

In The Workplace

Graphic Designers

Graphic designers design and create layouts for magazines and newspapers, brochures, advertisements, business marketing materials, Web pages, and other publications. Many graphic designers work in both print and electronic publishing, including film and videogame industries. The skills you are learning in this book are the same skills graphic designers use on the job

On the Job

Graphic designers often work with a variety of software such as illustration software, computer aided design (like CAD) software, two-dimensional (2-D) modeling software, or animation software. Being able to draw by hand is beneficial but not required. Images can be produced with software, downloaded from cameras or scanners, or created with pen tablets, which allow designers to draw or edit by hand.

Often graphic designers are part of a larger team. For example, to create this textbook, the designer worked with writers and editors, who provided the content, and a production coordinator, who used the design to lay out the book. Designers must have good communication skills to create the product that everyone envisions.

According to the U.S. Bureau of Labor Statistics, one-third of all designers work in their own homes as freelancers. Designers who freelance must find new employers when they finish work with one employer, and they also provide their own equipment and their own benefits, such as health care. All designers need a good portfolio (a collection of your best work) when meeting prospective employers.

Future Outlook

Demand for graphic designers is expected to increase as electronic publishing becomes more popular. For more information about this field, go to the following Web sites:

- **American Institute of Graphic Arts (www.aiga.org)** to learn more about the design industry
- **National Association of Schools of Art and Design (nasad.arts.accredit.org)** for information about schools for design education

Chapter 3 In The Workplace

Training

Training can come from 2–3 year design schools, 4-year colleges, or from apprenticeship programs. Most graphic designers need on the job training for 1–3 years. Student organizations such as Future Business Leaders of America (FBLA) and Business Professionals of America (BPA) also help prepare students for careers in design.

Salary Range

The median average earnings for graphic designers is between $20,000–$60,000, depending on experience, responsibilities, and location.

Skills and Talents
Graphics designers need to have:

- Knowledge of desktop publishing programs such as Illustrator, Photoshop, and InDesign
- A flair for good design
- Active imaginations
- Good problem-solving skills
- Good communication skills
- The ability to work independently and meet deadlines

Career

Why must freelance designers have a portfolio?

145

Outlook
Students are informed about the job prospects for the future.

How to Use the Assessments

The projects at the end of chapters and the Projects Across the Curriculum at the end of units have a cross-curricular focus and will help assess the different skill levels of students.

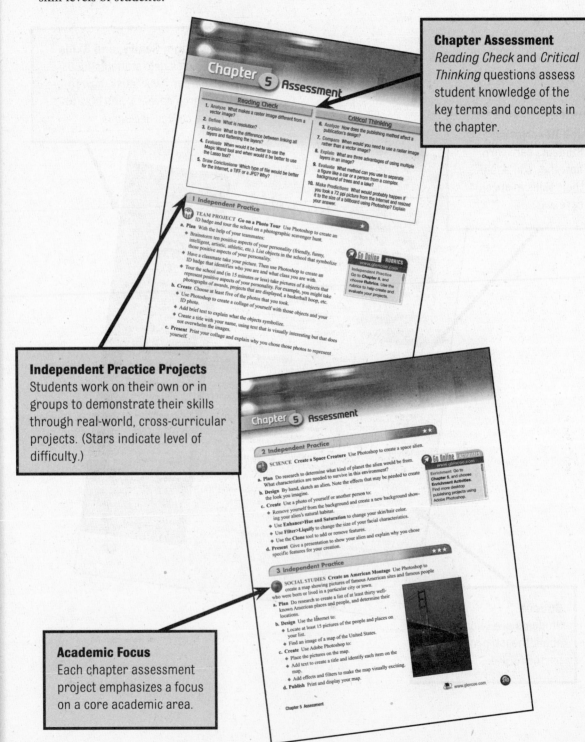

Chapter Assessment
Reading Check and *Critical Thinking* questions assess student knowledge of the key terms and concepts in the chapter.

Independent Practice Projects
Students work on their own or in groups to demonstrate their skills through real-world, cross-curricular projects. (Stars indicate level of difficulty.)

Academic Focus
Each chapter assessment project emphasizes a focus on a core academic area.

How to Use the Unit Review

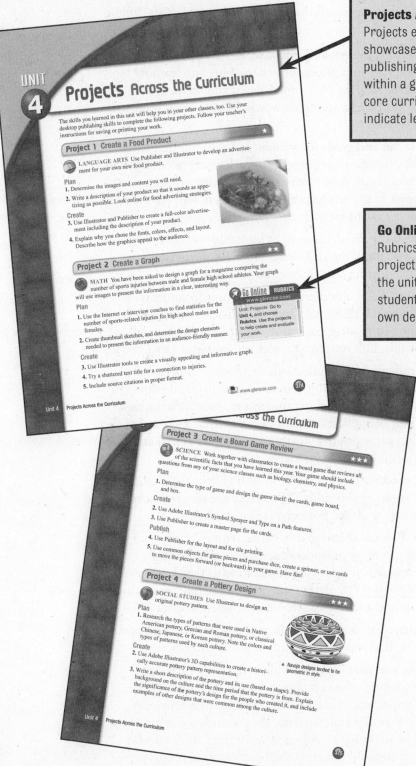

UNIT
4

Projects Across the Curriculum

The skills you learned in this unit will help you in your other classes, too. Use your desktop publishing skills to complete the following projects. Follow your teacher's instructions for saving or printing your work.

Project 1 Create a Food Product

LANGUAGE ARTS Use Publisher and Illustrator to develop an advertisement for your own new food product.

Plan
1. Determine the images and content you will need.
2. Write a description of your product so that it sounds as appetizing as possible. Look online for food advertising strategies.

Create
3. Use Illustrator and Publisher to create a full-color advertisement including the description of your product.
4. Explain why you chose the fonts, colors, effects, and layout. Describe how the graphics appeal to the audience.

Project 2 Create a Graph

MATH You have been asked to design a graph for a magazine comparing the number of sports injuries between male and female high school athletes. Your graph will use images to present the information in a clear, interesting way.

Plan
1. Use the Internet or interview coaches to find statistics for the number of sports-related injuries for high school males and females.
2. Create thumbnail sketches, and determine the design elements needed to present the information in an audience-friendly manner.

Create
3. Use Illustrator tools to create a visually appealing and informative graph.
4. Try a shattered text title for a connection to injuries.
5. Include source citations in proper format.

Go Online RUBRICS
www.glencoe.com
Unit: Projects Go to **Unit 4**, and choose **Rubrics**. Use the projects to help create and evaluate your work.

www.glencoe.com

374

Unit 4 Projects Across the Curriculum

...ross the Curriculum

Project 3 Create a Board Game Review

SCIENCE Work together with classmates to create a board game that reviews all of the scientific facts that you have learned this year. Your game should include questions from any of your science classes such as biology, chemistry, and physics.

Plan
1. Determine the type of game and design the game itself: the cards, game board, and box.

Create
2. Use Adobe Illustrator's Symbol Sprayer and Type on a Path features.
3. Use Publisher to create a master page for the cards.

Publish
4. Use Publisher for the layout and for tile printing.
5. Use common objects for game pieces and purchase dice, create a spinner, or use cards to move the pieces forward (or backward) in your game. Have fun!

Project 4 Create a Pottery Design

SOCIAL STUDIES Use Illustrator to design an original pottery pattern.

Plan
1. Research the types of patterns that were used in Native American pottery, Grecian and Roman pottery, or classical Chinese, Japanese, or Korean pottery. Note the colors and types of patterns used by each culture.

Create
2. Use Adobe Illustrator's 3D capabilities to create a historically accurate pottery pattern representation.
3. Write a short description of the pottery and its use (based on shape). Provide background on the culture and the time period that the pottery is from. Explain the significance of the pottery's design for the people who created it, and include examples of other designs that were common among the culture.

▲ Navajo designs tended to be geometric in style.

Unit 4 Projects Across the Curriculum

375

Projects Across the Curriculum

Projects encourage students to showcase their mastery of desktop publishing skills individually or within a group while reinforcing core curriculum content. (Stars indicate level of difficulty).

Go Online Rubrics

Rubrics are provided for every project in the textbook, including the unit review projects to help students create and evaluate their own designs and publications.

GUIDELINES FOR A SUCCESSFUL COURSE

To facilitate the success of the course and the progress of your students, follow these general guidelines:

◆ **Review course philosophy, theme, and purpose.** Review your philosophy and goals for the course. Has your philosophy of teaching and learning changed over the years? Review the philosophy, goals, and themes of the book. Write the course purpose in your own words. What do you want students to learn from this class?

◆ **Identify course objectives and goals for students.** Write your objectives and goals for the course. Review your purpose for each class period. Writing your objectives helps you clarify your methods, communicate expectations, and evaluate your success. It is often helpful for students to see your class objective(s) written on the board for each class period.

◆ **Encourage critical thinking.** Students need to learn how to solve problems, make decisions, and think through issues rationally. Help students use critical thinking skills during class discussions.

◆ **Make learning personal.** Each unit presents projects to help students develop and demonstrate their skills. Ask students to assess their progress and clarify personal and professional goals as they build knowledge and experience. When possible, link concepts to students' everyday experiences.

◆ **Educate the whole student.** Make certain you stress essential personal qualities throughout the course. Civility, character, integrity, and ethics can be woven throughout the course by asking students to share with the class situations from their jobs (if applicable), their personal lives, and current events. Be sure to collect some positive stories and examples as well and acknowledge positive attitudes in your students.

◆ **Link school and job success.** The instructor must highlight the usefulness and insight gained by studying this subject. Reinforce the idea that success in this course will enhance students' potential for job success.

◆ **Preview assignments.** Preview assignments with students to clarify your expectations. Previewing units helps students prepare, and it can also be a tool for showing how new information relates to what they have just studied and to their everyday work. Before you preview the unit, review and summarize the previous unit and discuss what students have learned.

◆ **Emphasize commitment.** Stress that commitment to study and consistent practice produce results. Real learning is based on positive habits.

◆ **Encourage attendance and participation.** Take attendance each class period and meet with students who miss twice. Even if this course is not graded, attendance is important. Point out that the course experience is built on classroom participation and exercises. Poor attendance or tardiness results in confusion, low motivation, and resentment from students who attend and are well-prepared and punctual. Full participation means preparation, commitment, and involvement.

The underlying principles that support the preceding guidelines are as follows:

◆ **Students are responsible for both the academic and social aspects of their education.** It is important that students plan and take charge of their courses and careers. Remind them that blaming others for their circumstances does not empower them to take charge of their lives. Blaming themselves is also a waste of time. Stress that empowerment is facing a problem directly, solving it, and performing the strategies that produce positive results.

◆ **Effort and commitment to excellence are essential.** To make the most of school and work, students must be willing to put in the time and effort required. Vague wishes, desires, half-hearted attempts, and hopes do not produce results. A commitment to make school a top priority is a key factor for success. Remind students that adopting strategies and turning them into daily habits are important both in school and at work.

◆ **Cooperative learning promotes interdependence.** Working in small groups is a key factor in getting students involved in their own learning and in the learning of other group members. Group exercises provide application of ideas and strategies. Interaction, interpersonal communication, and teamwork each play a powerful role in student success.

◆ **Expressing ideas effectively increases self-confidence and self-esteem.** Practicing public speaking skills is fundamental for students to improve their presentations. Group work encourages critical thinking, creative problem-solving, and respect for diversity. Listening to others and keeping an open mind helps reduce misunderstandings and celebrate the valuable experience of working with different kinds of people.

◆ **Learning how to learn best is important.** Attending school for many years does not guarantee that students know how they learn best. Give students the opportunity, space, and techniques to assess and discover how they learn best. Knowing how to learn and having the willingness to be a lifelong learner are essential to job success.

◆ **Successful people are positive, resourceful, and motivated.** The most productive, positive, flexible, and courteous people in school and at work are people who are emotionally mature and have developed strong personal qualities. Attitude affects relationships, work habits, and results.

PLANNING A COURSE

Planning a course from the bottom up can be both an exciting and daunting experience. Preparing to teach requires calculation. You need to factor the various assignments, tests, student dynamics, and instructional interactions. Creating a calculated pacing framework will help make your course function smoothly.

How to Develop a Pacing Chart

Estimating how much time it takes to teach the content of the textbook and assess students' knowledge of that content is not an exact science. Determining how long to spend covering course content and completing student activities and projects requires that teachers consider the amount of actual class time, the abilities of the students, and how motivated and prepared students generally are.

Suggested Course Pacing Charts

Pacing charts provided on the following pages suggest how the textbook and other activities might be used to teach a 9-week course (quarter), an 18-week course (semester), and a 36-week course (full year). During the course, take time to develop your own pacing chart and utilize that schedule the next time you teach the course. Depending on your students' knowledge and needs, you may want to spend more or less time covering specific material. Adjust the pacing charts as needed to meet your course's particular requirements. For example:

◆ You may choose not to cover Workshop articles or introductory chapters.

◆ Your advanced students may or may not need to review the Microsoft Word projects covered in Unit 1.

◆ You may choose not to cover advanced software such as Adobe Illustrator.

◆ Your course may or may not require students to learn team building, Excel, or PowerPoint skills covered in Unit 5.

◆ You may choose to have students complete only selected end-of-chapter and end-of-unit activities.

◆ Schedule in weeks during your class time that students might need to spend on testing.

◆ You may wish to take the final week of class to assess students' overall achievement in this course.

Suggested Course Pacing Chart

9-Week Course

Week	Chapters	Projects	Online Activities (optional)
Week 1	1	1-4, 1-5, 1-7, 1-11	Ch 1 PowerPoint, Worksheets, e-Review
Week 2	2	2-2, 2-5, 2-6	Ch 2 PowerPoint, Worksheets, e-Review
Week 3	3	3-1, 3-2, 3-3, 3-4	Ch 3 PowerPoint, Worksheets, e-Review
Week 4	4	4-1, 4-3, 4-4, 4-7	Ch 4 PowerPoint, Worksheets, and e-Review
Week 5	5	5-1, 5-2, 5-3, 5-4	Ch 5 PowerPoint, Worksheets, and e-Review
Week 6	5–6	5-4 (cont'd), 6-1, 6-2, 6-3	Ch 5 Worksheets, e-Review, Ch 6 PowerPoint
Week 7	6–7	6-4, 7-1, 7-2	Ch 6 Worksheets, e-Review, Ch 7 PowerPoint
Week 8	7–8	7-3, 8-1, 8-2, 8-3	Ch 7 Worksheets, e-Review, Ch 8 PowerPoint, Worksheets, e-Review
Week 9	10	10-2, 10-3	Ch 10 PowerPoint, Worksheets, e-Review

18-Week Course

Week	Chapters	Projects	Online Activities (optional)
Week 1	1	1-4, 1-5, 1-7, 1-8	Ch 1 PowerPoint
Week 2	1–2	1-9, 1-11, 2-2, 2-5, 2-7	Ch 1 Worksheets, e-Review, Ch 2 PowerPoint
Week 3	2–3	2-8, 2-9, 3-2	Ch 2 Worksheets, e-Review, Ch 3 PowerPoint
Week 4	3	3-4, 3-5, 3-8	Ch 3 PowerPoint
Week 5	3–4	3-9, 4-1, 4-3, 4-4	Ch 3 Worksheets, e-Review, Ch 4 PowerPoint
Week 6	4	4-7, 4-8, 4-9	Ch 4 Worksheets, e-Review
Week 7	5	5-1, 5-2, 5-3, 5-4	Ch 5 PowerPoint
Week 8	5–6	5-4 (cont'd), 5-5, 5-6, 6-1, 6-2	Ch 5 Worksheets, e-Review, Ch 6 PowerPoint
Week 9	6	Projects 6-3, 6-4, 6-5	Ch 6 PowerPoint, Worksheets, e-Review
Week 10	1–6	Independent Practice, Units 1–6 Review	
Week 11	7	7-1, 7-2, 7-3, 7-4	Ch 7 PowerPoint
Week 12	7–8	7-5, 8-1, 8-2, 8-3	Ch 7 Worksheets, e-Review, Ch 8 PowerPoint
Week 13	8	8-4, 8-5, 8-6	Ch 8 PowerPoint, Worksheets, e-Review
Week 14	9	9-4, 9-5	Ch 9 PowerPoint
Week 15	9–10	9-6, 9-7, 10-2	Ch 9 Worksheets, e-Review, Ch 10 PowerPoint
Week 16	10	10-3, 10-4	
Week 17	10	10-5, 10-6	Ch 10 Worksheet and e-Review
Week 18	6–10	Independent Practice	

Suggested Course Pacing Chart *(continued)*

		36-Week Course	
Week	**Chapters**	**Projects**	**Online Activities (optional)**
Week 1	1	1-1, 1-2, 1-3, 1-4, 1-5	Ch 1 PowerPoint
Week 2	1	1-7, 1-8, 1-9, 1-10	Ch 1 Worksheet and e-Review
Week 3	2	2-1, 2-2, 2-3, 2-4, 2-8	Ch 2 PowerPoint
Week 4	2	2-9, Independent Practice, Units 1–2 Review	Ch 2 Worksheet and e-Review
Week 5	3	3-1, 3-2, 3-3	Ch 3 PowerPoint
Week 6	3	3-4, 3-5	
Week 7	3	3-6, 3-7, 3-8, 3-9	
Week 8	3	3-9 (cont'd), Independent Practice	Ch 3 Worksheet and e-Review
Week 9	4	4-1, 4-2, 4-3, 4-4, 4-5	Ch 4 PowerPoint
Week 10	4	4-5, 4-6, 4-7, 4-8	
Week 11	4	4-9, Independent Practice, Units 3–4 Review	Ch 4 Worksheet and e-Review
Week 12	5	5-1, 5-2	Ch 5 PowerPoint
Week 13	5	5-3, 5-4, 5-5	
Week 14	5	5-6, 5-7, 5-8	
Week 15	5	5-8 (cont'd), 5-9, 5-10, Independent Practice	Ch 5 Worksheet and e-Review
Week 16	6	Independent Practice, 6-1, 6-2	Ch 6 PowerPoint
Week 17	6	6-3, 6-4, 6-5, 6-6	
Week 18	6	6-7, 6-8, Independent Practice, Units 5–6 Review	Ch 6 Worksheet and e-Review
Week 19	1–6	Independent Practice	
Week 20	7	7-1, 7-2, 7-3, 7-4	Ch 7 PowerPoint
Week 21	7	7-5, 7-6, 7-7, 7-8	
Week 22	7	7-9, Independent Practice	Ch 7 Worksheet and e-Review
Week 23	8	8-1, 8-2, 8-3	Ch 8 PowerPoint
Week 24	8	8-4, 8-5, 8-6	
Week 25	8	8-7, 8-8, 8-9, 8-10,	
Week 26	8	Independent Practice, Units 7–8 Review	Ch 4 Worksheet and e-Review
Week 27	9	9-1, 9-2, 9-3	Ch 9 PowerPoint
Week 28	9	9-3, 9-4, 9-5	
Week 29	9	9-6, 9-7, 9-8	
Week 30	9	Independent Practice	Ch 9 Worksheet and e-Review
Week 31	10	10-1, 10-2, 10-3, 10-4	Ch 10 PowerPoint
Week 32	10	10-4 (cont'd), 10-5, 10-6	
Week 33	10	10-6 (cont'd), 10-7, 10-8, 10-9	
Week 34	10	10-9, Independent Practice	Ch 10 Worksheet and e-Review
Week 35	10	Independent Practice, Units 9–10 Review	
Week 36	7–10	Independent Practice	Enrichment activities

WRITING A COURSE OUTLINE

A course outline adds order and organization to your course. Students want to know what to expect, so it is important to have a detailed written guide for them to follow and refer to throughout the semester. The course outline could include:

◆ Teacher's name

◆ Location of class (include building number, classroom number, etc.)

◆ Day(s) and time(s) the class meets

◆ Required textbooks and resources

◆ Course purpose and objectives

◆ Learning climate or teaching method

◆ Course requirements and expectations

◆ Daily outline

◆ Evaluation or grading methods

The example on the following page has been structured to follow the textbook. You can adapt this suggested course outline and student expectation guide to the specific needs of the class. Tell students that the course outline is a guide and that you may change the order of topics, exercises, and assignments when it is appropriate.

Before developing a course outline, you may want to write down some of your own expectations for the course.

Course Expectations _____

_____

_____

_____

_____

_____

_____

_____

_____

_____

_____

_____

_____

_____

Suggested Course Outline for Introduction to Desktop Publishing With Digital Graphics

Course Outline

Required Textbook

Introduction to Desktop Publishing With Digital Graphics

Course Purpose

Introduction to Desktop Publishing With Digital Graphics is an introductory course for students who are learning desktop publishing skills. Students will learn fundamental concepts about design, as well as key application skills in Microsoft Word, Microsoft Publisher, Adobe Photoshop, and Adobe Illustrator.

Course Objectives

After completing this course, you will be able to:

Key Concepts

◆ Understand the technology used for desktop publishing.
◆ Identify key steps of the design process.
◆ Analyze the elements of effective design, particularly the PARC principles (**P**roximity, **A**lignment, **R**epetition, **C**ontrast).
◆ Determine which software to use for different elements of design.
◆ Compare vector and raster images.
◆ Analyze use of layers in graphics.
◆ Identify design elements of desktop-published documents such as flyers, brochures, newsletters, booklets, business cards and stationery, posters, and banners.
◆ Compare layout, color, and design in print documents and Web pages.
◆ Evaluate resolution in images published in print and online.
◆ Compare file formats for different types of graphics.
◆ Describe options for professional printing.
◆ Explain the relationship between client and designer.
◆ Evaluate the importance of audience, budget, and deadlines on design.
◆ Discuss ethical issues associated with design.
◆ Identify the skills and tools necessary to work as a team.

Application Skills

◆ Identify the software tools used to create effective layout, text, and graphics in a document.
◆ Apply effective design principles, including PARC.
◆ Select appropriate typeface, font, and font styles for print and Web documents.
◆ Lay out text and graphics in documents using layout guides and grids.
◆ Create a variety of documents, including flyers, multi-fold brochures and cards, newsletters, booklets, business cards, stationery, posters, and banners.

- Choose appropriate software for desktop publishing projects.
- Create vector and raster images.
- Insert, edit, and resize graphics in documents.
- Manipulate images by using layers and masks.
- Identify tools and effects used to enhance graphic images.
- Customize templates.
- Save documents in formats that can be used with different types of desktop-publishing software.
- Design and tile print oversized publications.
- Add hyperlinks to Web pages.
- Apply tools, like Microsoft Excel and PowerPoint, for team projects that require budgets, timelines, and presentations.

Course Requirements and Expectations

- **Attendance** You are expected to attend each class and be on time.
- **Participation** You are expected to participate in class and complete all assignments. You will have opportunities to interact with and help other students, but remember that you are responsible for completing your own assignments.
- **Critical Thinking** You are expected to use critical thinking and creative problem solving to complete exercises. You will apply the new concepts that you learn as you complete activities and projects. Active, creative thinking will help you understand new concepts as you complete this course.
- **Activities and Projects** Frequent challenges appear throughout the course. You are expected to apply the skills you have learned to come up with creative, effective solutions to the problems presented.

Assessment

Assessment will be based on attendance, participation, and successful completion of various assignments and projects throughout this course. Quizzes and tests will be given periodically to test your knowledge and skills.

Grading

The following is an example of grading guidelines and a grading scale:

Grading Guidelines		Grading Scale
Attendance	= 25%	A = 90–100%
Quizzes/Tests	= 25%	B = 80–89%
Assignments	= 50%	C = 70–79%
		D = 60–69%
Total	**= 100%**	F = Less than 60%

GUIDELINES FOR THE TECHNOLOGY CLASSROOM

Students will use technology throughout the course. Use the following guidelines to help students use technology responsibly.

Using the Internet

Students are often instructed to access Web sites to complete activities and projects. Where possible, suggested Web sites are provided in the student edition and in this Teacher Resource Manual. Although suggested live sites have been reviewed, they are not under the control of Glencoe/McGraw-Hill. Site content and URLs may also change over time. We therefore strongly encourage teachers to preview these sites before assigning their students individual activities. Teachers may also want to let parents know that students will be using the Internet to complete activities and assignments for the class.

Acceptable Use Policies

Teachers should check with their school to learn about their district's acceptable use policy (AUP). Most AUPs provide a statement of responsibilities of educators, parents, and students for using the Internet, guidelines for appropriate online behavior, and a description of the consequences should the school district's AUP be violated. Teachers, parents, guardians, and students should all be familiar with their school's AUP before any Internet activities are assigned. Once online, teachers should continue to monitor students' Internet time and watch for objectionable content or for irresponsible computer use.

Downloading Files

For almost all projects, Data Files are either supplied or not required; however, students are occasionally instructed to locate and download files to complete activities and projects. Review your school's policies on downloading files from the Internet. If students will not have that capability, supply appropriate files and let students know where to find them. Students should always review a Web site's Terms of Use before downloading and using any files.

Copyright Guidelines

When necessary, students should include copyright information and credit lines on their pages to acknowledge their sources. You can use *Eyes on Ethics* throughout the book, and the *Technology Handbook* at the end of the student edition to review basic copyright guidelines with students. There is also a PowerPoint presentation about ethical issues that is available on the Teacher Resource CD and the student section of the Online Learning Center.

Students should be expected to know that:

1. It is illegal and unethical to use a person's or company's intellectual property without first obtaining their permission.

2. A person or company does not have to obtain a copyright notice to have rights over their intellectual property. Therefore, even if a site does not have a copyright notice, the content included on that site is still protected.

3. Another person's or company's intellectual property can only be used if written permission is obtained to use this property, or if it is stated on their Web site that all content is royalty free and can be used without permission.

4. If an individual places a copyright notice on a work, then he or she must defend that work if he or she knows that the work is being used without permission. Failure to defend a copyright can result in the loss of that copyright.

Suggested Classroom Resources

Students may want to use the following materials for reference when learning skills and completing activities and projects.

◆ Computer catalogs and magazines

◆ Online tutorials for using applications such as Microsoft Word, Publisher, PowerPoint, and Excel, as well as Adobe Photoshop and Illustrator.

◆ User guides for computer hardware and software

Publishing Web Sites

Students will be creating Web sites, but you should determine whether their work should be published online. Please review the options available at your school for publishing Web sites. Because of the potential legal ramifications of students publishing Web sites under the school's name or auspices, it is critical that the students understand their responsibility to avoid any content that is controversial. You may want to review appropriate and inappropriate content guidelines with students before they publish any sites.

Using the Student Data Files

To complete some projects in this book, student data files are required.

◆ When you see the Student Data File icon, locate needed files *before* beginning the activity.

◆ Student Data Files are available on the Teacher Resource DVD and on the book's Online Learning Center Web site at **www.glencoe.com**.

Teachers need to review how best to distribute these files to students depending on your computer setups and network capabilities. Some options may include:

1. Posting the files on the teacher's course Web site.

2. Saving the files in a folder or folders on the school network.

3. Saving the files to the hard drive of each computer with read-only access. Students can resave files to their location as a writeable file. (Due to limited hard drive space, you may wish to save selected files as they are needed.)

A chart outlining each data file and where it is used in the textbook is included on the following pages.

Using the Solution Files

Solution files are provided to teachers the Exercises and Guided Projects in which students create documents and save their work.

◆ Solution Files are available on the Teacher Resource DVD and on the book's Online Learning Center Web site at **www.glencoe.com**.

◆ These files are on the password-protected Teacher Center portion of the site so that only teachers have access. Visit the Online Learning Center for user name and password information (registration is *not* required).

Teachers might choose to use the Solution Files in the following ways:

1. Some projects require students to continue working on files created in previous projects. If a student did not complete the first project, then the solution file for that activity may be used as a starting point for the continuing activity.

2. Display a project's solution file on a projection screen before students begin, as a model for student work.

3. Display the solution file for all students to see as they complete their work so they can check their progress.

4. Print the solution files and give each student a copy. Let students swap seats and check their partner's work against the solution file. Students can then make changes or redo project steps as needed to make corrections.

An outline of each solution file and where it corresponds to the textbook is included on the following pages.

Student Data Files

Chapter 1 Data Files—Introducing Desktop Publishing			
Page	*Location*	*File Name and Description*	*Type of File*
7	Project 1-1	1-1 (Star-Spangled Banner)	Word
10	Project 1-2	1-2 (Poland's Prize essay)	Word
13	Project 1-3	1-3 (Font Families Table)	Word
15	Project 1-4	1-4 (Gettysburg Address text)	Word
20	Project 1-5	1-5a (Aesop's Fable text)	Word
		1-5b (bear clip art)	GIF image
25	Project 1-6	1-6 (watermark)	JPEG image
30	Project 1-7	1-7a (Meeting Demand text)	Word
		1-7b (HypothetiCo logo)	JPEG image
		1-7c (graph)	JPEG image
		1-7d (sidebar image)	TIFF image
36	Project 1-8	1-8a (recipe text)	Word
		1-8b (top clip art)	TIFF image
		1-8c (bottom clip art)	GIF image
46	Project 1-10	1-10 (Ben Franklin résumé text)	Word
49	Project 1-11	1-11 (time capsule clip art)	GIF image
Chapter 2 Data Files—Vector Graphics in Word			
64	Project 2-2	2-2 (guitar clip art)	GIF image
68	Project 2-3	2-3a (pizza image)	Word
		2-3b (chef clip art)	GIF image
75	Project 2-5	2-5 (card clip art)	GIF images
79	Project 2-6	2-6a (knight clip art)	GIF image
		2-6b (newsletter articles)	Word
84	Project 2-7	2-7 (castle photograph)	BMP photograph
89	Project 2-8	2-8 (concert program text)	Word
93	Project 2-9	2-9 (concert program clip art)	GIF image

Chapter 3 Data Files—Introducing Microsoft Publisher			
Page	Location	File Name and Description	Type of File
106	Project 3-1	3-1 (autumn clip art)	JPEG photograph
110	Project 3-2	3-2a (clock clip art)	GIF image
		3-2b (clock background)	JPEG image
115	Project 3-3	3-3 (babysitter clip art)	JPEG image
120	Project 3-4	3-4 (skier clip art)	JPEG image
125	Project 3-5	3-5a (future home clip art)	JPEG image
		3-5b (future home text)	Word
		3-5c (appliances text)	Word
		3-5d (robot-dog photograph)	JPEG image
		3-5e (computer chip clip art)	TIFF image
130	Project 3-6	3-6a (elephant clip art)	TIFF image
		3-6b (student photograph)	JPEG image
133	Project 3-7	3-7a (Course Description text)	Word
		3-7b (Lunch Menu text)	Word
		3-7c (Volunteer Opportunities text)	Word
137	Project 3-8	3-8a (restaurant logo)	EMF image
		3-8b (menu background)	JPEG image
140	Project 3-9	3-9a (Page 2 menu text)	Word
		3-9b (Page 3 menu text)	Word
		3-9c (nachos clip art)	JPEG image
		3-9d (salad clip art)	JPEG image
		3-9e (pasta clip art)	JPEG image
		3-9f (pastry clip art)	JPEG image
Chapter 4 Data Files—Focus on Design Makeovers			
154	Project 4-1	4-1 (Food Fair flyer)	Publisher
158	Project 4-2	4-2 (Food Fair clip art)	JPEG image
162	Project 4-3	4-3 (Auction flyer)	Publisher
167	Project 4-4	4-4a (Eye Care flyer)	Publisher
		4-4b (Eye Care photograph)	JPEG image
172	Project 4-5	4-5a (Internet brochure)	Publisher
		4-5b (style sheet)	Publisher
		4-5c (thought-bubble clip art)	JPEG image
177	Project 4-6	4-6 (Internet brochure text)	TXT file

180	Project 4-7	4-7a (Shakespeare Web page)	Publisher
		4-7b (scroll clip art)	GIF image
		4-7c (Shakespeare clip art)	GIF image
186	Project 4-8	4-8a (teacher newsletter)	Publisher
		4-8b (lined paper image)	JPEG image

Chapter 5 Data Files—Introducing Adobe Photoshop

Page	Location	File Name and Description	Type of File
203	Project 5-1	5-1 (gingerbread house)	PSD (Photoshop)
211	Project 5-3	5-3 (car photograph)	JPEG image
215	Project 5-4	5-4 (speedometer)	PSD (Photoshop)
220	Project 5-5	5-5 (Stonehenge)	PSD (Photoshop)
224	Project 5-6	5-6 (dog photograph)	JPEG image
229	Project 5-7	5-7 (baby in flower)	PSD (Photoshop)
240	Project 5-9	5-9a (soccer player photograph)	TIFF image
		5-9b (soccer background)	TIFF image
244	Project 5-10	5-10a (nameplate)	TIFF image
		5-10b (bar code)	TIFF image
		5-10c (corner callout)	TIFF image

Chapter 6 Data Files—Integrating Publisher and Photoshop

254	Project 6-1	6-1 (bluebonnet flowers)	JPEG image
261	Project 6-3	6-3 (gold banner)	PSD (Photoshop)
269	Project 6-5	6-5a (giraffe photograph)	TIFF image
		6-5b (Komodo dragon)	JPEG image
273	Project 6-6	6-6a (Animal Quick Facts text)	Word
		6-6b (Animal Description text)	Word
		6-6c (Animal Habitat text)	Word
		6-6d (map image)	TIFF image
278	Project 6-7	6-7a (Mexico photograph)	JPEG image
		6-7b (Road Trip article text)	Word
		6-7c (Teacher's Desk text)	Word
		6-7d (Student Poetry text)	Word
		6-7e (Ask Karen photograph)	JPEG image
		6-7f (Ask Karen text)	Word
		6-7g (Student Point text)	Word
		6-7h (Student Counterpoint text)	Word
		6-7i (Student Spotlight text)	Word
		6-7j (Spotlight bike photograph)	JPEG image
		6-7k (Final Word text)	Word

Chapter 7 Data Files—Design with Adobe Illustrator			
No data files			

Chapter 8 Data Files—Integrating Publisher and Illustrator			
Page	*Location*	*File Name and Description*	*Type of File*
342	Project 8-2	8-2 (dragon clip art)	GIF image
349	Project 8-4	8-4 (lab clip art)	JPEG image
354	Project 8-6	8-6 (fire background)	TIFF image
363	Project 8-9	8-9a (label text and image of can top)	AI (Illustrator)
		8-9b (strawberry clip art)	GIF image

Chapter 9 Data Files—Work with Teams			
400	Project 9-8	9-8 (mail merge data file)	Access

Chapter 10 Data Files—Create Marketing Materials			
413	Project 10-2	10-2 (Mars Quest brochure exterior text)	Word
416	Project 10-3	10-3a (Mars Quest brochure interior text)	Word
		10-3b (spaceship image)	BMP image
		10-3c (airtrain image)	GIF image
		10-3d (skier clip art)	GIF image
		10-3e (Mars mountain image)	GIF image
		10-3f (hotel exterior image)	TIFF image
418	Project 10-4	10-4a (Mars Quest booklet text)	Word
		10-4b (cover image)	JPEG image
		10-4c (Page 3 image)	JPEG image
		10-4d (dining room image)	TIFF image
		10-4e (luxury room image)	TIFF image
		10-4f (Presidential Suite image)	TIFF image
		10-4g (airtrain image)	GIFF image
		10-4h (spaceship image)	BMP image
		10-4i (Mars map)	TIFF image
423	Project 10-5	10-5a (Web page background)	JPEG image
		10-5b (Mars image)	TIFF image
431	Project 10-7	10-7a (presentation outline text)	TXT file
		10-7b (Slide Master background)	TIFF image
		10-7c (Title Master background)	TIFF image
436	Project 10-8	10-8a (business package)	TIFF image
		10-8b (brochure)	TIFF image
		10-8c (travel guide)	TIFF image
		10-8d (Web page)	TIFF image

Solution Files

Chapter 1 Solution Files—Introducing Desktop Publishing

Page	Location	File Name and Description	Type of File
7	Project 1-1	C1P1 Star Spangled Banner	Word
10	Project 1-2	C1P2 Poland's Prize report	Word
13	Project 1-3	C1P3 font chart	Word
15	Project 1-4	C1P4 Gettysburg Address	Word
20	Project 1-5	C1P5 illustrated Aesop's Fable	Word
25	Project 1-6	C1P6 certificate with watermark	Word
30	Project 1-7	C1P7 annual report with graphics	Word
36	Project 1-8	C1P8 recipe with symbols	Word
41	Project 1-9	C1P9 State Facts table	Word
46	Project 1-10	C1P10 Ben Franklin résumé	Word
49	Project 1-11	C1P11 time capsule flyer	Word

Chapter 2 Solution Files—Vector Graphics in Word

Page	Location	File Name and Description	Type of File
61	Project 2-1	C2P1 pizza illustration	Word
64	Project 2-2	C2P2 guitar lesson flyer	Word
68	Project 2-3	C2P3 pizza flyer with border	Word
71	Project 2-4	C2P4 pizza flyer with logo	Word
75	Project 2-5	C2P5 quad-fold card	Word
79	Project 2-6	C2P6 one-page newsletter	Word
84	Project 2-7	C2P7 completed newsletter with photo	Word
89	Project 2-8	C2P8 bi-fold concert program interior	Word
93	Project 2-9	C2P9 completed concert program	Word

Chapter 3 Solution Files—Introducing Microsoft Publisher

Page	Location	File Name and Description	Type of File
106	Project 3-1	C3P1 calendar	Publisher
110	Project 3-2	C3P2 business card	Publisher
115	Project 3-3	C3P3 babysitter flyer with tear-offs	Publisher
120	Project 3-4	C3P4 Sports World coupon mailer	Publisher
125	Project 3-5	C3P5 Future Home bi-fold brochure	Publisher
130	Project 3-6	C3P6 high school Web page	Publisher
133	Project 3-7	C3P7 completed Web pages with hyperlinks	Publisher
137	Project 3-8	C3P8 bi-fold menu exterior	Publisher
140	Project 3-9	C3P9 completed menu	Publisher

Chapter 4 Solution Files—Focus on Design Makeovers

Page	Location	File Name and Description	Type of File
154	Project 4-1	C4P1 Food Fair flyer	Publisher
158	Project 4-2	C4P2 Food Fair flyer with graphics	Publisher
162	Project 4-3	C4P3 Auction flyer	Publisher
167	Project 4-4	C4P4 Eye Care flyer	Publisher
172	Project 4-5	C4P5 tri-fold brochure exterior	Publisher
177	Project 4-6	C4P6 completed tri-fold brochure	Publisher
180	Project 4-7	C4P7 Shakespeare Web page	Publisher
186	Project 4-8	C4P8 children's newsletter, Page 1	Publisher
189	Project 4-9	C4P9 completed children's newsletter	Publisher

Chapter 5 Solution Files—Introducing Adobe Photoshop

Page	Location	File Name and Description	Type of File
203	Project 5-1	C5P1 gingerbread house, Part 1	PSD (Photoshop)
207	Project 5-2	C5P2 completed gingerbread house	PSD (Photoshop)
211	Project 5-3	C5P3 car image, Part 1	PSD (Photoshop)
215	Project 5-4	C5P4 completed car image	PSD (Photoshop)
220	Project 5-5	C5P5 Stonehenge image	PSD (Photoshop)
224	Project 5-6	C5P6 retouched dog photograph	JPEG image
229	Project 5-7	C5P7 baby in flower with vignette effect	PSD (Photoshop)
234	Project 5-8	C5P8 space image	PSD (Photoshop)
240	Project 5-9	C5P9 model with soccer ball	TIFF image
244	Project 5-10	C5P10 soccer magazine cover	TIFF image

Chapter 6 Solution Files—Integrating Publisher and Photoshop

Page	Location	File Name and Description	Type of File
254	Project 6-1	C6P1 image for Texas postcard	JPEG image
258	Project 6-2	C6P2 completed postcard	Publisher
261	Project 6-3	C6P3 image for banner	TIFF image
266	Project 6-4	C6P4 completed banner	Publisher
269	Project 6-5	C6P5 blended Komodo giraffe image	TIFF image
273	Project 6-6	C6P6 Komodo giraffe booklet	Publisher
278	Project 6-7	C6P7 laid out newsletter	Publisher
283	Project 6-8	C6P8 completed newsletter	Publisher

Chapter 7 Solution Files—Design with Adobe Illustrator

Page	Location	File Name and Description	Type of File
297	Project 7-1	No solution file	
301	Project 7-2	C7P2 crayon illustration	AI (Illustrator)
306	Project 7-3	C7P3 completed crayon box	AI (Illustrator)

Page	Location	File Name and Description	Type of File
311	Project 7-4	C7P4 eye illustration	AI (Illustrator)
315	Project 7-5	C7P5 completed eye illustration	AI (Illustrator)
317	Project 7-6	C7P6 flag illustration	AI (Illustrator)
321	Project 7-7	C7P7 flag with distort	AI (Illustrator)
325	Project 7-8	C7P8 lightbulb text illustration	AI (Illustrator)
328	Project 7-9	C7P9 completed text illustration	AI (Illustrator)
Chapter 8 Solution Files—Integrating Publisher and Illustrator			
Page	*Location*	*File Name and Description*	*Type of File*
337	Project 8-1	C8P1 coat of arms, Part 1	AI (Illustrator)
342	Project 8-2	C8P2 completed coat of arms	WMF image
346	Project 8-3	C8P3 tent card with coat of arms	Publisher
349	Project 8-4	C8P4 Live Trace illustration	AI (Illustrator)
351	Project 8-5	C8P5 shattered text illustration	PNG image
354	Project 8-6	C8P6 Lab Safety poster	Publisher
359	Project 8-7	C8P7 3D cylinder	AI (Illustrator)
361	Project 8-8	C8P8 juice drink logo	AI (Illustrator)
363	Project 8-9	C8P9 juice drink label	AI (Illustrator)
366	Project 8-10	C8P10 3D juice can	AI (Illustrator)
Chapter 9 Solution Files—Work with Teams			
382	Project 9-1	C9P1 flowchart	Publisher
385	Project 9-2	C9P2 timeline	Publisher
387	Project 9-3	C9P3 budget spreadsheet	Excel
391	Project 9-4	C9P4 logo	AI (Illustrator)
393	Project 9-5	C9P5 business card	Publisher
396	Project 9-6	C9P6 letterhead stationery	Publisher
398	Project 9-7	C9P7 letterhead envelope	Publisher
400	Project 9-8	C9P8 addressed envelope	Publisher
Chapter 10 Solution Files—Create Marketing Materials			
410	Project 10-1	No solution file	
413	Project 10-2	C10P2 brochure exterior	Publisher
416	Project 10-3	C10P3 completed brochure	Publisher
418	Project 10-4	C10P4 booklet	Publisher
423	Project 10-5	C10P5 formatted Web page	Publisher
426	Project 10-6	C10P6 completed Web pages with hyperlinks	Publisher
431	Project 10-7	C10P7 presentation with text and Master slides	PowerPoint
436	Project 10-8	C10P8 presentation with images	PowerPoint
439	Project 10-9	C10P9 completed presentation	PowerPoint

Recommended Hardware and Software

Specific directions and illustrations are given for the Microsoft Windows XP platform. Projects and figures in *Introduction to Desktop Publishing With Digital Graphics* were created using Microsoft Word 2003, Microsoft Publisher 2003, Adobe Photoshop CS2, and Adobe Illustrator CS2. However, teachers can easily tailor activities to previous versions of Windows and the above-mentioned software applications. (Note to Macintosh users: Material in this textbook can be modified and used in the Mac platform. Mac User icons have been provided in step-by-steps where the steps may be somewhat different from Microsoft Windows.)

Equipment and Software Needs		
	Hardware	**Software**
Required	• Computer • Color monitor • (Make sure your equipment meets or exceeds the system requirements of your software.) • Mouse • Keyboard	• Internet browser (such as Microsoft Internet Explorer or Mozilla Firefox) • Microsoft Windows XP, 2000, or 98 • Microsoft Word • Microsoft Publisher • Adobe Photoshop • Adobe Illustrator
Recommended	• Flash, CD, or DVD drive • Printer • Scanner • Digital camera	• Microsoft Excel • Microsoft PowerPoint

Using Equipment

This book does not discuss the specific ways to use technology tools such as scanners and digital cameras. Review the operating procedures for any technology tools that you have available in the classroom, and make sure that students understand how to use this equipment responsibly.

Saving Student Work

Students will need to save their work often.

◆ Identify where students should save their work before they begin working.

◆ Remind students to double check that they save to the correct location. Otherwise, they may not be able to find their work later.

CHECKLIST FOR CLASS PREPARATION

Teaching Tips

The following tips and recommendations from experienced teachers can help you achieve your optimum teaching level and will encourage your students to learn at the rate of their full potential.

1. **Be prepared and organized.**
   - ◆ Order books.
   - ◆ Write a course outline and student expectation guide.
   - ◆ Review files of past classes.
   - ◆ Meet with other teachers.
   - ◆ Meet with administrators about expectations.
   - ◆ Keep an idea file.

2. **Clarify expectations with students.**
   - ◆ Review attendance policy.
   - ◆ Review course outline.
   - ◆ Review expectations of class.
   - ◆ Answer students' questions.
   - ◆ Set high standards.
   - ◆ Reward good work.

3. **Get students involved.**
   - ◆ Create teams.
   - ◆ Use text exercises.
   - ◆ Use class discussions.
   - ◆ Go on field trips if feasible.
   - ◆ Have students give presentations.
   - ◆ Have regular one-on-one student conferences.

4. **Be an example for your students.**
   - ◆ Listen.
   - ◆ Respect different views.
   - ◆ Speak in a respectful tone.
   - ◆ Use supportive language.
   - ◆ Use direct eye contact.
   - ◆ Respect differences.

5. **Integrate different learning styles.**
   - ◆ Use visuals such as overhead transparencies.
   - ◆ Repeat important information.
   - ◆ Use exercises based on real-life examples.
   - ◆ Use computer-based exercises.
   - ◆ Have students explain class material to other students.

6. **Reward learning and positive behavior.**
   - ◆ Reward critical thinking.
   - ◆ Reward attendance and participation.
   - ◆ Reward excellent academic work.
   - ◆ Notice students being positive.
   - ◆ Notice students being respectful.

7. **Connect school and job success.**
   - ◆ Point out that school and job success are connected.
   - ◆ Bring in examples from the newspaper.
   - ◆ Ask students for examples.

8. **Model enthusiasm.**
   - ◆ Come to class positive and motivated.
   - ◆ Be flexible when finding solutions to problems.
   - ◆ Look for the best in students.

9. **Make learning fun and active.**
   - ◆ Humor can be an effective teaching tool.
   - ◆ Smile.
   - ◆ Encourage teamwork.

10. **Assess, adjust, and renew.**
    - ◆ Give student evaluations.
    - ◆ Assess your teaching. Audiotape your class.
    - ◆ Take responsibility for your teaching.
    - ◆ Seek to improve.
    - ◆ Find balance.
    - ◆ Attend professional conferences.
    - ◆ Focus on what works.
    - ◆ Keep a journal.
    - ◆ Take time to renew yourself.

Record Keeping

Some teachers like to keep note cards with students' names, interests, work experiences, record of absences, assignments completed, and so on, for daily use and then transfer major projects and final grades to a formal booklet. Keep your record-keeping system simple, flexible, and accurate. On the front side of the card include the student's:

◆ Name

◆ Phone number

◆ E-mail address

◆ Graduation year

◆ Expectation of class

◆ Grade expected

◆ Hobbies/interests

On the back of the card include the student's:

◆ Attendance (days missed)

◆ Assignments completed

GENERAL CLASSROOM GUIDELINES

Both students and teachers have a role in creating an effective classroom.

The Student's Role

The student's role is changing in today's classroom. Students are expected to be active learners, not passive receivers. The best learning methods incorporate reading and listening to lectures with active student participation. Be sure to review the following general classroom guidelines with your students:

◆ **Be prepared.** Have students come to class prepared with reading assignments and homework. If students are not prepared, they are less likely to participate and to grasp concepts during the lecture. Stress the importance of completing assigned exercises and coming to class prepared to discuss them. You may want students to complete certain assignments outside class so that classroom time can be devoted to discussion and review. Many of the exercises work well when they are discussed in small groups, and others work best when they are completed and reviewed in class.

◆ **Review objectives.** Read the chapter objectives at the beginning of each class so that the students know the class expectations. Review the instructions of the exercises out loud as students follow in their books so that everyone is on the same track, questions can be clarified, and everyone is ready to start on time.

◆ **Bring books to class.** Students should bring their books to each class period unless otherwise instructed.

◆ **Encourage responsibility.** Stress that students should take responsibility for their education by participating in class, looking for innovative solutions, and clarifying course expectations. Their teachers and advisors cannot tell them about all academic regulations. They must be aware of deadlines and procedures, and understand how the system works.

◆ **Encourage support groups.** Students need support from other students, teachers, advisors, and academic support groups. Encourage them to take responsibility for creating support groups. Point out that learning time management tips can help students in their future careers. Discuss with them the value of gaining the support of family members, classmates, and their community.

The Teacher's Role

A teacher must often exhibit a range of skills. In addition to understanding the course material, you must be able to communicate clearly and draw out important concepts from student questions and discussions.

◆ **Acknowledge the whole of intelligence.** Encourage students to use the whole of their intelligence. IQ is only one indicator of intelligence. Emotional maturity is also fundamental to school and job success. Students who have emotional control, have developed the ability to work well with others, have integrity and character, and have developed the tools to relate to others courteously can greatly increase their effectiveness.

◆ **Create a supportive climate.** Students will get involved in the exercises if they see that you are enthusiastic and interested, and value the assignments. Walk around while students do the exercises and check their progress, but do not help individuals or join teams. Give students lots of examples and reinforce the material.

◆ **Establish ground rules early.** Stress that not only is attendance required, but coming to class on time and prepared is also necessary. If students miss five or ten minutes, they have missed the introduction and review, and must interrupt to ask questions. You can always ease the schedule after students demonstrate that they are responsible and take charge of their own learning. Decide how long you need to spend on exercises, class discussions, and lectures.

◆ **Create diverse teams.** Students can learn from those who offer different perspectives, and diverse groups can foster understanding and respect for differences. Arrange groups to be diverse in gender, culture, interests, and so on. Many teachers like to have permanent teams throughout the course to add continuity, increase team skills, and build friendships.

◆ **Create classwide participation.** Encourage all students to participate. You may want to rotate the role of leader to encourage shy students to participate and learn leadership skills. Shift the location of teams so that those in the back of the classroom can respond more readily.

◆ **Emphasize communication skills.** Stress the importance of public speaking and interpersonal communication skills. One important communication skill is the ability to present short summaries of projects, exercises, or activities. Tell students that you will call on one of them to give a concise and brief summary of the main points covered in the last class meeting. This will not only encourage them to be prepared, but it will increase their public speaking skills and liven up the class as well. A summary also serves as a reminder and review of previous material. You can also add to the student's summary and connect it to the current lecture.

◆ **Make time for questions.** Have a set time when any topic is allowed, perhaps at the end of the class or once a week during an extended break.

◆ **Incorporate peer teaching.** Peer teachers and advisors are effective because they are able to relate to one another and they feel encouraged by working together. Students also have a chance to explain concepts in their own words. Peer teachers do not have to be the students with the best grades to be successful. Average students and struggling students can choose a topic and explain it effectively to others. Incorporate peer teaching throughout the course.

◆ **Make connections.** Education will be more relevant and meaningful if students see the connection between school and work. Throughout the course emphasize these connections:

   ❖ Student to student

   ❖ Student to teacher

   ❖ School to work

   ❖ Theory to practice

◆ **Encourage students to be open to new perspectives.** Sometimes students have set values and mind-sets. Discuss the value of seeing problems from a fresh perspective.

◆ **Be aware of other demands on students' time.** Many students have work, family, and community obligations that demand their time. Offer understanding but also discuss the necessity of backup plans. Have students discuss their many roles and concerns.

Instruction Style Guidelines

Students benefit from a variety of teacher input: introduction of new concepts and procedures through oral explanation, demonstration of new procedures and applications, and encouragement and immediate feedback on performance.

Building on Topics

Students need to know where they are headed, where they have been, and how the topics they are learning fit together.

◆ Always review old learning to be sure students are ready to move on to a new topic.

◆ Demonstrate new concepts and procedures to the class. Students learn many of their skills by following teacher demonstrations and solving relevant assignment materials.

◆ Relate new and advanced learning to the students' growing competency with overall skills. Explain how new skills reinforce and build on earlier skills.

Effective Questioning

Questioning is one way to stimulate student participation in class sessions to assess the extent of the learning that has taken place. Here are some suggestions for making your questioning as effective as possible.

◆ Ask precise questions that require exact responses when principles or procedures are involved.

◆ Ask questions that are relevant only to the subject matter.

◆ Direct your questions to the class as a whole. After a slight pause, call on one student for a reply.

◆ Ask questions that can be answered by the students to whom they are addressed, with special regard for each student's ability.

◆ Ask enough questions to reach everyone in the class during the period or during the week.

◆ Avoid questions that require simple yes or no responses. Ask why, how, and when to encourage students to show that they really understand the material.

◆ Plan your questions to cover the unit content as indicated by the unit objectives.

◆ Invite your students to ask questions. Have other class members attempt to answer these questions before you do. As you know, students can often explain things to one another very clearly if they are given the opportunity to do so.

◆ Take note of the questions that most often provoke discussion or are raised frequently. Include them in future quizzes and tests.

◆ Include some grade or mark for class participation in your overall appraisal of each student.

The Teacher's Attitude

Learning is a process centered around beliefs, attitude, and experience. Build a supportive environment as you create a learning community. As the teacher, you are key in creating this supportive classroom climate. Genuine interest and supportiveness are shown daily and may be enhanced by the following suggestions:

◆ Listen carefully to student comments and take notes when necessary.

◆ Respond seriously to students' questions and concerns. Be enthusiastic and positive and show that you enjoy teaching this class.

◆ Be available to meet with students if necessary.

◆ As the teacher, try to be seen as an open, supportive member of the team, as well as a coach and facilitator. Student discussion is important to a supportive learning climate.

◆ Encourage students to discover how their own answers can help facilitate class discussion.

Managing a classroom takes considerable interpersonal and management skills. When you feel discouraged or fatigued, try the following techniques for renewal:

◆ Talk with other teachers and share ideas.

◆ Take students on field trips.

◆ Find your own style of teaching.

◆ Focus on your strengths.

◆ Build a supportive learning environment.

◆ Be a mentor.

◆ Express your concerns and expectations to the class.

◆ Invite stimulating guest speakers to class.

LEARNING-STRATEGY GUIDELINES

The two most common reasons that students fail are poor study habits and lack of time management skills.

Helping Improve Study Habits and Time Management

Follow these guidelines to help students improve their study habits and time-management skills.

◆ Post reminders of due dates for homework, projects, and tests. Encourage students to break assignments into smaller tasks. They can work backward from the due date, planning all the steps necessary to complete the assignment. Students will be less prone to procrastinate, will find inspiration in completing smaller tasks, and will feel more in control.

◆ Encourage students to learn how to contact at least two students in their class. They can take notes for each other in an emergency, share information, and study together.

◆ Encourage study groups. Students will be most effective when they learn to use the skills and talents of others.

◆ Encourage students to get in touch with you as soon as they have a question or problem. Emphasize that they should not wait until the night before an exam to ask for clarification.

◆ Return phone calls and e-mails promptly.

Developing Critical Thinking Skills in Students

When your students enter the world of work, they will be required to process, analyze, interpret, and communicate information. Successful employees possess the ability to make insightful decisions, solve problems creatively, and interact with diverse groups.

Basic Elements of Critical Thinking

Critical thinking is the process of logically deciding on a course of action or a conclusion to a question or scenario. It involves the ability to:

◆ Compare and contrast

◆ Solve problems and make decisions

◆ Analyze and evaluate

◆ Synthesize and transfer knowledge

Benefits of Critical Thinking

◆ Help students investigate their own methods for solving problems.

◆ Lead students to investigations that compare and contrast knowns and unknowns.

◆ Allow students to make decisions about their own learning.

◆ Make students aware of their own learning processes.

Problem-Solving Strategies

1. **Define the problem.** Instruct students to work through the following question: What is the situation or the context of the problem? To define the problem clearly, state the problem in one or two sentences.

2. **Gather information and facts.** Next, students should make sure that they have all the necessary information about the situation. Ask questions and observe.

3. **Go from the general to the specific.** Encourage students to look at the big picture as they gain a general understanding of the context of the problem. Break down the problem into its smaller parts.

4. **Develop a plan.** Problem solvers formulate a potential plan of action based on the information gathered. Students should outline their plan step-by-step and evaluate how the problem will be affected if their plan is enacted.

5. **Make connections.** If students can learn to connect what they have learned in other classes to the problem at hand, they will become successful problem solvers.

6. **Be flexible and creative.** Problems often have a variety of acceptable outcomes. Students should approach the situation from different viewpoints and directions, exploring options. Speculation, intuition, and estimation are important in this process.

How to Teach Critical Thinking

All educational disciplines strive to teach critical thinking skills. Today's business environment is highly competitive and demands skilled employees who can make insightful decisions and solve problems creatively. Your students will need to apply critical thinking skills to make important personal and professional plans and decisions in their own lives now and in the future. When you teach your students critical thinking, you are equipping them with skills that are essential to success.

Since all learning requires thinking, your students will benefit from exposure to a variety of thinking exercises. Benjamin Bloom's Taxonomy of the Cognitive Domain is widely recognized for its schema of levels of thinking. Each of Bloom's cognitive categories includes a list of thinking skills and indicates the kinds of behavior students are expected to demonstrate when performing specific learning tasks. Here are some examples:

Bloom's Cognitive Categories

Thinking Skill	Behaviors Required
Knowledge	define, recognize, recall, identify, label, understand, examine, show, collect
Comprehension	translate, interpret, explain, describe, summarize, extrapolate
Application	apply, solve, experiment, show, predict
Analysis	connect, relate, differentiate, classify, arrange, check, group, distinguish, organize, categorize, detect, compare, infer
Synthesis	produce, propose, design, plan, combine, formulate, compose, hypothesize, construct
Evaluation	appraise, judge, criticize, decide

Integrating Critical Thinking Skills

The student text book and this Teacher Resource Manual provide you with a variety of activities and guidelines to help you incorporate and integrate critical thinking and problem-solving skills into your daily plans. The following are some guidelines for integrating and teaching these skills:

◆ Let students know they are engaging in aspects of critical thinking. Explain to students that finding solutions to problems is an example of analyzing and evaluating information. Extend these applications of critical thinking skills into your students' lives; point out that they constantly analyze and evaluate music, conversations with friends, magazine or newspaper articles, and television programs. This will help demonstrate to students that they have had experience in using these skills.

◆ Stress the importance of critical thinking in daily life. Students should learn to focus on sound decision-making processes, not snap judgments.

◆ Use activities that focus on open-ended problems to foster greater growth for creative problem-solving. Discuss how people use different thought processes to solve problems. When possible, have students share their ideas and discuss how they arrived at their solutions.

◆ Organize students in cooperative learning groups so they can see how others solve problems, give each other feedback, and try out new ideas. Divide students into small discussion groups to think in a cooperative setting.

◆ Use assessments that measure students' growth and performance. Challenge students to reflect on chapter concepts and apply their knowledge. Ask students to apply their analytical skills to solve a problem.

◆ Provide feedback and encourage students to feel comfortable experimenting with new ideas and new ways to solve problems.

Improving Basic Skills

As your students progress through their academic education, basic skills in reading, writing, listening, and math continue to evolve and expand. In the classroom there are many opportunities to expose students to activities and exercises that not only contribute to their understanding of the subject matter, but also strengthen basic skills.

Developing Active Reading Strategies for Students

How well do your students read? Do they understand what they read? Are they active readers or passive readers? By applying various strategies for reading, you can help your students understand even difficult concepts and theories.

To begin, have your students analyze their reading skills. Are they good at reading factual material? Is it easy or difficult for them to read and interpret data? Do they have a good vocabulary? Then discuss with your students the different skills needed when reading factual material as opposed to recreational material. In order to get the most from reading, your students need to learn how to become active readers, getting involved with and responding to the material. Active readers are effective readers.

Active reading requires focus and concentration. Becoming actively engaged in reading can mean employing a variety of techniques: taking notes, previewing, outlining main points, jotting down key words, finding definitions, looking for patterns, and summarizing information in written or verbal forms.

Using SQ3R "SQ3R" is known as one of the most successful and efficient study methods used by students. The initials stand for the five steps in the study process: Survey, Question, Read, Recite, and Review. At first, your students may find that the SQ3R method is difficult to master. Putting the steps into practice requires deliberate effort and active involvement. If your students find that they re-read information in order to absorb it, use of this study method will save them time and frustration.

A Reading/Study System The following method could be used by your students on a section-by-section basis for each unit of the text.

S = SURVEY

Students survey the piece of writing to establish its purpose and to prepare themselves for the main ideas. Students should do the following:

◆ Read the titles and section headings.

◆ Read the objectives and instructions to understand how each unit fits the author's purpose.

◆ Notice each boldface heading and subheading. Recognize the text's organization before starting to read. Build a structure for the thought and details to come.

◆ Notice any graphics (charts, maps, diagrams). They are presented to make a point.

◆ Notice reading aids like italics, highlighting, bold face print, unit objectives, and margin notations. They are presented to help the reader sort, comprehend, and remember the ideas of the unit.

Q = QUESTION

As students are surveying the piece, a good way to decide what they will be reading is to question as they survey. Writing down questions keeps students alert and focused on their work. Students should do the following:

◆ Divide a sheet of paper in half lengthwise.

◆ On the left half, write questions as they are surveying the section of writing.

◆ Turn the boldface headings into as many questions as they think will be answered in that section. The better the questions, the better their comprehension is likely to be. Students may always add further questions as they proceed. When their minds are actively searching for answers to questions, they become engaged in learning.

R1 = READ

As students read, they should also actively seek answers to their questions. Students should do the following:

◆ Read each section (one at a time) with their questions in mind. Look for the answers and write them down on the right side of the sheet of paper.

◆ Take notes on additional concepts that were not covered in their questions.

◆ Notice whether they need to make up some new questions and add them to their list.

R2 = RECITE

After students have read and answered all of their questions, it is helpful to recite the questions and their answers.

Students should do the following:

◆ Recite each question out loud, one at a time.

◆ Answer each question verbally according to the answer they have written down on the right side of the paper.

◆ Create flashcards for difficult concepts or procedures.

◆ After each section, stop, recall their questions, and see if they can answer them from memory. If not, look back again, but do not go on to the next section until they can recite the answers.

R3 = REVIEW

Once students finish the entire unit using these steps, they should review all the questions from the headings. They should do the following:

◆ Using their notes, questions, and answers, mentally go over the material within 24 hours of covering it.

◆ Review again after one week.

◆ Review approximately once a month until their exam.

◆ Be sure they can still answer all of the questions they posed in the Question phase of their study process. If not, look back and refresh their memory.

Remember to stress that reading is not a passive activity! Students must train their minds to actively learn!

GRID FOR SQ3R

Students can use the following grid to help them use the SQ3R system.

S = SURVEY: *Survey the piece of writing to establish its purpose.*	
Titles, Headings, and Subheadings	List unit, chapters, projects, etc.
Objectives/Instructions/Terms	List the major objectives, instructions, and terms used in the text.
Graphics/Visuals	List graphics/visuals in text.
Reading Aids	Objectives, section questions, bolded terms, etc., are all designed to emphasize important information.
Q = QUESTION: *Question as you survey the materials.*	
Ask questions based on main headings and titles.	For example: What is desktop publishing?
R1 = READ: *As you read, actively seek answers to your questions. Write them down as you find the answers in your reading.*	
For example: What is desktop publishing?	Desktop publishing is the use of a computer to combine text and graphics on a page.

Writing for Success

Effective writing skills are essential for communicating information. Emphasize these four basic steps to students as they attempt to communicate in writing:

1. **Prepare** Emphasize the importance of generating and focusing ideas through brainstorming, research, and observation.

2. **Organize** Review the importance of organizing an outline so students can keep focused on the theme, format, and ideas they want to express.

3. **Write** It is vital that students learn how to develop their main topic and supporting points. Encourage students to prepare a timetable for completing a written assignment and to use this schedule to meet a deadline.

4. **Edit** Emphasize the importance of revising their written work. Ask students how they think editing may help improve their grades.

Listening with Intent

Although attending lectures, taking notes, and gathering information are a daily part of your students' lives, they may not have devoted the proper attention to becoming effective listeners. Professionals in the world of business attend meetings, follow directions, work with clients and customers, take notes, and give and receive feedback. In order to successfully participate in these activities in the future, students must learn to be fully attentive with an intent to understand the topics presented. Active listening must include a desire to listen, a willingness to learn, the postponement of judgment of the teacher or speaker, a mindful approach, a respectful viewpoint, an observant mind-set, and an ability to ask questions. It is important for the listener to invest energy in the act of listening, to reduce distractions, and to be quiet while the speaker is delivering a message.

Strengthening Arithmetic/Mathematics Skills

Basic arithmetic computations are performed on a daily basis in the lives of your students when they compute percentages, keep track of their bank accounts, or calculate their wages after deductions. Draw upon these life experiences to strengthen math skills. Remind students that they can perform basic computations and approach practical problems by choosing appropriately from a variety of mathematical techniques.

Thinking Algebraically

Algebraic thinking recognizes various types of patterns and functional relationships and uses symbolic forms to represent and analyze mathematical situations and structures. Many life and work experiences can be expressed in algebraic terms. Your students' life experiences should provide a broad base of real-world ties that can be readily linked to the concepts of equation, function, and graphs. Use logic puzzles, tables and graphs, and concepts centered on equations to help build algebraic thinking.

COURSE ENRICHMENT GUIDELINES

The following guidelines will help students recognize the value of their efforts and attitudes toward promoting their social, ethical, and cultural awareness as it applies to the course.

Integrating Real-World Connections

Students want to see the relevance of what they are studying. Stress how the course brings them closer to reaching their personal and professional goals. Use practical applications when possible. Make certain that your examples are relevant to students and that you ask them for examples that illustrate concepts.

Value Students' Experiences

Students have a wealth of experience. Have them integrate course concepts with their experiences. Discuss their viewpoints and encourage classroom discussions.

Discuss School and Community Resources That Can Help Students

You can use many resources at school and in the community to help in teaching. Some schools have faculty development coordinators, special workshops, and speakers.

Invite Guest Speakers to Your Class

Guest speakers can be an important addition to your class because:

◆ They are experts in their area.

◆ They add variety.

◆ They help students see the resources available.

◆ They help students see the value of networking and contacts.

You should give your guest speaker this information:

◆ Purpose of the class

◆ Description of the students

◆ Purpose of the presentation

◆ Topic and what you would like to see covered

◆ Appropriate amount of time to talk

◆ Time, place, and directions to the classroom

Ask the speaker for a brief description of his or her background, how he or she would like to be introduced, and if he or she has questions for the students to answer. Remember to send a thank-you note and comments from students.

Evaluate guest speakers for your records by filling in this form:

Guest Speaker Form

Date: _____

Guest speaker: _____

Topic: _____

Students' reaction: _____

Teacher's assessment: _____

Possible alternatives for speakers in this area: _____

_____

_____

Integrating Ethics

When students begin to engage in business transactions and act as employees and managers, they will encounter ethical dilemmas requiring sound decision-making skills. Students should understand that unethical behavior is often perceived as unethical only after the action or decision has been taken or made.

The purpose of introducing ethics into your instruction is to help your students integrate ethical considerations and basic values into their decision-making process. Students are directed to develop a process for considering both the business and the ethical ramifications of a decision before that decision is made. Even though basic values are set in childhood, people do make different decisions as they gain knowledge and insight.

Teaching Ethics

Educational instruction of ethics as a discipline is an aspect of teaching that is commonly ignored. Yet, you do know how to make decisions and most likely have personal experiences with decisions involving ethical ramifications. You need not be an ethics theorist to incorporate discussions of ethical actions into your instruction.

The Ethical Decision-Making Model

This ethical decision-making model will help your students analyze a situation, evaluate alternatives, consider ramifications of each decision, and choose among the alternatives. The five-step model described on the next page is one possible approach to making an ethical decision.

- What are the ethical issues?
- What are the alternatives?
- Who are the affected parties?
- How do the alternatives affect the parties?
- What would you do?

CLASSROOM MANAGEMENT GUIDELINES

Even the most experienced teacher can have problems in the classroom. The following strategies are designed to help you handle the more common problems encountered by educators. Should you encounter situations that require stronger discipline than what is discussed here, contact your supervisor to learn your school's guidelines concerning student disciplinary procedures.

Attendance Problems

Sometimes students do not understand how important it is to attend every class. Here are some tips for handling attendance problems:

- **Expect regular attendance.** From the first day of class, announce that attendance, participation, and team cooperation will be graded. Stress that assessing the students' strengths, weaknesses, needs, and motivational levels is important for completing assignments and evaluating progress. Point out that when students miss class, they disappoint their teams. If a student misses class without telling you in advance, talk with the student in private and ask for a commitment.

- **Grade attendance.** Remind students that attendance and participation are large parts of their grade. Prompt attendance is important to a class, students, and teams, and promotes positive habits for the workplace.

Problems with Incomplete Work

You may have some students who are not turning in assignments. Here are some teaching tips to encourage students to complete their work:

- **Communicate expectations.** Explain the guidelines and expectations for receiving a good grade or credit for the course. Discuss what students want to learn from the course and what that means in terms of attendance, assignments, and participation. As suggested earlier, you may want to have students turn in note cards with their name, phone number, the grade they expect to earn, what they hope to learn from the course, and the areas they most want to work on. This is an excellent time to review their goals.

- **Contact students.** Call or e-mail students when they miss class, do not participate, or fail to turn in assignments. After this contact, it is up to students to produce results. Show your concern but avoid rescuing them. They need to be responsible for their behavior.

Attitude Problems

A few students may be unsure of what is expected or skeptical of the value of the course. Dealing with different attitude problems is an important part of classroom management.

Negative Attitude

Occasionally, you may have a student who is negative, argumentative, and refuses to participate in team activities or contribute to class discussions. A negative attitude may indicate a feeling of discomfort or fear. Here are some teaching tips for handling negative attitudes:

◆ **Expect responsibility.** Stress that students are responsible for their attitudes. Coaching and encouragement often inspire the negative student. Remind students they are responsible for motivating themselves and creating a resourceful state of mind. They cannot blame others and empower themselves at the same time.

◆ **Isolate the problem student.** Meet with the disruptive student. Indicate that students who are disruptive during team exercises or class discussion will be asked to leave. Indicate that students with negative attitudes affect the entire class. If students complain or are uncooperative, have them answer this question: What can I do to correct this situation?

Unmotivated Students

Increasing motivation is a major factor in helping students to try new strategies, perform the required work, and attend all classes. Here are some teaching tips for handling unmotivated students:

◆ **Review strategies.** As a group, discuss how students can cope with low motivation. Invite a guest speaker to address motivation and attitude.

◆ **Make learning active.** When energy is low (and it often is around mid-term), you may want to go on a field trip. You could also vary the assignments or discuss students' solutions for increasing motivation and creating a more positive attitude.

◆ **Model enthusiasm.** When you are excited and enthusiastic about class, students are more likely to be motivated. Enjoy what you are doing and do not get discouraged by a lack of motivation.

Personality Conflicts

At times you may feel that students do not like you. Here are some teaching tips for avoiding personality conflicts:

◆ **Do not take it personally.** Some students want to appear cool or tough and will not let anyone get close to them. Other students may be especially shy or unresponsive. These behaviors are rarely directed at you alone.

◆ **Clarify perceptions.** Perhaps there is a misunderstanding or students are unclear about expectations. Be open to listening and trying to improve communication.

◆ **Discuss learning styles.** Discuss different learning and relating styles. Explain to students that they will have many different kinds of teachers and employers, and it is important to be able to relate and communicate with all kinds of people. Sometimes people are uncomfortable with a teacher because he or she has a different teaching/learning style.

◆ **Be yourself.** Be confident, approachable, supportive, and a good listener. Your goal is to support students in being successful both inside and outside the classroom.

Behavior Problems

Behavior problems can disrupt the classroom and make it difficult for students to learn. Use the following guidelines to deal with common classroom disruptions.

Class Interruptions

Here are some teaching tips for avoiding interruptions:

◆ **Expect good manners.** The point of listening until others are finished talking should be stressed from the first day of class. Emphasize how important civility and etiquette are in school and in the workplace.

◆ **Model respect.** Show respect to students by modeling good listening skills. Discuss periodically the importance of listening without interrupting or criticizing in teams, classes, and relationships.

Too Much Socializing

Sometimes students seem to be having so much fun socializing in class that they do not complete their assignments. Here are some teaching tips for reducing student socializing:

◆ **Time exercises.** Set a certain amount of time for group and class discussions and exercises. This time limit helps students focus on the task at hand. You can always extend the time if necessary.

◆ **Do first things first.** Go over the first rule of time management: Do first things first. Set priorities, follow through, and then have fun. Tell students that they will gain confidence when they learn this important habit.

Side Talking in Class

Inappropriate side talking is disruptive and distracting. Side talking is especially common when friends sit in the back of the classroom. Here are some teaching tips to cut down side talking:

◆ **Encourage courtesy.** Restate your expectations and rules for the class and be consistent. Encourage students to be respectful of all speakers.

◆ **Illustrate the disruption.** Often students think that because they are in the back of the classroom, the teacher does not see or hear them. Demonstrate the effects of side talking on a speaker and the class. Choose a student to speak in front of the classroom. Have a few other students talk among themselves. Ask the speaker what it was like to try and speak over conversations. Stress that public speaking and giving presentations are already difficult without distractions or rude behavior.

◆ **Clarify your feelings.** Use the "I" message to communicate how you feel: "I feel that what I am saying is being ignored when students side talk."

Participation Problems

Active learning simply requires students to participate in class and to interact with classmates. Anticipating students who are reluctant to participate will help you adjust your teaching style to accommodate unequal participation in class.

Lack of Class Participation

Class participation helps you learn more about your students and encourages them to keep up with assignments. You will have some students who are not willing to participate or talk. Here are some teaching tips to help increase participation:

◆ **Talk about the benefits of cooperative learning.** Tell students that when they become professionals, they will find that organizations are run by teams and require employees to participate.

◆ **Review expectations.** Announce the first day of the class and several times thereafter that teamwork and participation are important factors in this course and essential in the working world. People who are successful learn to work with various types of people, regardless of whether they like them.

◆ **Emphasize that students be prepared.** If students do not keep up with assignments, then they cannot contribute to the rest of the class.

◆ **Get involved.** Indicate that participation and team sharing make the class much more effective and enjoyable. Some students may feel more comfortable talking and participating in a small group. You may want to have teams of four or five students discuss exercises and then spend a few minutes discussing the topic with the class. Teamwork brings out participation even with shy students.

Unequal Participation

Often it is only assertive students who lead the discussions. Here are some teaching tips for getting all students to participate:

◆ **Encourage all class members.** It is important for you to stress that this course depends on the participation of all class members. Occasionally call on the quieter members of the class. Sometimes this makes it easier for them to participate.

◆ **Encourage listening.** Listening is not only vital for healthy relationships; it is also an important job skill. Encourage students to listen and to monitor how much time they speak in groups. Communication is always enhanced when people listen and contribute.

Shy Students

You will always have some students who are shy and do not contribute as much as the more outgoing students. Here are some teaching tips for encouraging shy students:

◆ **Integrate learning styles.** Discuss the different learning styles with students. Point out that some people are more extroverted than others.

◆ **Take a risk.** If students are shy, ask them to reach out and be more involved. Extroverted students should listen more to draw out the shyer students. Encourage your outgoing students to be supportive, to listen, and to help others express their views. You might want to shift the seating about every four weeks so that shy students sit up front during some of the sessions.

◆ **Stress class participation.** Acknowledge that many students are shy but are often more comfortable working in small teams.

◆ **Give positive reinforcement.** Call on students who do not participate much, but who are otherwise doing well in class. If they get a positive response to their contributions, they may become less reluctant to talk in class.

COOPERATIVE LEARNING

Studies show that students learn faster and retain more information when they are actively involved in the learning process. Studies also show that in a classroom setting, students often learn more from each other about subject matter than from a traditional teacher-led lecture and discussion. Cooperative learning is one method that gets students actively involved in learning and at the same time allows for peer teaching.

Cooperative learning helps students acquire the interaction skills that are increasingly necessary in today's team-oriented workplaces. Working in teams is so much a part of the workplace that many employers give prospective employees inventories and assessments to determine their ability to function within a team framework. Through the use of cooperative learning, the teacher can emphasize the collaborative skills of team-building and team decision-making, and social skills such as how to listen, respond, agree, disagree, clarify, encourage, and evaluate.

The Basic Elements of Cooperative Learning

In traditional educational settings, students tend to work on their own and compete with one another. In the cooperative learning environment, students work in teams and contribute to each other's learning. Cooperative learning is structured for small group learning, which meets the basic needs for interpersonal relationships, personal growth, and enhanced learning. All members of the group benefit from each other's efforts, backgrounds, experiences, and viewpoints. Cooperative learning can provide invigorating classroom dynamics; increase respect for diversity; and encourage skills in effective listening and speaking, leadership, decision-making, and conflict resolution.

Cooperative learning involves assigning students to small groups to work together within a classroom setting. This learning structure is especially effective for more difficult learning tasks, such as problem-solving, critical thinking, and conceptual learning. Cooperative learning requires a supportive, student-centered, and non-competitive climate. It supplements rather than replaces traditional approaches, including lectures.

Cooperative learning groups emphasize:

◆ Supporting mutual goals rather than individual competition and achievement

◆ Completing structured tasks where each team member contributes

◆ Sharing equal responsibility for accomplishing group goals

◆ Learning social skills

◆ Rotating interdependent roles (discussion leaders, recorders, observers, listeners, and speakers)

- Maintaining equal participation
- Encouraging individual responsibility

The Benefits of Cooperative Learning Groups

Cooperative learning offers many benefits:

- Students are drawn into learning situations that require them to be directly involved. Each student must make a contribution as well as accept input from others.
- Students discover how to work with people of all types. Schools with racially or ethnically mixed populations often improve interracial and multicultural relationships between students.
- Students improve communication skills.
- Students learn valuable social and problem-solving skills that transfer to real-world occupations and work environments.
- Students learn to work through conflicts.

Preparation for Cooperative Learning

Before assigning a cooperative learning activity, prepare your students for the cooperative learning process. The following tips will help you set the stage for effective cooperative learning.

- **Classroom Arrangement** Move the furniture in the room so that students can face each other.
- **Group Size** Decide on the size of the group. Groups work best when composed of two to five students.
- **Group Assignments** Assign students to groups. Each group should be mixed racially, socially, ethnically, and by gender and range of ability.
- **Rotation of Group Members** Change groups periodically. For example, you can change the groups every four to six weeks, every quarter, every semester, or for every new chapter or section.
- **Student Preparation** Prepare students for cooperation. Students will work with each other to accomplish the same goal, but each student will be individually accountable for learning.
- **Initial Activities** Start small. It is not necessary to incorporate all the characteristics of cooperative learning into the first activity. Some ideas will be easy to adapt while others may be more difficult.
- **Group Roles** Explain group roles. Students need to learn the cooperative skills that are fundamental to each role before they begin interacting in cooperative activities. Their roles should be introduced to students one at a time so the students can learn the differences between them.

Create Heterogeneous Teams

Within the first or second class meeting, place students in four- or five-member teams. You can create heterogeneous class teams by mixing characteristics:

◆ Learning abilities

◆ Genders

◆ Cultures

◆ Ethnicities

Teachers and team members should assess their team's effectiveness and reflect on the learning process and outcomes. Is the team effective? Does everyone contribute? How can the team be more effective?

Teachers can ascertain how teams interact by completing a chapter exercise each class period. By starting the class with an exercise, you emphasize skills acquisition. Students get the opportunity to become acquainted with each other and exchange ideas.

Teacher and Student Responsibilities

The success of the cooperative learning groups depends largely on the teacher's ability to coach each of the groups and on the students' abilities to accomplish a goal as a team.

The Teacher:

◆ Creates the learning environment.

◆ Structures and guides the process of learning.

◆ Motivates students to learn.

◆ States the goals of the instruction.

◆ Teaches the fundamental concepts.

◆ Interacts with and guides the work of many groups.

◆ Acts as a resource to the groups as needed.

◆ Monitors student behavior.

◆ Evaluates the group process.

The Students:

◆ Work toward group goals, yet understand that individual responsibility is expected.

◆ Contribute their own ideas.

◆ Understand that they are responsible for one another's learning as well as their own.

◆ Draw upon their own creativity and on the strengths of their teammates.

◆ Communicate effectively with one another.

◆ Recognize that the differences among team members are a form of enrichment, not a deficit.

Results of Cooperative Learning

In most classrooms, only a few outspoken and articulate students actively participate. However, one of the goals of cooperative learning is to get all members of the class to share ideas, express opinions, and participate in group exercises. Emphasize the value of inclusive participation and the responsibility of outspoken students to encourage less talkative students to express their views. Stress the importance of listening and taking turns to talk.

CULTURAL DIVERSITY

Schools are becoming increasingly diverse environments. Diversity includes factors such as gender, race, age, sexual orientation, ethnicity, physical ability, social and economic background, and religion.

The Diverse Classroom

Your class may include students who have learning disabilities; students who are very goal-oriented; transfer students; students on probation; athletes; students of different races, cultures, and religions; and students who are physically impaired. Each of these students will have different needs and problems. The more you know about each individual, the more you will be able to use various strategies, learning methods, examples, and approaches to meet their specific needs.

Emphasize that we can all learn from each other by being open and sharing different views, values, ideas, and goals. Encourage all students to get to know people from different races, cultures, backgrounds, and religions. As contributing members of society, ask your students to assess their assumptions, judgments, prejudices, and stereotypes. Discuss how critical thinking can lead to changes in beliefs and attitudes.

Examine your own concerns, fears, prejudices, and assumptions. Avoid generalizations and make certain your lectures are sensitive to the needs and views of all your students. Be a model for tolerance and understanding, and increase your awareness of other cultures or ethnic groups.

Supporting Diversity

The population of the United States is becoming increasingly diverse. As students from many backgrounds enter our schools, it is becoming evident that versatility is the key for learning. The traditional delivery mode of the teacher lecturing to passive, inexperienced students is no longer relevant. Varied learning approaches and students' active involvement are necessary if students are to make meaningful connections to their classes and to the world of work.

Help prepare students to work with and celebrate differences between fellow students. Have students discuss situations in which they felt different because they were younger, older, of a different religion or culture, or a minority of some other type.

Explore the available resources in the school and community that support diversity. Post lists of noted speakers, events, and opportunities promoting increased awareness and understanding. Bring in speakers who discuss how to celebrate and promote diversity. Encourage students from different cultures to participate and assume leadership roles.

Teaching Tips for the Diverse Classroom

Here are some teaching tips that may help students learn to value and understand diversity:

◆ **Be inviting.** Students need to feel that they belong. Make your classroom and office inviting. Be personable, get to know students, and welcome them to your office. Ask questions about how they are adjusting and show that you are interested.

◆ **Invite outside speakers.** Bring in speakers from different cultural backgrounds.

◆ **Use peer facilitators.** Hire peer facilitators or tutors from different cultural backgrounds.

◆ **Plan outside events.** Investigate resources on campus and in the community. Have students attend different cultural events or take a field trip as part of the class experience.

◆ **Discuss resources.** Have a list of resources available for various cultural groups.

◆ **Encourage class discussions.** Encourage all students to discuss their viewpoints. Point out how people see things differently. Understanding and respecting differences are the foundations of building common bonds.

◆ **Encourage creativity and flexibility.** Stress that people can speak and act differently in different situations. Being flexible and relating to diverse people at home, at school, or in the community both expand options and build relationships. Relating to different people does not mean students are rejecting their own culture. They are expanding their communication and relationship skills.

Tips for Working with Diverse Students

High-Risk Students

The term "high-risk student" is often used today to describe students who are at risk of dropping out of school. Emphasize that everyone has some risk factors, and that the more students assess their strengths and weaknesses, the more likely they are to ask for help and thus succeed. Stress to students that the key is to take responsibility for who they are, where they are, and where they want to be.

Transfer Students

Transfer students are often most concerned with what credits are transferred and are acceptable for meeting the school's requirements. It is critical that transfer students see an advisor and plan their educational program. Transfer students may think they already know the rules. Stress that every school is different and students should not assume that the procedures are the same.

Student Athletes

Athletes have the same issues that other students have, plus they have a large commitment of time for sports practice and the additional stresses of competition, risk of injury, and the need to stay energized and focused on winning.

Here are some teaching tips for student athletes:

- **Clarify expectations.** Stress that attending and participating in all classes is important. Athletes' top priority should be school and not sports.

- **Help students clarify their goals.** Talk about their academic and career goals. What do they want to do when they finish school? How can this course help them reach their goals? What personal qualities and skills have they gained by playing sports?

- **Emphasize planning.** Show students the importance of planning and time management. Have them keep a time log so they can set their priorities and keep their commitments.

Students on Academic Probation

Many students do not understand how easy it is to fall behind and find themselves on academic probation. You may want to invite the principal or another administrator to discuss what "probation" and "disqualified" mean and how students can stay in good standing academically. At some schools a student will be placed on academic probation when his or her overall grade average falls below a C average.

Here are some teaching tips for students on academic probation:

- **Take fewer units.** Students on probation are advised to not take more than 12 units.

- ◆ **Compute GPA.** Show students how to compute their grade point average.
- ◆ **Talk to teachers.** Stress the importance of meeting with each of their teachers and obtaining regular progress reports or grades.
- ◆ **Meet with an advisor.** Students on probation need special attention. Stress the importance of students meeting with their advisors.

International Students

The number of international students is increasing dramatically at many schools. The adjustment to a new culture, language, and climate is tremendous.

Here are some teaching tips for international students:

- ◆ **Stress involvement.** Encourage students to form supportive relationships with various types of people by getting involved in school or community activities.
- ◆ **Explore resources.** Learn what resources are available both at school and in the community for international students.
- ◆ **Encourage mentoring.** Many schools have a mentoring program. Connect the international student with a student who has been at school for at least a year.
- ◆ **Speak clearly.** If the student's primary language is not English, speak clearly and slowly, avoid slang, and explain the meaning of common expressions and phrases.
- ◆ **Clarify assignments.** Make sure students understand what is expected of them. Put important information in writing. It is important that you do not come across as condescending, which can make the students feel uncomfortable.
- ◆ **Be warm and friendly.** International students need to see a friendly face. Smile and be welcoming.
- ◆ **Integrate learning styles.** As with all students, international students can benefit from seeing, hearing, doing, and utilizing information.
- ◆ **Learn about other cultures.** Cultural differences in body language, attitudes toward time, slang, and eye contact may be dramatic. Ask questions and be respectful.
- ◆ **Encourage students to talk.** All students can benefit from hearing the experiences of international students. Ask them to explain their customs, country, and background.

MEETING SPECIAL NEEDS

Your classroom contains learners who possess their own unique set of abilities, perceptions, and needs. In order to meet the special needs of students with physical or learning challenges, you may need to utilize more than one approach to teaching. Auditory, visual, or physical difficulties may interfere with an individual's ability to learn in the same way as other students, yet these special needs students have the same educational, social, emotional, and personality development goals. This Teacher Resource Manual provides a variety of teaching strategies to help you modify and creatively support the concepts that students need to learn.

Students with Special Needs

There are many definitions of what constitutes a learning disability. All of us have certain deficiencies and strengths. The point is to encourage all students to assess their strengths and to seek help in coping with their deficiencies.

Special needs and disabilities may be visible or invisible. Some students are deficient in certain skills. They may be required to take remedial math or English. Other students may have learning disabilities and have difficulty processing information. This difficulty may interfere with their abilities to take tests, write, read, solve math problems, or comprehend information. Other students may have physical or health disabilities.

The Americans with Disabilities Act disabled stipulates that disabled students are entitled access to public education. Students should investigate the available resources at their schools. Many schools have a disabled student support services office. Public schools provide accessibility to classrooms, labs, and the library.

Meeting Individual Needs and Learning Styles

One of your greatest challenges as a teacher is to provide a positive learning environment for all students in your classroom. Because each student is unique, their learning styles and physical abilities may vary widely.

Improve your teaching effectiveness by understanding how students learn and by integrating different learning styles. Students can improve their learning by discovering how they learn best. This understanding can empower them to take control of their learning.

To help you provide all your students with a positive learning experience, the text provides a variety of activities. This diversity will stimulate student interest, motivate learning, and facilitate understanding.

Teaching Students with Special Needs

Students in your classroom may have orthopedic impairments. They may have hearing or vision impairments, learning disabilities, or behavior disorders—all of which may interfere with their ability to learn. The learning styles of your students may also vary. Some students may be visual learners, while others may learn more effectively through hands-on activities. Some students may work well independently, while others need the interaction of other students. Students may come from a variety of cultural backgrounds, and some may be second-language learners.

Once you determine the special needs of your students, you can identify the areas in the curriculum that may present barriers to them. In order to remove those barriers, you may need to modify your teaching methods.

Preparing for Special Needs

In your classroom, you may encounter students who have special needs. A Special Needs Information and Resources chart (pages 76–79) describes some of those special needs and identifies sources of information. Also provided are tips for modifying your teaching style to accommodate the special needs of your students.

The Different Learning Styles chart (pages 80–83) will help you identify your students' learning styles, provides a description of each type of learner, the likes of each type, what each type is good at, and how each type learns best. Famous learners within each type are also listed.

As you prepare for the special learning needs of your students, follow these general guidelines:

◆ Identify the special needs of your students.
◆ Identify areas in the curriculum that may present barriers to some students.
◆ Define ways to remove any impediments to their learning.
◆ Modify your teaching methods to meet your students' needs.
◆ Consult with your school professionals about students with special needs.

Modifying Your Teaching Style

Learning can occur in a variety of ways and at different speeds. To maximize their learning experience, it is important to recognize how each of your students learns best. You can meet their various needs by offering activities, resources, and experiences that will help them learn effectively. This will help students reduce frustration, focus on their strengths, and achieve an understanding of the concepts.

Vary the way in which you present material so that you are appealing to all of the different learning styles. If you have traditionally relied on a lecture-question format, consider incorporating more visual aids into your instruction. Instead of explaining a concept only verbally, integrate the use of transparencies, handouts, or charts.

- **For visual learners:** Use visual aids, such as PowerPoint presentations, the board, and transparency masters.
- **For auditory learners:** Present lectures, use small group discussion, and repeat important material.
- **For kinesthetic learners:** Use field trips, student presentations, role-playing, case studies, and activities.

Assign class time for different activities. Use student speakers to add interest and information to the class. As you make adjustments for the benefit of your special needs students, it is important to avoid calling attention to these modifications. By developing good relationships with your special needs students, you can address their specific challenges and offer encouragement.

Another challenge in dealing with special needs learners is how to have them relay to you their understanding of the course material. Methods of assessment may have to be altered in order to fairly apply the same standards to all students. For example, a student who has difficulty writing may have to take a test orally or use a computer. A student who deals with physical challenges may not be equipped to participate in some group activities and may be better evaluated using a project designed for an individual.

Encourage special needs students to take leadership roles just as other students do. They should understand that they offer unique skills, talents, and perspectives to the activities and concepts they are learning.

Tips for Teaching Students with Special Needs

Here are some tips for teaching students with special needs:

- **Be aware of physical requirements.** When an activity requires students to write on a chalkboard or marker board, students who use wheelchairs may require that the board be lowered, or they may use an overhead projector. For students with visual impairments, an oral response is appropriate.
- **Encourage responsibility.** The student is responsible for documenting a disability and requesting accommodations and assistance. Encourage students to communicate what they need to be successful. Encourage them to take responsibility for their learning. Have students find resources available on campus and in the community.
- **Learn about the Americans with Disabilities Act (ADA).** As a teacher, you will want to know about guidelines and resources. Find out what resources are available to support students with disabilities.

◆ **See the whole student.** Do not allow disabilities to create a faulty perception of a student's talents, effort, and abilities.

◆ **Use various learning styles.** Use visual, auditory, and hands-on learning techniques. Have students discover how they learn and relate best. Knowing how they learn, process information, and relate to others is an essential tool that students can use for school and job success. Have students integrate different learning styles.

◆ **Use success tips and strategies.** Studying in teams, previewing chapters, sitting in the front row, attending all classes, actively participating in class, making learning active, taping lectures, planning daily schedules, and getting organized are just a few tips that can help students succeed.

◆ **Encourage students to meet with teachers and advisors.** One of the best tips is to encourage students to meet with each of their teachers and their advisors. Students should review course expectations, plan a course of study, and seek feedback.

◆ **Encourage students to use available resources.** Have students explore campus resources. For example, many schools have tutors, learning centers, free workshops, and study guides. Encourage students to seek tutors, and to ask teachers for extra help, more classroom discussions, explanations, alternative methods for completing projects or testing, and extended time for tests. Being assertive involves speaking calmly, concisely, directly, and courteously. Students do not need to be pushy or aggressive to ask for what they need.

◆ **Use individualized projects.** Students who are assigned to individual projects are free to progress at their own pace. You may ask your students to use tutorial software that allows learners to advance at their own pace.

Special Needs Information and Resources

The following table contains information and resources that may help teachers who have students with special needs. Teachers should always consult school professionals when working with students who have special needs

Subject	Description	Sources of Information
Students with Limited English Proficiencies	Multicultural and/or bilingual individuals often speak English as a second language. The customs and behavior of people in the majority culture may be confusing to these individuals. Cultural values may inhibit some of these students from full participation.	◆ Teaching English as a Second Language ◆ Mainstreaming and the Minority Child ◆ Children with Limited English: Teaching Strategies for the Regular Classroom ◆ Educational Services to Handicapped Students with Limited English Proficiency: A California Statewide Study/ PBN B621
Students with Behavior Disorders	Individuals with behavior disorders deviate from standards or expectations of behavior and impair the functioning of others and themselves. These learners may also be gifted or learning disabled.	◆ Exceptional Children ◆ Journal of Special Education ◆ Educating Students with Behavior Disorders
Students with Orthopedic Impairments	Individuals who have orthopedic impairments have restructured use of one or more limbs and require the assistance of wheelchairs, crutches, or braces. Other impairments may require the use of respirators or other medical equipment.	◆ The Source Book for the Disabled ◆ Teaching Exceptional Children ◆ Vocational Preparation and Employment of Students with Physical and Multiple Disabilities

Tips for Instruction

◆ Remember that students' ability to speak English does not reflect their academic ability.
◆ Try to incorporate students' cultural experiences into your instruction. The help of a bilingual aide may be effective.
◆ Include information about different cultures in your curriculum to help build students' self-image.
◆ Avoid cultural stereotypes.
◆ Encourage students to share their cultures in the classroom.

◆ Provide a clearly structured environment with regard to scheduling, rules, room arrangement, and safety.
◆ Clearly outline objectives and how you will help students obtain objectives.
◆ Work for long-term improvement; do not expect immediate success.
◆ Model appropriate behavior for students and reinforce it.
◆ Adjust group requirements for individual needs.

◆ Discuss with the student when you should offer aid.
◆ Help students and staff understand orthopedic impairments.
◆ Invite all students to participate in activities including field trips, special events, and projects.
◆ Learn more about special orthopedic devices; be aware of any special safety precautions needed.

continued on next page

Subject	Description	Sources of Information
Students with Visual Impairments	The visually disabled have partial or total loss of sight. Individuals with visual impairments are not significantly different from their sighted peers in ability range or personality. However, blindness may affect cognitive, motor, and social development, especially if early intervention is lacking.	◆ Journal of Visual Impairment and Blindness ◆ Education of Visually Handicapped ◆ American Association for the Blind
Students with Hearing Impairments	Partial or total loss of hearing may affect an individual's cognitive, motor, social, and speech development if early intervention did not occur. The ability range or personality of the hearing impaired is not significantly different from the hearing student.	◆ American Annals of the Deaf ◆ Journal of Speech and Hearing Research ◆ National Association of the Deaf
Students with Learning Disabilities	All learning-disabled students have an academic problem in one or more areas, such as academic learning, language, perception, social-emotional adjustment, memory, or ability to pay attention.	◆ Journal of Learning Disabilities ◆ The ABCs of Learning Disabilities ◆ Learning Disability Quarterly
Gifted Students	Gifted students are often described as those having above-average ability, task commitment, and creativity. Gifted students rank in the top five percent of their class. They usually finish work more quickly than others and are capable of divergent thinking.	◆ Journal for the Education of the Gifted ◆ The National Research Center on the Gifted and Talented

Tips for Instruction

◆ Help students become independent. Modify assignments as needed.
◆ Provide tactile models whenever possible.
◆ Team the students with sighted peers.
◆ Teach classmates to serve as guides.
◆ Tape lectures and reading assignments.

◆ Seat students where they can see your lip movements easily.
◆ Avoid verbal directions.
◆ Avoid standing with your back to the window or to a light source.
◆ Use an overhead projector to help you maintain eye contact while writing.
◆ Write all assignments on the board, or hand out written instructions.

◆ Create a classroom environment that leads to success.
◆ Provide assistance and direction; clearly define rules, assignments, and duties.
◆ Allow for peer interaction during class time; utilize peer helpers.
◆ Practice skills frequently.
◆ Use games and drills to help maintain interest.
◆ Allow students to record answers on tape, and allow extra time to complete tests and assignments.
◆ Provide outlines or tape lecture materials.

◆ Emphasize concepts, theories, relationships, ideas, and generalizations.
◆ Let students express themselves in a variety of ways including drawing, creative writing, or acting.
◆ Make arrangements for students to work on independent projects.
◆ Make arrangements for students to advance to selected subjects early.
◆ Utilize public services and resources, such as agencies providing free and inexpensive materials, community services and programs, and people in the community with specific expertise.

Different Learning Styles

Students often have different learning styles. Knowing how a particular student learns can be the key to academic success.

Type	Description	Likes to...
Verbal/Linguistic Learner	Intelligence is related to words and language, written and spoken.	read, write, tell stories, play word games, and tell jokes and riddles.
Logical/ Mathematical Learner	Intelligence deals with inductive and deductive thinking and reasoning, numbers, and abstractions.	perform experiments, solve puzzles, work with numbers, ask questions, and explore patterns and relationships.
Visual/Spatial Learner	Intelligence relies on the sense of sight and being able to visualize an object, including the ability to create mental images.	draw, build, design, and create things; daydream; do jigsaw puzzles and mazes; watch videos; look at photos; and draw maps and charts.
Naturalistic Learner	Intelligence involves observing, understanding, and organizing patterns in the natural environment.	spend time outdoors and work with plants, animals, and other parts of the natural environment; good at identifying plants and animals and at hearing and seeing connections to nature.

Is Good at...	Learns Best by...	Famous Learners...
memorizing names, dates, places, and trivia; spelling; using descriptive language; and creating imaginary worlds.	saying, hearing, and seeing words.	◆ Maya Angelou—poet ◆ Abraham Lincoln—U.S. President and statesman ◆ Jerry Seinfeld—comedian
math, reasoning, logic, problem solving, computing numbers, moving from concrete to abstract, and thinking conceptually.	categorizing, classifying, and working with abstract patterns and relationships.	◆ Stephen Hawking—physicist ◆ Albert Einstein—theoretical physicist ◆ Alexa Canady—neurosurgeon
understanding the use of space and how to get around in it, thinking in three-dimensional terms, and imagining things in clear visual images.	visualizing, dreaming, using the mind's eye, and working with colors and pictures.	◆ Pablo Picasso—artist ◆ Maria Martinez—artist ◆ I.M. Pei—architect
measuring, charting, mapping, observing plants and animals, keeping journals, collecting, classifying, and participating in outdoor activities.	visualizing, performing hands-on activities, bringing outdoors into the classroom, and relating home/classroom to the natural world.	◆ George Washington Carver—agricultural chemist ◆ Rachel Carson—scientific writer ◆ Charles Darwin—scientist

continued on next page

Type	Description	Likes to...
Musical/Rhythmic Learner	Intelligence is based on recognition of tonal patterns, including various environmental sounds, and on sensitivity to rhythm and beats.	sing and hum, listen to music, play an instrument, move body when music is playing, and make up songs.
Bodily/Kinesthetic Learner	Intelligence is related to physical movement and the brain's motor cortex, which controls bodily motion.	learn by hands-on methods, demonstrate skill in crafts, tinker, perform, display physical endurance, and challenge self physically.
Interpersonal Learner	Intelligence operates primarily through person-to-person relationships and communication.	have lots of friends, talk to people, join groups, play cooperative games, solve problems as part of a group, and volunteer help when others need it.
Intrapersonal Learner	Intelligence is related to inner states of being, self-reflection, metacognition, and awareness of spiritual realities.	work alone, pursue own interests, daydream, keep a personal diary or journal, and think about starting own business.

Is Good at...	Learns Best by...	Famous Learners...
remembering melodies; keeping time; mimicking beat and rhythm; noticing pitches, rhythms, and background and environmental sounds.	rhythm, melody, and music.	◆ Henry Mancini—composer ◆ Marian Anderson—opera singer ◆ Paul McCartney—singer, songwriter, musician
physical activities such as sports, dancing, acting, and crafts.	touching, moving, interacting with space, and processing knowledge through bodily sensations.	◆ Jackie Joyner-Kersey—Olympic gold medalist ◆ Katherine Dunham—modern dancer ◆ Dr. Christian Barnard—surgical pioneer
understanding people and their feelings, leading others, organizing, communicating, and mediating conflicts.	sharing, comparing, relating, cooperating, and interviewing.	◆ Jimmy Carter—U.S. President, statesman, winner of Nobel Peace Prize ◆ Eleanor Roosevelt—humanitarian ◆ Lee Iacocca—former president of Chrysler Corporation
understanding self, focusing inward on feelings/dreams, following instincts, pursuing interests, and being original.	working alone, doing individualized projects, and engaging in self-paced instruction.	◆ Marva Collins—educator ◆ Mara Montessori—educator and physician ◆ Sigmund Freud—psychotherapist

STUDENT PERFORMANCE ASSESSMENT

Assessing the level of understanding that your students have gained is both an administrative necessity and a useful tool for motivating students. When grading, promote a positive attitude. Grades should provide positive reinforcement of your assessment of students' performance. Grades can also help students feel proud of their accomplishments and motivate them to work at improving their overall performance.

Vary your grading standards according to time and purpose. For example, you may be lenient at the beginning of the course to help students develop feelings of success and confidence. Later, when your expectations are higher, your standards may be more rigid.

Quizzes and tests should be scored and ranked but not necessarily graded. Sometimes percentage grades may be misleading or even confusing. Since many quizzes and some tests, especially short tests, cannot be scored on the basis of 100 percent, many teachers maintain a cumulative record of points earned and make no association with letter grades or percentages.

In determining a student's final grade, do not depend entirely on a mathematical average. Also give consideration to the general quality of the student's homework, the quantity and quality of the student's class participation, and evidence of improvement in skills, knowledge, habits, and attitudes.

As the teacher for this course, you may want to consider the purpose of assessment:

◆ What is it you want to evaluate and why?

◆ What are your goals for the course?

◆ How do you meet your goals and objectives?

Assessment Strategies

You may need a variety of ways to assess what your students have learned. One traditional method of measuring student progress is the written test that evaluates recall of subject content. This course offers students assessment opportunities at the chapter and unit levels. Use *ExamView Assessment Suite* software for Windows® Microsoft® and Macintosh® to evaluate and assess student progress. The companion Online Learning Center Web site also offers self-assessment exercises for your students.

Performance Assessment

It is important to assess more than students' rote learning skills. Performance assessment gives you the opportunity to evaluate whether or not a student has learned to analyze and plan under different sets of circumstances. A traditional paper-and-pencil test will not demonstrate your students' skills in these areas.

The assessment process for this course is designed to be multidimensional and provides you with many activities, projects, and situations that create opportunities for performance assessment. Cooperative learning, discussion activities, and research projects provide opportunities for students to practice new skills and to apply what they have learned to hands-on projects.

Skills Development

Skills development is the application of learning. It is the concept that skills can be taught and that practice of those skills improves learning. The assumptions underlying skills development accept that students:

◆ Are responsible for their learning, their behavior, and their actions.

◆ Must be active participants in the learning process.

◆ Must participate in cooperative and experiential learning.

◆ Must be open and willing to experiment and to learn new ideas, information, and skills.

Ask students to complete the following questions at the end of each chapter or at the end of each week:

◆ What is the most important thing I learned in class this week?

◆ How can I apply what I learned to my other classes?

◆ How can I apply what I learned to the workplace?

Project Assessment Rubric

The rubric on the following page may be used to assess projects, research assignments, and class presentations. You may wish to work with individual students to set more specific goals and use those goals to assess student work. Using this rubric, a student can receive a maximum score of 20 points. The point grade can be assessed as a letter grade following the information below:

Total Possible Points = 20		
Score		**Grade**
18–20	=	A
15–17	=	B
10–14	=	C
5–9	=	D
0–4	=	F

Project Assessment Rubric

	1	2	3	4
Technical Requirements Has the student met the technical requirements of the project as assigned?	No technical requirements have been met.	The student has met some of the technical requirements.	The student has met the technical requirements.	The student has exceeded the technical requirements.
Content Does the project contain the required content as assigned?	No content requirements of the project have been met.	The student has met some of the content requirements.	The student has met the content requirements of the project.	The student has exceeded the content requirements of the project.
Organization Is the information in the project well organized and appropriate to the goals of the project?	The information in the project is not understandable.	The organization of information can be followed with difficulty but is not appropriate to the goals.	The organization of information is adequate and appropriate to the goals.	The organization is logical and interesting; the goals are met in creative ways.
Design Is the design understandable and appropriate to the goals of the project?	The design detracts from the clarity of the project.	The design is somewhat understandable but is not appropriate to the goals.	The design is clear and adequate to the goals.	The design is compelling and creative and serves the goals.
Mechanics Is the text or the speech (for oral presentations) grammatically correct?	The text has more than ten grammatical errors. The student has great difficulty speaking clearly and correctly.	The text has six to nine grammatical errors. The student has some difficulty speaking clearly and correctly.	The text has two to five grammatical errors. The student has little difficulty speaking clearly and correctly.	The text has no grammatical errors. The student's speaking is clear and correct.

Portfolio Assessment

If they are used, student portfolios can also provide assessment opportunities. Have students include in their portfolios:

◆ Work that reflects an achievement of SCANS skills and competencies.

◆ Work that reflects growth as a critical thinker.

◆ Work that demonstrates presentation skills.

◆ Work that shows interdisciplinary thinking.

◆ Something that reflects growth in professional behavior.

◆ Something that shows application of logical reasoning.

◆ Something that shows application of scientific reasoning.

◆ Work that shows an ability to effectively communicate.

◆ Something that shows an aesthetic analysis or evaluation of artwork.

◆ Something from an extracurricular activity that reflects personal or professional growth or understanding.

DETERMINING ASSESSMENT STRATEGIES

The chart below can help you determine which assessment strategies will work best for you and your students.

Assessment Strategies	Advantages	Disadvantages
Objective Measures Multiple choice Matching True/False Fill in the blank	◆ Reliable, easy to validate ◆ Objective, if designed effectively ◆ Low cost, efficient ◆ Automated administration ◆ Lends to equating	◆ Measures cognitive knowledge effectively ◆ Limited on other measures ◆ Not a good measure of overall performance

continued on next page

Assessment Strategies	Advantages	Disadvantages
Written Measures Essays Restricted response Written simulations Case analysis Problem-solving exercises	◆ Face validity (real life) ◆ In-depth assessment ◆ Measures writing skills and higher level skills ◆ Reasonable developmental costs and time	◆ Subjective scoring ◆ Time consuming and expensive to score ◆ Limited breadth ◆ Difficult to equate ◆ Moderate reliability
Oral Measures Oral examinations Interviews	◆ Measures communications and interpersonal skills ◆ In-depth assessment with varied stimulus materials ◆ Learner involvement	◆ Costly and time consuming ◆ Limited reliability ◆ Narrow sample of content ◆ Scoring difficult, need multiple raters
Simulated Activities In-basket Computer simulations	◆ Moderate reliability ◆ Performance-based measure	◆ Costly and time consuming ◆ Difficult to score, administer, and develop
Portfolios and Product Analysis Work samples Projects Work diaries and logs Achievement records	◆ Provides information not normally available ◆ Learner involvement ◆ Face validity (real life) ◆ Easy to collect information	◆ Costly to administer ◆ Labor and paper intensive ◆ Difficult to validate or equate ◆ Biased toward best samples or outstanding qualities

continued on next page

Assessment Strategies	Advantages	Disadvantages
Performance Measures Demonstrations Presentations Performances Production work Observation	◆ Job-related ◆ Relatively easy to administer ◆ In-depth assessment ◆ Face validity (real life)	◆ Greater training required ◆ Hard to equate ◆ Subjective scoring ◆ Time consuming if breadth is needed
Performance Records References Performance rating forms Parental rating	◆ Efficient ◆ Low cost ◆ Easy to administer	◆ Low reliability ◆ Subjective ◆ Hard to equate ◆ Rater judgment
Self-Evaluation	◆ Learner involvement and empowerment ◆ Learner responsibility ◆ Measures dimensions not available otherwise	◆ May be biased or unrealistic

COURSE ASSESSMENT AND EVALUATION

The first place to start in the evaluation process is to examine goals and objectives against outcomes.

Assessment of Teachers

The point of giving teacher and course evaluations is to receive comments from students concerning their opinions of the course and the teacher's teaching. Students can use many standard evaluation forms to evaluate teachers. You may also want to have students give you verbal or written suggestions.

Teacher Self-Assessment

A good place to start when designing your own instructional assessment plan is to review your goals. Give some thought to what it is you want to accomplish. You may have a long list. Review your list carefully and choose the goals that are most important.

◆ What were the goals and objectives of the class?

◆ Did the course meet these goals and objectives?

◆ Did students make connections to other courses?

◆ Did students make connections to the workplace?

◆ Did students use critical thinking and creative problem solving?

◆ Did students learn how to learn?

◆ Did lectures integrate learning styles?

◆ Did students understand the value of cooperative learning?

◆ How can you make the class more experiential and active?

◆ Were guest speakers effective?

◆ What topics did students enjoy most?

Student Assessments of Course

Alternatively, you may want students to evaluate the course. Students can answer the same questions listed above under teacher self-assessment, you may perfer that students complete an evaluation form. An evaluation form should ask specific questions to help students focus on particular topics and concerns that you may have.

Assessment of Outcomes

You may want to gather data and work with staff in research and development to measure outcomes. Compare students who took the class with those who did not. Investigate:

◆ The retention rates of students over several years

◆ GPAs

◆ Graduation rates

You may also want to look at other factors considered important in the success of the class. For example:

◆ The class is limited to 25 students.

◆ The class is taught by experienced teachers.

◆ The class includes peer teachers.

◆ The textbook is new and required.

◆ The course is offered at a reasonable time.

◆ The teachers are given training and support.

Student Advisory Committee

You may want to suggest that a student advisory committee be established to collect data, set goals, and assess the success of the program. This committee may be composed of teachers, administrators, and staff interested in student success and retention. It should be stressed that data not be used punitively, and there should also be multiple measures. The data should be a basis for ongoing conversations. This committee may want to:

◆ Develop a historical database.

◆ Set goals and objectives.

◆ Monitor results and outcomes.

◆ Meet with employers.

◆ Analyze student performance.

◆ Integrate data and goals into strategic planning and budget procedures.

◆ Collect data for program review and accreditation.

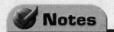

PART 2

Lesson Plans and Answer Keys

UNIT 1

Design with Microsoft Word

Getting Started

About the Unit

This unit is intended to teach students the fundamentals of word processing and desktop publishing by starting with a program that most students are familiar with and have easy access to—Microsoft Word. The unit has two chapters which cover important basic concepts and skills that prepare students for more advanced desktop publishing using layout software.

In **Chapter 1**, students will learn what desktop publishing is and get a general introduction to design and typography. In the process of creating one-page documents such as flyers, certificates, illustrated stories, and résumés, they will practice skills that reinforce the standards of professional word processing. These skills include setting tabs, creating tables, manipulating graphics, and using symbols including em- and en-dashes.

Once students have reviewed essential word processing skills, they are ready to explore Word's drawing tools and learn the fundamentals of creating and editing images. In **Chapter 2**, they will practice using layers, grouping objects, and creating more complicated layouts in documents such as newsletters, bi-fold brochures, and quad-fold cards.

Quick Write Activity

Ask your students to make a list of the similarities and differences between a drawing and a photograph. Both are graphic images, but they are still very different from each other. You can have them use the Venn Diagram, Graphic Organizers from Part 3 of this Teacher Resource Manual. Based on students' lists, determine when students might use a photograph in a publication and when they might use a drawing. For example, a drawing might have more appeal in a children's book, but a photograph would be better in a fashion magazine.

Unit 1 Design with Microsoft Word	Articles, Activities, and Exercises
Chapter 1 **Introducing Desktop Publishing** (pages 1–54)	**Workshop: Foundations,** Desktop Publishing, pg. 3–4 **Workshop: Toolbox,** Introducing Word, pg. 5–6 ⓘ **Go Online PowerPoint Presentations Preview,** pg. 7 DF Ⓡ **Project 1-1** Format with Fonts, pg. 7 DF Ⓡ **Project 1-2** Design with Font Attributes, pg. 10 DF Ⓡ **Project 1-3** Design with Font Families, pg. 13 DF Ⓡ **Project 1-4** Format with Word Tools, pg. 15 DF Ⓡ **Project 1-5** Insert and Wrap Clip Art, pg. 20 DF Ⓡ **Project 1-6** Create a Certificate, pg. 25 DF Ⓡ **Project 1-7** Create a Business Flyer, pg. 30 DF Ⓡ **Project 1-8** Design with Symbols, pg. 36 Ⓡ **Project 1-9** Create a Table, pg. 41 DF Ⓡ **Project 1-10** Create a Résumé with a Template, pg. 46 DF Ⓡ **Project 1-11** Create a Flyer, pg. 49 ⓘ **Go Online Enrichment Activities,** pp. 48 **In The Workplace,** Administrative Assistants, pg. 52 Ⓣ **TechSIM**
Chapter 2 **Vector Graphics in Word** (pages 55–98)	**Workshop: Foundations Understanding Graphics,** pg. 56–57 **Workshop: Toolbox Word's Drawing Toolbar,** pg. 58–60 ⓘ **Go Online PowerPoint Presentations Preview,** pg. 61 Ⓡ **Project 2-1** Drawing Basics, pg. 61 DF Ⓡ **Project 2-2** Group Drawing Objects, pg. 64 DF Ⓡ **Project 2-3** Layer Drawing Objects, pg. 68 Ⓡ **Project 2-4** Create a Logo and Add Callouts, pg. 71 DF Ⓡ **Project 2-5** Create Quad-fold Documents, pg. 75 DF Ⓡ **Project 2-6** Create a Newsletter, pg. 79 DF Ⓡ **Project 2-7** Crop and Resize a Photograph, pg. 84 DF Ⓡ **Project 2-8** Design a Brochure, pg. 89 DF Ⓡ **Project 2-9** Lay Out a Front Panel, pg. 93 ⓘ **Go Online Enrichment Activities,** pg. 88 **In The Workplace, Writers and Editors,** pg. 96 Ⓣ **TechSIM**
Unit Assessment **Projects Across the Curriculum** (pages 99–100)	Ⓡ **Project 1** Draw a Castle, pg. 99 Ⓡ **Project 2** Create a Visual Report, pg. 99 Ⓡ **Project 3** Create a Greeting Card, pg. 100 Ⓡ **Project 4** Create a Travel Brochure, pg. 100

Assessments

Workshop Foundations Reading Check, pg. 4
Workshop Toolbox Reading Check, pg. 6

End of Chapter 1 Assessment
    Reading Check, pg. 53
    Critical Thinking, pg.53
Ⓡ Independent Practice 1: Create a Daily Schedule, pg. 53
Ⓡ Independent Practice 2: Illustrate a Poem, pg. 54
Ⓡ Independent Practice 3: Create a Pet Flyer, pg. 54

⊙ **Additional Assessments You May Wish to Use**
ExamView Assessment Suite Testbank, Chapter 1

Workshop Foundations Reading Check, pg. 57
Workshop Toolbox Reading Check, pg. 60

End of Chapter 2 Assessment
    Reading Check, pg. 97
    Critical Thinking, pg. 97
Ⓡ Independent Practice 1: Create a Logo, pg. 97
Ⓡ Independent Practice 2: Create a Flyer, pg. 98
Ⓡ Independent Practice 3: Create a Brochure with a Map, pg. 98

⊙ **Additional Assessments You May Wish to Use**
ExamView Assessment Suite Testbank, Chapter 2

ⓘ **Go Online e-Review Self Checks** Chapter 1 and Chapter 2

Estimated Time to Complete Unit

  9 Week Course = 4–5 days
18 Week Course = 7 days
36 Week Course = 9–10 days

To help customize lesson plans, use the Pacing Guide on pages 29–30 and the Standards Charts on pages 98–99.

Key to Recommended Materials

ⓘ Internet access required

Ⓡ Scoring Rubrics

ⅅⅎ Data Files

⊙ *ExamView Assessment Suite* CD

Ⓣ TechSIM (Technology Simulations available on CD and the Online Learning Center)

The Teacher Resource DVD contains Data Files, Solution Files, Rubrics, Reproducible Worksheets, and PowerPoint Presentations.

Data Files for Unit 1 provided on the Teacher Resource DVD and Online Learning Center

Chapter 1	Chapter 2
1-1	2-2
1-2	2-3a to 2-3b
1-3	2-5
1-4	2-6a to 2-6b
1-5a to 1-5b	2-7
1-6	2-8
1-7a to 1-7d	2-9
1-8a to 1-8c	
1-10	
1-11	

Inclusion Strategies
For **Differentiated Instruction Strategies** refer to the **Inclusion in the Computer Technology Classroom** booklet.

ISTE NETS Foundation Standards

1. Basic operations and concepts	4. Technology communications tools
2. Social, ethical, and human issues	5. Technology research tools
3. Technology productivity tools	6. Technology problem-solving and decision-making

Performance Indicators	Textbook Correlation
1. Identify capabilities and limitations of contemporary and emerging technology resources and assess the potential of these systems and services to address personal, lifelong learning, and workplace needs. (NETS 2)	3, 15–16, 20–21, 46–47, 48, 52, 53, 56–57, 58, 88, 96
2. Make informed choices among technology systems, resources, and services. (NETS 1, 2)	4, 15–16, 20–24. 25–29, 36–40, 46, 56, 59, 75, 89, 93, 96
3. Analyze advantages and disadvantages of widespread use and reliance on technology in the workplace and in society as a whole. (NETS 2)	3, 4, 5, 13, 16, 21, 22, 52, 79, 96, 97
4. Demonstrate and advocate for legal and ethical behaviors among peers, family, and community regarding the use of technology and information. (NETS 2)	4, 36, 41, 43, 59
5. Use technology tools and resources for managing and communicating personal/professional information (e.g. finances, schedules, addresses, purchases, correspondence). (NETS 3, 4)	7–9, 10–12, 15–19, 20–24, 25–29, 30–35, 46–47, 52, 53, 55, 56–57, 58–60, 61, 75–78, 88–92, 93–95, 96
6. Evaluate technology-based options, including distance and distributed education, for lifelong learning. (NETS 5)	4, 5, 6, 8, 10, 13, 15, 16, 21, 26, 30, 31, 37, 48, 49, 52, 54, 57, 71, 88, 89, 96, 98
7. Routinely and efficiently use online information resources to meet needs for collaboration, research, publications, communications, and productivity. (NETS 4, 5, 6)	7, 52, 53, 54, 61, 88, 96, 97, 98, 99, 100
8. Select and apply technology tools for research, information analysis, problem-solving, and decision-making in content learning. (NETS 4, 5)	31, 37, 41–45, 53–55, 98, 99–100
9. Investigate and apply expert systems, intelligent agents, and simulations in real-world situations. (NETS 3, 5, 6)	52, 53–54, 71, 79–87, 88–95, 96, 97–100
10. Collaborate with peers, experts, and others to contribute to content-related knowledge base by using technology to compile, synthesize, produce, and disseminate information, models, and other creative works. (NETS 4, 5, 6)	49–51, 54, 79–87, 88–95, 97–100

21st Century Skills

Core Subjects Language arts, math, science, social studies	3, 4, 6, 10, 15, 20, 30, 36–38, 41, 46, 53–54, 56, 57, 60, 68–70, 75, 79, 89, 93–94, 98–100
Learning Skills Information and media literacy; communication skills; critical thinking and systems thinking; problem identification, formulation, and solution; self-direction; accountability	2, 3–4, 5–6, 13–14, 30–31, 48–51, 53–54, 55, 56–57, 58–60, 68–70, 75–78, 88–95, 97–100
21st Century Tools Communication, information processing and research tools; problem-solving tools, personal development and productivity tools	5–6, 7, 10, 13, 15, 16, 20, 36, 46, 52, 53–54, 58–60, 61, 93, 96, 97–100

Foundation Skills

Basic Skills Reading, Writing, Math, Listening, and Speaking	3, 4, 6, 30, 36–38, 53–54, 56, 57, 60, 68–70, 93–94, 97, 98–100
Thinking Skills Creative thinking, decision making, problem solving, reasoning	2, 3, 4, 6, 52, 53–54, 55, 56, 57, 59, 96, 97–100
Personal Qualities Self-esteem, responsibility, self-management, and integrity/honesty	4, 36, 52, 59, 96, 97

Workplace Competencies

Resources Allocate time, money, materials, facilities, and human resources	2, 4, 53, 54, 55, 97, 98, 99–100
Interpersonal Participate on teams, teach others, serve clients and customers, exercise leadership, negotiate to arrive at decisions, and work with cultural diversity	2, 52, 55, 96, 97, 98
Information Acquire, evaluate, organize, maintain, interpret, communicate, and use computers to process information	2–6, 53–54, 58–60, 97–100
Systems Understand, monitor, correct, improve, and design systems	2, 3, 4, 52, 55, 96
Technology Select, apply, maintain, and troubleshoot technology	5–6, 16, 49, 53–54, 58–60, 97–100

Introducing Desktop Publishing

Skills You Will Learn

Workshop Foundations: Introducing Desktop Publishing
- Identify elements of desktop publishing
- Apply design process skills

Workshop Toolbox: Introducing Word
- Define interface
- Identify Word's commands and toolbars

Project 1-1 Format with Fonts
- Format fonts
- Change font size

Project 1-2 Design with Font Attributes
- Apply formatting attributes

Project 1-3 Design with Font Families
- Use font families

Project 1-4 Format with Word Tools
- Cut and paste
- Align text
- Insert a drop cap
- Add a page border
- Check spelling

Project 1-5 Insert and Wrap Clip Art
- Find and replace text
- Insert a text box
- Add a fill color
- Insert a graphic
- Move and resize an object

Project 1-6 Create a Certificate
- Change page orientation
- Format a page border
- Insert a watermark
- Add WordArt
- Apply kerning

Project 1-7 Create a Business Flyer
- Adjust leading
- Add a bulleted list
- Kern text
- Insert page numbers

Project 1-8 Design with Symbols
- Create a numbered list
- Insert symbols

Project 1-9 Create a Table
- Create a table
- Sort data
- Add footnotes
- Resize columns
- Format a table
- Center vertically

Project 1-10 Create a Résumé with a Template
- Create a résumé
- Use a template

Skills Studio

Lay Out One-Page Flyers
Project 1-11 Create a Flyer
- Determine message, audience, and content
- Design flyer layout

Start-Up Skills

Ingredients of a Design Start students thinking about why publications are designed in different ways. For example, why do books not look like magazines even though they have many similarities? Answer: the audience's purpose for reading is different. Magazines have advertisements, pull-quotes, and sidebars, and the stories are frequently interrupted by pictures, captions, and section headers. Magazine readers usually want to skim the publication to find information quickly, while book readers want to be absorbed in the story without disruption.

Design Process: Overview

Compare Design Issues Students will recognize that all sorts of printed publications have to be designed. Ask students to brainstorm the kinds of things that have a design and write their responses on the board. They will most likely mention magazines and brochures, advertisements, and posters. They may forget to mention T-shirts, CD covers, labels on products like vitamins, shampoo, or any commercial item, cereal boxes, display signs, and even receipts and forms. Virtually any commercial product has had to have someone design its look and functionality.

Quick Write Activity

Review the Design Process Chart Discuss with students the Design Process chart and go over the questions to make sure they understand it. Then have them choose a particular type of publication and answer each question in regard to the publication. To avoid duplication, you can prepare slips of paper with different types of publications and hand a slip out to each student.

LEARNING LINK

Chapter 1 reviews many basic word-processing skills that students may already know from previous classes. If you feel that you would like to jump immediately to using layout software rather than starting with Microsoft Word, you should still review many of the skills taught in this chapter. Microsoft Publisher has many of the same tools as Word, and using its word-processing tools will help build a strong foundation for using text in desktop-published documents.

When creating their projects, encourage students to use the rubrics and PowerPoint presentations in the Online Learning Center, as well as the *Review and Revise* checklists in the textbook. Students can use these tools to evaluate their own projects, or their classmates', to make sure that they have completed all the key steps.

Workshop Foundations

Pages 3–4

Desktop Publishing

FOCUS

Focus Activity

Discuss Changes in Publishing In this article, students learn where desktop publishing originated and the foundations of the design process. Publishing has been around for quite a long time, though it was not until Gutenberg invented the movable-type printing press in 1450 that it became possible to create and distribute printed materials easily. The invention of the movable-type press is associated with the beginning of the Renaissance period. Ask students what has changed in publishing since 1985, when desktop publishing began.

> **You Will Learn To:**
> - Identify elements of desktop publishing
> - Apply design process skills

Page 3

Before You Read Activity

Key Terms Journal While you are taking attendance, tell the students to add new terms to their own desktop publishing dictionaries. Have students write down each key term and see if they can fill in any of the columns: *Definition* (What Is It?), *What Else Is It Like?* (or *What Does it Remind Them of?*), and an *Example*. For example, for the term *desktop publishing*, the definition would be "the use of a computer to combine text and graphics together on a page." Students might say that it reminds them of a regular printing press. An example could be anything from a newspaper to a CD cover to a billboard advertising a movie.

As you go through the book, stop at each key term and have students refine their dictionaries. Occasionally collect this dictionary for a grade, or allow students to use it on classroom quizzes.

Page 3

Key Term Activity

Multiple-Choice Questions Have students create multiple-choice test questions for each key term in the chapter. Students can then practice and share these questions and use them for test reviews. The best test questions could be included on the next exam.

Key Term Definitions

publication A work that is produced and distributed for an audience. It can be printed or electronic. (page 3)

layout software An application that is designed to combine text and graphics together on a page. (page 3)

WYSIWYG (What You See Is What You Get) An acronym that means that the computer monitor shows what a document will look like when it is printed. (page 3)

desktop publishing The use of a desktop computer to combine text and graphics together on a page. (page 3)

Answers to Workshop Foundations Activities

Page 3

Caption

This flyer suggests that this company has a limited operating budget and could not afford to produce the highest quality product. The WordArt (amateurish), the misspellings, the poor choice of clip art, and the boring layout all suggest an unprofessional operation. If the business is careless even when attempting to attract customers, what level of customer service will they provide during and after the sale?

Page 4

Eye on Ethics

Almost anything that can be physically expressed can be copyrighted. This includes logos, pictures, music, books, movies, machines, software, and processes. Names, common phrases, and ideas cannot be copyrighted. Works are considered copyright protected as soon as the creator of the work prints, publishes, or saves the work to any medium. Since it can be difficult to prove when a work was first created and saved, it is best to file important works with the U.S. Patent Office for a small fee. This ensures protection and a record of the item's unique nature. See **www.copyright.gov** for more information.

ASSESS

Use the following questions and any Sidebar and Eye on Ethics features to access students' understanding of the workshops. Students can write answers to these questions in their desktop publishing journals.

Page 4

 Reading Check

1. Desktop Publishing is the use of a computer to combine text and graphics together on a page.

2. To develop design skills, you should look for examples of good design, and carefully consider the audience's needs and the purpose of the design. You should then sketch several ideas on paper, before you even begin working on the computer, and get feedback from others.

CLOSE

Class Discussion The textbook uses the term "revolution" for describing desktop publishing. Do students believe that this is a fair and accurate use of the word? In what ways has the ability to cheaply and quickly produce and publish documents with text and graphics changed society? *(Possible answers: It has made it easier to spread information and ideas. It has made owning books possible for all classes of society, not just the wealthy. It has made reading a common skill for most people.)*

Workshop Toolbox   Pages 5–6

Introducing Word

FOCUS

Focus Activity

Overview In this Toolbox feature, students will learn the basic areas of Microsoft Word's user interface. This section will help students locate commands more easily and become familiar with terminology related to Microsoft Word.

You Will Learn To:

- Identify Words' toolbars
- Identify Word's menu bar
- Find the scroll bars and rulers

Evaluate Prior Knowledge Have students complete Worksheet 1A in Part 3 of this TRM. It is a survey of the skills they will need for this course. It should help students understand what they can expect in the course and where they might have holes in their knowledge.

Page 5

Key Term Activity

On the Board Have students use each of the key terms in a sentence which demonstrates that they understand the word. Write some of the best sentences on the board for other students to copy.

Key Term Definitions

interface The onscreen elements that allow the user to communicate with the computer. (page 5)

Print Layout View A way to display a document on the monitor so you can see how text and graphics will print on the page. (page 5)

icon A picture button that activates a command when it is clicked with a mouse. (page 6)

TEACH

Teach Activity

GUI and Desktop Publishing Explain that Paul Brainerd and Art Agnos invented desktop publishing in 1985 for the Macintosh computer. Until then, personal computers were not GUI and WYSIWYG was not possible. Additionally, most PC monitors were monochrome, and few people saw the need for a computer mouse. Also, computers at that time would have had a hard time storing or processing large amounts of data. Finally, a laser printer is needed for true typeset quality and this kind of technology was beyond the means of most. If allowed, have students visit the computer museum at **www.computerhistory.org** to find information about computers before 1985.

Manipulate Toolbars Demonstrate to students how toolbars are opened and closed, then show how they can be moved and placed on different areas of the screen. Show what happens when they are moved to the end of another toolbar at the top of the screen. Have students use the View menu to open the Standard, Formatting, and Drawing toolbars, which they will need throughout this unit.

Answers to Workshop Toolbox Activities

Page 5

Sidebar

A graphical user interface (GUI) is a picture-based method for communicating with the computer. The previous method required keying in commands, which required memorizing many command codes, and often ran into syntax problems.

Page 6

Sidebar

The View menu allows the user to open and close items displayed on screen including toolbars and rulers. It can also be used to change views from Normal to Print Layout, Web Layout, or Outline.

ASSESS

Use the following questions and any Sidebar and Eye on Ethics features to access students' understanding of the workshops. Students can write answers to these questions in their desktop publishing journals.

Reading Check

1. A user interface refers to the onscreen elements that allow the user to communicate with the computer.

2. The menu bar is similar to a toolbar because they both provide access to commands. They are different because the toolbars contain only the most commonly used commands, while the menu bar contains most all commands. Also, the toolbars use a graphical interface.

CLOSE

Compare Software Interfaces Programs with complex interfaces can discourage certain kinds of users, and programs with user-friendly interfaces are simpler in nature, though they may also be somewhat limited in power. Give students a preview of the other interfaces they will be using in this course. Show them the Microsoft Publisher screen on page 104 of the student text, the Adobe Photoshop screen on page 201, and the Adobe Illustrator screen on page 295. See if students can recognize similarities and differences in the interfaces, particularly between Microsoft and Adobe products.

Chapter 1 Projects

Pages 7–51

FOCUS

Focus Activity

Identify Fonts The term *font* used to refer to the drawer where printers would keep the metal stamps of an entire typeface. Large alphabetic letters were kept in the upper cases, while the small ones were kept in the lower cases.

Pass out full-color, full-page advertisements from national magazines. Have students identify the number of different typefaces used in these magazines. As a class, create a chart using the columns: *Advertisement's Tone* and *Number of Fonts*. See if students can identify a pattern.

 Go Online PREVIEW

Before You Begin Students can use the chapter **PowerPoint** presentations and **rubrics** at the Online Learning Center to determine what is expected *before* they complete a project. Students can view the PowerPoint slides on their own computers, or you can project them to preview chapter concepts and show examples of the finished projects. You might also display project solutions so students can easily refer to them while they work. (Presentations and rubrics are also provided on the Teacher Resource DVD for your convenience).

glencoe.com

Projects

Project 1-1
Format with Fonts

Project 1-2
Design with Font Attributes

Project 1-3
Design with Font Families

Project 1-4
Format with Word Tools

Project 1-5
Insert and Wrap Clip Art

Project 1-6
Create a Certificate

Project 1-7
Create a Business Flyer

Project 1-8
Design with Symbols

Project 1-9
Create a Table

Skills Studio

Project 1-10
Create a Résumé with a Template

Key Term Activity

Group Like Terms Before reviewing the key term definitions, see if students can arrange the words below into groups of related words. For example, *kern* and *leading* both refer to spacing; a *gridline* is a type of *border*. Write their word groups on the board. Then have students explain why they put the words together and discuss the definitions.

Key Term Definitions

font A specific typeface combined with variations such as size, style, and spacing. (page 7)

sans serif A type of typeface without small cross strokes (see *serif*). (page 7)

scalable The ability to be resized (scaled) without a loss of image quality. (page 7)

serif A typeface with small cross strokes at the top and bottom of most letterforms. (page 7)

typeface A design for a set of characters. (page 7)

typography The study of type and its characteristics. (page 7)

points A font size measurement, where 1 point is 1/72 of an inch. (page 8)

font attributes The stylized characteristics of a typeface such as bold, italics, superscript, or emboss. (page 10)

letterform The shape of a character in a particular typeface. (page 13)

drop cap A large decorative letter used at the beginning of a paragraph. (page 16)

footer Information that appears at the bottom of every page. (page 16)

header Information that appears at the top every page. (page 16)

sizing handle A small circle or rectangle along the edges of an object that indicates the object has been selected and can be resized. (page 21)

text box A rectangular graphic element that can serve as a holder for text and graphics. (page 21)

wrap When text is set to flow around an object. (page 21)

watermark A lightly visible image in the background of a design. (page 25)

white space The empty space in a design that sets off text and graphics. (page 25)

WordArt Decorative text found in Microsoft Word and Microsoft Publisher. (page 25)

kern To adjust the horizontal spacing between two letters. (page 26)

landscape orientation A page layout where the long edge of the paper is at the top. (page 26)

portrait orientation A page layout where the short edge of the paper is at the top. (page 26)

leading The spacing between lines of text in a paragraph. (page 30)

dingbat A font that uses graphic icons and symbols, rather than alpha-numeric characters. (page 36)

gridlines The border lines (visible and invisible) in a table. (page 41)

sort To arrange information into an order determined by the user. (page 41)

table A grid of columns and rows used to organize information. (page 41)

template A pre formatted document designed to be easily customized. (page 46)

thumbnail sketch Simple drawings used to give a sense of the layout and basic elements of a design. (page 49)

TEACH

Teach Activity

Saving Files Before you begin, make sure that students understand how and where to save their files. They will also need these skills in order to open Data Files and previous projects that they have already started. The TechSim Tutorials on the Online Learning Center can be used to review basic skills in file management.

Show students how to navigate through the file structure to open a document and save a document. Encourage students to save a document immediately after it is opened, and then to press CTRL + S from time to time to save their latest changes as they work in a document.

Remind students to name their documents something that will make it easy to find the file later, and not random letters like "zxcgfsdf." You might want to assign a naming convention, such as the Project number followed by the student's last name. Also, point out that certain symbols, such as !, ?, *, ., /, |, ~, should not be used in a file name. Many of these symbols mean something to the computer and can create trouble finding or opening files.

Web Resources You might want to use these online resources if you or students need additional information about typography. (Note: Before sending your students to any Web site, make sure that the content is acceptable to you and your school district.)

- www.microsoft.com/typography
- www.paratype.com/help/class

Teaching Tips and Troubleshooting Tips ⚠ for Projects

Pages 7–9

Rubric

Student Data File

> **Project 1-1** ▷

Format with Fonts Students format the text used to key the lyrics of the national anthem. Discuss with students how a font is a design's "voice." Just as 90 percent of all communication is non-verbal, we need to be able to control our voice on paper. This is the first, most basic, most important thing we need to learn in desktop publishing. **(Data File 1-1, Solution File 1-1, Rubric 1-1)**

Pages 8

Answer to Sidebar Since a monitor is low resolution and documents are usually printed in high resolution, fonts may not look the same when displayed and printed. This is particularly true of fonts with serifs and ornamentation, which may not look as clear on a monitor.

Choose Appropriate Fonts Ask students when it would be appropriate to use fonts such as Jokerman, Old English, Freestyle Script, Goudy Stout, or Stencil (see the chart on page 13). What should designers consider when choosing a font?

Key Text If you prefer that your students key the document rather than use the Data File, remind them that they should use only one space after most punctuation (except opening parentheses and quotations) and that the Enter key is used to end a paragraph and move to the next line. Encourage your students to use tabs and the alignment buttons—not the spacebar—when moving text horizontally.

Pages 10–12

Rubric

Student Data File

Project 1-2 ▶ **Design with Font Attributes** Students align text and apply font attributes, such as bold, all caps, subscript, and superscript, to a one-page report with a title page. If you prefer not to use the Data File, provide students with a copy of the text so they can key the document themselves. **(Data File 1-2, Solution File 1-2, Rubric 1-2)**

Page 10

Answer to Sidebar CTRL + B is the shortcut for Bold.

Identify Typeface Show students an example of simple text, such as the word "text" or your name. Then, using the same font, apply different attributes from the Format>Font dialog box. Ask your students how many different typefaces you are using. The answer, of course, is that you are using the same typeface: one. Also, emphasize to students that to keep special effects special, they should use them sparingly and only to enhance the message of the design.

Explore the Font Dialog Box Display the Format>Font dialog box. Show students how special effects can be created by applying a variety of tools together. For example, you can choose the Emboss (or Engrave) effect and change the font color from its default white to black. The effect is subtle, but effective when printed. The Character Spacing tab is where kerning and tracking can be adjusted. These skills will be studied later in greater detail. The Text Effects tab is for creating Web pages, though most of these effects are considered quite unprofessional.

Problems with Text Effects Not every type of effect is available with every font, so some effects may be "grayed out" (unavailable) when a student tries to use them. Students frequently have problems with superscript and subscript text because these features must be turned off in order to return text to its normal size. Hidden text effects will not appear to have changed anything, but the text that is identified as "hidden" will not print. Check your print preview before printing.

Pages 13–14

Rubric

Student Data File

Project 1-3 ▶ **Design with Font Families** Students complete a table listing font families. Advanced students can create their own table rather than using the Data File. **(Data File 1-3, Solution File 1-3, Rubric 1-3)**

Answer to Sidebar It is important that publications be readable to encourage people to read the entire message and to make sure the message is clearly understood.

Classify Fonts Show students three fonts from different font families. Have students develop a list of ways that they would classify these fonts based on their characteristics. Guide students into considering the shape of the letters, the thickness of the letters, the tone of the font, etc. Explain that this is what designers do. While there are many kinds of classifications and some fonts that are difficult to categorize, learning a classification strategy can help make the decision about which font to use much easier.

Identify Font Characteristics Explain that fonts are classified by the following characteristics:

- Serifs: Small cross strokes at the top or bottom of the character.
- Transitions: The change from thick to thin parts of the letterform.
- Stress: The slant of the typeface. (Roman fonts have no slant.)
- Weight: The heaviness of the font.

Make a copy of the chart below and have students copy it in their notebooks.

Font	Serifs	Transitions	Stress	Weight
Oldstyle	Yes	Smooth	No	Light
Slab Serif	Yes	None–Slight	No	Heavy
Modern	Yes	Radical	No	Heavy
Sans Serif	No	None	Varies	Light
Script	No	Yes	Yes	Varies
Decorative	Varies	Varies	Varies	Varies
Dingbats	n/a	n/a	n/a	n/a

Fonts and Message Ask students to consider the following examples: an advertisement for surgery written in Comic Sans, or a sign advertising a sporting event using a Script font. Guide students to the conclusion that mood is part of the design's message and that font choice plays an important part in communicating this element.

Pages 15–19

Rubric

Student Data File

Project 1-4

Format with Word Tools Students format the Gettysburg Address using cut, copy, and paste; alignment options; a drop cap; a page border; and a header and footer. They also perform a spell check. If you prefer that students key the document, rather than using the Data File, provide a hard copy of the Data File so that they can then perform the formatting activities in the project. **(Data File 1-4, Solution File 1-4, Rubric 1-4)**

Page 15

Answer to Sidebar Keyboard shortcuts allow users to continue keying text without having to move their hands off the keyboard to use the mouse.

Page 16

Answer to Sidebar When you select text or need to cut and paste, it is useful to be able to see where there are spaces, breaks, and hard returns so that you know where to place your insertion point. Also, if your document seems to be formatting itself with odd breaks and indents, Show/Hide lets you see hidden commands that you may not know are there.

Add Page Borders Ask students for examples of graphics and how the graphic can enhance a design's message. Students are likely to say that graphics could include a picture, a map, a chart, or a graph. Guide the students into understanding that even lines are graphic elements and can serve to create visual interest. Graphics are all elements that are not text. Lines alone can be used to send a professional tone, organize space, and create visual interest. Maps, graphs, and pictures can be used to visually present complex information, while page borders, rules, and simple designs can be used to set a mood or group elements in the design.

Ask students to consider how the design looked before and after the page border. The design now looks more complete. Consider what the design looks like with other borders. How does the mood of the design change with the change in border? Which border works best? Why? Which kinds of borders are most versatile?

Insert Headers and Footers Show students that when they select View>Header and Footer, a special area of the page becomes available. Like a master page, the contents of this area are repeated on every page. Notice that the Header and Footer toolbar also becomes available. Show students how this toolbar allows them to switch from the header to the footer area, change the page setup, and add page numbers and time/date stamps. Students can use the vertical ruler to expand the space of the header/footer areas, and graphic elements can even be placed there.

When writing reports, students should be encouraged to key their names in the header and the name of the document in the footer. Using the AutoText feature in the Header/Footer toolbar, students can even have the file path automatically placed in the footer. People often use this feature to find files easily.

Apply the Show/Hide Tool Turn on the Show/Hide button and show students how it displays the hidden commands that do not normally print: spaces, hard returns, tabs, page and column breaks, etc. Students should use this button when proofreading work or when troubleshooting a design. If the computer seems to be doing something strange, many times the problem can be found by using the Show/Hide button.

Cut and Paste Some beginning students will have a hard time recognizing the difference between copy/paste and cut/paste. Many will copy the area, then go back and delete the area copied. Be sure to monitor students and encourage effective strategies.

Pages 20–24

Rubric

Student Data File

Project 1-5 **Insert and Wrap Clip Art** Students add clip art and a text box to add visual interest to an Aesop's fable story. Students will then resize and wrap text around these elements, and they will apply the Thesaurus and Find/Replace tools to the document. Students may key the text instead of using the Data File. **(Data Files 1-5a and 1-5b, Solution File 1-5, Rubric 1-5)**

Page 21 **Answer to Sidebar** The Thesaurus can be quite useful when searching for synonyms to better match tone and audience.

Wrap Text Display a page full of text, and then use the Oval tool on the Drawing toolbar to create a circle in the middle of the text. Fill the circle with a color so that students can see it more easily. The circle should have white, circular handles. Ask students how the text is "reacting" to the circle's presence. Most likely, the text is behind the circle and not moving, no matter how you move the circle.

Choose Format>AutoShape, and click the Layout tab. (Notice that the dialog box is the same as Format>Picture and Format>WordArt. The name changes based on what kind of object is selected.) Show students the dog icons showing the different layout options and ask them to predict what will happen when you click each.

Choose the Square option. Repeat for the other types of text wrapping (Tight, Behind text, In front of text, and In line with text). Ask students if their predictions were correct. See if they can explain the difference between Square and Tight. *(Answer: Tight follows the shape of the object itself, while square will create a square area around the graphic.)*

Use Text Boxes Have students evaluate the layout for this design. How is it different from that in previous projects? Many students have probably never created text in a text box, and they probably never knew they could rotate the text 90° using this tool. Additionally, the placement of the clip art is a bit different. How does this help to enhance the message of the fable? Both the layout and the conclusion of the story are a bit unexpected. There is also a lot of white space in the design to encourage reading.

Move Clip Art Students may do tasks ineffectively when they have to figure out problem for themselves. Students often have problems moving clip art that they have inserted, so they often put clip art into text boxes. Watch to make sure that students are not using text boxes for graphics. Instead, students should insert clip art, and then use Format>Picture>Layout to change the wrapping to something other than *In line with text*. Anything other than this first option will allow them to move the graphic easily, though they must choose the most effective type of text wrapping.

Pages 25–29

Rubric · Student Data File

Project 1-6 ▷ **Create a Certificate** Students create a certificate with a watermark. Besides inserting an image, they will use WordArt, change page orientation, and learn how to kern. **(Data File 1-6, Solution File 1-6, Rubric 1-6)**

Page 26 **Answer to Sidebar** Some letters are confusing when placed together. For example, in the "fi" combination, the line of the f and the dot on the i run into the other letter. Ligatures are letter combinations that avoid this problem by designing a new letter. In the Insert>Symbol menu, you will find a few common ligatures, such as fi and fl (in the Alphabetic Presentation Forms category).

Design Tips Ask students when they might use kerning or watermarks in a design. Guide students to consider that business forms will frequently watermark "Confidential" or "Copy" on a business form. Kerning is important for large text like titles on flyers or posters, where awkward spacing will be very noticeable. Kerning may seem like a very small detail, but it is often these small things that make a difference creating professional designs.

Kern Text Have students key the word "awkward" in a 36 point font. Have them select the word and choose Format>Font, then choose the Character Spacing tab. In the Spacing option, have students condense the spacing by 10 points. Are the results surprising? Are they readable? Have students expand the spacing by 20 points. What has happened now?

In the word "awkward," students might notice the odd spacing between the *a* and the *w*. Have them select the first *a* and condense the spacing a bit (try 1.25) until the spacing between the letters looks consistent. They can then adjust the spacing around other letters that need kerning.

Create Watermarks Watermarks can be created using Format>Background> Printed Watermark, or the effect can be better controlled when you select a picture in the document and choose Format>Picture. In the Picture tab, adjust the Brightness and Contrast sliders to the desired setting. Unfortunately, though, you cannot preview the effect when you use this method.

Another way is to select the picture and use the Picture toolbar. It should appear whenever a picture is selected. Four buttons—the two Brightness buttons and the two Contrast buttons—will allow you to also create a custom effect, and you can preview the effect as it is being applied.

Print the Full Page Printers all have different areas in which they can print. Have students use File>Print Preview to make sure that the entire border will print. If the border appears to be inconsistent, students can use Format>Border>Page Border and adjust the settings for the border to ensure that it will print correctly.

Page 30–35

Rubric

Student Data File

Project 1-7 ▶ **Create a Business Flyer** Students create one page of a company's annual report. They will insert graphics, create a bulleted list, and apply line space (leading). (**Data Files 1-7a to 1-7d, Solution File 1-7, Rubric 1-7**)

Page 30

Answer to Sidebar Lines of text using small fonts would appear very close together on a page and be difficult to read. By increasing the leading, the space between lines is more generous and might help readability.

Page 31

Answer to Sidebar One example of a new bulleted item would be: Received top customer-service awards from leading travel organizations worldwide.

Discuss Instant Evaluations Studies suggest that audiences make decisions about a product after seeing it for about one third of a second. How might that affect design? Discuss how using readable fonts, generous leading, plenty of white space, and graphics help promote readability and understanding.

Line Spacing and Text Density Discuss with students the concept of density when laying out text. If possible, bring in some examples of documents with dense text (often legal disclaimers at the bottom of ads are dense). What kinds of publications tend to use denser text? Students might mention college textbooks or technical books versus textbooks for middle school. Also, legal documents are often dense.

Display a paragraph written in Times New Roman at 12 points. Have the students squint at the paragraph. They should see the text as a dark region. Select the text and choose **Format>Paragraph** to set the Line Spacing to **Exactly 4 points**. The lines of text should be overlapping each other. When students squint at the paragraph, they should see that this version looks darker than it did before. Change the Line Spacing of the paragraph to **Exactly 17 points**. (141.5% leading) Students should see that the paragraph appears much lighter and less dense.

Customize Bullets Bullets help to break information into smaller chunks so that the reader can more easily skim the highlights. Like leading, this can increase readability, and bullets can be customized to help set the mood of the document.

Create a list of five different things. Select the list, and click the Bullets button. Show students that the bullet and indents that are added to the list this way are the current bullet settings. To change the bullet and its settings, they must use Format>Bullets and Numbering, then use the Customize options as described in the project. Students will frequently need help with bulleted text. Be sure to walk around and observe students, and encourage students to help each other.

Page 36–40

Rubric — Student Data File

Project 1-8 **Design with Symbols** Students insert symbols and add a numbered list to a recipe. Students can key the text or use the Data File. **(Data File 1-8a to 1-8c, Solution File 1-8, Rubric 1-8)**

Page 36 **Answer to Eye on Ethics** The copyright, registered, and trademark symbols indicate that a work is copy protected by the US Patent Office. Works can be copyright protected without these symbols, as well. See **www.copyright.gov** for more information.

Page 37 **Answer to Sidebar** The AutoCorrect feature forces the computer to automatically correct or change certain keystrokes. Common misspellings such as "teh" are automatically corrected to "the" and common symbols such as © can be created by using (c).

Identify Symbols Have students create a three-column table with columns for the symbol, how it is used, and the shortcut key. As a class, have students tell you the symbols they encounter in everyday life, and write their answers on the board. (Some possibilities are $, ¢, Σ, ≈, Δ, ¿, ñ, ™, etc.) Once you have a good selection, have students work independently. Ask them to choose ten symbols and look for the symbols in the Insert>Symbols dialog box. They should then use the information from the Symbols box to fill in the table. Have them try out the shortcuts, displayed at the bottom of the Symbols box. Remind them that they must enter numbers using the number pad, with Num Lock turned on.

Identify Subset Locations Symbols are categorized by subsets. In the Symbols box, choose the *normal text* font and show students the Subset window. Click some of the symbols and see what subsets are displayed. See if students can guess the subsets for the symbols listed in the table below. They might be surprised that many are listed in Latin-1, which is the alphabet in which these symbols are used. Have students create their own tables with the names and subsets of the listed symbols, or symbols of their own. Show them where the symbol name is displayed in the bottom left of the Symbols dialog box.

Symbol	Name	Subset Location
≤	Less than or Equal to	Mathematical operators
π	Pi	Basic Greek
™	Trademark Sign	Letterlike Symbols
¢	Cent	Latin-1
÷	Division Sign	Latin-1
é	Accent ague	Latin-1
€	Euro sign	Currency Symbols
♪	Eighth Note	Miscellaneous Dingbats

Pages 41–45

Rubric

Project 1-9 **Create a Table** Students create and format a table comparing populations and other data about U.S. states. They also add a citation showing where the information is from. Demonstrate how to move from cell to cell by using the cursor keys or by using Tab (or Shift + Tab to move left). **(Solution File 1-9, Rubric 1-9)**

Use Tables to Format Ask students why menus are not formatted in paragraphs. Answer: relating the information as a table better suits the needs of the audience. They want to see the information in an easy-to-understand format. There are two ways to format information in a tabular layout: using the Tables menu or with tabs. Most people find tables much easier, but there are times when setting tabs works better in a document. We will look at formatting with tabs in Project 2-8.

AutoFormat Tables The Table menu includes all the options you need to format tables. One feature that is useful if you are in a hurry is the Table AutoFormat feature. Select the table, and choose Table>AutoFormat. Then select the table design you like best. You can choose to change borders, font, colors or any combination thereof.

Arrange Content Tables are such an important concept that you might want students to create other types of tables. Show students examples of tables from newspapers, magazines, and Web sites like **www.infoplease.com** (an online almanac). Discuss the different ways that information is categorized and sorted. Sometimes it might be sorted alphabetically and sometimes numerically. Discuss different ways the table they create in this project can be sorted.

Ask students what column headers they would use for a table showing their top ten favorite movies of all time. Have them create the table, sorting the information at least two different ways.

Sorting Data When using Data>Sort, some students will try to sort all of the data at the same time. Pay attention to Figure 1.39; the data for US will not be sorted with the states. They should highlight only the states for their sorts.

When students try to use the Sort feature, they may select lines outside the table, as well as the table itself. In this event, Word will not display "Column 2" as an option. Have students try again, and more carefully select only the table itself.

Page 46–47

Rubric

Student Data File

Project 1-10 **Create a Résumé with a Template** Students modify a Microsoft Word template to create Ben Franklin's résumé. Explain to students that most professional graphic designers avoid using templates because the information is not being presented in a creative, original way for a specific message or audience.

However, templates can be useful when a design must be finished quickly, when originality is not necessary or desirable (such as when a company already has a design), or as a good starting point for creating an original design. **(Data File 1-10, Solution File 1-10, Rubric 1-10)**

Evaluate Résumés Have students list the information that an employer would need to know before they hired someone. Students might think of experience, education, references, interests or hobbies, and contact information. These all could be included on a résumé.

When a job is posted, a company may easily receive several thousand résumés to read. How does a company go through all those résumés? If reading them by hand, companies will be looking at the résumés only briefly, so important information needs to stand out. Messy or hard-to-read résumés will simply never be read. If résumés are scanned electronically, they must use a standard font and format that is easy for the computer to read. They must also use a compatible file format and contain specific words that match the criteria for which the company is looking.

Using Templates Some students feel that Word's templates are not easy to use. Have students open the résumé template, and then choose Table>Show Gridlines. This will show the non-printing lines that make up the table grid. Then students will see that the template is simply a table, much like Project 1-9.

Rather than selecting and deleting entire rows of text at one time, students will probably find it easiest to select each section of text that needs to be changed, and then key the new data. In Unit 2, students will use templates again in Microsoft Publisher, and they will probably find that those templates are far easier to use than Word's.

Skills Studio

Pages 48–51

Lay Out One-Page Flyers

Flyers are one of the most commonly used forms of advertising. However, they are usually created as quickly and inexpensively as possible. Often they are printed from a local printer or on a copy machine.

Have students consider the limitations of a copy machine as described in the Sidebar on page 49. With that in mind, have them look at the thumbnail sketches on page 50. Why is the design that was finally used the best design to use on a copy machine? (*Possible answers: Some of the designs would probably look best in full-color, which would be expensive. Other designs would require details or effects that might not print clearly on a copy machine. The chosen design is the simplest and works well in either black and white or color.*)

Page 49–51

Rubric

Project 1-11 ⟩ **Create a Flyer** Students create a flyer advertising a school project. They will go quickly through the design process, drawing thumbnail sketches based on the needs of the project. You can have students create an original flyer based on their own sketches and peer evaluation, or use the example provided in the textbook. **(Data File 1-11, Solution File 1-11, Rubric 1-11)**

Page 49

Answer to Sidebar The first thing a designer should consider is how the work will be published. Knowing this can help to determine which software will need to be used and what kinds of effects can be incorporated into the design.

✍ **Center Objects on the Page** To place a drawing object exactly in the center of the page, select the object and choose Format>(AutoShape, WordArt, or Object). Then choose the Layout tab. Click the Advanced button at the bottom of this tab. Change the settings so the Horizontal Alignment is Centered relative to the Page.

Students can then move the object up and down into position. To "nudge" an object, select the object and hold Ctrl, then use the arrow keys. If other objects on the page move when the object is moved, the text wrapping may be set incorrectly. Select the object, open the Layout tab again, and choose In Front of Text (or Behind Text).

⚠ **Work with the Drawing Canvas** In recent versions of Word, a Drawing Canvas appears when you use the Drawing toolbar to insert an object on a page. When you create a drawing within the canvas, all objects in the drawing work together more easily. If you prefer not to use the drawing canvas, you can press Delete each time it appears, or draw outside the drawing canvas, and it will go away by itself. You can also turn it off by choosing Tools>Options. In the General tab, uncheck *Automatically create drawing canvas when inserting AutoShapes.*

ASSESS

Encourage students to use the Review and Revise checklists to be sure that they have completed the key steps to this project. Encourage students to proofread and assist each other. Students learn best when they are teaching each other. Consider giving bonus points for well-designed projects for both the student and the student who evaluated his/her work.

It is recommended that for these first four chapters you evaluate student printouts carefully, looking for a standard set of problems. You might purchase a do-it-yourself stamp kit and create a stamp with the following grading criteria:

Font Style	Balance
Font Size	Alignment
Leading	Proximity
Repetition	Spelling and Grammar

Take off 5 points for each type of mistake and 10 points for skipping skill sets in the lessons. For a grade, have students chart the kinds of mistakes they have been making. Hopefully, they will begin to see a pattern of mistakes and you will be finding fewer problems, making grading faster in the future.

CLOSE

Activities for Students You have a number of options for students who finish projects early or need more challenges. The Online Learning Center has additional activities, including more projects. Students also can choose from the projects in the Chapter Assessment. See the Enrichment Activities for this chapter on page 121.

Students who may need additional reinforcement should be encouraged to use the worksheets for this chapter in Part 3 of this TRM. Worksheet 1A will allow them to assess the skills they have learned. See The Reteaching Activities for this chapter on page 121.

Page 52

IN THE WORKPLACE

ADMINISTRATIVE ASSISTANTS

Career Activity

Administrative Assistants must have desktop publishing skills due to the number of publications they are responsible for creating. Often, Administrative Assistants may be responsible for creating company newsletters, financial reports, advertisements, or catalogs. Without special skills, these documents can reflect poorly upon the company's perceived professionalism.

Use the following Reading Check and Critical Thinking answers as a guide to help evaluate student understanding of the core concepts. Requiring that your students write in complete sentences will help you grade faster and promote good writing skills. You can have students write answers in their desktop publishing journals, or students can answer these questions at the computer by accessing the Reading Check and Critical Thinking activities on the Online Learning Center at **glencoe.com**.

Chapter   1   Assessment Answers

Page 53

Reading Check

1. Sans serif fonts are fonts whose typeface has no cross-strokes on the letter-forms. Some examples are Arial, Tahoma, and Verdana.

2. Scalable fonts are vector-style graphics. Vector graphics are graphics drawn by using math. These can be scaled easily because the computer simply redraws these objects using a scale multiple, and they are resized perfectly every time.

3. Check the title bar to make sure you are in the correct document.

4. You can align text on the page by selecting the text, then using the Formatting toolbar's align buttons to align the text on the left, on the right, in the center of the page, or justified from margin to margin.

5. You should use fonts from different font families in order to differentiate text as in titles and body text, to provide good contrast, and to add visual interest.

Critical Thinking

6. You should use oldstyle fonts for long bodies of information and slab serif fonts for titles.

7. Underlining is no longer used much because it reduces readability. The underline often interrupts the descenders in a word and can cause difficulty reading the text on the next line, as well. Italics are often used instead.

8. The Spelling and Grammar tool will not identify correctly spelled words that are used incorrectly, such as their, there, and they're.

9. Correcting two spaces after every period would be easily fixed through the Edit>Replace command.

10. Students might describe the following advantages for tables: tables present information in a visual way that is easy to understand, data can be easily added to a table, tables can be easily formatted to look good, and tables can be easily moved on the page.

Evaluate Assessment activities allow students to demonstrate their understanding of concepts and skills learned throughout this project. Because of time constraints, students may not be able to complete every activity suggested. Match assignments to student ability levels using the leveled projects (★ Easy, ★★ Medium, and ★★★ Challenging). Rubrics are available to evaluate projects on the Teacher Resources DVD and the Online Learning Center at **glencoe.com**.

Page 53

Rubric

1. Independent Practice ★

Create a Daily Schedule Remind students that pre-planning is important and that they should briefly sketch out what they intend to put into their table. Keep in mind, though, that most everything they will need for creating and formatting tables is under the Table menu, so if they need to add or remove rows or columns, they can do it at any point. **(Rubric IP 1-1)**

- Documents should be free of misspellings or other inaccuracies and information should be presented in a logical and clear manner.

- Information in the table should be made more readable by using effective leading and different colors or shading.

- Documents may contain a footnote citing the source of the information.

- A header and footer may be added with proper student contact information and the file name.

- For an additional challenge or credit, students might add a border and insert a single piece of clip art consistent with the tone of the document.

Page 54

Rubric

2. Independent Practice ★★

Illustrate a Poem Provide books of poetry anthologies or allow students to bring in their own resources. Remind students that pre-planning is important and that they should briefly sketch out what they intend to put into their illustration. Have students look at the Color Theory appendix to help them choose a color appropriate to the mood of the poem. Students should consider the audience: Who will be reading this design? Have students search for relevant clip art or other illustrations they can use. Students should then conduct pre-planning and briefly sketch out what they intend to put into their design. **(Rubric IP 1-2)**

- Designs should use artwork, colors, graphics (like a border), and fonts that represent the mood of the poem.

- Students should check their work for typos or errors.

- Students might include information about the author at the bottom of the page, and add a footnote to cite any sources.

- A header and footer may be added with proper student contact information and the file name.

Rubric

3. Independent Practice ★★★

Create a Pet Flyer Have students brainstorm five unusual animals that might make interesting pets. Students should then do some research to determine the best one to use for an advertisement. Students should choose specific features to include in the flyer. They should also consider the audience: Who would want this pet? Have students do pre-planning and create some sketches for their design, then search for relevant clip art or other graphics. **(Rubric IP 1-3)**

- The text should use an easily readable font and be presented as a bulleted list. It should provide accurate information about the animal's appearance (size, coloring), eating habits, and personality traits.

- Fonts, colors, and graphics should be created for a specific audience, and match the tone and message of the advertisement.

- Students should cite their information sources either in a textbox on the flyer, or in a separate document.

Reteaching Activities

Evaluate Font Families Have students use advertisements from magazines to find examples of all the different font families identified on page 13 of the textbook. Have them cut, glue, and label these examples on paper to create a poster or a booklet.

Complete Worksheets Have students complete Worksheets 1A and 1B, which can be found in Part 3 or this TRM, on the Teacher Resource DVD, at the Online learning Center at **glencoe.com**.

Enrichment Activities

Create Electronic Portfolios Have students create electronic portfolios of their best work, as a way of tracking their progress and also as examples for college or employment. Professional designers often host their work on Web sites or create PowerPoint presentations. If these are not an option for students, have them insert images of their design into a Word or Publisher document, where they can also add descriptive text.

To create images of their Word documents, students will need to use the Print Screen button to capture the document as it appears on their monitor. They can then paste it into another application such as a PowerPoint slide or a Publisher document. They should crop the image, as necessary, and then write an explanation of the document's purpose and why specific design decisions were made.

Enrichment If students need an additional challenge, have them complete the activities in the Online Learning Center at **glencoe.com**.

Chapter 2

Vector Graphics in Word

Skills You Will Learn

Workshop Foundations: Understanding Graphics

- Identify vector and raster graphics
- Compare vector and raster graphics

Workshop Toolbox: Word's Drawing Toolbar

- Display the Drawing toolbar
- Identify drawing tools

Project 2-1 Drawing Basics

- Apply color fill options
- Draw and format lines

Project 2-2 Group Drawing Objects

- Apply different font styles
- Add a page border
- Edit and resize clip art
- Group drawing elements
- Wrap text
- Add a header

Project 2-3 Layer Drawing Objects

- Create shapes
- Group drawing objects
- Resize clip art
- Duplicate clip art

Project 2-4 Create a Logo and Add Callouts

- Format WordArt
- Combine text and graphics
- Add callouts
- Add a background color

Project 2-5 Create Quad-fold Documents

- Lay out a quad-fold document
- Use the zoom tool
- Rotate images
- Print four pages on a sheet

Project 2-6 Create a Newsletter

- Create a masthead
- Format columns
- Create styles

Project 2-7 Crop and Resize a Photograph

- Crop and resize a photograph
- Add a caption

Skills Studio

Create a Bi-fold Brochure

Project 2-8 Design a Brochure

- Add tabs with leaders
- Format columns
- Apply Format Painter

Project 2-9 Lay Out a Front Panel

- Design a front panel
- Add a texture background

Page 55

Start-Up Skills

Identify Graphics Use examples from publications to show students the different kinds of art and graphics that are used in each. See if they can identify clip art, boxes, borders, rules, etc. Explain that even the simplest line is considered a graphic, and a line's color, weight, design, and placement can enhance a design or detract from it. In this chapter, students will be learning how to create and manipulate different graphics, using Word's drawing tools.

Design Process: Flyers and Brochures

Compare Flyers and Brochures Whenever you begin a chapter, you will see a Design Process chart discussing the different elements that must be considered when designing a particular type of publication. Later in the chapter, students create the document that is evaluated in the chart, and the skills they learn in the chapter will help them understand the design choices.

Before beginning the bi-fold brochure in the Skills Studio (Projects 2-8 and 2-9), have students review the Design Process chart on this page one more time. See if they can identify the purpose, audience, and content from the completed brochure shown on page 95. Use the same example and the illustration on page 88 to discuss layout and publication of a brochure.

Compare the design elements of the brochure to the flyers that students create in Projects 2-2 and 2-4. How are they the same and how are they different?

Quick Write Activity

Evaluate Brochures and Flyers Have students bring in examples of brochures and flyers that were created for different purposes and audiences. Have each student choose one example to evaluate, using the Design Process chart on page 55 to determine what to look for. Afterwards, choose a few of the best examples and discuss the different elements as a class.

LEARNING LINK

This chapter is intended to teach the foundations of using drawing tools. Many of these same drawing tools are also available in Microsoft Publisher and will be used in Unit 2. In Units 3 and 4, when students learn Adobe Photoshop and Adobe Illustrator, they will need to rely on the skills that are introduced in this chapter.

Workshop Foundations
Pages 56–57

Understanding Graphics

FOCUS

Focus Activity
Compare Graphics Have students read the discussion on vector and raster graphics in this section. Give students a copy of the Venn diagram from Part 3 of this manual or have them create their own. Students should use the Venn diagram to compare the differences and similarities of vector and raster graphics.

You Will Learn To:
- Identify vector and raster graphics
- Compare vector and raster graphics

Page 56

Before You Read Activity
Survey Before You Read This activity is a good way to get students interested in what they will be learning before they start a chapter. It will also help you determine how much they know and which students may need extra help.

Give students five minutes to look at the titles, headings, objectives, and illustrations in the chapter. Then discuss with them what the chapter is about. See if they can get a sense of some of the skills they will be learning, even if they do not yet understand specific terminology. Ask them what parts of the chapter look most interesting, and have them explain why.

Page 56

Key Term Activity
Illustrate Terms Most professions have certain words, or jargon, that refer to industry-specific concepts. Raster, bitmap, vector and pixel are these sorts of words. By using these terms, you are identifying yourself as a professional to others and are better able to explain specific circumstances.

Understanding vector and raster graphics is a very important part of this course, and it is crucial that students know what these terms mean. Discuss the concepts with them and have them look at the illustration on page 56.

Key Term Definitions

vector graphic A type of graphic where the information used to redraw the picture is stored as mathematical formulas. (page 56)

raster graphic A graphic that is made up of pixels that work together to form an image. Also called *bitmap graphic*. (page 56)

bitmap graphic See *raster graphic*. (page 56)

pixel Short for *picture element*, the smallest unit of color in an image or on a computer monitor. (page 56)

TEACH

Teach Activity

Compare Clip Art If allowed, have students go to **office.microsoft.com/clipart** or display the Web site to the whole class. Do a search for *dog* clip art for *all media types*. Students should immediately be able to identify which of the results are photographs and which are drawings. Discuss how they can tell the difference. Double-click on a few of the clip art examples to open the Properties window. Here, students can see if the image is clip art or a photograph and whether the image is considered resizable. Notice the file extension. Do not just assume that because it looks like a drawing that the file is a vector image.

 Homework Suggestion Assign and collect homework on a weekly basis. This will train students to look at the ways design is used in the world around them. It will force them to be more attentive and give them a background to draw upon when creating their own designs. Keep their findings in a swap file that all students can use. For this chapter, have students bring in examples of graphics, then discuss the basic shapes that make up each object.

● Answers to Workshop Foundations Activities

Page 57

Sidebar

Pixel is short for "picture element."

ASSESS

Page 57

✓ Reading Check

1. Raster and vector graphics are both pictures. They are different in the way the computer stores the information. Vector graphics usually look like drawings, while raster (bitmap) images usually look like photographs. Vector images are usually smaller files than Raster images. Vector images can be resized without loss of image quality.

2. Clip art is often a vector graphic. However, though clip art often looks like a drawing, it may not be scalable. It is always best to check the file name extension to make sure that it is in a vector format (see page 294).

CLOSE

Compare Drawings and Photographs When do students think that it would be more appropriate to use photographs over drawings, or the other way around? Look at file sizes for drawings and photographs and have students determine which is larger and why.

Workshop Toolbox
Pages 58–60

Word's Drawing Toolbar

FOCUS

Focus Activity

Add Visual Interest In this chapter, students begin to learn how to use graphics to make a document more attractive to readers.

> **You Will Learn To:**
> • Display the Drawing toolbar
> • Identify drawing tools

Studies show that a reader's interest must be captured within a fraction of a second. In the past, that was not the case. For example, advertisements used a lot more text than today's advertisements. Ask students why they think this is so. Is it MTV's fault? Is it only recently that people have such short attention spans, or have people always been this way?

Have students look at the ways publications use images and graphics to attract readers' attention. How do images in a newspaper differ from those in an advertisement? What kinds of information are these pictures conveying? You might mention that newspaper images usually provide details to clarify or complement the text. Advertisements may provide little information, but set a mood or unconscious message.

Page 58

Key Term Activity

Restore Default Settings The term *default* is used frequently in this textbook. It is particularly important because, on computers that are used by many people, the default settings have often been changed. For example, students' Word toolbars might not look like the toolbars shown in their textbooks. Buttons might have been added or deleted. To restore toolbars to their default settings, you would click **Tools>Customize**. In the **Options** tab, click **Reset menu and toolbar usage data**.

> **Key Term Definitions**
>
> **Default** The automatic or built-in setting for a feature in a computer program. (page 58)

TEACH

Teach Activity

Review the Drawing Toolbar Make sure students understand how to display the Drawing toolbar. They can click View>Toolbars>Drawing, or right-click on the arrow on the end of a toolbar, then check Drawing from the drop-down menu. If the toolbar is not automatically placed at the bottom of the screen, review with students how to move it there. Walk through each tool on the Drawing toolbar, demonstrating the purpose and usefulness of each. Be sure to show students that the Draw button also has many useful tools.

Answers to Workshop Toolbox Activities

Page 59

Eye on Ethics

Before copyright laws, writers were not protected from having their work stolen and republished. People who created intellectual property risked working on something and not being compensated for their time, effort, or the expenses related to developing the work.

ASSESS

Use the following questions and any Sidebar and Eye on Ethics features to access students' understanding of the workshops. Students can write answers to these questions in their desktop publishing journals.

Reading Check

1. Answers will vary. Evaluate students' responses based on their understanding of the drawing tool indicated and how it would be used.

2. One must be familiar with a variety of drawing tools since there is no one tool that meets all needs and expectations. Just as a carpenter needs more than a hammer, we need to be familiar with a variety of drawing tools to create a range of products.

CLOSE

Preview Icons In the steps of each project, students have probably noticed the icons representing the buttons on the toolbars. Have students quickly look over the steps in Projects 2-1 and 2-2, and see if they can identify the drawing tools that they will be using. Have them explain how each of these tools is used.

Chapter 2 Projects

Pages 61–95

FOCUS

Focus Activity

Focus on Clip Art Go to the Microsoft online clip art to show students how to search for examples of clip art and evaluate clip art properties. You can access the Web site by clicking the Insert Clip Art button on the Drawing toolbar, then choosing *Clip art on Office Online* in the Clip Art task pane. Or you can access it directly at **http://office. microsoft.com/clipart**.

Show students the drop-down menu for Media Types and choose *Clip Art*. Then, in the search box, enter a subject, such as *chef*. Double-click on one of the clip art options to show students the properties box. In this box, they can see whether the clip art is scalable and its size. There is also a Copy button, so they can copy and paste the clip art into a document. If allowable, you can demonstrate how to download clip art to their computers.

 Go Online PREVIEW

Before You Begin Students can use the chapter **PowerPoint** presentations and **rubrics** at the Online Learning Center to determine what is expected *before* they complete a project. Students can view the PowerPoint slides on their own computers, or you can project them to preview chapter concepts and show examples of the finished projects. You might also display project solutions so students can easily refer to them while they work. (Presentations and rubrics are also provided on the Teacher Resource DVD for your convenience).

glencoe.com

Projects

Project 2-1
Drawing Basics

Project 2-2
Group Drawing Objects

Project 2-3
Layer Drawing Objects

Project 2-4
Create a Logo and Add Callouts

Project 2-5
Create Quad-fold Documents

Project 2-6
Create a Newsletter

Project 2-7
Crop and Resize a Photograph

Project 2-8
Design a Brochure

Project 2-9
Lay Out a Front Panel

Key Term Activity

On the Board Write five key terms on the board, and then have students come up and add their own definitions next to each term. Discuss any terms that may be unclear. Have students write all the terms and definitions in their Key Term journals.

Key Term Definitions

parallel When two lines stay an equal distance from each other and never intersect. (page 61)

perpendicular When two lines intersect to form a 90° right angle. (page 61)

pull squares or circles around a graphic image that are dragged to make objects larger or smaller. (page 61)

group To combine separate elements into a single, more complex object. (page 64)

ungroup To break apart a single complex object into its separate parts. (page 64)

scale The size of an object. (page 68)

layers The separate objects on different levels that make up a complex image. (page 68)

ratio The relationship between vertical and horizontal width of an image. (page 68)

callout A type of text box that calls attention to parts of an image. (page 71)

leader A line or series of dots used to connect information. (page 71)

logo A design combining text and graphics, used to identify an organization or product. (page 71)

scalable The ability of a graphic to be resized without losing image quality. (page 71)

quad-fold A document that is folded in half twice to create four folds. (page 75)

byline A credit line showing the name of an article's writer, usually below an article's title. (page 79)

masthead A title of a newsletter, newspaper, or other periodical that stands out from the rest of the text. (page 79)

style sheet Formatting rules that allow the user to set guidelines for text that ensure consistency throughout a publication. (page 79)

crop To trim an image. (page 84)

resize To increase or reduce the size of an image. (page 84)

bi-fold A document that has been folded in half like a book. (page 89)

leading (page 89)

duplex printing A feature that allows a printer to print on both sides of the paper before going on to the next copy. (page 93)

TEACH

Teach Activity

Demonstrate Drawing Tools Review some basic functions that are common to many drawing programs:

- Click on the Line tool and drag it onto the workspace. Word will display a Drawing canvas. Drawing in here automatically "groups" all the objects so that they can be moved together. This feature can save some steps, but it can be confusing. Students can turn this feature off by choosing the Tools>Options>General tab and then checking *Automatically create Drawing Canvas with new AutoShape*.

- Show students that they can create lines at any angle with the Line tool. The lines have pull handles and can be reformatted at any time. Show how the tool is inactive when the line has been drawn and the mouse button is released.

- Select the Line tool again and hold the Shift key, then click and drag in the workspace. Holding Shift limits the angle in which the line can be drawn to exactly 90°, 180°, or 45°.

- Double-click on the Line tool. You can draw any number of lines in the workspace. Notice that the line tool does not release after drawing a line. In Microsoft Word 2003 or later, you can double click drawing tools. This option is not available in earlier versions of Word. (**Note:** Visit the Online Learning Center to see tips for using earlier versions of Microsoft Word.)

- Select the Line tool again, and hold the Alt key when creating a line. This allows you to draw objects with more precision.

- Hold the Shift key while demonstrating the Rectangle and Oval tools to show how this allows you to create perfect squares and circles.

- Show students how clicking on a shape selects it and displays the pull handles for moving and resizing. Objects can be filled with color, and line color can be changed.

- Hold the Control key, and click on a few objects to demonstrate how more than one object can be selected. The Select Objects tool can also be used to drag a selection box around all the objects that you want to select.

Teaching Tips ✍ and Troubleshooting Tips ⚠ for Projects

Pages 61–63

Rubric

Project 2-1 → **Drawing Basics** Students create a drawing of a pizza using a number of simple shapes and drawing tools. They will also learn some keyboard tips that will help them use the drawing tools more precisely. (**Solution File 2-1, Rubric 2-1**)

✍ **Draw a Venn Diagram** Challenge students to explain how they could create their own Venn Diagram by using the drawing tools in Microsoft Word. Students would need to use two circles and three text boxes. To see the section where the boxes overlapped, they would need to choose *No Fill*.

Look for More Students will see in this project that they have the option of choosing *More Colors* in the Fill Color drop-down menu. This opens a new window with many more options. Other drawing tools, including AutoShapes and Arrow Style also have the "More" option. Have students open these features to see the extra formatting options.

Zoom In Students tend to create their drawings without zooming in closer to see what they are doing. For example, in this drawing, if students do not zoom in when they draw the lines on the pizza, they may not extend them all the way to the edge of the crust. Encourage students to draw their images, then zoom in closely and check the details. Make sure they hold the Alt key for more precision when using their drawing tools.

Remove the Drawing Canvas Although the drawing canvas can be useful, it can also be confusing to students. If it pops up when they click one of the drawing tools, they simply have to press the Delete key to remove it. To turn off the option completely, use Tools>Options>General, and uncheck the option *Automatically create drawing canvas when inserting AutoShapes.*

Pages 64–67

Rubric

Data File

Project 2-2 → **Creating Complex Objects** Students will create a flyer using clip art. They will learn how to edit the clip art, and in the process, learn the concept of grouping. (**Data File 2-2, Solution File 2-2, Rubric 2-2**)

Create Complex Drawings When artists draw a figure like a dog, they usually do not start by drawing the entire dog. Rather, they create the individual shapes that make up the dog's head, body, legs, and tail. Then they join them together to form the dog, and perhaps they will add more shapes and details, like the shading of the hair. Have students look at the dog illustration on page 64 and identify the shapes that are used (circles, trapezoids, etc.). When all these individual objects are grouped together, they form the complex drawing of the dog's head.

Edit Clip Art Show students that most clip art from Microsoft Word can be ungrouped. This allows you to recolor clip art and remove unwanted elements. Some objects that look like clip art cannot be ungrouped. This is most likely because the object was saved as a raster graphic, even though it may look like a drawing.

In some versions of Word, you will see that when an object is ungrouped, the drawing canvas appears. The drawing canvas is a tool that keeps together the different elements that make up a drawing object like clip art. When you change the layout of the drawing canvas, you change the layout for the clip art. To do this choose **Format>Drawing Canvas.** If you prefer not to use the canvas, you can drag the drawing off the canvas, and then delete the canvas.

Group Objects Show students that when they wish to group objects, they must select more than one object before they are allowed to use the Group command.

⚠️ **Resize the Clip Art** The real challenge to this lesson will be resizing the clip art without disrupting the text layout. Help students pay close attention to this possibility and come up with solutions to the problem. Removing the drawing canvas should help. Students can also crop the edges of the drawing canvas or create soft returns (Shift+Enter) for lines that do not wrap correctly.

Pages 68–70

Rubric

Project 2-3 ➤ **Layer Drawing Objects** Students will use the pizza illustration they created in Project 2-1 to create a flyer advertising a restaurant. In this project, they will learn how to layer objects and create a border from clip art. They will complete the flyer in Project 2-4. If students have not completed Project 2-1, you have the option of letting them use Data File 2-3a. **(Data Files 2-3a and 2-3b, Solution File 2-3, Rubric 2-3)**

✍️ **Duplicate Objects** In Microsoft Word, most students know about copying and pasting, but few know that a third option—that only works for drawing objects—is duplicating an object. The advantage to duplicating is that the relative space between the original object and its copy is preserved. In today's lesson, students will be using this concept to create their own page border.

✍️ **Mask Objects** When you use a mask, you are using a shape (the mask) to cover part of another object in order to hide part of it. (This concept will become more important when working with Adobe projects in later units.) Many programs come with this feature, but in Microsoft Word, this effect must be created manually. In this case, we will be creating our own mask to hide the pizza layer. While the concept may be a bit strange, it is much easier than trying to actually draw a pizza with a slice missing.

⚠️ **Save Files** If students are using Project 2-1 as a starting point for this project, make sure that they use the **Save As** command to resave the file under a new name. Otherwise, they will lose the image they created specifically for Project 2-1. This is a good point to review saving procedures with your class.

⚠️ **Align Objects** Students will find the border to be relatively challenging. To ensure that all the elements are aligned and evenly distributed, students can select all the objects on one side of the border and choose **Draw>Align or Distribute>Align Center** and **Draw>Align or Distribute>Distribute Horizontally** (or Vertically, depending upon the side). Both of these options will ensure that elements are lined up with each other and are spaced out evenly. Students should repeat this procedure for each side as needed.

Pages 71–74

Rubric

Project 2-4 **Create a Logo and Add Callouts** Students finish the flyer that they started in Project 2-3, adding a logo, callouts, and text to the flyer. **(Solution File 2-4, Rubric 2-4)**

Page 71

Answer to Sidebar Answers will vary. This can be done as a class discussion or as an assignment. Evaluate responses based on whether two logos are described and whether the explanation on how the logo relates to the company or product is logical. Many students may have trouble explaining logos like the Nike swoop, though they may wish to try. Encourage students to do some research on company Web sites regarding the logo's meaning.

Evaluate Logos Have students come up with a list of logos. You can write their responses on the board, or they can create a list in their notebooks. Students are likely to list McDonald's, Nike, and other popular companies, but they are probably oblivious to the logos on the computers in front of them, on their textbooks, or others they can see in the classroom at this very moment.

Ask students to tell you who published this textbook. Students should be able to find the answer in a matter of seconds. Without the logo, finding out the publisher would have taken a little longer. The graphic element of the logo helps to set it apart and (hopefully) help customers recognize the manufacturer more quickly.

Design Logos Many logos are red. Can students predict why? Have them look in the Color Theory appendix on color associations (p. 494). If every logo were red, would this lessen its impact? Have students explain their answer.

Logos can be expensive to have professionally produced. A successful logo will get the audience's attention, convey the purpose of the company, and appear simple. McDonald's logo is a perfect example. It uses bright, warm colors. The red background helps to capture attention. The yellow symbol looks like an "M" for McDonald's and it also resembles a pair of french fries twisted together, symbolizing the product itself.

Save Resources Show students how to use File>Print Preview before printing a document, so they can notice any problems before wasting resources. To save toner, omit Steps 20–24. If you want a colored background without using colored ink, you can have students print on colored paper. Show students how colored paper might affect the colors used in the document. This is called *color metamerism.*

Fit Text in Text Boxes If students have a difficult time getting all the text to fit into a callout text box, they can adjust the size of the boxes and/or the size of the text. Advanced users can select the text box by clicking the border, then choose Format>Text Box>Text Box to adjust the internal margins of the text box. Setting the internal margins to 0 inches saves a lot of space.

⚠ **Add Background Color** Students will often try to use Format>Background to add a background color and effects behind text. While this works fine on screen, students will be surprised when it does not print. The Format>Background feature is for Web pages and the effects do not print.

Pages 75–78

Rubric

Student Data File

▶ **Project 2-5** **Create Quad-fold Documents** Students lay out and create quad-fold party invitations, using WordArt to create text that can be rotated. (**Data File 2-5, Solution File 2-5, Rubric 2-5**)

✍ **Lay Out Quad-fold Documents** Since Microsoft Word is a word processor, it does not have tools for creating documents with a complex layout, such as a quad-fold invitation. Still, these publications can still be created with a little bit of ingenuity. Have students look at the figures on page 75. What do they notice about the layout of the document? Ask how would they turn text upside down for pages 2 and 3? Notice that pages 1 and 4 and pages 2 and 3 are not the direction we would normally expect, from left to right.

✍ **Create a Model** Have students follow the steps on page 75 to create a model for this activity. Students can use a scrap sheet of paper and fold it properly, then number or label the panels: front (1), back (4), inside left (2) and inside right (3). They should then open the page and compare it to the figure on page 75. The layout of the panels may change if the page is folded differently from the illustration.

⚠ **Print Quad-fold Documents** If your printer does not allow you to print multipage documents on one sheet, as described on page 78, there is another way to lay out the quad-fold document. Students can create a large table with two rows and two columns (2 × 2), and then size it to fit on as much of the page as possible. They would then choose **Table>AutoFit>Distribute Rows Evenly** and **Distribute Columns Evenly** to ensure that all four panels on the table are equal. Although this is not extremely precise, it should help students to lay out the document.

Pages 79–83

Rubric

Student Data File

▶ **Project 2-6** **Create a Newsletter** Students begin to lay out a one-page newsletter, which they will complete in Project 2-7. They will create a masthead, format columns, and use style sheets. (**Data Files 2-6a and 2-6b, Solution File 2-6, Rubric 2-6**)

✍ **Compare Newsletters** Ask students if they have ever seen a newsletter before. Most likely they have seen newsletters from their school, from different businesses, and from family friends and relatives at Christmas. Bring in a few newsletters or have students look at the example on page 79. What would make a student pick up one of those newsletters to read? They might mention that they only read newsletters that address their interests. If the text and graphics immediately convey that connection, they would read it. It is vital for a document to reach its intended audience and to be designed to specifically attract that audience.

Apply Style Sheets Ask students if they would like to use software that keeps track of all the fonts and font attributes used in various documents. We all like to make work easier, so students should be pleased to learn about styles. Often it is difficult to manage leading, margins, fonts, font sizes, and font styles. Keeping the formatting consistent throughout an entire publication is complicated. Graphic designers use *style sheets* to help with this. Style sheets not only maintain consistency, but they also make it easy to apply format changes throughout an entire document.

To demonstrate how style sheets work, key four words on four separate sheets of paper. Format one of the words with a different font, color, size and add a border and shading (Format>Borders and Shading). Select the formatted word. In the Style window on the Formatting toolbar, key a name (like "Test Word") for the style.

Select a word on a different page, then open the drop-down menu from the Style window and choose the "Test Word" style. Notice that this new word will change to reflect the appearance of the first word. Repeat for the other two pages.

Reformat one of the words, Select the word, and then click the **Styles and Formatting** button on the far left of the Formatting toolbar. In the resulting task pane, find the *Test Word* style. Open the style's drop-down menu, and choose *Update to Match Selection*. Show students that the text on all pages has changed. Using this method, it is easy to fix even a 100 pages in a single click!

Walk Around More than likely, students have never even heard of style sheets before, much less ever used them. They will need help. Be sure to walk the classroom and assist students in assigning and using style sheets. Encourage students to assist each other. This way you will not have to be everywhere at once, and students learn better by teaching others.

Page 84–87

Rubric

Student Data File

> Project 2-7

Crop and Resize a Photograph Students complete their newsletter by adding a text box and a photograph, which they will crop and resize. They will also add drop caps and captions to complete the design. **(Data File 2-7, Solution File 2-7, Rubric 2-7)**

Create a Focal Point Ask students to consider how movie makers direct the audience's attention towards a specific character on the screen. That character may say lines, move toward the camera, be in the center of the screen, be the only one in focus, or wear a different color. Ask students to explain how we might use some of these same tricks to redirect the audience's attention in a document. The spot where we want a reader to look is called the focal point.

Crop a Photograph The Picture toolbar has a tool that *crops*, or trims, the edges of a picture. This feature is commonly used to reshape a picture to fit into a specific area or to remove unneeded information so the reader's attention is directed towards the most important elements in the image. Show students a picture of a group of people sitting together, having fun. Use the crop tool on Word's Picture toolbar to crop the picture in order to redirect attention toward a specific person in the group.

One advantage to cropping in Word, rather than a photo editor like Photoshop, is that cropping in Word is not permanent. In Word, the crop tool acts more like a mask, simply hiding the edges of the image. Since it is a nondestructive process, the picture can be uncropped later if necessary. This is helpful for placing a picture and showing the content to the client. If the client wishes to crop the picture differently, then this can be performed without becoming time consuming. Since the image information is merely hidden, however, the file size is not reduced by cropping images.

Insert Symbols If students have trouble with Step 9, have them use Insert>Symbol and change the font to Wingdings. They should be able to find the banner symbol more easily this way. If they were to select the Wingdings font from the Formatting toolbar, they would use an uppercase P to insert the symbol.

Add Captions Step 16 tells students to right-click on the photo to choose the Caption option. If your version of Word does not have that option in the right-click menu, students can choose Insert>Reverence>Caption. They can also use a text box for adding captions.

Align Columns If students have problems balancing the columns as shown in Figure 2.34, they can:

- Click in front of Sir Gawain and choose Insert>Break>Column Break to force the new column to start at this point, or
- Click at the end of the second column and choose Insert>Break>Continuous Section Break. This usually evens out the columns.

Skills Studio

Pages 88–95

Create a Bi-fold Brochure

Have students list the possible uses of a bi-fold brochure, such as the example shown on page 88 that they will create in the Skills Studio. Students will notice that this is a concert program. What are some activities in your school that could use bi-fold brochures? Students are likely to mention music programs, but there are also sports programs (basketball, volleyball, and football), theater arts productions, school orientation brochures, fundraising leaflets, and more.

Both newsletters and brochures are challenging to design due to the amount of information that needs to be relayed, yet they still must be inviting to read. Have students create a Venn diagram to compare the two different types of designs.

Page 89–93

Rubric

Student Data File

Project 2-8 → **Design a Brochure** Students format the inside pages of a bi-fold brochure, creating a two-column layout and using tabs with leaders. They also apply styles by using the Format Painter. They will complete the outside of the brochure in Project 2-9. **(Data File 2-8, Solution File 2-8, Rubric 2-8)**

Page 89

Answer to Sidebar A tri-fold brochure template is useful in Word because it is difficult to lay out brochures in Word, which is a word processor, not layout software.

Apply Format Painter The Format Painter is a powerful tool, especially when combined with style sheets. As in the Teaching Tip in Project 2-6, begin by keying four words on four separate pages. Select one of the words, and change the size, color, font, alignment and add a shade and a border.

Use the Style Sheet window to define a style for the word, such as *My New Style*. Then triple-click the word you formatted. Triple-clicking treats this word as a paragraph and will load the word and its alignment into the Format Painter. Double-click the Format Painter on the Standard toolbar. Next to your insertion point should be a small paint brush to indicate that the Format Painter is active.

Move to the next page, and use the Format Painter insertion point to highlight the word on the page. It should change to the same format as the first word. Notice, also, that the style you had defined is also assigned to this word. This is a faster and easier way to assign styles than using the Style Window drop down menu.

Format Columns After inserting the column break, some students may notice that the second column is not lining up with the first column. It is an important design concept that the tops of all columns should be aligned. Misalignment commonly occurs when the break is put into the wrong place.

To assess the problem, turn on the Show/Hide ¶ button and look for the ¶ symbol, which indicates the use of a hard return. This is usually the problem. The hard return can be deleted, or students can use the backspace key to bring the lines back up to an even alignment.

For some students, this may not solve the problem. Try clicking on the first line and checking Format>Paragraph. Under Spacing, make sure that a "0" is in the *Before* window.

Fix Formatting There are times when working with Microsoft Word that the text does not do what you expect it to do. The last number or bullets in an automatic list look different than the others in the list, or paragraphs are not aligning with other paragraphs. One way to fix this is to triple-click a line (or double-click if it is just a single word) that is behaving normally, then use the Format Painter to paint the good formatting on top of the problem one. Many times, this will solve the problem!

Pages 92–95

Rubric

Student Data File

Project 2-9

Lay Out a Front Panel Students complete the outside of the brochure they started in Project 2-8 and add graphics to unify the design. **(Data File 2-9, Solution File 2-9, Rubric 2-9)**

Free Fonts If you and your school allow it, have students go online to a site for free fonts like **www.fontfreak.com** or **www.fonts.com**. Have students look through the available fonts and make a list of fonts that would be good for this brochure's winter holiday theme. With your permission, allow students to choose a font to download and install on the computer for future use.

Use Text Boxes Show students that text boxes are easy to use and have many advantages. Text boxes can be moved so that text can be placed anywhere on the page without tab stops or having to create tables. They can also be filled with a color that contrasts with the text within them or the page around them.

Text boxes can even be linked together. Simply create two text boxes, then select one. Click **View>Toolbars>Text Box**, and on the Text Box toolbar click the *Create Text Box Link* button. A pitcher icon will appear next to your cursor. Clicking the second text box will then link the two boxes together. When the first text box runs out of room for text, the text will flow into the second text box. Your students will use this tool in Project 3-5 and elsewhere.

ASSESS

Evaluate Projects Encourage students to use the rubrics and the Review and Revise checklists to be sure that they have completed the key steps to these projects. Whenever possible, have students proofread and assist each other. Students learn best when they are teaching each other. Consider giving bonus points for well-designed projects for both the student and the student who evaluated his/her work.

It is recommended that for the first four chapters you evaluate student printouts carefully looking for a standard set of problems. You might purchase a do-it-yourself stamp kit and create a stamp with the following grading criteria:

Font Style	Balance
Font Size	Alignment
Leading	Proximity
Repetition	Spelling and Grammar

Take off 5 points for each type of mistake and 10 points for skipping skill sets in the lessons. For a grade, have students chart the kinds of mistakes they have been making. Hopefully, they will begin to see a pattern of mistakes and you will be finding fewer problems, making grading faster in the future.

CLOSE

Preview Unit 2 Discuss with students the difficulties of formatting certain layouts in Word, such as the quad-fold card in Project 2-5 with its upside-down text. Explain that, although Word can be used for basic desktop publishing, it is word processing software. In Unit 2, students will be working with Microsoft Publisher layout software. Students will see how layout software simplifies many of the tasks that were so complicated in Unit 1.

Page 96

IN THE WORKPLACE

WRITERS AND EDITORS

Career Activity

Writers and editors must often create their own publications, such as newsletters, or they must work with designers or layout specialists to create a publication. In both cases, it is important for writers and editors to understand how the text they create or edit will be laid out on a printed page. They might even have to work directly in a document created in layout software.

Notes

Chapter 2 Assessment Answers

Use the following Reading Check and Critical Thinking answers as a guide to help evaluate student understanding of the core concepts. Requiring that your students write in complete sentences will help you grade faster and promote good writing skills. You can have students write answers in their desktop publishing journals, or students can answer these questions at the computer by accessing the Reading Check and Critical Thinking activities on the Online Learning Center at **glencoe.com**.

Page 97

Reading Check

1. Vector images are rescalable graphics where the information used to recreate the image is stored as math. Raster images are graphics whose information to recreate the image is stored as pixels.

2. To draw a perfect circle, hold the Shift key and use the Oval tool.

3. If you were creating a bi-fold brochure, the right side of the document would be the front of the brochure. The left side would be the back.

4. To create a complex drawing object out of several simple objects, you would group the simple objects. To do this, select all the objects, then click Draw on the Drawing toolbar, and choose Group.

5. When you resize a picture, the entire picture becomes larger or smaller. When you crop a picture, you remove part of the picture.

Critical Thinking

6. The Edit Picture command will ungroup the clip art and display the Drawing Canvas. The individual pieces of the clip art can then be deleted or altered.

7. The only way to turn text to any angle (or even upside down) in Word is to use WordArt.

8. A doughnut can be drawn two ways:

   • Create a small circle within a larger circle. The outer circle (the ring shape) should be the color of the doughnut. The inner circle would be the color of the background to mask the interior of the doughnut.

   • The other option is to use the AutoShapes>Basic Shapes and choosing the Donut shape.

9. Student answers will vary. Their responses should describe a specific logo. If you are not familiar with it, see if they can include a picture or Web site so you can view it. Their answers should take into account design elements like graphics, color, fonts, etc.

10. Vector images can be resized without losing image quality. These images are also usually smaller and make for faster downloading and printing times.

Evaluate Assessment activities allow students to demonstrate their understanding of concepts and skills learned throughout this chapter. Because of time constraints, students may not be able to complete every activity suggested. Match assignments to student ability levels using the leveled projects (★ Easy, ★★ Medium, and ★★★ Challenging). Rubrics are available to evaluate projects on the Teacher Resources DVD and the Online Learning Center at **glencoe.com**.

Page 97

Rubric

1. Independent Practice ★

Create a Logo Students can work with a partner or individually, if they prefer. Try to have a collection of logos available in the classroom, both professional ones and examples that students have created. When brainstorming, provide students with a specific number of ideas to come up within a specific amount of time. Remind students that a brainstorming list includes any responses that come to mind, without spending time to evaluate them.

Assign a value to each part of the project, and grade the project according to the guidelines as described in the Plan, Design, Create and Present sections on page 97. Use the rubric to help students evaluate their own projects and to help you assign a grade. **(Rubric IP 2-1)**

Page 98

Rubric

2. Independent Practice ★★

Create a Flyer Encourage students to develop a theme for their ice cream shop flyer. They should pick a theme they think might sell their ice cream to a particular audience, be it nature, action heroes, music, etc. Have them use this theme to pick names for the store, flavors, and menu offerings. Encourage students to carry the theme throughout their design.

Require students to create several thumbnail sketches, each with different designs. Have them evaluate each other's sketches and, from the feedback, create a final sketch that incorporates all their best ideas into one final design. Evaluate the student project by assigning point values for the theme, application to the audience, the thumbnail sketches, and the design elements described on page 98. **(Rubric IP 2-2)**

Page 98

Rubric

3. Independent Practice ★★★

Create a Brochure with a Map Have students brainstorm what information they would include in a brochure about the school. Set guidelines as to whether you will allow serious or silly brochures (such as avoiding the cafeteria on days when it serves Casserole Surprise). Encourage students to choose a theme for their brochure. Possible themes might be using the school mascot and colors, or designing it as if it were a travel guide. Award bonus points for creativity and carrying the theme throughout the entire design: clip art, fonts, and text.

Require that students create several thumbnail sketches, each with different designs. Then have them share their ideas before deciding on a final design. Evaluate the student project by assigning point values for the theme, application to the audience, the thumbnail sketches, and the design elements described on page 98. **(Rubric IP 2-3)**

Reteaching Activities

Evaluate Folded Documents Have students bring in a variety of publications that use folds as part of the design. They might choose bi-fold or tri-fold brochures, menus, booklets, pamphlets, or folded cards. Have them sketch out the layout of each of these publications to use as models for later designs. Make sure they clearly mark which panels are the front, back, and pages in the center. If text needs to be rotated, they should include that in their models.

Complete Worksheets Have students complete Worksheets 2A and 2B, which can be found in Part 3 of this TRM, on the Teacher Resource DVD, or on the Online Learning Center at **glencoe.com**.

Enrichment Activities

Work with Clients Encourage students to create a list of clients that they could approach for real world work. Have them interview the person to determine what information that client would want to publish, the best type of publication (i.e., a flyer, newsletter, brochure, etc.), and the audience meant to receive the publication. Require that the students create the flyer, newsletter, or brochure for the client.

Enrichment If students need an additional challenge, have them complete the enrichment activities on the Online Learning Center at **glencoe.com**.

Notes

Projects Across the Curriculum

Evaluate Understanding These projects allow students to demonstrate their understanding of concepts and skills learned throughout this unit. Because of time constraints, students may not be able to complete every activity suggested. Match assignments to student ability levels using the leveled projects (★ Easy, ★★ Medium, and ★★★ Challenging). Rubrics are available to evaluate projects on the Teacher Resource DVD and the Online Learning Center at **glencoe.com**.

Page 99

Rubric

Project 1 Draw a Castle ★

Encourage students to do research on actual castles and require items such as a drawbridge, a tower, and a moat. Add callouts to label these and other features. Encourage students to use patterns to establish texture to show the difference between the castle and its surrounding countryside. Evaluate projects based on realism, accuracy, perspective and texture. **(Rubric PAC 1-1)**

Page 99

Rubric

Project 2 Create a Visual Report ★★

If possible, work with a science teacher to come up with a project that students can do for your class and the science class. Evaluate the student project by assigning point values to the design elements described on page 99. Designs should also have original, complete, and accurate text; properly cited sources; follow font rules; present information clearly and effectively; and contain relevant illustrations. **(Rubric PAC 1-2)**

Page 100

Rubric

Project 3 Create a Greeting Card ★★

If possible, work with a Language Arts teacher to help students write poems for their cards. Encourage students to review the quad-fold model created in Project 2-5. Bring in examples of cards to show them. Evaluate student projects based on whether the layout is accurate, the graphics complement the poem and theme of the card, and that all the design elements on page 100 are included. **(Rubric PAC 1-3)**

Page 100

Rubric

Project 4 Create a Travel Brochure ★★★

Have students brainstorm destinations and then do some online research to determine the information and images they will use in their brochures. Brochures can include information about hotels, popular sites, hours of operation, history, or anything else students find relevant. Evaluate student projects based on the entire design process: brainstorming ideas, performing accurate research, creating thumbnail sketches, and creating a sound design.

Assess whether layout is accurate, graphics illustrate the text, design elements are consistent throughout the brochure, and all the design elements on page 100 are included. Designs should also have original, complete, and accurate text and properly cited sources. **(Rubric PAC 1-4)**

Design with Microsoft Publisher

Getting Started

About the Unit

In this unit, students will learn how to use layout software, specifically Microsoft Publisher, to create and design publications. The **Workshop Foundations** and **Workshop Toolbox** articles introduce students to layout software with an easy-to-understand comparison to Microsoft Word. Later, students will be introduced to design guidelines that will help them create and evaluate their work according to professional standards.

In **Chapter 3**, students create a wide variety of publications including flyers, business cards, brochures, Web pages, and a menu. Students will learn how to design effective advertisements. The Design Process table, on page 102 in the textbook, will help students focus on the importance of advertisements in everyday life.

The design process and design principles of proximity, alignment, repetition, and contrast (PARC) are introduced in **Chapter 4**. Students will enjoy using their layout design skills to do publication design makeovers. In each project, students identify design flaws and blunders and then redesign the publication while adhering to the PARC principles.

Quick Write Activity

Up to this point, students have been exposed to general design concepts, allowing them to focus on basic desktop publishing skills. In this unit, design concepts will become more important, and by the time students complete Chapter 4, they should have a good sense of what goes into effective design.

Before beginning the unit, have students write a list of all the design principles they have already learned in the first two chapters. As a class, discuss these guidelines and write their responses on the board. Have students copy the full list in their notebooks. They can then add to it as they progress through the unit.

Unit 2 Design with Microsoft Publisher	Articles, Activities, and Exercises
Chapter 3 **Introducing Microsoft Publisher** (pages 101–147)	**Workshop Foundations** Layout Software, pg.103 **Workshop Toolbox** The Publisher Interface, pg. 104 ⓘ **Go Online PowerPoint Presentations Preview,** pg. 106 DF R **Project 3-1** Create a Calendar with a Template, pg. 106 DF R **Project 3-2** Design a Business Card, pg. 110 DF R **Project 3-3** Add Tear-Offs to a Flyer, pg. 115 DF R **Project 3-4** Create a Coupon Mailer, pg. 120 DF R **Project 3-5** Design a Bi-fold Brochure, pg. 125 DF R **Project 3-6** Create Web Pages Using a Master Page, pg. 130 DF R **Project 3-7** Add Hyperlinks to Web Pages, pg. 133 DF R **Project 3-8** Design the Menu Exterior, pg. 137 DF R **Project 3-9** Design the Menu Interior, pg. 140 ⓘ **Go Online Enrichment Activities,** pp. 136 **In The Workplace,** Graphic Designer, pg. 145 Ⓣ **TechSIM CD**
Chapter 4 **Focus on Design Makeovers** (pages 148–193)	**Workshop Foundations** The Design Process, pg. 149–150 **Workshop Toolbox** PARC Design Principles, pg. 151 ⓘ **Go Online PowerPoint Presentations Preview,** pg. 154 DF R **Project 4-1** Evaluate Design in a Flyer, pg. 154 DF R **Project 4-2** Add Contrast and Focal Points, pg. 158 DF R **Project 4-3** Apply the Golden Ratio, pg. 162 DF R **Project 4-4** Apply Styles in a Flyer, pg. 167 DF R **Project 4-5** Revise a Tri-fold Brochure, pg. 172 DF R **Project 4-6** Apply PARC to the Brochure Interior, pg. 177 DF R **Project 4-7** Apply PARC to a Web Page, pg. 180 DF R **Project 4-8** Design for a Young Audience, pg. 186 R **Project 4-9** Complete Your Newsletter, pg. 189 ⓘ **Go Online Enrichment Activities,** pg. 185 **In The Workplace,** Layout Artist, pg. 191 Ⓣ **TechSIM CD**
Unit Assessment **Projects Across the Curriculum** (pages 194–195)	R **Project 1** Create a Flyer with Tear-offs, pg. 194 R **Project 2** Create a Personal Budget Planner, pg. 194 R **Project 3** Create a Brochure with a Coupon, pg. 195 R **Project 4** Add Hyperlinks to a Web Site, pg. 195

Planning Guide UNIT 2

Assessments

Workshop Foundations Reading Check, pg. 103
Workshop Toolbox Reading Check, pg. 105

End of Chapter 3 Assessment
  Reading Check, pg. 146
  Critical Thinking, pg.146

Ⓡ **1.** Independent Practice: Create a Friendship Coupon, pg. 146

Ⓡ **2.** Independent Practice: Create a Plant Brochure, pg. 147

Ⓡ **3.** Independent Practice: Create Community Service Web Pages, pg. 147

⊙ **Additional Assessments You May Wish to Use**
ExamView Assessment Suite Testbank, Chapter 3

Workshop Foundations Reading Check, pg. 150
Workshop Toolbox Reading Check, pg. 153

End of Chapter 4 Assessment
  Reading Check, pg. 192
  Critical Thinking, pg. 192

Ⓡ **1.** Independent Practice: Evaluate and Design an Advertisement, pg. 192

Ⓡ **2.** Independent Practice: Create a *Tips for Teens* Brochure, pg. 193

Ⓡ **3.** Independent Practice: Practive for FBLA Event, pg. 193

⊙ **Additional Assessments You May Wish to Use**
ExamView Assessment Suite Testbank, Chapter 4

ⓘ **Go Online e-Review Self Checks** Chapter 3 and Chapter 4

Estimated Time to Complete Unit

9 Week Course = 5–7 days
18 Week Course = 7–8 days
36 Week Course = 13–15 days

To help customize lesson plans, use the Pacing Guide on pages 29–30 and the Standards Charts on pages 148–149.

Key to Recommended Materials

ⓘ Internet access required

Ⓡ Scoring Rubrics

🅳🅵 Data Files

⊙ *ExamView Assessment Suite* CD

Ⓣ TechSIM (Technology Simulations available on CD and the Online Learning Center)

The Teacher Resource DVD contains Data Files, Solution Files, Rubrics, Reproducible Worksheets, and PowerPoint Presentations.

Data Files for Unit 2 provided on the Teacher Resource DVD and Online Learning Center

Chapter 3	Chapter 4
3-1	4-1
3-2a to 3-2b	4-2
3-3	4-3
3-4	4-4a to 4-4b
3-5a to 3-5e	4-5a to 4-5e
3-6a to 3-6b	4-6
3-7a to 3-7c	4-7a to 4-7c
3-8a to 3-8b	4-8a to 4-8b
3-9a to 3-9f	

Inclusion Strategies
For **Differentiated Instruction Strategies** refer to the **Inclusion in the Computer Technology Classroom** booklet.

ISTE NETS Foundation Standards

1. Basic operations and concepts
2. Social, ethical, and human issues
3. Technology productivity tools
4. Technology communications tools
5. Technology research tools
6. Technology problem-solving and decision-making

Performance Indicators	Textbook Correlation
1. Identify capabilities and limitations of contemporary and emerging technology resources and assess the potential of these systems and services to address personal, lifelong learning, and workplace needs. (NETS 2)	103, 104–105, 106, 110, 125, 130, 133, 136, 145, 147, 158, 162, 170, 172, 180, 185, 191, 193
2. Make informed choices among technology systems, resources, and services. (NETS 1, 2)	103, 105, 106, 115, 120, 125, 130, 133, 145, 147, 150, 152–153, 158, 172, 173, 180, 193, 194
3. Analyze advantages and disadvantages of widespread use and reliance on technology in the workplace and in society as a whole. (NETS 2)	129, 130, 145, 146, 147, 191, 192, 193
4. Demonstrate and advocate for legal and ethical behaviors among peers, family, and community regarding the use of technology and information. (NETS 2)	105, 130, 147, 152, 153
5. Use technology tools and resources for managing and communicating personal/professional information (e.g. finances, schedules, addresses, purchases, correspondence). (NETS 3, 4)	106–109, 110–114, 115–119, 130–132, 133–135, 145, 146–147, 148, 185–186, 187–188, 189–190, 191, 192–193, 194
6. Evaluate technology-based options, including distance and distributed education, for lifelong learning. (NETS 5)	136, 145, 147, 162, 185, 191
7. Routinely and efficiently use online information resources to meet needs for collaboration, research, publications, communications, and productivity. (NETS 4, 5, 6)	106, 136, 145, 146, 147, 154, 162, 185, 191, 192, 192, 194–195
8. Select and apply technology tools for research, information analysis, problem-solving, and decision-making in content learning. (NETS 4, 5)	126–129, 145, 146–148, 162–166, 180–184, 191, 192–193, 194–195
9. Investigate and apply expert systems, intelligent agents, and simulations in real-world situations. (NETS 3, 5, 6)	110–114, 115–119, 120–124, 125–129, 130–135, 136–144, 145,146–147, 151–153, 154–161, 162–171, 172–179, 180–184, 185–190, 191, 192–195
10. Collaborate with peers, experts, and others to contribute to content-related knowledge base by using technology to compile, synthesize, produce, and disseminate information, models, and other creative works. (NETS 4, 5, 6)	102, 125–129, 130–135, 147, 148, 186–190, 193, 194–195

21st Century Skills

Core Subjects Language arts, math, science, social studies	103, 105, 110–112, 117, 125–129, 130–132, 136–144, 146–147, 149, 150, 153, 155–157, 162–166, 167, 169–171, 186–190, 192, 193, 194–195
Learning Skills Information and media literacy; communication skills; critical thinking and systems thinking; problem identification, formulation, and solution; self-direction; accountability	102, 103, 104–105, 130–135, 136–144, 146–147, 162–166, 180–184 185–190, 192–193, 194–195
21st Century Tools Communication, information processing and research tools; problem-solving tools, personal development and productivity tools	104–105, 106–109, 115–119, 130–135, 136–139, 145, 151–153, 180–184, 191, 194–195

Foundation Skills

Basic Skills Reading, writing, math, listening, and speaking	103, 105, 110–112, 117, 146–147, 149, 150, 153, 162–166, 167, 169–171, 192–193, 194–195
Thinking Skills Creative thinking, decision making, problem solving, reasoning	103, 105, 120, 130, 140, 145, 146–147, 148, 149, 150, 151–153, 154, 163, 167, 172–173, 181, 191, 192–193, 194–195
Personal Qualities Self-esteem, responsibility, self-management, and integrity/honesty	105, 116–119, 145, 147, 152, 153, 191, 193

Workplace Competencies

Resources Allocate time, money, materials, facilities, and human resources	146–147, 192–193, 194–195
Interpersonal Participate on teams, teach others, serve clients and customers, exercise leadership, negotiate to arrive at decisions, and work with cultural diversity	102, 146–147, 148, 192–193
Information Acquire, evaluate, organize, maintain, interpret, communicate, and use computers to process information	102–105, 173–180
Systems Understand, monitor, correct, improve, and design systems	103, 104–105, 149–150, 151–153, 174–176, 177–179
Technology Select, apply, maintain, and troubleshoot technology	103, 107, 109, 110, 112, 114, 116, 130–135, 140, 146–147, 173, 180, 189, 192–193, 194–195

Introducing Microsoft Publisher

Skills You Will Learn

Workshop Foundations: Layout Software

- Define layout software
- Compare layout and word processing software

Workshop Toolbox: The Publisher Interface

- Identify Publisher's interface and features
- Compare Word's and Publisher's Interface

Project 3-1 Create a Calendar with a Template

- Use templates and wizards
- Rotate a shape
- Add clip art/pictures
- Add/change color

Project 3-2 Design a Business Card

- Modify a template
- Apply layout guides
- Change brightness and contrast
- Add a background image

Project 3-3 Add Tear-Offs to a Flyer

- Insert and format WordArt
- Create and format a bulleted list
- Flip an image
- Insert a Design Gallery object
- Create tear-offs

Project 3-4 Create a Coupon Mailer

- Create a custom-size document
- Crop an image
- Create a coupon
- Insert and resize dingbats

Project 3-5 Design a Bi-fold Brochure

- Lay out a two-page brochure
- Apply ruler guides
- Link text boxes
- Add pull quotes

Project 3-6 Create Web Pages Using a Master Page

- Lay out Web pages
- Create a master page
- Publish a file as a Web page

Project 3-7 Add Hyperlinks to Web Pages

- Insert hyperlinks
- Publish a file as a Web page

Skills Studio

Design a Menu

Project 3-8 Design the Menu Exterior

- Apply layout guides
- Lay out text and graphics
- Create a master page

Project 3-9 Design the Menu Exterior

- Apply styles to text
- Create and apply a second master page

Page 102

Start-Up Skills

Introduce Layout Software Start students thinking about how layout software organizes a document to achieve the desired visual appeal. Cut apart the design elements from magazine spreads and brochures. Without showing students the original layout, ask them to try putting the layout together. You can do the activity by taping the elements on poster paper as the students tell you where each design element should go. This activity emphasizes the power of a layout software program. Before it was developed, people did have to literally cut and paste to lay out documents.

Design Process: Advertisements

Compare Advertisements Students should enjoy talking about the advertisements they are exposed to on a daily basis. Ask students how they feel about advertising. Has an ad ever persuaded them to make a purchase? Bring in various ads aimed at the high school market, and discuss how ads influence attitudes, beliefs, and behavior. Then ask students to brainstorm on tips and advice to help them become savvy about advertising and list these strategies on the board.

Quick Write Activity

Evaluate Advertisements Ask students to identify at least one print advertisement aimed at the high school market that they think is effective. Have them use the Design Process chart on page 102 to help them describe why they think the ad's message works so well. Ask students to be specify how, as the targeted audience, the ad makes them feel.

LEARNING LINK

Chapter 3 introduces students to Publisher layout software. Explain to students that there are many layout software programs on the market. Adobe InDesign is one professional layout program which has gained recent popularity with graphic designers. Quark manufacturers other commonly used layout software.

Have students look at the table of contents in their textbooks, and ask them why Chapter 6 integrates Publisher with Adobe Photoshop and Chapter 8 integrates Publisher with Adobe Illustrator. Students should realize that images alone are not considered desktop publishing. Documents are created when images are imported into layout software and combined with text.

Workshop Foundations Page 103

Desktop Publishing

FOCUS

Focus Activity

Compare Word and Publisher Ask students to read the table on page 103. Explain that Word is an appropriate tool for creating many basic publications, such as flyers, reports, or résumés. However, it does not include all the tools for layout, art, graphics, and formatting that are needed for more complex designs such as brochures or booklets. Call on students to name other examples of publications that would require complex layouts. They might suggest books, magazines, posters, banners, newsletters, greeting cards, CD covers, and catalogs.

> **You Will Learn To:**
> - Define layout software
> - Compare layout and word processing software

Page 103

Before You Read Activity

Adjust Reading Speed Find an easy-to-understand article in *USA Today* and a more difficult subject (like finance) in *The Wall Street Journal*. Ask one student to read aloud the first few paragraphs from the *USA Today* article at a fast, but comprehensible speed. Ask another volunteer to summarize it. It should not be too difficult.

Have another student read *The Wall Street Journal* article at the same speed. It should be more difficult for students to grasp the idea and summarize it. Have the reader reread the article more slowly, stopping after each important point. See if it is now easier for students to summarize it. Explain to students that reading speed should be adjusted to the level of difficulty, whether reading aloud or to oneself.

Page 103

Key Term Activity

On the Board Write the following on the board: *He will revise the layout. He will lay out the design for the brochure. He will use layout software.* Discuss how *layout* and *lay out* are used and whether the term is used as a noun (the first sentence), verb (the second sentence), or adjective (the third sentence). Ask students how this determines if one or two words is needed.

Key Term Definitions

layout software An application that is designed to combine text and graphics together on a page. (page 103)

TEACH

Teach Activity

Preview Publisher To fully emphasize the power of a layout software program, display several eye-appealing publications that have been done by students from prior desktop publishing classes with Publisher software (or other layout software). Posters, banners, and bumper stickers will always catch students' interest.

 School Newspaper Invite the teacher sponsor or one of the editors for the school newspaper to briefly describe the layout process and the software used for the publication.

ASSESS

Page 103

Reading Check

1. A five-page research paper with three graphics can be created best using a word processor. Layout software is designed to handle documents with complex layouts and printing needs.
2. Layout is easier in Publisher than in Word because text and images can be placed exactly where you want them to appear on the page.

CLOSE

Assign Homework For this chapter, have students bring in newsletters or brochures they think are well designed and present them to the class, along with an explanation of what they liked about the design. At this point, they may have a hard time explaining why they like the designs. That is okay, as long as their explanations show a thoughtful response. Have students keep these examples in folders that are labeled "Swap File," for effective design, and "Morgue," for poor design. Students should file these examples as an Advertisement, Brochure, Flyer, Newsletter, Postcard, etc. They will have opportunities to refer to these examples throughout the course.

Workshop Toolbox Pages 104–105

The Publisher Interface

FOCUS

Focus Activity

Introduce the Object Toolbar Show students the Object toolbar and tell them that this toolbar contains many of the tools they will need in Publisher. See if they can identify the icons. The buttons on this toolbar are similar to Word's Formatting toolbar and its Drawing toolbar. Explain that the tools are slightly different in Publisher because they create frames for the objects and text that are placed in a Publisher document.

You Will Learn To:

- Identify Publisher's interface and features
- Compare Word's and Publisher's features

Page 104

Key Term Activity

Review Previous Knowledge Before discussing the key terms, see if students can define any of them based on what they have read previously or from their own real-world experience. They might remember that the drawing canvas and text boxes in Word were frames, and that headers and footers were actually created on a master page. If you mention that "spread" refers to multipage documents like books and magazines, they may be able to guess the definition.

Key Term Definitions

frame A holder for an object, such as text or a picture, in a publication. (page 104)

spread Pages that face each other, like in an open book. (page 104)

master page A special layer that allows design elements to be repeated automatically on any number of pages. This layer is usually behind all other layers. (page 104)

TEACH

Teach Activity

Moving the Ruler Have students use Help in Publisher to find out two things about the ruler: 1) How to move the rulers, and 2) How to reset the 0 inch (origin) point on the ruler. *(Answers: 1) Hold the Shift key, then click and drag the ruler. Dragging the point where the horizontal and vertical rulers intersect moves both rulers at once. 2) Hold the Shift key and right-click the ruler to place the 0 inch setting at that point.)* Explain that these features are useful for measuring the space between objects. Measuring the objects themselves is done by selecting the object and looking at measurements on the Status bar at the bottom of the screen.

⚠️ **Display Different Views** Show students that there are different view buttons in the bottom left corner of the screen and demonstrate each view. Explain that people sometimes accidentally click these buttons, and causing the screen layout to suddenly change.

● ## Answers to Workshop Toolbox Activities

Page 105

Eye on Ethics

Fair use means you can use material without permission under certain conditions. If you use copyrighted work for limited educational purposes, as in a classroom, the material will often fall under the category of fair use. It can be used without permission, though the source should still be cited.

ASSESS

Reading Check

1. The scratch area is used for holding objects that you may need to later place back into a document.
2. To move from page to page in a Publisher document, you must use the Page Navigation Control at the bottom of the screen, unlike Word, where you can use scrollbars.

CLOSE

Class Discussion Review with the class the similarities and differences between Microsoft Publisher and Microsoft Word. Students should know that both applications are manufactured by the same company and have similar interfaces, but they serve vastly different purposes.

- Word is an excellent word processor, but it is primarily designed to enter and edit text. Although it can do much more than these simple things, when documents become too complex and contain many graphics, it becomes somewhat unstable.

- Publisher is designed to incorporate text and graphics together on a page. Many layers of graphics and long bodies of text are no trouble for Publisher. Its whole purpose is to create complex documents such as brochures, newsletters, banners, posters, and greeting cards. All of these designs would be challenging— or even impossible— in Word.

- Publisher is also meant for publishing professionally printed documents. Publisher can do color separations and print reports that tell professional printers the exact settings that are needed. These tools and utilities are not available in Word.

Chapter 3 Projects

Pages 106–144

FOCUS

Focus Activity

Preview Publisher Skills Have students look at the photograph in the Unit opener (page 101). Ask someone to describe what is happening in the photograph. Students should see that someone is looking at a display of flyers—some with tear-offs— and probably making a call regarding the information in a flyer. What does this tell them about the skills they will learn in this unit? Some responses might be that they will learn how to create flyers with graphics, tear-offs, and other design elements. They will learn how to create designs that attract people's attention and provide the information a reader needs. Also, students will be able to immediately use their skills for real-world, everyday needs, not just for a professional job in the future.

Projects

Project 3-1
Create a Calendar with a Template

Project 3-2
Design a Business Card

Project 3-3
Add Tear-offs to a Flyer

Project 3-4
Create a Coupon Mailer

Project 3-5
Design a Bi-fold Brochure

Project 3-6 Create
Web Pages Using a Master Page

Project 3-7
Create a Business Flyer

Skills Studio

Project 3-8
Design the Menu Exterior

Project 3-9
Design the Menu Exterior

 Go Online PREVIEW

Before You Begin Students can use the chapter **PowerPoint** presentations and **rubrics** at the Online Learning Center to determine what is expected *before* they complete a project. Students can view the PowerPoint slides on their own computers, or you can project them to preview chapter concepts and show examples of the finished projects. You might also display project solutions so students can easily refer to them while they work. (Presentations and rubrics are also provided on the Teacher Resource DVD for your convenience).

glencoe.com

Key Term Activity

Draw Conclusions Write key terms on the board before you begin each project. See if students can infer the meaning of the terms by looking at the illustrations in the Spotlight on Skills or the steps, or from previous knowledge. Have volunteers write their definition on the board. When you have completed the project, see if the class thinks the original definition was accurate, or if it should be modified. Add any changes to the definition. If the original definition is correct, give the volunteer extra credit or points that can add up to a small award.

Key Term Definitions

template A pre-formatted, fill-in-the-blank document (page 106)

layout guides Also called layout grids, layout guides are evenly spaced lines that form the basic framework under a design, allowing objects to be precisely aligned and sized. (page 110)

gutter The space between columns of text or between the binding and the first column in a page spread. (page 110)

snap A feature that pulls objects to align with the nearest guide, ruler position, or object. (page 110)

tear-off A tab that can easily be torn off a flyer or advertisement and contains contact information such as an address or phone number. (page 115)

synchronization A tool that makes it possible to create or edit one object and have all related objects automatically display the same information. (page 115)

dingbat A variety of graphic icons and symbols included in the Wingdings and Webdings fonts. (page 120)

link This command connects text boxes so that information flows automatically from the one text box to the next, no matter where the boxes are located. (page 125)

HTML (Hypertext Markup Language) A common computer language used to create Web pages. (page 130)

master page A special layer that allows design elements in a document to be repeated automatically on any number of pages. This layer is usually behind all other layers. (page 130)

hyperlink A clickable area in a document, often represented as colored text or a graphic, that takes you to information within the same document or to another location. (page 133)

hot spot A hyperlink location on a Web page or electronic document that takes you to another location in the publication. (page 133)

duplex printing A feature that allows a printer to print on both sides of the paper before going on to the next copy. (page 140)

TEACH

Teach Activity

Introduce Publisher's Publications Open the New Publications task pane, and review some of the options with students:

- The *Blank Publications* menu shows different types of blank documents with no other design features. There are different folds and sizes, though later students will learn to create their own custom documents.

- *Publications for Print* has thumbnail pictures showing the various templates that are available. Briefly review template categories and sub-categories with students. Show that in some categories, such as brochures, flyers, and business cards, there is a sub-category called *Special Paper*. To use designs in this section, you would need to purchase special paper that already has the design pre-printed upon it. Students should also be aware that many of the designs—such as business cards, advertisements, and banners—are different sizes and are not the standard 8½ × 11 inches.

- *Publication Designs* are useful for companies that want all documents looking consistent. The chosen design can be applied to any type of publication, sending a single, consistent, professional message to clients.

Teaching Tips ✍ and Troubleshooting Tips ⚠ for Projects

Page 106–109

Rubric

Student Data File

Project 3-1 ▸ **Create a Calendar with a Template** Students modify a calendar template by changing the color theme and adding clip art and text boxes. They also are introduced to the Design Checker tool. **(Data File 3-1, Solution File 3-1, Rubric 3-1)**

✍ **Modify Dates** Although this project provides a specific month and year and holidays for the calendar, you can have more advanced students create their own calendars. Allow them to choose the current month and year, and they can add holidays, birthdays, important school or class events, and so on. They should also add an image that effectively illustrates a theme associated with the month.

✍ **Design Gallery Calendars** Show students that calendars are not only in the Publications for Print task pane, but they are also available in the Design Gallery Objects, if they need a calendar smaller that a standard sheet of paper. Ask students when they might use a calendar in another publication. Students might suggest a date book, a newsletter, or a Web page for a business that takes reservations.

⚠ **Text in Templates** Point out the Instant Message on page 109 to students. Since classroom computers are shared by a number of people, students may find that the text they see on the screen is different from the example in the book. Explain that Publisher has a Personal Information feature that automatically saves information that is entered into a template. The book shows the default text for the template.

Page 110–114

Rubric Student Data File

Project 3-2 → **Design a Business Card** Students use layout guides to modify a business card template. Students should be aware of the special layout features of business cards, including the size. (**Data Files 3-2a and 3-2b, Solution File 3-2, Rubric 3-2**)

Page 114

Answer to Sidebar AutoFit automatically resizes text in a text box so that it has the best fit—not too big or too small for the box.

Display Rulers Make sure rulers are displayed so students can see that the actual printed size of the card is 3.5 × 2 inches, even if the workspace fills the entire screen. See if students can figure out by themselves how to display the rulers (View>Rulers). Ask students why business cards are that standard size. Answers might include that they are easy to carry, and they fit well in wallets, day planners, and rolodexes.

Design Options for Business Cards Have students bring in business cards or show students business cards that you have acquired. Ask students what they should consider when designing a business card. (Possible answers: They need to be readable, eye catching, and clearly provide contact information. They may also describe the business's services or key features.) Business cards can be landscape or portrait. Cards that need to list features, services, or directions can use duplex printing. Business cards, in general, should not look too busy. They should have one or two alignments and look simple and clean.

Read Troubleshoot Tips Make sure students read and understand the Sidebar on page 114. There are quite a few boxes and graphics in the card they are creating, and text might move in unexpected ways. The sidebar provides strategies they can use to fix these problems.

AutoFit Text Show students the **Format>AutoFit Text** tool. They should use *Best Fit or Shrink Text on Overflow* to ensure that information in text boxes does not get cut off. The problem with this feature, however, is that the text may look different from other text in the design, causing the design to look inconsistent. If students find this feature getting in the way, they can turn it off with Format>AutoFit Text>None.

Pages 115–119

Rubric Student Data File

Project 3-3 → **Add Tear-Offs to a Flyer** Students are introduced to the **Design Gallery Object** tool. They use the Phone Tear-Off option in a flyer advertising babysitting services. (**Data File 3-3, Solution File 3-3, Rubric 3-3**)

Publish with Tear-Offs Ask students when they would use a tear-off in a document. They should realize that this tool is only necessary when the document is being publicly displayed. This feature would not be used if the design were going to be mailed to someone, posted on a Web site, or posted in a place (like a display case) where the audience could not remove a tear-off.

Edit Design Gallery Objects Open a new, blank document, and click Design Gallery Object on the Objects toolbar. Choose a calendar to insert into the document. Near the calendar, students should see an icon that allows them to edit the calendar like a template. Click the icon to show the task bar that opens and its options. Even when the editing icon does not show, as in the tear-offs, students can still make changes to it, such as changing text, fonts, colors, or size.

Copying Tear-Offs Students may think they need to use copy and paste to add another set of tear-offs because the tear-offs do not fit all the way across the page. Show students that they can click on the tear-offs, then drag a pull handle to create more or fewer tear-offs.

Page 120–124

Rubric

Student Data File

Project 3-4 **Create a Coupon Mailer** Students use layout guides and dingbat fonts to create a mailer with a coupon. The mailer is a custom size that will allow them to print more than one copy per sheet, if you would like them to try that option. **(Data File 3-4, Solution File 3-4, Rubric 3-4)**

Page 120

Answer to Sidebar Dingbat fonts are useful in several ways: a) they can be used as clip art; b) they can be used as bullets that stand out from the usual dots; c) they can be used as symbols (such as the scissors) that can visually convey directions.

Class Discussion Ask students why companies want to invest the time and money to design, mail, and pay for coupons. Answer: Companies use coupons to attract customers. They hope that once a customer discovers the quality product offered by the company, the company will increase its sales. Additionally, companies are able to use coupons to track the effectiveness of particular ad campaigns. If coupons mailed to potential customers generate more sales than coupons in newspapers or ads on the radio, then this is the best way to reach that company's audience. More advertisement dollars should be spent in that method of advertising than other, less effective ways.

Create Coupons Show students that creating coupons is so common in Publisher that it actually has a faster way of doing this than using the scissors dingbat. You can create a rectangle, click the Line/Border Style button on the Formatting toolbar, and choose *More Lines*. In the Colors and Lines tab, click the Border Art button. Scroll down until you find the style labeled *Coupon Cutouts Dots* (or *Dashes*).

Review Symbols Most fonts have an extended set of characters that are used so rarely they are not included on standard keyboards. In Microsoft Word and Publisher, you can access this extended set of characters by using Insert>Symbol. Here you will find characters for several languages, some common symbols, and even some pictures. Change the font from "normal text" to a symbol font and view even more pictures. Symbol graphics, or dingbats, work like a combination of clip art and a font. When inserted into a design, they cannot be moved and resized like a graphic. Instead, they must be moved and resized like any other character.

Draw Thumbnail Sketches Have students create a thumbnail sketch of the design on page 120, then have them create at least two variations on the design. Sketches should be simple, showing the placement of graphics and text, with notes to show colors or fonts. Only major words need to be written out. The rest can be indicated by squiggly lines to show their placement. Reinforcing this skill will help to prepare students for designs they create on their own.

Position the Text It may be necessary to nudge the text box or the picture slightly so that the letters fall to one side or the other of the graphic. Students will need to select the object they want to move, then hold the ALT key and use the arrow keys on the keyboard to nudge the object.

Position the Dingbat Students may have problems placing the globe dingbat in the Sports World logo. The dingbat may have to be resized to fit within the word. Students can select the dingbat and click CTRL+Shift+< to reduce its size. They may also key a font size (even using decimal places like 54.5) in the Font Size window.

Page 125–129

Rubric

Student Data File

Project 3-5 ➤ **Design a Bi-fold Brochure** Students will design a bi-fold brochure, seeing how Publisher's tools make it easier than it was in Word to design multiple page documents. They will continue to use layout guides and also link text boxes. **(Data Files 3-5a to 3-5e, Solution File 3-5, Rubric 3-5)**

Evaluate Layout Guides Have students consider how they used layout guides to help format the page. What are advantages to using layout guides? Students might answer that layout guides help to place objects accurately and consistently on the page, between different pages, and between different designs.

Share Layouts Explain that layout guides make it easier for designers to work on a design together. Project two versions of a simple design. The first shows only measurements explaining where objects should be placed. For example, you might show two rectangles that are 3.25 inches wide by 1.75 inches high. Both are placed 2.15 inches from the left of the page. One is placed 1.25 inches below the top of the page and the other is 1.65 inches above the bottom of the page. The second version shows the same design with layout described by using layout guide settings.

Have half your students create the design in Publisher without guide lines and the other half create it using the guides. See how quickly and accurately they create the design. Ask students which they think is a better way to describe where things go on the page. Some students may disagree, but most students will see that the grid is a far easier method of describing and recreating a page layout. You can also remind students that other professionals such as carpenters and tailors use rulers and other measurement tools to do their work for the same reason designers use layout guides.

Introduce Gutters In this lesson, not only will layout guides be set to create a standard layout, but also to standardize the spacing between columns of text. Show students the gutter lines in Figure 3.29 on page 126. Go to **Arrange>Layout Guides>Grid Guides tab,** and demonstrate the Spacing option. Also show students the Center Guides option, which places red lines exactly in the center of each gutter.

Practice Kerning In Steps 7 and 13, students are asked to change the spacing between characters. Students may ask you whether there is any standard amount to kern letter pairs. Let students know that there is no particular standard except to keep the spaces between the letters looking consistent. Kerning is something that is normally done for large titles, but not for body text.

Pages 130–132

Rubric

Student Data File

Project 3-6 ➤ **Create Web Pages Using a Master Page** Students create a master page and home page for a Web site. They will add hyperlinks to the Web pages in Project 3-7. **(Data Files 3-6a and 3-6b, Solution File 3-6, Rubric 3-6)**

Page 130

Answer to Sidebar On free Web sites, you will frequently see advertisements, such as banner ads, sidebars, and pop-up ads. If a Web site cannot get income from subscribers, it needs to earn money some other way. By placing advertisements, Web sites can offer many services free.

Evaluate Web Pages Have students look at page 130 of their textbooks. In the illustration on the page, both Web pages are from the Web site. While the content is different, you can tell they are from the same source. Have students answer the following questions in their journals: What elements about the structure of the Web pages indicates they are from the same source? What are some advantages to using the same underlying structure? Lead students to understand that not just the text and graphics are common, but the arrangement of the pages, and even the white space, is common as well. These pages were most likely created using tables, layout guides, and master pages.

Set Layout Grids Ask students to preview Projects 3-6 and 3-7. The Web pages they are designing have far more layout guides than previous designs. Why would a designer choose to use this many gridlines? Answer: the number of gridlines depends upon the needs of the design. Here, the gridlines help to make the buttons a certain size, and to keep the placement of graphics, text, and titles consistent from page to page.

Apply a Master Page A master page allows elements to be repeated on several pages. Using them makes it easier to change an element over multiple pages. You only have to make the edit on one page, and the change is applied throughout. Also, master pages can reduce the size of a file because many of the graphics are in one place.

Monitor the Task Pane Students may get confused about whether they are working in the master page or in the publication. Make sure that students pay attention to what they are doing. They can easily see which page they are in by looking at the task pane to see if the Edit Master Page or Apply Master Page panes are displayed. If they are in Edit Master Page, then they are working on the master page.

Pages 133–135

Rubric

Student Data File

Project 3-7 → **Add Hyperlinks to Web Pages** Students continue the Web pages they began in Project 3-6. They add new pages and add hyperlinks to allow users to easily move between pages. Tell students that once they can create hyperlinks in Microsoft Publisher, they can also use the same skills to create hyperlinks in Word and PowerPoint. **(Data Files 3-7a to 3-7c, Solution File 3-7, Rubric 3-7)**

Diagram a Web Site Show students different examples of hyperlinks on Web sites. Explain to students that Web sites can often have very complex structures, where clicking on enough hot spots can make it difficult to get back to the original where a user first entered the site. Web designers frequently use flowcharts to help diagram the paths that users can take and to ensure the completeness and accuracy of their designs. The Web site that students are creating has a very simple structure. Have students create a simple flowchart that diagrams how this Web site works. Use Graphic Organizer 3 as a model.

Test Hyperlinks Demonstrate how to create a hot spot or a hyperlink for students so they see the process. Point out to students that on each of the pages, the selected page button is slightly different to help the visitor navigate the site. Have students allow time to test their hyperlinks using your Web browser, if possible. It is easy to forget to link something or link something to the wrong page.

Skills Studio

Pages 136–144

Design a Menu

Students will use skills that they learned in both this chapter and the Word unit to complete this menu. Have students look at the illustration on page 136. What types of publications have similar layouts? Students might recognize that the layout is similar to ones used for bi-fold brochures, cards, and newsletters. Besides content, what elements make a menu design different from a newsletter or a brochure? Answers may vary, but students should be considering the size and placement of various elements on the page.

Pages 137–139

Rubric

Student Data File

Project 3-8 **Design the Menu Exterior** Students start to create a menu. In this project they will complete the exterior using a master page and booklet layout. They will complete the interior in Project 3-9. **(Data Files 3-8a and 3-8b, Solution File 3-8, Rubric 3-8)**

Lay Out as a Booklet Have students review the layout they used for the brochure they created in Project 3-5. They should notice that the brochure has two pages, and the first page actually shows the front and back panels of the brochure. After they have completed Step 2 of the project, ask them what the difference is between a booklet and the brochure layout. Guide them to see that the booklet layout has four, rather than two, pages. The first page is the front panel, pages 2–3 are laid out as a spread, and the fourth page is the back panel.

Compare Publications Ask students to list the things that make designs look like the kinds of designs they are. What is it that makes a brochure, newsletter, or menu look like the type of design that it actually is? Students are likely to decide that the size of the fonts, the size and placement of graphic elements, the placement of titles, headers, and body text all contribute to the design's function. Use one of the graphic organizers in Part III, or have students create their own chart, to compare and contrast two types of multi-page publications.

Pages 140–144

Rubric

Student Data File

Project 3-9 **Design the Menu Interior** Students complete the menu that they started in Project 3-8. They will apply a different master page to the interior pages and apply a style sheet. **(Data Files 3-9a to 3-9f, Solution File 3-9, Rubric 3-9)**

Page 140

Answer to Sidebar Often when the spacebar is used to align text, the text does not align correctly. It can also change the special relationship between words, and problems can result. It is actually easier and more effective to use the Tab key to align objects horizontally on the page.

Page 144

Answer to Sidebar The keyboard shortcut for an en-dash is CTRL+minus on the numeric keypad.

Apply Multiple Master Pages Students will see in this lesson that it is possible to set up different master pages to use in designs. When creating a book, for instance, a master can be for chapter titles, a different master for the interior, and a different master for indexes and glossaries. Find examples that you can show students, or have them bring in examples as a homework assignment.

Review Style Sheet Activity See if students can remember how they created and applied new styles in Project 2-6 (and review the tips for that project in this teacher's manual). To reinforce how to use style sheets, go over the steps on page 140.

Print a Booklet The brochure that students created in Project 3-5 printed much the same way as the four-page booklet they are printing in this project. To demonstrate Publisher's power, however, create a booklet with 6–8 pages. Place a large page number on each page and print it. Show students how Publisher automatically prints the pages so that they will be placed correctly in booklet layout.

ASSESS

Encourage students to use the rubrics and the Review and Revise checklists to be sure that they have completed the key steps for the projects in this chapter. Encourage students to proofread and assist each other. Students learn best when they are teaching each other. Consider giving bonus points for well-designed projects for both the student and the student who evaluated his/her work.

It is recommended that for these first four chapters you evaluate student printouts carefully looking for a standard set of problems. You might purchase a do-it-yourself stamp kit and create a stamp with the following grading criteria:

Font Style	Font Size
Balance	Leading
Alignment	Proximity
Repetition	Spelling and Grammar

Take off 5 points for each type of mistake and 10 points for skipping skill sets in the lessons. For a grade, have students chart the kinds of mistakes they have been making. Hopefully, they will begin to see a pattern of mistakes and you will find fewer problems, making grading faster in the future.

CLOSE

Preview Chapter 4 Now that students are comfortable with Publisher's tools and the desktop publishing concepts they have learned to this point, they are ready to tackle design. In the next chapter, they will look at unsuccessful designs, evaluate the problems, and do "design makeovers" on the publications. Give students a quick peak at some of the documents they will revise, and ask them to find some examples of bad design to share when they start Chapter 4.

IN THE WORKPLACE

GRAPHIC DESIGNERS

Career Activity

All designers need to have a portfolio to show prospective employers the work that best showcases their extensive ability and imagination. Freelance graphic designers must find their own clients and will find a varied portfolio especially useful.

Notes

Chapter 3 Assessment Answers

Use the following Reading Check and Critical Thinking answers as a guide to help evaluate student understanding of the core concepts. Requiring that your students write in complete sentences will help you grade faster and promote good writing skills. You can have students write answers in their desktop publishing journals, or students can answer these questions at the computer by accessing the Reading Check on the Online Learning Center at **glencoe.com**.

Page 146

Reading Check

1. Layout software is an application designed for professionals to combine text and graphics together on the page. It is used when a design must be professionally printed, when a design is long and graphic intensive, or when it requires special folds or complex layouts.

2. Unlike Word, Publisher's interface has the Objects toolbar, a scratch area, Page Navigation Controls, an Object Size and Object Position tools, new buttons like Design Gallery Objects, catalog of templates, layout grids and ruler guides, and movable rulers.

3. In Publisher, rulers can be moved and zero mark can be repositioned so as to measure elements on the page. Rulers can be used to place and manage tab stops and margins. You can also use the ruler to see if elements are aligned, though this is an imperfect method and it would be much better to use ruler guides, also found in the ruler itself.

4. Master pages should be used to consistently place graphics and other design elements and multiple pages. It makes it easy to edit design elements that are applied throughout the publication.

5. Hyperlinks contain instructions for the computer to access a particular location on a page, a document, or a file. They are commonly used to add interactivity to a Web page.

Critical Thinking

6. Creating brochures in Publisher is easier because Publisher contains templates that can help you create designs and difficult layouts, master pages to add consistent design elements, and layout grids to create a consistent framework.

7. Layout guides help to set a consistent framework beneath a design. They can also set up special relationships between elements, which gives an organized structure to documents, even when different page layouts are used throughout.

8. Answers will vary. Ensure that students mention two real Design Gallery Objects and accurately give an example of each item's usefulness.

9. The newsletter would link text boxes on both pages so that the article could easily flow from the first to third page.

10. Templates are a fast way to create a publication, but they are not original and may duplicate designs used by other businesses. Modifying the template allows original designs with little time and a small budget.

Evaluate Assessment activities allow students to demonstrate their understanding of concepts and skills learned throughout this project. Because of time constraints, students may not be able to complete every activity suggested. Match assignments to student ability levels using the leveled projects (★ Easy, ★★ Medium, and ★★★ Challenging). Rubrics are available to evaluate projects on the Teacher Resources DVD and the Online Learning Center at **glencoe.com**.

Page 146

Rubric

1. Independent Practice ★

Create a Friendship Coupon Evaluate student projects based on whether students complete the entire design process: brainstorm ideas, create thumbnail sketches, and execute a sound design. Designs should be required to have elements similar to Project 3-3 (if a flyer with tear-offs) or Project 3-4 (if a coupon). Evaluate designs based on whether the required design elements are included as described on page 146. Flyers must include 2 to 3 fonts and follow the font rules as discussed in Chapter 1. Grammar and spelling should be accurate. **(Rubric IP 3-1)**

Page 147

Rubric

2. Independent Practice ★★

Create a Plant Brochure Give students time to research content and images for their brochures. If possible, bring in information from your local nursery for students to use.

Evaluate student projects based on whether they complete the entire design process: brainstorm ideas, perform accurate research, create thumbnail sketches, and execute a sound design. Designs should have original, complete, and accurate text; properly cited sources; follow font rules; contain relevant illustrations, and follow the requirements described on page 147. **(Rubric IP 3-2)**

Page 147

Rubric

3. Independent Practice ★★★

Create Community Service Web Pages Help students form teams of two or more people. To ensure that all group members contribute to the design, have students create a task list and a timecard. If possible, bring in an assortment of information from local community groups, or have students brainstorm ideas as a class before starting. Make sure all the required information described on page 147 has been obtained before students begin their Web pages.

Evaluate student projects based on whether they have completed the entire design process, they have followed proper design practices, and that there are at least five Web pages, applying a master page and hyperlinks. Require that students create several thumbnail sketches, each with different designs. Have them create one, final sketch that incorporates all their best ideas into one, really good, design. **(Rubric IP 3-3)**

Reteaching Activities

Use Microsoft Help Have students open Microsoft Publisher and use Help to search for tutorials or training. Help them find *Get Started Designing Professional Publications*. Have them go through the training at their own pace whenever they have time.

Complete Worksheets Have students complete **Worksheets 3A and 3B**, which can be found in Part 3 or this TRM, on the Teacher Resource DVD, and at the Online Learning Center at **glencoe.com**.

Enrichment Activities

Create Professional Work Samples Encourage students to create a list of clients that they could approach for real world work. Require that the students create a flyer, newsletter, or brochure for one or more of the clients on their list.

Create Gift Calendars Students can create their own calendars as gifts. They should use pictures, holidays, and relevant family dates for the year. Have students create a cover page for the calendar, printed on card stock and bound to finish. Encourage students to give these calendars away as holiday gifts. See Project 3-1 for help on these skills.

Enrichment If students need an additional challenge, have them complete the activities in the Online Learning Center at **glencoe.com**.

Focus on Design Makeovers

Skills You Will Learn

Workshop Foundations: The Design Process

- Identify the steps of the design process
- Apply the design process
- Determine client needs in relation to design

Workshop Toolbox: PARC Design Principles

- Identify PARC design principles

Project 4-1 Evaluate Design in a Flyer

- Create repetition
- Adjust white space

Project 4-2 Add Contrast and Focal Points

- Add contrasting color
- Insert an Attention Getter

Project 4-3 Apply the Golden Ratio

- Apply the Golden Ratio
- Group related content

Project 4-4 Apply Styles in a Flyer

- Apply PARC to a list
- Create new styles
- Apply style sheets

Project 4-5 Revise a Tri-fold Brochure

- Import a style sheet
- Apply CMYK custom colors
- Align objects

Project 4-6 Apply PARC to the Brochure Interior

- Link text boxes
- Re-align orphan text

Project 4-7 Apply PARC to a Web Page

- Resize a Web page
- Resize a Design Gallery object

Skills Studio

Create a Children's Newsletter

Project 4-8 Design for a Young Audience

- Lay out a booklet
- Position and resize graphics
- Apply style sheets
- Link text boxes

Project 4-9 Complete Your Newsletter

- Insert a calendar template

Start-Up Skills

Introducing Design Principles In Chapters 1–3, students had a chance to create designs with only a basic introduction to design principles. This allowed them to learn new skills and experiment without worrying too much about rules and processes. Now that they know how to use some desktop publishing tools, they are ready to develop a more systematic approach to understanding design. Remind your students, however, that the design principles that they learn about in this chapter are guidelines only. They must be considered along with the client's needs, the limitations of time, budget, software, and hardware; and the creativity of the designer.

Design Process: Newsletters

Newsletters and Design If your school publishes a newsletter or newspaper, bring some examples to class. Try to bring in other types of newsletters from a variety of sources. It would be helpful if you can find business newsletters, personal newsletters (like the kind that families send at holidays or the new year), and newsletters from other schools. If you cannot find a sufficient selection of newsletters, bring in different examples of newspapers or magazines.

As a class, compare the different elements that go into the design of the examples. Ask what the purpose is for the publication, and for what audience it has been created. How does the purpose and audience affect content and layout? For example, what kind of images and text might be used on the front page of a school newsletter compared to a newsletter from a bank or a dentist? Which newsletters probably have the biggest budgets? How can you tell?

Quick Write Activity

Evaluate Newsletters Have each student choose one of the newsletters you brought in, and then have them use the Design Process chart on page 148 to evaluate the example. If you prefer, you can also have students use the chart to compare the newsletters in the textbook on pages 185–190 and 277–285. They should see that the purpose of those two newsletters is similar, but the audience is different, making the two designs very different.

> ## LEARNING LINK
>
> In this textbook, students will have an opportunity to create a number of newsletters, requiring a number of skills. They will also create other publications, including Web pages, brochures, and pamphlets. Whenever possible, use the design process charts to discuss and compare the different publications. Use the graphic organizers in Part 3 of this manual to help students clearly and succinctly evaluate documents and note their observations.

Workshop Foundations

The Design Process

FOCUS

Focus Activity

Design for an Audience Ask students what kinds of things are designed besides publications. They might come up with answers such as clothes, textbooks, cell phones, computer interfaces, buildings, cars, and so on.

Choose one designed product and have students determine how it might be redesigned for at least three different clients or audiences. Determine if different audiences might also affect the product's purpose and development. For example, if the product were jeans, students might discuss what they look for when they buy jeans compared to their parents, who likely would consider features such as cost and materials.

You Will Learn To:
- Identify the steps of the design process
- Apply the design process
- Determine client needs in relation to design

Page 149

Before You Read Activity

Use Bookmarks Students may not be familiar with or remember vocabulary they encounter when reading. They may also be introduced to concepts that they do not understand at first.

Let students know that when that happens, they should not be afraid to ask questions. However, sometimes it is not convenient to answer a question right at that moment. If so, students can mark their books with a sticky note or a scrap of paper. Have sticky pads or scrap paper available. Also make it very clear that students cannot make marks in their book with pen, pencil, or highlighter, nor should they dog-ear a corner.

Page 149

Key Term Activity

Relate Concepts Have students add the definitions to their desktop publishing vocabulary dictionaries. For variety, have students write a sentence that contains both terms. The sentence should clearly show how the terms are related. For example: *Working with a client is important throughout the design process.*

Key Term Definitions

design process A step-by-step system used to create effective designs and documents. (page 149)

client The person or group of people who commission a publication. (page 149)

TEACH

Teach Activity

Evaluate Processes An entertaining way to reinforce the importance of processes is to have students create a peanut butter sandwich. Bring in some slices of bread, a jar of peanut butter, a plastic knife, and a paper plate. Have students write the steps to make a sandwich. Then read a few responses while one student tries to follow the steps to make the sandwich. Chances are students will neglect to include important steps such as "Twist the lid counter-clockwise to open the jar," "Put the knife in the jar and remove a scoop of peanut butter," "Repeat until the bread is covered," and so on.

Use the exercise to explain that having a clear procedure 1) helps us know what to do next, 2) helps others know what we are doing, and 3) makes it easy for us to repeat what we have done. Although these steps are to be used as guidelines, not rules, they can help use time efficiently and encourage collaboration with clients.

Answers to Workshop Foundations Activities

Page 150

Sidebar

Responses to this assignment will vary. Require that students are specific and explain their reason for finding the advertisement effective. Do not accept, "Because it got my attention." Require that students explain what exactly got their attention.

ASSESS

Page 150

✓ Reading Check

1. The design process is more of a spiral than a list because there is often the need to revise work throughout the design process. So you may be repeating a task you had done previously, but at a higher level in the process.

2. By committing to an exact budget, the expectations of the publication are clear for everyone involved. The designer knows how much time to put into a publication and which kinds of effects can and cannot be included in the design.

CLOSE

Review the Design Process Have students create a visual interpretation of the design process. It can be a flowchart, a spiral, or any creative way to portray the steps, as well as the continuous review and revisions that are needed to fine-tune their work. Students should include as many details as they can from this Foundations text.

Workshop Toolbox Pages 151–153

PARC Design Principles

FOCUS

Focus Activity

Overview Have students preview the designs in this chapter. How can they tell when a design is good or bad? Tell students that in this chapter, they will learn how to use the concepts of proximity, alignment, repetition, and contrast (the PARC principles) to evaluate a design.

You Will Learn To:
- Identify PARC design principles

Page 151

Key Term Activity

Visual Interpretations Display a solution file from the textbook or bring in a good example that demonstrates the PARC principles. Then have students use the example to explain each of the key terms.

Key Term Definitions

proximity How close objects are on a page in order to create visual groups. (page 151)

white space Empty space that sets off the text or graphics on a page. (page 151)

alignment The horizontal and vertical placement of objects. (page 152)

repetition The consistent use of important design elements are echoed, or repeated, in some way throughout the design. (page 152)

contrast Design elements that look different from surrounding features to create visual interest or specific focal points. (page 153)

focal point An area to which your eye is drawn. (page 153)

TEACH

Teach Activity

Applying PARC Principles Remind students that the PARC principles should be thought of as a checklist when reviewing their designs. Using these principles will ensure that a design looks competent, attractive, and easy to read. However, these principles are not absolute law. While they should be included in every design, in some rare designs, these principles may be violated if the message is better served. Students must also realize, to be truly outstanding, a design needs imagination. Creativity is what makes one design stand out from the rest.

● Answers to Workshop Toolbox Activities

Page 152

Eye on Ethics

Free pictures may have certain limitations that will only be known if the terms and conditions are read. Most free pictures are often free for non-commercial use, such as a picture that is used in a class project or distributed among friends. However, when a picture is published for wide distribution, especially for commercial interests, one must have permission—usually at a price.

Page 153

Eye on Ethics

Herman Melville, the writer most famous for *Moby Dick*, died in 1891. Since an author's works are copyright protected for 70 years after death, his works went into the public domain in 1961. However, if someone translated his work into Spanish in 2001, the translation would still be copyrighted.

ASSESS

 Reading Check

1. A user interface is the onscreen elements that allow the user to communicate with the computer.

2. The menu bar is similar to a toolbar because they both provide access to commands. They are different because the toolbars contain only the most commonly used commands, while the menu bar contains most all commands. Also, the toolbars use a graphical interface.

CLOSE

Homework Activity Have students locate and bring to class full-page, full-color designs from a national magazine each week. On their example, have them:

• Circle examples of proximity.
• Draw arrows along lines edges of aligned objects.
• Highlight examples of the use of repetition.
• Draw stars next to areas of high contrast.

Chapter 4 Projects

Pages 154–190

Pages 154–190

FOCUS

Focus Activity

Real World Design Have students look around the room to see if they can find examples that illustrate PARC principles. They can look at everything from simple signs, to posters, to the layout of their textbooks (both covers and interior pages), and even the design of their cell phones or MP3 players.

Go Online PREVIEW

> **Before You Begin** Students can use the chapter **PowerPoint** presentations and **rubrics** at the Online Learning Center to determine what is expected *before* they complete a project. Students can view the PowerPoint slides on their own computers, or you can project them to preview chapter concepts and show examples of the finished projects. You might also display project solutions so students can easily refer to them while they work. (Presentations and rubrics are also provided on the Teacher Resource DVD for your convenience).
>
> **glencoe.com**

Projects

Project 4-1
Evaluate Design in a Flyer

Project 4-2
Add Contrast and Focal Points

Project 4-3
Apply the Golden Ratio

Project 4-4
Apply Styles in a Flyer

Project 4-5
Revise a Tri-fold Brochure

Project 4-6
Apply PARC to the Brochure Interior

Project 4-7
Apply PARC to a Web Page

Skills Studio

Project 4-8
Design for a Young Audience

Project 4-9
Complete Your Newsletter

Key Term Activity

Determine Previous Knowledge Before going over the key term definitions, see if students recognize any of the words and can define them. Some of the terms may be familiar from earlier chapters, and some they might know from other classes or previous experience.

For concepts they may not know, like *dithering* and *spot color*, you can have them review the definitions in the chapter, then see if they can add to the definition by reading about color theory in Appendix A.

Key Term Definitions

negative space Another term for white space, or the space without text or graphics. (page 155)

spot color A color not created by combining cyan, magenta, yellow, and black. These colors are premixed and can be special ordered when printing at a professional print shop. (page 158)

ratio The relationship between objects based on size or quantity. (page 162)

style sheet Formatting rules that allow you to easily format specific text consistently.(page 167)

export To send out a product or file to be used in another location. (page 172)

import To bring in a file or product. (page 172)

link To connect. (page 177)

widow The last word of a paragraph carried forward to the top of the next page or column. (page 177)

orphan A first line of a paragraph (or other text group) that is left at the bottom of a page or column. (page 177)

dithering When a visiting computer substitutes colors on Web pages that use colors that are not included in the standard 216 colors. (page180)

TEACH

Teach Activity

Design Makeovers Your students have probably seen shows on TV that involve "design makeovers" of some type. In this chapter, they will have a chance to do their own makeovers of publications with definite flaws. Each project will begin with a "Before" example and a chart that evaluates the problems.

Before discussing the chart, have students look at the original design and see if they can use the PARC principles to determine what the problems are. Ask them for suggestions as to how to improve it. After you have discussed the "Before" version, show them the "After" solution (at the end of the project). Does it address the problems? How would they have revised the design? Why or why not?

This chapter gives you the opportunity to challenge more advanced students. They can be given the option of following the steps to create the solution in the textbook, or they can be allowed to create a "design makeover" of their own.

Teaching Tips ✍ and Troubleshooting Tips ⚠ for Projects

Pages 154–157

Rubric

Student Data File

Project 4-1 ➤

Evaluate Design in a Flyer Students evaluate and revise a flyer using PARC principles. Discuss the design for the illustration on page 154 before going over the information in the chart or displaying the solution file for the project. In this example, everything is evenly spaced apart and there are no groups. Since this is the first time students are applying the PARC principles, review the concepts thoroughly. In this project, students will be mostly concerned with proximity. Other PARC principles will be applied to the flyer in Project 4-2. **(Data File 4-1, Solution File 4-1, Rubric 4-1)**

Evaluate White Space Ask students to look at the illustration page 155. The figure on the left represents the flyer on page 154. It is blacked out to show how the white space flows in that layout. Students should notice how the text is all blocked together. The design to the right shows a more open layout, with small chunks of text grouped together. This illustrates the concept of proximity. Ask students why a document using the layout on the right might be easier to read than the layout on the left.

Group Information Ask students why it is that phone numbers are written the way that they are. Why not just write them as 11895376192? Why do we break phone numbers and social security numbers into smaller groups of information?

Obviously, we can remember 1-189-537-6192 much more easily than we can the first long group of numbers. The human mind finds it easier to process information this way. Breaking things into smaller pieces can be a helpful study technique, making it easier to memorize important information. Ask students how this concept relates to the use of proximity in design.

Alignment Tips Alignment has been discussed in previous chapters, but you can review the following concepts:

- The word alignment contains the word *line*. That should help students remember that all elements in a document should line up with something else.

- Alignment helps readers to organize and group information, so content should be aligned for best readability.

- Alignment should not only be applied horizontally, but vertically, too.

- Multiple columns of text should have the tops aligned, though it is not usually important to align the bottoms.

- Ruler guides, layout guides, margin guides, and alignment commands in the Arrange>Align or Distribute menu can be used to apply both horizontal and vertical alignment.

- Break alignment only to draw attention to one thing in particular. This effect will not work, however, if other elements are also out of alignment.

- Alignments contribute to the mood of the design. Center alignment can be elegant and sophisticated, but also boring and predictable. Left alignment is more exciting that center, but very common and ordinary. Right-aligned items can make a design look daring and different.

- Justified text generally works well with any other alignment.

Know What to Group Remind students that the principle of proximity says that, "Things that logically belong together, physically belong together." The corollary to this rule is that, "Things that do not belong together should be separated." To group information effectively, the designer must read and understand the work. This helps the reader to digest the information as well. Some studies suggest that the reader has less than a second to make a decision as to whether the information is interesting or relevant. Given so little time, disorganized information is unlikely to be considered.

Either print out or project on a board Data File 4-1. (It will look like the original document on page 154.) Have students read through it carefully. Then have them use circles and arrows to group the information, either by writing on the printouts or on the board where the document is projected.

Review Grouping Techniques Before students view the revised flyer on page 157, have them write down or discuss the different techniques they can use to group the information in the original flyer on page 154. They might suggest:

- Creating white space around groups of information.
- Adding lines to separate items.
- Adding boxes.
- Using different fonts and font sizes.
- Applying different colors (or shades of gray) to fonts or backgrounds (in text boxes).

Review the suggestions for creating proximity on page 151. Then have students determine which techniques were used in the solution.

Pages 158–161

Rubric

Student Data File

> Project 4-2

Add Contrast and Focal Points Students continue revising the flyer they began in Project 4-1. In this project they will add color and an attention getter to add contrast and focal points. (**Data File 4-2, Solution File 4-2, Rubric 4-2**)

Add Contrast to Alignment Point out to a student that, since the alignment in this document is all centered, the attention getter and graphic should both break the alignment. The added color will also help the design from looking too monotonous.

Apply the AutoFit Tool The Attention Getter contains a text box for writing a message. If the AutoFit Text tool is not turned on, students may have a difficult time inserting their new text. Remind them that if they are having problems, they should use Format>AutoFit Text and choose either *Best Fit* or *Shrink Text on Overflow*. There will be other times when students do not want to use this feature, in which case they should turn it off by using Format>AutoFit Text>None.

Pages 162–166

Rubric

Student Data File

Project 4-3 ▷ **Apply the Golden Ratio** Students use the concept of the *Golden Ratio* to lay out an advertisement. Have students compare the original and the final advertisement, and ask them to describe why the ratio is an effective way of meeting PARC principles. **(Data File 4-3, Solution File 4-3, Rubric 4-3)**

✍ **Team Teach** If possible, invite a math teacher to discuss the Golden Mean (Golden Ratio) and to walk your students through the example as described on page 162.

Introduce the concept as an ancient Greek secret. The Greeks saw this ratio being repeated throughout nature, from the relationship between parts on the ideal body or face to the size of the spirals in a nautilus shell. The Greeks based architecture and art on this concept. Even the dimensions of the Parthenon, considered to be the world's most perfect building, were based on this concept.

⚠ **Supply the Math** If students are confused by the math, do not spend too much time trying to explain it. The exact settings that students need are included in the project steps so that every student can succeed (see Figure 4.12 and Steps 3–5). If advanced students wish to experiment with the formula in their design, you should encourage them.

Pages 167–171

Rubric

Student Data File

Project 4-4 ▷ **Apply Styles in a Flyer** Students add consistency to an advertisement by creating and applying styles, using a style sheet. Students should find that this flyer lacks consistency and focus, which can be fixed by applying repetition and contrast. **(Data File 4-4, Solution File 4-4, Rubric 4-4)**

✍ **Stay Consistent with Style Sheets** Students should not have any problems seeing that the text, bullets, and alignment are inconsistent in this document. Before they begin revising the design, ask them what styles they would assign to the different text in the document. How do they determine how the text should be grouped, which text should act as headers, what kind of spacing they would use to separate lines, and what style they would use to help important text stand out?

✍ **Compare Flyers** The contrast between the original flyer and the final flyer is so extreme that students should take a few minutes to evaluate the changes that were made and why they are effective. Have them use a graphic organizer from Part 3 of this manual, or have them create their own chart comparing the two flyers. They should include brief explanations of how design principles were applied. See if students can suggest other ways that the original flyer could have been redesigned. Advanced students might want to create a completely different design for the original flyer.

⚠ **Insert Graphics** Remind students that if the image seems to fill the screen when they insert it, they should Zoom Out so that they can see the edges of the picture. This makes it easier to resize. Once it is the approximate size that they need, they can Zoom In again to make sure there are no design problems.

Pages 172–176

Rubric · Student · Data File

Project 4-5 ▶ **Revise a Tri-fold Brochure** Students revise the exterior of tri-fold brochure that is difficult to read and that overuses boxes as a design element. The interior of the brochure will be revised in Project 4-6. **(Data Files 4-5a to 4-5c, Solution File 4-5, Rubric 4-5)**

Page 173

Answer to Sidebar The Align and Distribute option in the Arrange menu makes it possible to align objects in relation to the margins or in relation to another object in the document.

✍ **Effective Use of Repetition** The principle of repetition says that, "Dominant design elements should be echoed in some way throughout the design." Repetition is the design principle most responsible for creating a professional looking publication, but it is also the most difficult principle to apply. When used well, it creates harmony within a design. Overuse of repetition, however, can lead to monotony and an amateurish design.

⚠ **Adjust Text Box Colors** Students might find that the sheer number of text boxes (a common design problem) and the lack of contrast in some of the boxes is a bit overwhelming. Show students that they can select text boxes and then remove the fill color by pressing CTRL + T or by changing the fill to white. This will make it easier to change the font typeface, size, and color when they start the steps.

Pages 177–179

Rubric · Student · Data File

Project 4-6 ▶ **Apply PARC to the Brochure Interior** Students continue working on the brochure that they started in Project 4-5, revising the interior to make it more readable. **(Data File 4-6, Solution File 4-6, Rubric 4-6)**

✍ **Find Dominant Design Elements** The key to making repetition work is to create a *dominant design element* that is repeated throughout a design, tying the parts together. This element could be an interesting shape in a piece of clip art or a shape or color in a logo that can be used again elsewhere. Perhaps a title font has a distinct style.

Dominant design elements are not hard to create or identify. By definition, they are noticeable. Have students look over the brochure exterior that they redesigned in Project 4-5. See if anything naturally catches their eye. Which elements would they repeat in the brochure's interior?

Create Dominant Design Elements Sometimes it is difficult to find a dominant design element. In that case, one must be consciously added to the design. Rules (lines) can create a sense of elegance and sophistication. Be careful, though. Lines can distract a reader and lead his or her eyes off the page. Adding simple objects (rectangles, circles, triangles) will work in virtually any situation. Consistent use of fonts will also add repetition to the publication.

Pages 180–184

Rubric

Student Data File

Project 4-7 → **Apply PARC to a Web Page** Students redesign a Web page by changing the layout, making text more readable, and choosing more effective graphics. Make sure students view the Web page on their computers, using Web Page Preview. Otherwise, they will not see that there is animated clip art in the design. (**Data File 4-7a to 4-7c, Solution File 4-7, Rubric 4-7**)

Page 180

Answer to Sidebar MIDI files are used to add music to a Web site.

Identify Poor Web Design Ask students if they have ever seen a poorly designed Web site and what made it bad. Some answers that students might volunteer are that there was too much text, too much scrolling, it was difficult to find important information, hyperlinks were not clear, the background made it difficult to read, there was too much going on (like too much animation), or the music was annoying. Guide students into realizing that Web pages should also follow PARC principles, though there are certain design issues unique to Web pages.

Web Design Principles Along with PARC principles, students should follow a few more guidelines when designing Web pages. Have them create a list of Web page guidelines from the bulleted list on page 180 of their textbooks. You can also add the following tips:

- Web pages must be in landscape mode, though they may be of any length. Do not allow the pages to be too wide because scrolling to the right and left can be frustrating to the reader.

- Web pages should use sans serif text for the main body text. Monitors simply do not have the resolution necessary to make Oldstyle characters clear enough for easy reading.

Align Objects on a Web Page If students have difficulty aligning objects by using the layout grid, encourage students to use Arrange>Align or Distribute>Align Center (or left or right) to align objects in relation to each other.

Skills Studio

Pages 185–190

Create a Children's Newsletter

The Design Process table on page 148 discusses the elements for designing a newsletter. Newsletters are meant to provide up-to-date information to a specific audience. Often they are sent by mail or distributed automatically to the intended audience. If potential readers look at a newsletter and it does not attract their attention, they will throw it out without reading it. So it is particularly important that the exterior of a newsletter be designed so that a reader is likely to open it and read the inside.

Before students begin this newsletter, have them first read the Spotlight on Skills for Projects 4-8 and 4-9. Then look over the table on page 148 and discuss with them how each step of the design process relates to this newsletter. They should pay particular attention to the audience. Even though it is a fourth-grade newsletter, it most likely is aimed at both the young student and the student's parents. Both audiences must be satisfied with both the content and the design.

Pages 186–188

Rubric

Student Data File

Project 4-8 **Design for a Young Audience** Students revise a newsletter aimed at a fourth-grade audience. They will redesign the front page in this project and finish the interior and back pages in Project 4-9. **(Data Files 4-8a and 4-8b, Solution File 4-8, Rubric 4-8)**

Evaluate Publishing Options Ask students to look at the final paragraph on page 186. What information about Mrs. Arias and the newsletter is most important? How does this information affect the design? Three things are most important: 1) The design is 8½″ × 11″. This will affect the paper size settings and layout. 2) Although the newsletter cannot be longer than two pages, it will be printed on a duplex printer. This means that it can be printed front and back, allowing a four-panel layout, with no need to staple pages together. It will also save paper costs. 3) The document can be printed in color, which allows a greater variety of graphic and design options.

Analyze the Newsletter Design Unlike previous projects in this chapter, this project does not have a "Design Blunders" chart to evaluate the design in relation to the PARC principles. Ask students to look at the figure on page 186. As a class or individually, have students create their own Design Blunders chart for this newsletter. (See page 154 as a model.)

Students should explain why this design does not work in terms of PARC principles. They might mention that it looks like a worksheet, rather than a newsletter. This has to do with the layout and placement of elements. It is difficult to tell where one section ends and another begins. Other problems are the use of a monotype font, poor alignment, and clip art that seems completely unrelated to the material.

⚠️ **Place the Graphic** Students may have difficulty placing the lined paper graphic on the page. They should tilt it and size it so that most of it fits on the workspace. Any parts that go beyond the edge of the workspace will not print.

They must also remember to use the Send to Back command for the paper so that the text can be placed above it. You may have to help students place the text so that it is placed effectively on the lines of the paper. If the text does not all fit on the first page, that is okay. The overflow will be flowed to the next page.

Pages 189–190

Rubric

▶ **Project 4-9** **Complete Your Newsletter** Students finish the newsletter they started in Project 4-8. They will insert and modify a calendar template and redesign the last page. **(Solution File 4-9, Rubric 4-9)**

✍️ **Preview Changes** Before students continue the newsletter, make sure they understand how elements in the previous design are adapted to the new design. *Dates to Remember* will be entered into the new calendar, *Family Fun Corner* will move to the back page, and the continuation of *From the Teacher's Desk* will be on the second page.

⚠️ **Set Tab Stops** If students are confused about creating tabs, go over Steps 5–6 with them. Show them that they can create a right tab in two ways.

• They can press Shift and then click the Tab Selector on the left side of the horizontal ruler until the Right Tab icon shows. Then they can click on the ruler to set the tab where they want it.

• They can choose **Format>Tabs** and choose the **Right** option under Alignment. Then they can key the exact **Tab stop position**.

ASSESS

Evaluate Projects Encourage students to use the Review and Revise checklists to be sure that they have completed the key steps. Encourage students to proofread and assist each other. Students learn best when they are teaching each other. Consider giving bonus points for well-designed projects for both the student and the student who evaluated his/her work.

Students can also use the rubrics to evaluate their own work or their classmates'. You can then use the criteria listed in the rubric and the stamp (described on page 118 to help grade students' work. Take off 5 points for each type of mistake and 10 points for skipping skill sets in the lessons. For a grade, have students chart the kinds of mistakes they have been making. Hopefully, they will begin to see a pattern of mistakes and you will be finding fewer problems, making grading faster in the future.

CLOSE

Relate to Real World Problems Ask students why makeover shows are so popular. They will probably come up with many answers. You might lead them to see, however, that makeover shows understand that a new look can often provide new motivation, new confidence, and a better chance of success.

The design problems we have seen in this chapter are similar to ones that can easily be found in the real world. Understanding how to improve a design gives it a better chance of getting a client's message out to the world. Ask students which design principles or tricks from this chapter they have found to be most useful outside of the classroom. How might they use this knowledge?

IN THE WORKPLACE

LAYOUT ARTIST

Career Activity

A layout artist is a bit different from a graphic designer, though their jobs do often overlap. The graphic designer is the one who creates the page design and illustrations, while the layout artist uses the design to create the published product. Layout artists place new content into the design template and create the pages that will then be printed.

Notes

Chapter 4 Assessment Answers

Use the following Reading Check and Critical Thinking answers as a guide to help evaluate student understanding of the core concepts. Requiring that your students write in complete sentences will help you grade faster and promote good writing skills. You can have students write answers in their desktop publishing journals, or students can answer these questions at the computer by accessing the Reading Check and Critical Thinking activities on the Online Learning Center at **glencoe.com**.

Page 192

Reading Check

1. PARC: Proximity, Alignment, Repetition and Contrast. Proximity: establishing groups; Alignment: creating harmony and order through lining up all objects with something; Repetition: creating harmony through repeating dominant design elements; Contrast: creating visual interest by making differences and setting up a focal point.

2. An orphan is a short, abandoned group of text at the bottom of a column or page, while a widow is a short, abandoned group of text at the top of a column or page.

3. The design process includes planning, developing, and publishing a design. It often requires revision at every stage of the process and, therefore, is more like a spiral than like a list.

4. The Golden Ratio has been applied throughout all the visual arts because the proportions are considered to be "ideal" standards based on observations of nature.

5. By exporting and importing style sheets, different designers and documents can share styles and maintain a consistent design.

Critical Thinking

6. Proximity can be created with white space, lines, boxes, color, alignment, fonts, or font size.

7. An entry point allows the reader to focus on one part of the design before reading the rest. Focal points can be created by using high contrast, with color, font or font size, alignment, or a graphic.

8. In the planning stage of a project, the printing needs and budget are established, the content is researched, and design ideas are sketched out. This stage is important to determine the exact project requirements and the features that can be incorporated without breaking the client's budget. Sketches are important to help determine a final design that is approved by the client and can then be created on the computer.

9. Designing a Web page is different from the regular printed page because: the design is landscape, fonts must look clear on a monitor's low resolution display, graphics must be a low resolution to facilitate fast download times, and interactive elements like hyperlinks and animation can be added. Colors for Web page must be limited to Web-safe colors, but publishing the designs do not cost any extra for using the color.

10. Both a bank and high school newsletters would have lots of text, multiple pages, linked stories, and graphics. They would be different because the bank newsletter would be more conservative, and graphics would probably be charts and tables rather than pictures. The high school newsletter might use more interesting fonts, lots of photographs and graphics, and possibly use brighter colors. Content would also be very different. The bank's would discuss banking and business-related information. The school's would address student activities and stories that interest teenagers.

Assessment activities allow students to demonstrate their understanding of concepts and skills learned throughout this project. Because of time constraints, students may not be able to complete every activity suggested. Match assignments to student ability levels using the leveled projects (★ Easy, ★★ Medium, and ★★★ Challenging). Rubrics are available to evaluate projects on the Teacher Resources DVD and the Online Learning Center at **glencoe.com**.

Page 192

Rubric

1. Independent Practice ★

Evaluate and Design an Advertisement Require that students conduct thoughtful evaluations of a poorly designed advertisement. Examples of ineffective ads can often be found in phone books, free newsletters, and grocery store ads. Assign points to the evaluation of the original ad.

After the Planning and Design stages of the design process, have students conduct peer evaluations (in writing) that considers PARC principles for the design and count this as a grade. Students who turn in sloppy peer reviews should lose points for not making the effort to get good reviews.

The final advertisement should follow the guidelines described on page 192. Grade the work using the criteria in the rubric and the stamp described in the Assess section on page 118. **(Rubric IP 4-1)**

Page 193

Rubric

2. Independent Practice ★ ★

Create a *Tips for Teens* Brochure If possible, see if you can bring in examples of literature from the Chamber of Commerce. This will give students an idea of their client's preferences. Encourage students to come up with a design that will appeal to teenagers, but still conform to the style of the client.

Students might have to do some research to find examples and information for the three categories of food, recreation, and culture. You might provide a list of acceptable resources, or have a class discussion to get suggestions.

Evaluate student projects based on whether they complete the entire design process: brainstorm ideas, perform accurate research, create thumbnail sketches, and execute a sound design. Designs should have original, complete, and accurate text; properly cited sources; follow font rules; and contain relevant illustrations. The tri-fold brochure must be laid out effectively. Ensure that projects follow the guidelines described in the Plan and Create sections on page 193. **(Rubric IP 4-2)**

Page 193

Rubric

3. Independent Practice ★★★

Practice for an FBLA Event FBLA events are challenging events whose winners gain national recognition. The design competition is a fun event to prepare for and includes both a written exam and a performance exam. To participate, students must be accompanied by a sponsor who is an FBLA member, but students will find memberships rewarding—particularly if they intend to enter the workforce. Contact a local FBLA club leader for more information, or visit the FBLA Web site for information on starting your own chapter.

Evaluate student projects based on whether they complete the entire design process: brainstorm ideas, perform accurate research, create thumbnail sketches and execute a sound design. Require that students create several thumbnail sketches, each with different designs. Have them create a final sketch that incorporates all their best ideas into one very good design.

Have students then share their ideas and begin to create them. Evaluate the student project by assigning point values for the theme, how well it addresses the audience and message, the thumbnail sketches, and criteria described on page 193. The publication must follow the FBLA Competitive Event Guidelines. Designs should also have original, complete, and accurate text; properly cited sources; follow font rules; and contain relevant illustrations. **(Rubric IP 4-3)**

Reteaching Activities

Redesign a Project Have students choose one of the "Before" designs in this chapter to revise using their own ideas. They should first draw thumbnails of new design before creating a completely new version of the document. They can use the data files for their revision, but the final product should look very different from the solution file for that project.

Complete Worksheets Have students complete Worksheets 4A and 4B, which can be found in Part 3 of this TRM, on the Teacher Resource DVD, and at the Online learning Center at **glencoe.com**.

Enrichment Activities

Evaluate Poor Design Bring in examples of flyers, advertisements, brochures, or other publications that are poorly designed. Have students bring in any that they can find. Keep a selection of these in your classroom. Have students choose an example and evaluate it according to PARC principles. If possible, have students create their own versions of the publication, using effective design techniques. If the example is too difficult for them to revise, have them create a thumbnail sketch and write a description explaining how they would redesign it.

Enrichment If students need an additional challenge, have them complete the activities in the Online Learning Center at **glencoe.com**.

Notes

Projects Across the Curriculum

Evaluate Understanding These projects allow students to demonstrate their understanding of concepts and skills learned throughout this unit. Because of time constraints, students may not be able to complete every activity suggested. Match assignments to student ability levels using the leveled projects (★ Easy, ★★ Medium, and ★★★ Challenging). Rubrics are available to evaluate projects on the Teacher Resource DVD and the Online Learning Center at **glencoe.com**.

Page 194

Rubric

Project 1 Create a Flyer with Tear-offs ★

You might invite a science teacher to the class to discuss some possible astronomical events that students can use in their brochures. See if students can find some interesting images to add to the flyer and encourage them to create an imaginative theme that might use space images or stars or anything that will attract their audience. The Web site **www.nasa.gov** has a lot of good information and images that students can use without permission (though they should still be credited!).

Have students then share their ideas and begin to create them. Evaluate student projects based on whether they complete the entire design process: brainstorm ideas, perform accurate research, create several thumbnail sketches, and execute an effective final design. Assign point values for the theme, relevance to the audience and message, the thumbnail sketches, and the requirements described on page 194. Designs should also have original, complete, and accurate text; properly cited sources; follow font rules; contain relevant illustrations; and follow PARC design principles. **(Rubric PAC 4-1)**

Page 194

Rubric

Project 2 Create a Personal Budget Planner ★★

Students can use their own expenses and income to create their budget planner, or they can interview their parents (or another adult) and use their income and the type of expenses that they might incur in a week. Include gas, food, recreation, housing, etc. Students can then create their Publisher document based on the data that they have gathered.

Students that are familiar with Microsoft Excel can create a spreadsheet with formulas, and then copy and paste information in the Publisher document. Evaluate the student project by assigning point values for the requirements described on page 194. **(Rubric PAC 4-2)**

Page 154

Rubric

Project 3 Create a Brochure with a Coupon ★★

If possible, have students use an historical place that they are studying in their social studies class. Have students spend time researching the time and place that they want to visit, and make sure that they find suitable illustrations and all the information they will need to complete the Plan section of the project. Encourage students to be imaginative and create a theme that is appropriate to the trip they are planning.

Evaluate student projects based on whether they completed the entire design process and included all the projects requirements described on page 195. Designs should have original, complete and accurate text; properly cited sources; follow font rules; contain relevant illustrations; and follow PARC principles of design. **(Rubric PAC 4-3)**

Page 195

Rubric

Project 4 Add Hyperlinks to a Web Site ★★★

Tell students to look at the buttons on the Shakespeare Web page in Project 4-7 for information about the new Web pages they should create. Students can look at the High School Web site in Chapter 3, Projects 3-6 and 3-7, to review how to add hyperlinks and master pages to Web pages. Students should do research on Shakespeare in order to create effective pages. They should add illustrations whenever possible and continue the theme that is used on the home page. They can make up information about the production, including the names of their friends for the roles.

Ensure that projects follow the criteria on page 195, and make sure that all the hyperlinks work correctly when the document is previewed as a Web page. If your class has its own Web site, you could publish the best of your students' Shakespeare sites. **(Rubric PAC 4-4)**

Notes

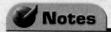

Notes

Design with Adobe Photoshop

Getting Started

About the Unit

This unit is intended to teach students how to use the main features of Adobe Photoshop to create and edit digital images. The unit has two chapters which cover important basic concepts and skills. **Chapter 5: Introducing Adobe Photoshop** introduces students to the key concepts of image creation and manipulation using Photoshop. **Chapter 6: Integrating Publisher and Photoshop** teaches advanced techniques of image manipulation and shows students how to integrate Photoshop and Publisher to create documents using both text and images.

In Chapter 5, students will learn how to create and manipulate digital images. The chapter provides a general introduction to raster graphics, the Photoshop interface, object selection, layers, masking, retouching, and filters. In the process of creating collages, retouching a photograph, and manipulating images with filters, students will practice skills that introduce the techniques of professional image manipulation.

In Chapter 6, students will learn the fundamentals of combining graphics with text using Microsoft Publisher layout software. Students will practice using Publisher and Photoshop to create a postcard, a banner, and a booklet. They will learn how to blend images and print oversized documents.

Quick Write Activity

Ask students to make a list of publications they would like to create that incorporate both text and images. These might include a CD cover for their favorite band, a magazine cover for National Geographic, or a poster advertising the latest action movie.

Based on students' lists, ask them to identify which elements of their design might use Photoshop and which elements will rely on Publisher. They should understand that Photoshop is used for manipulating photographs, but it can also be used to add text and create other types of illustrations, as they will learn in this unit. Publisher can also be used to add text, but its main function is to place the image in a publication like an advertisement, poster, cereal box, greeting card, and so on.

Assessments

Workshop Foundations, Reading Check, pg. 200
Workshop Toolbox, Reading Check, pg. 202

End of Chapter 5 Assessment
   Reading Check, pg. 248
   Critical Thinking, pg.248
[R] **1.** Independent Practice: Go on a Photo Tour, pg. 248
[R] **2.** Independent Practice: Create a Space Creature, pg. 249
[R] **3.** Independent Practice: Create an American Montage, pg. 249

⊙ **Additional Assessments You May Wish to Use**
   ExamView Assessment Suite Testbank, Chapter 5

Workshop Foundations Reading Check, pg. 252
Workshop Toolbox Reading Check, pg. 253

End of Chapter 6 Assessment
   Reading Check, pg. 287
   Critical Thinking, pg. 287
[R] **1.** Independent Practice: Create a Postcard, pg. 287
[R] **2.** Independent Practice: Create a Banner or Poster, pg. 288
[R] **3.** Independent Practice: Create a CD Cover and Insert, pg. 288

⊙ **Additional Assessments You May Wish to Use**
   ExamView Assessment Suite Testbank, Chapter 6

ⓘ **Go Online e-Review Self Checks** Chapter 5 and Chapter 6

Estimated Time to Complete Unit

9 Week Course = 5–7 days
18 Week Course = 7–8 days
36 Week Course = 13–15 days

To help customize lesson plans, use the Pacing Guide on pages 29–30 and the Standards Charts on pages 194–195.

Key to Recommended Materials

ⓘ   Internet access required

[R]   Scoring Rubrics

[DF]   Data Files

⊙   *ExamView Assessment Suite* CD

ⓣ   TechSIM CD (Technology Simulations available on CD and the Online Learning Center)

The Teacher Resource DVD contains Data Files, Solution Files, Rubrics, Reproducible Worksheets, and PowerPoint Presentations.

Data Files for Unit 3 provided on the Teacher Resource DVD and Online Learning Center

Chapter 5	Chapter 6
5-1	6-1
5-3	6-3
5-4	6-5a to 6-5b
5-5	6-6a to 6-6d
5-6	6-7a to 6-7k
5-7	
5-9a to 5-9b	
5-10a to 5-10c	

Inclusion Strategies
For **Differentiated Instruction Strategies** refer to the **Inclusion in the Computer Technology Classroom** booklet.

ISTE NETS Foundation Standards

1. Basic operations and concepts
2. Social, ethical, and human issues
3. Technology productivity tools
4. Technology communications tools
5. Technology research tools
6. Technology problem-solving and decision-making

Performance Indicators	Textbook Correlation
1. Identify capabilities and limitations of contemporary and emerging technology resources and assess the potential of these systems and services to address personal, lifelong learning, and workplace needs. (NETS 2)	197–200, 201–202, 203, 224, 239–240, 247, 249, 251–252, 253, 254, 258–259, 266, 277, 283, 286, 289–290
2. Make informed choices among technology systems, resources, and services. (NETS 1, 2)	197–200, 203, 211, 240, 251–252, 253, 258–259, 266, 287–288, 289–290
3. Analyze advantages and disadvantages of widespread use and reliance on technology in the workplace and in society as a whole. (NETS 2)	202, 224, 239, 247, 248, 252, 266, 269, 273, 286, 287
4. Demonstrate and advocate for legal and ethical behaviors among peers, family, and community regarding the use of technology and information. (NETS 2)	202, 251–252, 273, 287, 289
5. Use technology tools and resources for managing and communicating personal/professional information (e.g. finances, schedules, addresses, purchases, correspondence). (NETS 3, 4)	197, 224–228, 229–233, 239, 240–243, 244–246, 247, 248–249, 251–252, 254–257, 258–260, 266–268, 273, 277–278, 286, 287–288, 289–290
6. Evaluate technology-based options, including distance and distributed education, for lifelong learning. (NETS 5)	247, 249, 277, 286, 288
7. Routinely and efficiently use online information resources to meet needs for collaboration, research, publications, communications, and productivity. (NETS 4, 5, 6)	203, 239, 247, 248–249, 254, 277, 286, 287, 288, 289, 290
8. Select and apply technology tools for research, information analysis, problem-solving, and decision-making in content learning. (NETS 4, 5)	234–238, 240–243, 247, 248–249, 250, 269–272, 273–276, 286, 287–288, 289–290
9. Investigate and apply expert systems, intelligent agents, and simulations in real-world situations. (NETS 3, 5, 6)	211–219, 220–223, 224–228, 229–234, 239–246, 247, 248–249, 254–260, 261–268, 269–276, 277–285, 286, 287–290
10. Collaborate with peers, experts, and others to contribute to content-related knowledge base by using technology to compile, synthesize, produce, and disseminate information, models, and other creative works. (NETS 4, 5, 6)	197, 240–246, 248–249, 250, 278–282, 288, 290

21st Century Skills

Core Subjects Language arts, math, science, social studies	198, 199, 202, 203–206, 211–214, 220–223, 224–228, 234–238, 240–246, 248–249, 251, 252, 253, 254–257, 269–272, 274–276, 287–288, 289–290
Learning Skills Information and media literacy; communication skills; critical thinking and systems thinking; problem identification, formulation, and solution; self-direction; accountability	187, 197, 198, 199, 200, 202, 203–206, 211–214, 224–228, 240–246, 274, 248–249, 250, 251, 252, 253, 266, 278–282, 286, 287–288, 289–290
21st Century Tools Communication, information processing and research tools; problem-solving tools, personal development and productivity tools	198–200, 201–202, 239–243, 247, 248, 251–252, 253, 258–259, 266–268, 286

Foundation Skills

Basic Skills Reading, Writing, Math, Listening, and Speaking	198, 202, 203–206, 211–214, 224–228, 240–246, 248–249, 251, 252, 253, 287–288, 289–290
Thinking Skills Creative thinking, decision making, problem solving, reasoning	187, 197, 199, 200, 202, 247, 248–249, 250, 252, 253, 266, 278–282, 286, 287–288, 289–290
Personal Qualities Self-esteem, responsibility, self-management, and integrity/honesty	198–202, 247, 248, 251–252, 273, 286

Workplace Competencies

Resources Allocate time, money, materials, facilities, and human resources	248–249, 287–288, 289–290
Interpersonal Participate on teams, teach others, serve clients and customers, exercise leadership, negotiate to arrive at decisions, and work with cultural diversity	197, 247, 248–249, 250, 286, 289
Information Acquire, evaluate, organize, maintain, interpret, communicate, and use computers to process information	200, 240–243, 248–249, 252, 253, 258–259, 266, 278–282
Systems Understand, monitor, correct, improve, and design systems	197, 198–200, 240, 258–259, 266–268, 278, 293–294
Technology Select, apply, maintain, and troubleshoot technology	199, 200, 205, 207, 208, 211, 220, 224–228, 240–243, 253, 254, 258–259, 266–268, 269, 287–290

Chapter 5

Introducing Photoshop

Skills You Will Learn

Workshop Foundations: Explore Raster Graphics

- Identify raster images
- Determine resolution
- Identify raster image file formats

Workshop Toolbox: The Photoshop Interface

- Identify parts of the Photoshop interface
- Identify toolbox tools

Project 5-1 Select Objects

- Apply the zoom tool
- Select with the Polygonal Lasso, Magic Wand, and Marquee tools
- Copy, move, and flip an object
- Scale an object

Project 5-2 Complete a Collage

- Select with the Magnetic Lasso
- Separate background images
- Resize and rotate objects
- Crop an image

Project 5-3 Create a Photo Collage

- Use the Navigator palette
- Add to selection
- Subtract from selection
- Add a layer

Project 5-4 Add Layers

- Change color
- Create and reorder layers
- Add a new background
- Adjust contrast
- Insert a new image
- Erase parts of an image

Project 5-5 Apply a Mask

- Resize a document
- Add a layer mask
- Set an RGB color
- Add text

Project 5-6 Retouch a Photo

- Straighten a photo
- Remove red eye
- Apply the Clone Stamp
- Adjust color levels

Project 5-7 Create a Photo Montage

- Add a layer for a selection
- Add a shadow and filter
- Flatten an image
- Create a vignette effect

Project 5-8 Create Effects and Images with Filters

- Change the workspace color
- Apply filters
- Apply the Magic Eraser
- Add a gradient fill

Skills Studio

Create a Magazine Cover
Project 5-9 Take a Digital Photograph

- Take a digital photograph
- Upload a photo from a camera
- Remove a background
- Insert a picture into an image

Project 5-10 Lay Out a Cover

- Group layers
- Add magazine cover objects
- Add text

Start-Up Skills

Understand Pixels Examining the artistic technique called pointillism is a good way to help students understand how the computer draws images on screen. In pointillism, all the colors and shading in the painting are created with tiny dots or strokes of primary colors. Bring in some examples of pointillism by artists like Georges Seurat, or ask students to find examples of pointillist art on the Internet or in art books from the library.

Have students examine the pointillist paintings and compare and contrast them to the raster image on page 198. Students should see that the dots in the painting are similar to the pixels in raster images. Just as the artist combines dots to create colors and images, the computer combines pixels.

Ask students to make a simple drawing on paper using colored markers. Tell them that they cannot use the markers to draw as they normally would, but must outline, color, and shade using only dots.

Design Process: Photographs

Compare Design Issues Students will recognize that photographs are used to provide visual information in a wide variety of contexts. Ask them to brainstorm the various places photographs appear, including books and magazines, billboards, products, and Web sites. Ask students to analyze how and why photographs are used in these contexts and what messages they are meant to convey. Students may mention that advertising photographs might be used to display a product clearly or to create a specific "image" of a product. Photographs are also used to convey an artistic vision or express ideas.

Quick Write Activity

Analyze Photos Bring in pictures from magazines and display them in the front of the room. Ask students to choose two or three of the photographs and write several sentences explaining how each of the pictures may have been altered. They may notice that colors have been enhanced or changed, images outside a window replaced, or blur effects added to draw the reader's attention toward the image that is in focus. Some students may even discover minor flaws in the image. All of these alterations may be evidence that the photograph was "Photoshopped."

LEARNING LINK

Photoshop is not, by itself, desktop publishing software. However, it is an important tool that is used with layout software to create publications. Explain to students that designers and layout artists usually need to be able to use software that allows them to create and manipulate images in publications. The illustrations that they create in this chapter can all be used in some type of documents, such as advertisements, product packaging, books, magazines, brochures, or posters. In Chapter 6, they will have a chance to see how Photoshop works in conjunction with layout software.

Workshop Foundations Pages 198–200

Explore Raster Graphics

FOCUS

Focus Activity

Discuss Scalability Ask students to read pages 198–200 of the text. Call upon a few students to explain why raster images are not scalable the way vector images are. Answers should demonstrate their understanding that the computer stores vector images as math formulas so when vector images are resized, the computer can recalculate the dimensions without losing any image clarity. When raster images are enlarged however, the actual pixels in the image become larger. The more the picture is enlarged, the more noticeable the pixels become.

You Will Learn To:
- Identify raster images
- Determine resolution
- Identify raster image file formats

Page 198

Before You Read Activity

Reading for a Purpose Have students follow the instructions in the *Before You Read* feature for the Foundations section of the chapter. After they have looked over "You Will Learn To" and the headings and the questions, ask them what the purpose will be for reading the section. Many students might say that they have already learned about raster graphics earlier in the book. Ask them how they think the information they learn here will be different.

Page 198

Key Term Activity

Multiple-Choice Questions Have students create multiple-choice test questions for each key term in the chapter. Students can then practice and share these questions and use them to review. The best test questions could be included on the next exam.

Key Term Definitions

pixel Short for *picture-element*, the smallest unit of color in an image or on a computer monitor. (page 198)

raster graphics Graphics made up of tiny colored squares (pixels) that work together to form an image. (page 198)

resolution The clarity of an image, expressed in number of pixels per inch (ppi) on the monitor, or dots per inch (dpi) on the printer. (page 198)

scalable The ability of a graphic to be resized without losing image quality. (page 198)

pixilated Refers to the distorted appearance of an image when the pixels that make up the image become visible. (page 199)

file name extension The letters displayed after a file name that describe the type of file format, such as .jpg, .exe, .doc. (page 200)

TEACH

Teach Activity

Study Advertising Layouts Have students bring in examples of full-page, full-color ads from a national magazine. Ask students to discuss the visual relationship between the text and the image. What elements of the advertisement immediately catch their eye? Do they read the text before looking at the image or do they see the image first? Which elements do they think are most memorable or effective?

Answers to Workshop Foundations Activities

Page 199

Sidebar

The total pieces of information displayed on a screen can be calculated as follows: 800 pixels (width of a computer screen) × 600 pixels (height of a computer screen) × 3 (RGB colors) = 1,440,000.

Page 200

Sidebar

GIF is a good format to use for e-mailing a photo to a friend. GIF uses only 256 colors so the file size of a photo is small. JPEG is also a good general-purpose format for sharing photographs on the Internet. A TIFF file might be so large that it would take a long time for the photo to download.

ASSESS

Reading Check

1. A computer stores information for recreating a raster image by storing values for the red, green, and blue colors (RGB) for every pixel in an image.

2. A 300 dpi image has a higher resolution, since it has more dots per inch.

CLOSE

Discuss Image Manipulation Explain to students that nearly every image that they see in the media has been altered with photo editing software like Photoshop. Challenge students to doubt, question, and analyze every image they see. Have students look closely at images of models, cars, foods, and other products to see how photo editing tools can be used to make things look more appealing. Ask students to consider the implications of digital image manipulation. Do they believe it is dishonest to alter photographs?

Workshop Toolbox
Pages 201–202

The Photoshop Interface

FOCUS

Focus Activity
Locate Elements Have students draw a diagram of the figure on page 201 into their journals. Ask them to indicate the location of the following elements: *menu bar, Options toolbar, toolbox, status bar, workspace and palettes.*

> **You Will Learn To:**
> - Identify parts of the Photoshop interface
> - Identify Toolbox tools

Page 201

Key Term Activity
Identify Palettes Have students look at page 201. Ask them how many palettes are currently open. (*Answer: Three palettes are clearly visible, while 11 palettes are open. The tabs for the other palettes are visible behind the top palette.*) This is one way that the interface for Adobe products differs from that of Word and other Microsoft products.

> **Key Term Definitions**
>
> **palette** A set of tools, located in a separate floating toolbar, that relates to a particular action, such as adding color or working with layers. (page 201)

TEACH

Teach Activity
Identify Parts of the Photoshop Interface Introduce the user interface to the students, especially the *workspace, palettes, Toolbox,* and the *Options toolbar.*

- Show students that the Toolbox has hidden tools located under tools with a small triangle (delta) in the corner. Show that students can position their mouse over a tool to learn the tool's name.

- Point out that the Options toolbar changes options when different tools are selected.

- Show how the three buttons at the bottom of the Toolbox change the view.

- Identify parts of the palettes. Point out the buttons at the bottom and the small triangle in the upper right corner. In the text, the triangle is referred to as an Options button. It opens a menu related to the palette.

- Have students open a palette by choosing Window>Info. Notice that at the bottom of the Info palette, students can find out a little bit about the tools they have selected.

Compare and Contrast Interfaces Ask students to create a matrix similar to Graphic Organizer 6 on page 368. They will then use it to compare the Adobe and Microsoft interfaces. Features unique to Microsoft products should be listed in the first column, while Adobe features should be listed in the third column. The column in between should list elements that both interfaces share. (*Students are likely to notice that Adobe products have palettes, with more tools at the bottom of each palette. Both Microsoft and Adobe products have a toolbar and a menu bar. Microsoft tends to include most commands as a menu choice, with toolbars being more or less optional. Not so with Adobe products, whose palettes have commands not found in the menu bar.*)

Erase Settings To erase previous settings, have students open Adobe Photoshop, while holding CTRL+ALT+Shift. Doing this will reset Photoshop so that students can more easily follow instructions found in the chapter.

● Answers to Workshop Toolbox Activities

Page 202

Eye on Ethics

A photograph posted on the Internet may be owned by the photographer or person who originated the image, the owner of the Web site on which it is posted, an image archive, or a licensing agency. For both legal and ethical reasons, it is important to contact the creator or owner before using an image.

ASSESS

Reading Check

1. Tool buttons that have hidden tools underneath are marked with a small triangle (a delta) in the bottom right corner of the tool.
2. When you select a tool in the Toolbox, a new set of options appears on the Options toolbar.

CLOSE

Preview Palettes Photoshop has a great many tools and features that enable the user to create compelling and realistic effects. In this unit, we will be exploring many of these tools and features, though people can spend years learning to use the software effectively. The interface is somewhat different from what students are likely to be used to, but they will get it, and it will be fun!

Open the Window menu, and show students some of the palettes they will be using in the chapter. See if students can guess how the palettes can be used, and get them thinking of the interesting skills they will be learning.

Chapter 5 Projects

Pages 203–246

FOCUS

Focus Activity

Discuss Selection Tools Ask students how they selected objects in Microsoft Word or Publisher. Generally, they just had to click on an object to select it. Explain that in Adobe there are many more ways to select objects, and it will require some more thought. However, with names like Marquee tools, Lasso tools, Magnetic Lasso, and Magic Wand, students will see that selecting images will be both more complex and more interesting.

Go Online PREVIEW

Before You Begin Students can use the chapter **PowerPoint** presentations and **rubrics** at the Online Learning Center to determine what is expected *before* they complete a project. Students can view the PowerPoint slides on their own computers, or you can project them to preview chapter concepts and show examples of the finished projects. You might also display project solutions so students can easily refer to them while they work. (Presentations and rubrics are also provided on the Teacher Resource DVD for your convenience).

glencoe.com

Key Term Activity

Define Key Terms Write each key term on an index card. On a separate index card, write the definition. Create several sets of cards, divide the class into small groups, and give each group a set of cards. Have students quiz each other by matching each key term to its definition. You can also create a Jeopardy-type game where you supply an answer that is either a term or a definition and students have to come up with the correct question.

Key Term Definitions

anchor point The spot where you begin or end a new line segment. (page 203)

marquee A dotted outline around sections you want to select. (page 203)

polygon A multisided geometric figure (page 203)

fastening points Points that anchor the line and start a new line segment. (page 207)

collage A collection of assembled images. (page 211)

blending modes Tools that control the way the pixels on one layer blend with the pixels in underlying layers. (page 215)

hue A synonym for *color.* (page 215)

opacity Noun form of the adjective *opaque.* In Photoshop, this is used to adjust an image's transparency. (page 215)

opaque A quality which makes an object too dark to see through. (page 215)

saturation The intensity of a color. (page 215)

transparency The level at which an object can be seen through in order to see another object behind it. (page 215)

mask A feature that hides areas of an image so that the data cannot be edited. (page 220)

clone To copy a range of pixels for placement elsewhere in an image. (page 224)

retouch To fix or edit an image. (page 224)

histogram A graph that shows the number of pixels for each color and tone in an image. (page 225)

flatten To merge all layers in Photoshop into a single layer. (page 229)

highlight An effect showing the light reflected off a surface. (page 229)

montage Similar to a collage, except that the separate images combine to create a new image. (page 229)

vignette An image that has a border that fades into the background. (page 229)

filter A tool that can create effects like distortions, textures, blurs, and more. (page 234)

megapixel A unit that contains over one million pixels. (page 240)

optical zoom A lens in a camera that magnifies the subject without losing image quality. (page 240)

single lens reflex (SLR) A single lens reflex camera, which allows the photographer to look through the camera's viewfinder and actually see the exact image that will be captured by the camera lens. (page 240)

TEACH

Teach Activity

Selection Tools Have students look at the figures and read the descriptions on page 203. Notice that while there are several kinds of individual selection tools, there are really three different kinds of groups of selection tools: the Marquee, the Lasso, and the Magic Wand. Have students write brief explanations of each kind of selection tool into their journals.

Teaching Tips and Troubleshooting Tips ⚠ for Projects

> **Project 5-1** ▶ **Select Objects** Students learn to use Photoshop's selection tools to move, format, and manipulate objects. In this project, they will create an image of a gingerbread house. **(Data File 5-1, Solution File 5-1, Rubric 5-1)**

⚠ **Use Undo** If students drop off a piece of the gingerbread house, they will find that they cannot move the piece afterwards without "tearing a hole" in the picture. Encourage students to use the Undo feature since they have not yet learned how to work with various layers in a document. They can undo by pressing CTRL+Z or Edit>Undo.

⚠ **Select Magic Wand** When using the Magic Wand tool, students might find they are selecting colors all over the workspace. Have students check the Options toolbar to ensure that "Contiguous" is selected. If students are getting too big a range of color or too small, have students adjust the "Tolerance" level on the Options toolbar.

> **Project 5-2** ▶ **Complete a Collage** Students continue to learn about Photoshop's selection tools as they complete the gingerbread house they started in Project 5-1. They will use the Magnetic Lasso and Magic Wand and resize objects using the "Show Transform Controls" option for the Move tool. **(Solution File 5-2, Rubric 5-2)**

 Review Tools Do a quick review of the last assignment and the three groups of selection tools: the Marquee, the Lasso, and the Magic Wand. Locate the tools and identify their purpose. *The Marquees are used to select objects of a definite shape. The Lasso tools are used when selecting objects whose shape is irregular. The Magic Wand is used to select objects with a consistent color.*

 Add and Subtract from Selection When a selection tool is activated, the Options toolbar displays settings particular to that specific tool, but there are four buttons that are consistent for all of the selection tools: the New Selection, Add to Selection, Subtract from Selection, and Intersect Selections buttons. Explain to students that the Add to Selection and Subtract from Selection options can be helpful in selecting unusual shapes, as they will see in this project, and again in Project 5-3.

> **Project 5-3** ▶ **Create a Photo Collage** In this project, students begin to create a collage, placing a photograph of a car into a new background image. They will continue to practice using selection tools, including the Add to Selection and Subtract from Selection options. They will also be introduced to the Layers palette. **(Data File 5-3, Solution File 5-3, Rubric 5-3)**

 Zoom Tools The Navigator palette is useful if students are working on a small section of a large image. It also has a slider for zooming in and out. However, if they have a wheel on their mouse, they can use CTRL+wheel, which is a faster way to zoom in and out.

Work with Layers The Layers palette is one of the most useful palettes, and it should always be left open. Use the Eye icon to make layers visible and editable or invisible and unable to be edited. The Layers palette can also give students control over the order of the layers.

Control the Magnetic Lasso Remind students that if the Magnetic Lasso tool starts to follow the wrong pathway, they can use CTRL+Z or the Delete or Backspace key to erase their last fastening point. The can start over by pressing CTRL+D. They can also click to add fastening points.

Pages 215–219

Rubric

Student Data File

Project 5-4 ▶ **Add Layers** Students finish modifying the car image they started in Project 5-3. They will change the color of the car using the Hue and Saturation command and add a new background using the Layers palette. **(Data File 5-4, Solution File 5-4, Rubric 5-4)**

Manipulate Layers Look at the figure of the Layers palette on page 215. Ask students how many layers are visible in the figure. *(Three: a Background layer, a Frost layer, and a Frame layer)*. Point out that the Frame layer is selected. The layer's opacity is set to 47 percent. Tell students that this means that the Frame layer is partially transparent. Notice, also, that a Blending mode has been set to Lighten. This means that this layer will interact with the layers below it. In this case, the Frame layer will lighten the Frost and Background layers for a compelling effect.

Order Layers Make sure that students check their details, particularly the order of their layers. The Reflection layer should be under the New Car layer, or it will violate our sense of belief.

Pages 220–223

Rubric

Student Data File

Project 5-5 ▶ **Apply a Mask** Students use a layer mask to alter a photograph of the ancient structure, Stonehenge, to make it look more dramatic. **(Data File 5-5, Solution File 5-5, Rubric 5-5)**

Provide Flexibility with Masks There will be times when a client will request a minor change in an image. This minor change may require major work, unless the graphic designer has already planned for the possibility by using masks, which let you make changes without having to completely redo the entire picture. If a client would like more or less detail in the image, the mask will simply need to be changed with a black or white brush.

Choose Grayscale Colors Masks are always grayscale images and cannot be edited with color brushes. Shades of grey can be painted to create various levels of transparency. Grayscale gradients can also be used on masks for a smoother effect.

Modify Masks Students may need to know that masks can be modified. They must: 1) click on the mask in the Layers palette (there will be no visible change), 2) choose a black or white color from the Color Picker, and 3) use a paintbrush to paint in the workspace. Black will hide the image beneath the mask, while white will make the image visible. Shades of grey create different levels of transparency.

⚠️ **Erase with Care** Using an eraser tool, rather than a mask, is not recommended because erasers actually destroy information, which you may not be able to recover.

⚠️ **Control Proportions** Students may accidentally squish or squash images when resizing them. Encourage students to get into the habit of holding the Shift key when resizing objects in order to constrain the proportions. Students may also use the Image>Image Size command to key an exact set of dimensions.

Pages 224–228

Rubric

Student Data File

Project 5-6 ➤ **Retouch a Photo** Students retouch a photograph that has many common image problems, including red eye, a blemish, and poor lighting. They will use the Clone Stamp tool and adjust histogram color levels to modify the photograph. (**Data File 5-6, Solution File 5-6, Rubric 5-6**)

✍️ **Improve Pictures** Ask students if they have ever taken a picture that they liked a lot, but one little thing in the photo ruined it. Discuss with students what kind of little things can ruin a picture. Students are likely to mention red eyes, blemishes, messed-up hair, or something odd in the background. All these things can be corrected with the proper use of Photoshop.

✍️ **Edit with the Histogram** Read about histograms on page 225. Students may have learned about histograms in math class. In Photoshop, a histogram is a chart that shows the color values in an image. Remind students that all colors have a specific, numerical value to the computer. When editing tonal ranges in Photoshop, using the histogram can create reliable results.

✍️ **Select Brushes** When they are using the Clone tool, suggest that students use a hard-edged, round brush with a 35 percent opacity. They should choose a size that is suitable for the size of the image they are painting over. For objects with straight sides or rectangular shape, students should use a square brush.

⚠️ **Add an Adjustment Layer** To avoid directly editing pixels (and preserve the original data in case of future changes), students will be adding an "adjustment layer." The adjustment layer will adjust the view of all the layers below it. Double-clicking adjustment layers allows students to refine the adjustments. Students can also single-click on the adjustment layer mask and use a black or white paintbrush to make modifications.

Pages 229–233

Rubric

Student Data File

Project 5-7 ➤ **Create a Photo Montage** Students create an imaginary photo montage framed by a vignette effect. Students also learn to flatten the image when they save it. (**Data File 5-7, Solution File 5-7, Rubric 5-7**)

Observe Shadows Students have very little practice observing their world and tend to be uncertain about how to create compelling shadows. Point students to page 229, and observe that shadows are opposite the light source. Also, point out that shadows follow the shape of the surface upon which they lie. If possible, use a direct light to create shadows and highlights on objects in your classroom. This way students can directly observe the way light effects can be used to add realism.

Select the Right Layer Many students will forget to select the flower layer before using Layer>New Layer>Via Copy and will instead create a disembodied baby arm in their document. If students do this accidentally, make sure they undo the previous action and select the flower layer first.

Save Flat and Layered Versions Advise students to save two versions: one that is flat and one that still has layer information. This gives the designer a version they can share with the client and printers and a different version that can be easily edited. Save the layered version of this assignment as **Flower Baby.psd**, and save the flat version as **Flower Baby FLAT.psd**. Saving as a TIFF may help to avoid problems since TIFFs can now contain layering information.

Pages 234–238

Rubric

| Project 5-8 > | **Create Effects and Images with Filters** Students use filters to create images of a planet, stars, and a nebula. Students learn

how to apply effects with many Photoshop filters. Since students are actually creating images, rather than just modifying them, their final image may look different from the solution file and Figure 5.56 on page 238. Encourage them to be creative. **(Solution File 5-8, Rubric 5-8)**

Go Online Have students look at the final figure on page 238. Tell students that in this project they will not be manipulating an image; they will be create an image from scratch. Encourage students to look at images of planets on the Web sites of The Jet Propulsion Laboratory (www.jpl.nasa.gov) or NASA, National Aeronautic Space Agency (www.nasa.gov). Challenge students to find examples of nebulae and gas giants and to explain what they are. *(Nebulae are interstellar space gas. Gas giants are planets—like Jupiter, Saturn, Uranus, and Neptune—that are composed primarily of gasses and contain very little actual solid matter.)*

Preview Filters Filters can be used to create textures, adjust lighting, or create a variety of other effects. Stacking filters lets you combine effects. Photoshop CS2 has a way to preview the effects in the Filter Gallery (see the figure on page 234). To open the Filter Gallery, choose **Filter>Filter Gallery**. Click the **New Effect Layer** icon at the bottom of the Stack Filters pane. Select the new layer, and click one of the effects in the gallery. Repeat for as many filters as you need to apply the desired effect to an object. Have students try this to experiment with filters.

Skills Studio

Create a Magazine Cover

Students will be creating a cover by using a "green screen" technique. They will photograph a model in front of a green or blue background (or use a data file) and then replace the background with photograph of a soccer field. Students might already know that many special effect movies, and even realistic movies, use this effect to create interesting locations, like huge space ship interiors, or to add digital effects like monsters or laser saber lights. Ask students to consider why green or blue are good choices for backgrounds. *(The colors green and blue occur least frequently in human skin. Therefore, these colors are easiest to remove when you want to isolate the subject so you can add a new background.)*

Pages 240–243

Rubric

Student Data File

Project 5-9 ▶ **Take a Digital Photograph** To create a compelling magazine cover, students photograph their subject in front of a blue or green screen (or use a data file) so they can easily remove the background from the picture and replace it with another image. If a digital camera is not available in the classroom, use Data File 5-9 and begin this project at Step 10. **(Data File 5-9, Solution File 5-9, Rubric 5-9)**

Set up the Shot Use the diagram in Figure 5.58 on page 241 to help set up an area for students to take their own picture. Use green or blue butcher paper along a wall. If these are not available, virtually any plain background (such as a door) will work, though it may be more challenging. Encourage students to leave a little distance between themselves and the wall, since cast shadows and reflected light are harder to remove from the picture. If possible, place a soft light behind the student to reduce the chance of casting a shadow onto the paper.

Reduce Shadows Students may find it challenging to remove themselves from shadows against the background. Remind students that they can add a layer mask which can be altered by clicking on the mask and using a small, round-feathered black or white paintbrush to hide or reveal details as needed.

Pages 244–246

Project 5-10 ▶ **Lay Out a Magazine Cover** Students use Photoshop to create a magazine cover that combines text with the photograph they created in Project 5-9. **(Data Files 5-10a to 5-10c, Solution File 5-10, Rubric 5-10)**

Analyze Covers Ask students to look at the final figure on page 246. Have them identify ways that the magazine cover attempts to capture the reader's attention. They might say that the model looks directly at the camera, the photo overlaps the nameplate, and the callouts and titles get our attention. Notice that the name of the magazine is not covered enough to affect readers' recognition.

Manage Layers Ask students to look at the images of the Layers palette in this project. Instruct them to pay particular attention to the order of the layers and to notice that some layers have been grouped in folders. This helps to manage the many layers in this document and reduce confusion. Show students how to create folders by clicking on the Create New Group button at the bottom of the Layers palette.

Name Layers Encourage students to name their layers something that is recognizable, since the thumbnail image in the Layers palette is not always easy to identify.

Prevent Problems with Text In general, Photoshop does not handle text very well. The text rasterizes upon printout and can appear quite blocky. This situation can be avoided by: a) using a high resolution like 300 ppi, b) using a word processor or layout software to key the text, or c) using a drawing program like Illustrator to lay out the text.

Print with Bleeds Most printers will not print to the edge of the page because it can cause paper jams. If yours does not, have students print on paper that is 11 × 17 inches and use crop (trim) marks where the page should be trimmed to create the size they want. This will allow students to create a "bleed," which takes the image all the way to the edge of the page. In the professional world, this feature costs a little extra money.

ASSESS

Evaluate Encourage students to use the project rubrics and the Review and Revise checklists to be sure that they have completed the key steps to their projects. Encourage students to proofread and assist each other. Students learn best when they are teaching each other. Consider giving bonus points for well-designed projects for both the student and the student who evaluated his/her work.

CLOSE

Compare Print Images to Monitor Images Ask students to compare printouts of their work with the image on the computer monitor. Some students may have chosen colors outside the CMYK range of your printer or have a better understanding of bleeds and crop marks, while other students may have a better insight into resolution and its effects. Ask students to exchange their printouts with each other and evaluate one another's work.

IN THE WORKPLACE

GRAPHIC DESIGNERS

Career Activity

All designers need to have a portfolio to show prospective employers the work that best showcases their extensive ability and imagination. Freelance graphic designers must find their own clients and will find a varied portfolio especially useful.

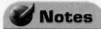
Notes

Chapter 5 Assessment Answers

Use the following Reading Check and Critical Thinking answers as a guide to help evaluate student understanding of the core concepts. Requiring that your students write in complete sentences will help you grade faster and promote good writing skills. You can have students write answers in their desktop publishing journals, or students can answer these questions at the computer by accessing the Reading Check and Critical Thinking activities on the Online Learning Center at **glencoe.com**.

Page 248

Reading Check

1. Raster images are made of pixels, while vector images are stored using math. Raster images, therefore, often look more realistic than vector images, use a large file size, and are not easily scalable without degrading the content.

2. Resolution refers to image quality, often measured in terms of pixels per inch.

3. When layers are linked in Photoshop, they still retain their independent nature and can be unlinked later, similar to the grouping feature in Microsoft Word and Publisher. When layers are flattened, actual pixel information is destroyed and cannot be easily recalled.

4. The Magic Wand selection tool would be better to use when selecting images with consistent coloring. Use the Lasso selection tools when an object has an unusual shape.

5. A JPG is better for the Internet due to its high compression. TIFFs are generally far too large for the Internet.

Critical Thinking

6. The method of publishing affects the design in many ways. Some of the design elements affected include the choice of fonts, the number of colors, the orientation of the document, and the number of pixels per inch.

7. Use a raster image when realism is important, and the image will not need to be resized significantly for different purposes.

8. Use multiple layers to create interaction and compelling effects, to help with editing, and to avoid damaging original data.

9. Use a combination of selection tools like the different Lassos and the Add/Subtract commands on the Options toolbar to select a complex image and separate it from a complex background.

10. Because of the image's small size and low ppi, the image would pixelate, becoming blurry and/or blocky. Resizing a raster image more than 10 percent is not recommended for professional-grade work.

Evaluate Assessment activities allow students to demonstrate their understanding of concepts and skills learned throughout this project. Because of time constraints, students may not be able to complete every activity suggested. Match assignments to student ability levels using the leveled projects (★ Easy, ★★ Medium, and ★★★ Challenging). Rubrics are available to evaluate projects on the Teacher Resource DVD and the Online Learning Center at **glencoe.com**.

Page 248

Rubric

1. Independent Practice ★

Photo Tour Introduce the project by giving some examples of symbolism. Have student groups brainstorm a list of characteristics and work as a group to determine objects in the school that can symbolize those characteristics. Encourage them to be creative and original. To save time and encourage students to be prepared, emphasize the time factor and award points for meeting the timed deadline when taking pictures. Create a rubric that rewards originality and positive traits. If possible, have students present their projects to the class through a PowerPoint presentation. Give a specific time frame that their presentation should use (such as 5 minutes), and award students points based on presentation style and whether they hit the 5 minute mark precisely. **(Rubric IP 5-1)**

Page 249

Rubric

2. Independent Practice ★★

Create a Space Creature Discuss how various animals are uniquely equipped for their surroundings. Animals who live at the bottom of the sea, for instance, are able to withstand immense pressures and temperatures and have limited eyesight. Bats, being nocturnal, are blind but they can emit sonic waves, which allow them to "hear." Ask students to research a particular planet in our solar system or give them the statistics for a make-believe planet. Ask them to develop a hypothesis as to how a space alien might be uniquely adapted to that particular environment. Use Photoshop filters and photographs to create a unique space alien for that habitat. Have students write an explanation citing three adaptive features, or have students deliver an oral report to the class. **(Rubric IP 5-2)**

Page 249

Rubric

3. Independent Practice ★★★

Create an American Montage As a class, or in small groups, have students brainstorm important locations in the United States. They might include famous battlefields, monuments, famous companies, cities, or national parks. Have students pick a theme and do some research. Ask students to find pictures related to the theme and the exact location of each element. Students should then create an American montage, complete with photographs, callouts to the exact location, and a brief description of each item. Students may find Google Maps a useful feature. **(Rubric IP 5-3)**

Reteaching Activities

Peer Teaching Some of the concepts in this chapter, such as layers and masks, might be difficult for students to understand. If any students are having difficulties, pair them with more advanced students who are comfortable using these skills. Then have them work as a team to review any projects and skills that might have caused problems.

Complete Worksheets Have students complete Worksheets 3A and 3B, which can be found in Part 3 of this TRM, on the Teacher Resource DVD, or at the Online Learning Center at **glencoe.com**.

Enrichment Activities

Retouch Photographs Students who are comfortable with the skills taught in this chapter might be eager to apply these skills to their own photographs. Have them bring in digital photographs that need to be retouched, and have them experiment with Photoshop's tools. If possible, allow them to scan old family photographs so that they can create a digital family album.

 Enrichment If students need an additional challenge, have them complete the activities in the Online Learning Center at **glencoe.com**.

Notes

Integrating Publisher and Photoshop

Skills You Will Learn

Workshop Foundations: Find Photo Resources

- Find resources for photographs
- Determine legal use of a photograph

Workshop Toolbox: Image Resolution

- Evaluate resolution needs
- Identify printer resolutions

Project 6-1 Create a Postcard

- Insert a custom shape
- Add filters
- Apply a type mask
- Add styles
- Save in a new format

Project 6-2 Add Text with Publisher

- Insert a Photoshop file
- Lay out a postcard
- Print multiple copies on a sheet

Project 6-3 Create a Banner

- Saturate colors
- Add layer masks
- Apply gradients
- Add a layer style

Project 6-4 Print an Oversized Document

- Set print specifications
- Assemble printed pages

Project 6-5 Blend Images

- Blend layers
- Apply the Clone tool
- Apply the Smudge tool

Project 6-6 Create a Booklet

- Apply PARC principles

Skills Studio

Create a Newsletter

Project 6-7 Lay Out a Newsletter in Publisher

- Lay out text elements and images in a multi-page newsletter
- Link text boxes
- Add a masthead
- Add Design Gallery objects

Project 6-8 Add Photoshop Effects

- Add a textured background
- Apply a master page
- Insert page numbers

Page 250

Start-Up Skills

Find Images Online In this chapter, students learn how to integrate Photoshop and Publisher to create complex documents using text and images. Ask students where they can find images to use in a design. They might answer that they can create original images, scan pictures, buy a photograph, or search the Internet.

Have students go online to look at some Web sites that offer images. The Smithsonian Institute (**www.si.edu**) and NASA (**www.nasa.org**) offer many photos that students can use in their publications. There are also *stock photography* sites, such as **www.corbis.com** and **www.gettyimages.com**, which sell a wide range of images to be used in professional publications.

These sites also allow the user to download "composite" images ("comps" for short) that can be used when creating a design. Designers use the comps in the layout, and then show the designs to the client. If the client likes the photograph, then the designer buys the rights to use the image and bills the client for the costs. (**Note:** These Web sites have material that may be inappropriate for a classroom. Know your students and your district policy. Be sure to carefully monitor student activity when using any sort of image search engine.)

Page 250

Design Process: Posters and Banners

Describe Images and Oversized Publications Ask students to describe photographs they have seen in large formats like posters, banner, or billboards. They might describe advertisements, movie posters, signs for local organizations, and so on. Have them use the chart on page 250 to describe some of the specific design requirements needed to create an oversized image in the formats they have discussed.

Quick Write Activity

Justify Copyrights Ask your students to imagine that they are professional photographers who discover that someone has downloaded one of their photos from the Internet and used it without permission in a printed brochure for a fast food restaurant. Ask students to write a short letter to the person who violated their copyright explaining why it is important to respect the ownership rights of photographers and other creators. Students should explain why they feel entitled to receive compensation and/or acknowledgment for their work.

LEARNING LINK

This chapter teaches the foundations of integrating Photoshop and Publisher to create documents using both text and images. Students will need to rely on the Photoshop skills that were introduced in Chapter 5. Since Photoshop is primarily a graphics program, it is important for students to learn to use layout software such as Publisher, which contains powerful text-editing tools.

Workshop Foundations   Pages 251–252

Find Photo Resources

FOCUS

Focus Activity

Study Photos in Advertisements Ask students to bring in magazine advertisements that feature photographs. Have them determine whether the featured photographs could have been licensed from a stock photography agency or if they were most likely commissioned for the specific ad. Explain that stock photographs cover a wide range of subjects, and the images are meant to be placed in any context relating to the subject. For example, textbooks often use stock photographs of high school students. Have them evaluate when a designer might choose a stock photograph and when the designer requires an original image.

> **You Will Learn To:**
> - Find resources for photographs
> - Determine the legal use of a photograph

Page 251

Before you Read Activity

Study with a Buddy Students might find it easier to study and evaluate information when they pair up with another person. Help students find partners that complement each other. They might have different strengths or just have fun challenging each other to see who knows more. This is a good way to encourage peer tutoring. Building this relationship helps in other ways. Students who need help will have someone to rely on besides you. More advanced students can polish their skills by teaching them to others.

Page 251

Key Term Activity

Respect Copyrights Write the three key terms in three columns on the board and define them. Ask students to identify when materials can be used under: fair use guidelines (*when they are copied for educational purposes or used in news programs and some documentary films*); public domain (*government-owned images and very old books*); or require a royalty (*music, films, and material used for profit*).

Key Term Definitions

fair use An exception to Copyright Law that allows for limited copyright infringement for the purposes for teaching and criticism. (page 251)

public domain Materials that are so old that they no longer have a copyright, or materials that are published by the government or are declared free to the public. (page 251)

royalty A fee that is paid in order to use copyrighted materials. (page 251)

TEACH

Teach Activity

Explore Images in the Public Domain Ask students to research Web sites that feature images that are in the public domain. Good resources for public domain material include the American Memory Collection at the Library of Congress (**www.loc.gov**). The collection of images contains a Copyright and Restrictions page with clear instructions regarding use. NASA's excellent images are also in the public domain at **www.nasa.gov/multimedia/imagegallery/index**.

 Understand Intellectual Property Like other works of art, photographs are considered intellectual property. *Intellectual property* is the ownership of the expression of ideas, like books, music, art, films, photographs, software, and even fonts. A person or organization that took the time, effort, and expense to create or develop these works should be compensated. Violating somebody's copyright can lead to a lawsuit, fines, and a loss of credibility. While most schools can use copyrighted materials under the fair-use guidelines that allow limited free use for the purposes of instruction, the business world (for which we are training our students) must follow copyright laws.

ASSESS

Reading Check

1. Photographs can be obtained by 1) taking your own pictures, 2) scanning photographs or pictures from magazines or books, or 3) using the Internet.

2. When working professionally, it is very important to carefully research who owns the photograph and determine whether it is possible to license the right to use it. It is also important to determine if the image is of sufficient quality to meet your needs. Spending time and effort working with photographs that you cannot use is not an efficient way to work.

CLOSE

Understand Fair Use Explain to students that nearly every image that they can locate is copyrighted material. Unless the image is from an original source over 100 years old, somebody owns the rights to the image. While schools have more lenient copyright obligations under fair-use guidelines, they are still liable for training students to function outside the school environment. Encourage students to know their copyright obligations and limitations.

Workshop Toolbox Page 253

Image Resolution

FOCUS

Focus Activity

Reduce Resolution for Web Images Ask students to describe the experience of waiting for an Internet page to load. Ask them if they waited patiently or simply moved on to another site. Explain that most images on the Internet are small, low-quality pictures. Many Internet pictures will be around 200 kilobytes, while professional grade pictures may be 10 megabytes. The reason for this discrepancy is that, in order to avoid driving away potential customers, Web sites reduce picture quality to limit the amount of time it takes to download a Web page.

> **You Will Learn To:**
> - Evaluate resolution needs
> - Identify printer resolutions

Page 253

Key Term Activity

Choose the Right Resolution Have students fold a sheet of paper in half to make two columns, one labeled "High Resolution," the other labeled "Low Resolution." Brainstorm a list of items they might print themselves or take to a printer and write students' responses on the board. These could include brochures, business cards, an announcement for a meeting, a book report, or a book of poetry.

Ask students to list which items they would ideally prefer to print at high resolution (greater ppi) and which items they would print using a low resolution (lower ppi) setting. Students may indicate that more important items such as business cards or books, and documents containing images, such as brochures or annual reports, should be printed at high resolution for better quality. Documents such as meeting announcements, handouts without images, or rough drafts can be printed more quickly and inexpensively at a lower resolution.

> ### Key Term Definitions
>
> **pixels per inch (ppi)** The measurement used in order to keep track of an image's resolution. (page 253)

TEACH

Teach Activity

Control File Size Remind students that graphic artists control file size by managing image resolution, based on the medium for publication. If the image is to be displayed on screen, then the images do not need to be any larger than screen resolution (72 ppi for PCs or 96 ppi for Macs). A higher resolution image will simply slow down the computer and will not add to the image quality. Most desktop printers can print 150 ppi fairly well, while laser printers print 300 ppi images. Special paper and higher resolution settings can also produce incredible results, but these settings can be expensive and time consuming. Professional printing presses (such as offset presses or imagesetters) may need higher resolution images.

Answers to Workshop Toolbox Activities

Page 253

Sidebar

To determine the ppi setting for a printer, double the linescreen setting. A printer with a 150 linescreen can print a 300 ppi image. Anything more would be a waste of time with no increase in quality.

ASSESS

Reading Check

1. To create a Web site, use 72 ppi for PCs or 96 ppi for Macs.
2. To show an image, a computer must remember color data for each pixel in an image. When Photoshop images are created with multiple layers, masks, and blending modes, the amount of data is multiplied. Images with higher resolutions have more information to remember and can cause a computer to slow down.

CLOSE

Review Resolution Students may have a hard time understanding resolution concepts if they are not printing documents. If there are no printing restrictions in your classroom, create your own examples of documents printed at different resolutions. Show students one of the projects on their monitors, and then show them printouts at 72 ppi, 150 ppi, and 300 ppi (if possible).

Chapter 6 Projects

Pages 254–285

Pages 254–285

FOCUS

Focus Activity

Integrate Programs Explain to students that this new chapter is different because this is the first time students will integrate software programs. They have learned about several specialized programs: Word (word processor), Publisher (layout software), and Photoshop (bitmap editor). To combine programs, students will first have to determine the needs of the project, then create the individual pieces using the appropriate software, and finally lay out the page. In this chapter, most designs will use Publisher after the supporting images are created in Photoshop. (The Skills Studio is the only exception.)

 Go Online **PREVIEW**

Before You Begin Students can use the chapter **PowerPoint** presentations and **rubrics** at the Online Learning Center to determine what is expected *before* they complete a project. Students can view the PowerPoint slides on their own computers, or you can project them to preview chapter concepts and show examples of the finished projects. You might also display project solutions so students can easily refer to them while they work. (Presentations and rubrics are also provided on the Teacher Resource DVD for your convenience).

glencoe.com

Projects

Project 6-1
Create a Postcard

Project 6-2
Add Text with Publisher

Project 6-3
Create a Banner

Project 6-4
Print an Oversized Document

Project 6-5
Blend Images

Project 6-6
Create a Booklet

Skills Studio

Project 6-7
Lay Out a Newsletter in Publisher

Project 6-8
Add Photoshop Effects

Key Term Activity

Add Definitions to Dictionaries Have students add the definitions to their desktop publishing vocabulary dictionaries. For variety, have students create fill-in-the-blank sentences with enough information to help determine the missing word. Use the best of these sentences on your next test or quiz, and watch students become motivated to make the best sentences they can!

Key Term Definitions

JPEG, also JPG (Joint Photographic Experts Group) A raster file format commonly used for photographs and images. This efficient format is frequently used on the Internet, for low to medium resolution needs, or for pictures that do not require transparency. (page 254)

native format A file format created specifically for a single software program. (page 258)

grayscale A color system that changes from white to black with shades of gray in between. (page 261)

tile print A method of printing an image that is larger than what the printer could normally print. The document is divided and the parts printed on separate pages that are later assembled into the complete image. (page 266)

clone To copy a range of pixels and paste the pixels into another location in an image. (page 269)

plagiarism Name given to the practice of using someone else's material without crediting the source. It is like stealing, and can result in stiff penalties. (page 273)

TEACH

Teach Activity

Preview Chapter Projects In Chapter 5, students created images but did not combine them with text to create a publication. Have students look through this chapter, and have them explain how Photoshop images are integrated with Publisher documents. See if students can identify the type of document, the way the images are used, and the audience and purposes of the final publications.

⚠ **Resave Solution Files** Photoshop solution files are provided in native format. Follow directions in the projects to resave the files for use with Publisher.

Teaching Tips ✍ and Troubleshooting Tips ⚠ for Projects

Pages 254–257

▶ **Project 6-1**

Create a Postcard Students create the image for a postcard from Texas, using filters, layer styles, and a type mask. They will complete the postcard in Project 6-2. **(Data File 6-1, Solution File 6-1, Rubric 6-1)**

✍ **Identify Postcard Formatting** Ask students to identify the features of a postcard. Typically, there is a graphic on the front, and the back is split into two areas: one for the address and one to write a quick note. The location for a stamp is indicated in the upper right-hand corner, and a brief description of the image is printed at the top, bottom, or middle of the card.

⚠ **Save Two Versions** Make sure that students save two versions of this assignment. One version is saved as a PSD for historical purposes in case they need to make editing changes or they want to use pieces of what they have already created. The other version should be saved as a JPEG document for integration with Publisher in the next lesson.

Pages 258–260

Rubric

Project 6-2 → **Add Text with Publisher** In this project, students will insert the image they created in Project 6-1 into a postcard created with Publisher. Students should check the ruler to see the actual size of the document. **(Solution File 6-2, Rubric 6-2)**

Review Native and Compatible Formats Students need to understand why Photoshop files must be saved in different formats in order to work with Publisher. Photoshop and Illustrator are both published by Adobe, while Word and Publisher are made by Microsoft. Each application produces files using its own native file format: .PSD (Photoshop), .AI (Illustrator), .DOC (Word), and .PUB (Publisher). To make these programs work together, we must use compatible, or interchangeable, file formats. Interchangeable file formats are formats that can be read by different software applications. Examples of picture file formats include .GIF, .JPEG, and .TIFF.

Identify Compatible Formats Have students copy the chart on page 259 into their notebooks. Discuss the advantages of each of the formats and whether the format supports transparent information. Transparent information becomes important when an image must fade into the background or when the image is not a rectangle. Images that are not rectangular will have a white box behind them if a file format that does not support transparency is used.

Insert Pictures Students will frequently try to just copy and paste images from one program to another. This is not an effective method because Windows will use WMF as the compatible file format between programs. The WMF format can reduce image quality and make it more difficult to work with the image. Instead, students should always use Insert>Picture>From File.

Save Ink To save ink when printing the postcard, you may prefer that students print only one copy per sheet. Choose **File>Page Setup**, click **Change Copies per Sheet**, and then check **Single copy per sheet**.

Pages 261–265

Rubric

Student Data File

Project 6-3 → **Create a Banner** In this project, students create a custom-sized banner, adding effects and using layer masks. They will print the banner in Project 6-4. **(Data Files 6-3, Solution File 6-3, Rubric 6-3)**

Analyze the Banner's Message The banner students are creating uses the proverb, "A handful of trade is a handful of gold." Ask students to write in their notebooks, or discuss as a class, what this phrase could mean and how the image complements this message. Explain that "trade," in this case, refers to a vocation, a job, not the trading of goods. Students should see that the proverb suggests that learning a new career or skill is worth money, like finding a treasure. The image illustrates this idea by showing gold at the end of the rainbow. Ask students to explain how the font, the keyboard, and the high-rise office buildings also reinforce the message.

Enrichment Activity If students are not sure what a proverb is, explain that they are wise sayings that have been passed down from generation to generation. Some common examples are: "A journey of a thousand miles begins with a single step" and "A stitch in time saves nine." Ask students what these two sayings mean, and see if they know any other proverbs. As an enrichment assignment, ask students to create an image that illustrates a favorite proverb.

Integrate Software Students may wonder why the text for their banners is created in Photoshop, rather than Publisher. Creating effective text can be challenging because each software application has strengths and weaknesses. Word processing and layout software generally do not create spectacular effects. Photo editors like Photoshop can create special text effects relatively easily, but the software may have problems creating text that does not rasterize or become difficult to read at different sizes.

In this project, Photoshop is used to create the large titles and add effects to the text. However, if more text was needed, or if there were more complex layouts, students would need to use layout software. As students become more skilled, they will learn how to integrate programs to use the strongest features of each.

Explain Layer Masks Students will have a number of opportunities to use layer masks in projects. It may be difficult for them to understand how the masks respond to black and white foreground colors. Demonstrate the effects of different grayscale colors by using a brush with a mask. For example, after Step 9 of this project, do not immediately apply a gradient. Instead, show students what happens to the City image when they use a white, gray, or black brush. Black adds pixels, covering the image more. White removes pixels, revealing more of the image beneath the mask.

Pages 266–268

Rubric

Project 6-4 ▶ **Print an Oversized Document** Students use Publisher to tile print the banner they created in Project 6-3. They will then assemble the individual pages to create one large banner. Students will have another opportunity to apply tile printing skills in Project 8-6. **(Solution File 6-4, Rubric 6-4)**

Tile Print Documents Ask students to tell you the size of the banner they created in Project 6-3. Students should notice that the banner is 28 inches long. Since a piece of paper is 11 inches long, how will they print the design? Students basically have three choices: 1) buy and use special paper to print a long banner, 2) take the design to a professional print shop, or 3) tile print the design. This is where layout software really shines. No application other than layout software can tile print.

Allow Enough Time With tile printing, the computer will recognize an oversized document and will divide the image onto separate pages and print each section separately. Parts of the design will be printed on two pages to allow the pages to overlap. When you overlap the pages in a tile printed project, the seams are a little less noticeable. It takes some time to align the pages properly, so be sure to allow about 20 minutes for all students to assemble their projects.

⚠ **Expect Imperfect Printing** Some pages might not print perfectly. Printers must load pages using rollers and moving parts. When a page slips slightly, it is out of register. It is normal for some pages to be slightly out of register. With better printers, this will happen less often, but even expensive offset presses sometimes get out of register. The only solution is to reprint, but if that is not an option in your class, students have to do the best they can with their printouts. Have students decide whether it is better to line up the text first or the image first. Generally, the results are better when students align the text first.

Pages 269–272

Rubric

Student Data File

Project 6-5 ▶ **Blend Images** Students use Photoshop to blend two different animals together to create a new species. They will use cloning to fill in the background in the image. They will then use their new creature as the subject of a booklet in Project 6-6. (**Data File 6-5a and 6-5b, Solution File 6-5, Rubric 6-5**)

✍ **View Photoshop Images** If it is permitted at your school, and you feel the content is suitable, direct students to **www.worth1000.com**. This site contains contests and tutorials for using Photoshop, as well as many imaginative Photoshop pictures, including animal crossbreeds.

⚠ **Modify Masks** Show students how the mask is modified in Step 10 by using either a black, white, or gray brush. The mask prevents the image below from being damaged. Have students look at page 272 and see the end product before they begin. Remind students that they can use the History palette if they do not like the results of their blending.

Pages 273–276

Rubric

Project 6-6 ▶ **Create a Booklet** Students use Publisher to make a booklet that describes the Komodo giraffe they created in Project 6-5. The booklet will include a reference page to cite the information sources. (**Data Files 6-6a to 6-6e, Solution File 6-6, Rubric 6-6**)

✍ **Identify Reliable Sources** In Project 6-5, students saw how images can be altered and manipulated using software. Ask students how they can tell if the images and information they find on a Web site are trustworthy. Students can use the following guidelines for evaluating a site's reliability.

- Check the URL. Sites with ".edu" or ".gov" are generally reliable, as the source is an educational institution or the U.S. government. A "~" indicates that the site is being rented from another source, a sign that it should not be trusted.
- Look for reliable, recognizable sources like **www.nationalgeographic.com**.
- Check for bibliographic references. Reliable sites often include references to source and bibliographic material.
- Be wary if links are dead, and the page layout, graphics, and special effects look unprofessional.
- Make sure the information can be verified with other reliable sources. Information that is unsubstantiated should be treated with suspicion.

⚠ **Apply Style Sheets** Students are likely to have a hard time keeping track of the fonts, font sizes, colors, leading, and margins, so that they are consistent across the entire document. Encourage them to use style sheets.

Skills Studio

Pages 277–285

Create a Newsletter

The Skills Studio will show students a different way to integrate Photoshop and Publisher. Rather than first creating a graphic in Publisher and then inserting it into a Publisher document, these projects will create a Publisher document and then add graphic effects with Photoshop. This will allow students to see how to create an eye-catching newsletter by combining Photoshop's filter effects with Publisher's master page feature.

Pages 278–282

Rubric   **Student Data File**

Project 6-7 ➤ **Lay Out a Newsletter in Publisher** Students lay out a newsletter in Publisher. They will finish the newsletter by adding graphic effects using Photoshop tools in Project 6-8. **(Data Files 6-7a to 6-7k, Solution File 6-7, Rubric 6-7)**

✍ **Increase Readability** Newsletters contain a lot of information in a small amount of space. See if students can identify all the tricks newsletter designers use to make information as readable as possible. Students might point out the use of captions, pictures, wide leading, wide margins, and articles that continue on inside pages to allow more headlines on the first page.

⚠ **Time-Saving Tips** Creating newsletters can be time consuming and tedious. To preserve class time, this assignment can be shortened by creating the layout in advance as a data file, allowing students to practice with the style sheets. You can also have students lay out and create only one of the four pages.

Pages 283–285

Rubric   **Student Data File**

Project 6-8 ➤ **Add Photoshop Effects** Students finish the newsletter they started in Project 6-7 by creating a background texture using in Photoshop and applying it to a master page in Publisher. **(Solution File 6-8, Rubric 6-8)**

✍ **Design for Effective Communication** Ask students to look at the final layout of the newsletter, as shown on page 285. Which of the four pages is the most important? Answer: The bottom half of the fourth page is the most important. Since most newsletters are mailed (including this one), the last page is the one that the audience will see first. It is this page that will encourage them to open the document or not. Be sure to place a table of contents or other information to attract the reader's attention on this page.

⚠️ **Save in a Compatible Format** Make sure students do not overlook Steps 10 and 11, or they will get confused. After creating the texture in Photoshop, they will save the Photoshop document in a suitable format, like TIFF or JPEG. Then they will leave Photoshop while they set up a master page for the newsletter in Publisher. It is not until Step 16 that they actually insert the background into the Publisher file.

ASSESS

Evaluate Encourage students to use the project rubrics and the Review and Revise checklists to be sure that they have completed the key steps to their projects. Encourage students to proofread and assist each other. Students learn best when they are teaching each other. Consider giving bonus points for well-designed projects for both the student and the student who evaluated his/her work. Use the stamp described in Chapters 1–4 of this section of the manual to grade projects.

CLOSE

Class Discussion Finish this unit by discussing with students what they learned about working with images in Photoshop. They should understand that the pictures they see every day may not show the "real thing" and that Photoshop can be used to manipulate pictures and the people that view them. Ask students how this knowledge affects the way they judge any media that uses images.

Page 286

IN THE WORKPLACE

DIGITAL IMAGING TECHNICIANS
Career Activity

Since digital imaging technicians work with sophisticated techniques for editing photographs, it is helpful for these technicians to be familiar with photography, photographic terminology, and photographic principles. They have to be able to communicate effectively with photographers and designers to create an image that meets the client's needs.

Chapter 6 Assessment Answers

Use the following Reading Check and Critical Thinking answers as a guide to help evaluate student understanding of the core concepts. Requiring that your students write in complete sentences will help you grade faster and promote good writing skills. You can have students write answers in their desktop publishing journals, or students can answer these questions at the computer by accessing the Reading Check and Critical Thinking activities on the Online Learning Center at **glencoe.com**.

Page 287

Reading Check

1. Native file formats are file formats used for a particular software application, while interchangeable file formats allow documents to be inserted or edited in other applications.

2. For on-screen resolutions, use 72 ppi for PC's or 96 ppi for Mac computers.

3. Use a black paintbrush to hide the image underneath a mask or a white paintbrush to reveal parts of an image.

4. Answers will vary. Adobe's Text Warping feature will produce more professional results, but Publisher's WordArt feature is much easier to use. Being an opinion question, grade the reasoning behind the explanation.

5. Tile printing divides an image larger than a single page onto separate pages so it can be printed on multiple sheets.

Critical Thinking

6. Before you print a document, you need to know how the document will be distributed to its audience. Documents to be published in a magazine will need different handling from documents to be printed in a school newsletter. A magazine would probably be printed professionally, using high-resolution printers, especially for images. A newsletter could probably be printed on a local printer and copied, and it would not need such high resolution.

7. Word processors and layout software are the easiest programs to use for text documents, and drawing programs can be used for limited text, since the text is not rasterized, but remains a vector image. Bitmap editors (photo editors and painting programs) will rasterize the text, which will create a blocky or blurry image.

8. After using Photoshop, students should be able to see all the ways that images might be manipulated. Pictures with people may have eliminated skin blemishes or wrinkles, advertisements may use techniques that enhance the product's appearance, and even news photographs may be modified to create a more dramatic image.

9. When working with a client, find out how the design will be published. This information will help you determine the software application, or applications, you will need and the resolution necessary to get the best results possible.

10. When printing to a local desktop printer, 72 ppi is the most cost-effective method. While print quality will not be as good as 150 or 300 ppi, the print-out will be faster and use less ink.

Assessment activities allow students to demonstrate their understanding of concepts and skills learned throughout this project. Because of time constraints, students may not be able to complete every activity suggested. Match assignments to student ability levels using the leveled projects (★ Easy, ★★ Medium, and ★★★ Challenging). Rubrics are available to evaluate projects on the Teacher Resources DVD and the Online Learning Center at **glencoe.com**.

Page 287

Rubric

1. Independent Practice ★

Create a Postcard Students should create this project using both Photoshop and Publisher. Reward students for using the complete design process, accurate research, creating a thoughtful design, imaginatively relating the postcard to a particular location. Postcard designs should follow PARC principles, and both the image and the text should reinforce local area features and interests. Postcards should also contain standard postcard layout. Text should be clear, without pixelation, so students should plan to key smaller text in layout software. Use the requirements described on page 287 as a guide. **(Rubric IP 6-1)**

Page 288

Rubric

2. Independent Practice ★★

Create an Earth Day Banner Earth Day is celebrated April 22. You might want to coordinate this project with other classes, such as science or social studies, and actually get students involved in an Earth Day event. Have students research events and brainstorm project ideas. Encourage students to create a slogan for their banner and develop a theme that relates the graphics to the message. Students should use the bulleted text on page 288 as a guide for their design process and create designs based on PARC principles. **(Rubric IP 6-2)**

Page 288

Rubric

3. Independent Practice ★★★

Create a CD Cover and Insert Have students bring in their favorite CDs and analyze the elements in them and what features particularly stand out. Students may choose to create their CD cover using pictures of themselves, pictures of their favorite band members or a Photoshopped combination of both. Have students create a band name, logo, front and back cover art, and a booklet insert. Encourage them to have some fun with this project. Remind them that most albums will have around eight different songs. The insert should include songs and song descriptions. Students may choose to use already existing lyrics, gibberish, poetry, or original lyrics. Remind students that albums have a common design theme that should be carried throughout the entire booklet, from cover art to the final page. Layout grids and style sheets will keep booklet pages consistent. Students should follow the instruction on page 288. **(Rubric IP 6-3)**

Reteaching Activities

Experiment with Formats Have students open one of their Photoshop files and resave it in at least three other formats. (**Note:** Make sure that when they save, they use the Save As command.) Then have them insert the Photoshop file in its native format and the three new formats into a Publisher document. Have them try copying and pasting the Photoshop image into Publisher. If possible, let them print documents to see if there is a difference in print. Have them write down what happens with each attempt, making sure to include the format and procedure they used each time.

Finish Worksheets Have students complete Worksheets 6A and 6B, which can be found in Part 3 of this TRM, on the Teacher Resource DVD, or at the Online Learning Center at **glencoe.com**.

Enrichment Activities

Scan Photographs If you have a scanner in your classroom, show students how to use it and how to save the images that they scan. Then have students bring in photographs from home or magazines that they would like to use to create a movie poster. Have them decide the title and theme of the movie, and then use Photoshop to create a montage with the scanned photographs and the text for the poster. The poster should be tile printed.

Enrichment If students need an additional challenge, have them complete the activities in the Online Learning Center at **glencoe.com**.

Projects Across the Curriculum

Assessment activities allow students to demonstrate their understanding of concepts and skills learned throughout this project. Because of time constraints, students may not be able to complete every activity suggested. Match assignments to student ability levels using the leveled projects (★ Easy, ★★ Medium, and ★★★ Challenging). Rubrics are available to evaluate projects on the Teacher Resources DVD and the Online Learning Center at **glencoe.com**.

Page 289

Rubric

Project 1 Create a Personal Calendar ★

Encourage students to make these calendars as personal as possible, adding birthdays, special events that are important to the student, and recognized federal holidays. Encourage students to use scanners and digital cameras to create collages and custom calendars. Evaluate student projects based on the project requirements on page 289. (**Rubric PAC 3-1**)

Page 289

Rubric

Project 2 Create a Book Cover ★★

Have students create book covers for hypothetical books, their favorite books, or for books they are reading in other classes. Be sure to have them create graphics related to the story, a short description of the story, a biography of the author, and a teaser, such as an interesting quote, for the back cover. The text, images, and themes, should clearly be related and designed for a specific audience. Evaluate student projects based on the project directions on page 289. See how well the covers fit a real books and reward students for creating book jackets that fit correctly. (**Rubric PAC 3-2**)

Page 290

Rubric

Project 3 Create a Geometric Shapes ★★

Before students begin, make sure they have found six different-shaped objects to use on their cards. The images should be photographs of real objects, not just shapes. For example, they can use a beverage can or glass for a cylinder, an ice cube for a cube, an ice cream cone for a cone, and so on. They can scan photographs, find them online, or even take their own photographs. Although they do not have to, students might want to show the objects as cutouts placed on a solid background. Students can create a poster or other related items to help reinforce content and understand how designs change according to the different media used. (**Rubric PAC 3-3**)

Page 290

Rubric

Project 4 Create a Hybrid Animal ★★★

Encourage students to create a realistic creature, similar to the Komodo Giraffe project. If you consider it appropriate, direct students to **www.worth1000.com** for other animal crossbreed ideas. Have students research real characteristics of two or three animals and use the data to create information related to their own hybrid. Evaluate student projects based on technical expertise (shadows, lighting, convincing appearance), accurate research, consistent and compelling animal "facts," PARC principles, and quality printout. Keep copies of these projects in a binder as a reference and source of inspiration for future students. (**Rubric PAC 3-4**)

Design with Adobe Illustrator

Getting Started

About the Unit

In this unit, students will learn how to use Adobe Illustrator, a professional vector-based drawing program. Illustrator is used to design, create, and edit artwork. The Workshop Foundations will review vector graphics and provide new information that will add to students' understanding of the new software. The Workshop Toolbox will introduce students to the new interface. Students will quickly recognize many elements from previous software. As they complete the projects, however, they will begin to get a better sense of how unique Illustrator's tools are. Although Illustrator may be difficult to use at times, the projects have been created to give students strong basic skills that will soon allow them to create their own drawings.

In **Chapter 7**, students create varied illustrations and are introduced to some of the many effects that can be created using gradients, blending modes, and distort effects. Students will also learn how to design illustrations using text. The Design Process table on page 292 in the student textbook will help students focus on the importance of illustrations in everyday life.

Chapter 8 brings Adobe Illustrator artwork and Microsoft Publisher together to design engaging publications. The Design Process table on page 333 focuses on logos, and the chapter helps students understand why an illustration program is the right choice for creating logos and other types of graphics.

Quick Write Activity

Before beginning this unit, have students bring in copies of favorite illustrations from books, CDs, videogames, advertisements, and so on. You should also have a variety of illustrations on hand to supplement those brought in by students. If possible, have a collection of examples that were created in Illustrator that employ a variety of drawing techniques. For example, you can have examples of simple drawings, scientific illustrations, 3D illustrations, drawings that look like paints, text illustrations, and so on.

Have students choose an illustration that they find particularly appealing. Ask them to write a paragraph explaining what features in the picture attract them. If possible, project some of the illustrations for the whole class, and ask volunteers to share their evaluations of the pictures.

Unit 4 Design with Adobe Illustrator	Articles, Activities, and Exercises
Chapter 7 **Introducing Microsoft Illustrator** (pages 292–332)	**Workshop Foundations**, Work with Vector Graphics, pg. 293–294 **Workshop Toolbox**, The Illustrator Interface, pg. 295–296 ⓘ **Go Online PowerPoint Presentations Preview**, pg. 297 Ⓡ **Project 7-1** Use Illustrator Tools, pg. 297 Ⓡ **Project 7-2** Create an Illustration, pg. 301 Ⓡ **Project 7-3** Set Colors, pg. 306 Ⓡ **Project 7-4** Apply Gradient Fills, pg. 311 Ⓡ **Project 7-5** Apply Blending Modes, pg. 315 Ⓡ **Project 7-6** Create a Drawing with the Blend Tool, pg. 317 Ⓡ **Project 7-7** Add Distort Effects, pg. 321 Ⓡ **Project 7-8** Create a Text Illustration, pg. 325 Ⓡ **Project 7-9** Enhance Your Text Illustration, pg. 328 ⓘ **Go Online Enrichment Activities**, pg. 324 **In The Workplace**, Illustrators, pg. 330 Ⓣ **TechSIM**
Chapter 8 **Integrating Publisher and Illustrator** (pages 333–373)	**Workshop Foundations** Assess Project Needs, pg. 334–335 **Workshop Toolbox** Layers Palette in Illustrator, pg. 356 ⓘ **Go Online PowerPoint Presentations Preview**, pg. 337 Ⓡ **Project 8-1** Create Shapes with Tools, pg. 337 DF Ⓡ **Project 8-2** Design Vector Images, pg. 342 Ⓡ **Project 8-3** Create a Tent Card, pg. 346 DF Ⓡ **Project 8-4** Apply Live Trace, pg. 349 Ⓡ **Project 8-5** Create Shattered Text, pg. 351 DF Ⓡ **Project 8-6** Lay Out a Poster, pg. 354 Ⓡ **Project 8-7** Create a 3D Cylinder, pg. 359 Ⓡ **Project 8-8** Design a Product Logo, pg. 361 DF Ⓡ **Project 8-9** Design a Product Label, pg. 363 Ⓡ **Project 8-10** Add Symbols to a Label, pg. 366 ⓘ **Go Online Enrichment Activities**, pg. 358 **In The Workplace**, Brand Identify Designer, pg. 371 Ⓣ **TechSIM**
Unit Assessment **Projects Across the Curriculum** (pages 374–375)	Ⓡ **Project 1** Create a Food Product, pg. 374 Ⓡ **Project 2** Create a Graph, pg. 374 Ⓡ **Project 3** Create Board Game Review, pg. 375 Ⓡ **Project 4** Create a Pottery Design, pg. 375

Assessments

Workshop Foundations Reading Check, pg. 294
Workshop Toolbox Reading Check, pg. 296

End of Chapter 7 Assessment
- Reading Check, pg. 331
- Critical Thinking, pg. 331
- Ⓡ **1.** Independent Practice: Prepare an Illustration for a Publication, pg. 331
- Ⓡ **2.** Independent Practice: Create Food Illustrations, pg. 332
- Ⓡ **3.** Independent Practice: Create a Technology Illustration, pg. 332

⊙ **Additional Assessments You May Wish to Use**
ExamView Assessment Suite Testbank, Chapter 7

Workshop Foundations Reading Check, pg. 335
Workshop Toolbox Reading Check, pg. 336

End of Chapter 8 Assessment
Reading Check, pg. 372
Critical Thinking, pg. 372
- Ⓡ **1.** Independent Practice: Create a Language Arts Poster, pg. 372
- Ⓡ **2.** Independent Practice: Create a Proverb Banner, pg. 373
- Ⓡ **3.** Independent Practice: Design Cereal Box Packaging, pg. 373

⊙ **Additional Assessments You May Wish to Use**
ExamView Assessment Suite Testbank, Chapter 8

ⓘ **Go Online e-Review Self Checks** Chapter 7 and Chapter 8

Estimated Time to Complete Unit

9 Week Course = 5–7 days
18 Week Course = 7–8 days
36 Week Course = 13–15 days

To help customize lesson plans, use the Pacing Guide on pages 29–30 and the Standards Charts on pages 238–239.

Key to Recommended Materials

ⓘ Internet access required

Ⓡ Scoring Rubrics

Ⅾⅎ Data Files

⊙ *ExamView Assessment Suite* CD

Ⓣ TechSIM (Technology Simulations available on CD and the Online Learning Center)

The Teacher Resource DVD contains Data Files, Solution Files, Rubrics, Reproducible Worksheets, and PowerPoint Presentations.

 Data Files for Unit 4 are provided on the Teacher Resource DVD and Online Learning Center.

Chapter 7	Chapter 8
No data files	8-2
	8-4
	8-6
	8-9a to 8-9b

 Inclusion Strategies
For **Differentiated Instruction Strategies** refer to the **Inclusion in the Computer Technology Classroom** booklet.

ISTE NETS Foundation Standards

1. Basic operations and concepts
2. Social, ethical, and human issues
3. Technology productivity tools
4. Technology communications tools
5. Technology research tools
6. Technology problem-solving and decision-making

Performance Indicators	Textbook Correlation
1. Identify capabilities and limitations of contemporary and emerging technology resources and assess the potential of these systems and services to address personal, lifelong learning, and workplace needs. (NETS 2)	293–294, 295–296, 297, 301–302, 306–307, 324, 330, 333, 334–335, 346, 349, 351, 354, 358, 359, 366, 370, 371
2. Make informed choices among technology systems, resources, and services. (NETS 1, 2)	292, 293–294, 297, 321, 331, 332, 333, 334–335, 346, 349, 359, 372, 373, 374, 375
3. Analyze advantages and disadvantages of widespread use and reliance on technology in the workplace and in society as a whole. (NETS 2)	292, 330, 331–332, 333, 355, 358–359, 361, 363, 366, 370, 371, 372–373
4. Demonstrate and advocate for legal and ethical behaviors among peers, family, and community regarding the use of technology and information. (NETS 2)	292, 330, 331–332, 333, 255, 258–359, 361, 363, 366, 370, 371, 372–373
5. Use technology tools and resources for managing and communicating personal/professional information (e.g. finances, schedules, addresses, purchases, correspondence). (NETS 3, 4)	292, 294, 301–302, 307, 330, 331–332, 334–335, 346–348, 354, 358, 359–360, 361–362, 363–365, 366–370, 371, 373, 374–375
6. Evaluate technology-based options, including distance and distributed education, for lifelong learning. (NETS 5)	324, 330, 332, 358, 371, 373
7. Routinely and efficiently use online information resources to meet needs for collaboration, research, publications, communications, and productivity. (NETS 4, 5, 6)	297, 324, 330, 331–332, 337, 358, 370, 371, 372–375
8. Select and apply technology tools for research, information analysis, problem-solving, and decision-making in content learning. (NETS 4, 5)	317–320, 321–323, 330, 331–332, 337–341, 342–345, 351–353, 354–367, 370, 372–373, 374–375
9. Investigate and apply expert systems, intelligent agents, and simulations in real-world situations. (NETS 3, 5, 6)	325–329, 330, 331–332, 334–335, 354–357, 358–359, 361, 363, 366, 370, 372–375
10. Collaborate with peers, experts, and others to contribute to content-related knowledge base by using technology to compile, synthesize, produce, and disseminate information, models, and other creative works. (NETS 4, 5, 6)	292, 331–332, 333, 354–357, 372–373, 374–375

21st Century Skills

Core Subjects Language arts, math, science, social studies	293, 294, 296, 297–300, 311–314, 315–316, 318–320, 322–323, 331–332, 334, 335, 336, 337–341, 344–345, 349–350, 355–357, 366–370, 372–373, 374–375
Learning Skills Information and media literacy; communication skills; critical thinking and systems thinking; problem identification, formulation, and solution; self-direction; accountability	292, 293, 294, 296, 297–300, 302, 311–314, 315–316, 321, 325, 330, 331–332, 333, 334, 335, 336, 337–341, 344–345, 349–350, 355–357, 366–370, 371, 372–373, 374–375
21st Century Tools Communication, information processing and research tools; problem-solving tools, personal development and productivity tools	293–294, 295–296, 297, 306, 325, 330, 332, 334–335, 336, 337, 359, 371

Foundation Skills

Basic Skills Reading, writing, math, listening, and Speaking	293, 294, 296, 297–300, 311–314, 315–316, 331–332, 334, 335, 336, 337–341, 344–345, 349–350, 355–357, 366–370, 372–373, 374–375
Thinking Skills Creative thinking, decision making, problem solving, reasoning	292, 294, 296, 302, 321, 325, 330, 331–332, 333, 334–335, 336, 349, 371, 372–373, 374–375
Personal Qualities Self-esteem, responsibility, self-management, and integrity/honesty	293, 330, 331–332, 334, 335, 352–353, 355–357, 371, 372–373, 374–375

Workplace Competencies

Resources Allocate time, money, materials, facilities, and human resources	331–332, 372–373, 374–375
Interpersonal Participate on teams, teach others, serve clients and customers, exercise leadership, negotiate to arrive at decisions, and work with cultural diversity	292, 331–332, 333, 372–373, 374–375
Information Acquire, evaluate, organize, maintain, interpret, communicate, and use computers to process information	253, 258–259, 294–296, 302, 335–336
Systems Understand, monitor, correct, improve, and design systems	293–294, 333, 334–335, 358, 359–360, 361–362, 363–365, 366–370
Technology Select, apply, maintain, and troubleshoot technology	294, 296, 300, 301, 302, 307, 322, 331–332, 334, 335, 336, 338, 342, 346, 349, 354, 372–374

Chapter 7

Introducing Adobe Illustrator

Skills You Will Learn

Workshop Foundations: Work with Vector Graphics

- Identify vector graphics software
- Combine vector graphic file formats

Workshop Toolbox: The Illustrator Interface

- Identify Illustrator's interface
- Identify Toolbox drawing tools
- Identify Illustrator palettes

Project 7-1 Use Illustrator Tools

- Create geometric shapes
- Apply the Selection tool
- Add fill color
- Drag objects
- Apply the Direct Selection tool

Project 7-2 Create an Illustration

- Display grids and guides
- Apply the Zoom tool
- Align objects
- Format a line
- Add text
- Rotate an object

Project 7-3 Set Colors

- Duplicate an image
- Work with the Color palette
- Work with the Swatches palette

Project 7-4 Apply Gradient Fills

- Work with the Gradient palette
- Create colors with the Color Picker

Project 7-5 Apply Blending Modes

- Use the Transparency palette
- Compare opacity levels

Project 7-6 Create a Drawing with the Blend Tool

- Apply blending options

Project 7-7 Add Distort Effects

- Distort an image
- Add a drop shadow
- Warp text

Skills Studio

Design with Text Illustrations

Project 7-8 Create a Text Illustration

- Add shape to area
- Apply text outlines

Project 7-9 Enhance Your Text Illustration

- Create a text path
- Apply a gradient
- Apply Envelope Distort

Start-Up Skills

Identify Drawing Tools Start students thinking about drawing. Ask them if they like to sketch or doodle. Explain that Adobe Illustrator is a tool that will give them the ability to create sophisticated and professional-looking artwork quickly and easily. Then ask students to describe details and effects that they would like to add to their sketches to make them more interesting or realistic. You might help students by showing them examples of effects such as shadowing, lighting effects, feathering, gradient colors, warping, blending effects, 3D effects, and so on. Explain that once they begin to master Illustrator, they will be able to change a simple sketch into a compelling drawing.

Design Process: Illustrations

Compare Illustrations Bring in an assortment of illustrations for students to evaluate using the Design Process chart on page 292. (If you or your students brought in illustrations for the Quick Write Activity on page 231, you can use those.) Find five different examples that you can project for the whole class to see. Have the class go through each item in the chart, identifying the purpose and audience of the illustration, how the illustration conveys a particular message, and in what type of publication the illustration might be used.

Students may have more than one way of evaluating an illustration, and you should encourage different points of view. For example, to what audience would a science fiction video game appeal? Some of your students might think it is meant to appeal to teenage boys and young men, but others might think it appeals to girls and women too. If that is the case, what message is conveyed to the different audiences? How might an advertisement for this game use the images to appeal to the different audiences?

Quick Write Activity

Evaluate an Illustration After having the class discussion described above, see if students can do their own evaluations of an illustration, based on the Design Process chart. You can have students write about an illustration of their own choice, or you can project one illustration that they can all write about.

LEARNING LINK

Chapter 7 introduces students to Illustrator drawing software. Explain that a drawing program gives them creative freedom to express ideas quickly and powerfully. The vector artwork created in Illustrator can be used in print, video, the World Wide Web, and mobile devices.

In Chapter 8, students will learn how to use their illustrations in real-world publications. Students should realize that images alone are not considered desktop publishing. Publications are created when images are imported into layout software such as Publisher or InDesign and combined with text.

Workshop Foundations   Page 293

Work with Vector Graphics

FOCUS

Focus Activity

Choose the Right Tools Ask students to describe what it is like to cook a meal in somebody else's kitchen. Chances are, students will say it is somewhat frustrating. They know what they need, but it is usually in a different place in the kitchen. Even when the right tools are located, cooking times and temperatures on someone else's oven or stove often vary. Point out that Illustrator is a lot like cooking in someone else's kitchen. Many of the tools in Illustrator are similar to the ones they have already seen in Microsoft Word, Microsoft Publisher, and Adobe Photoshop, though some of the tools act a bit differently than they may expect or are located in a different place than they would guess. There is a bit of a learning curve with Illustrator, but learning this software is well worth the effort.

> **You Will Learn To:**
> - Define vector graphic software
> - Compare vector graphic file formats

Page 293

Before You Read Activity

Prior Knowlege Metacognition—the art of knowing what you know and what you do not know—is critically important to the reading process. Too often students complain that they read the chapter, but did not understand the material. This can lead to great frustration. Have students briefly preview each workshop section or project before they read it. Ask them to note what sections of the chapter look difficult to them and answer any questions they have.

Pages 293–294

Key Term Activity

At the Computer The concept of file formats and file name extensions may be difficult to understand until students have experience using various file formats. Review the illustrations on page 294. Direct students to explore a specific directory on the computer. See how quickly they can locate WMF, EMF, AI, PICT, EPS, and SVG files on their computer.

Key Term Definitions

vector graphics Images that are created by using mathematical reference points. Vector graphics can be resized without losing clarity. (page 293)

scalable The ability of a graphic to be resized without losing image quality. (page 293)

file name extension The letters displayed after a file name that describe the file format. (For example, Word documents end with .doc). (page 294)

TEACH

Teach Activity

Discuss When to Use Vector Graphics Explain to students that there are many instances when it is best to use vector-based graphics, as opposed to raster graphics. The determining factor is whether the resulting graphic will need to be scalable (especially in the area of logos). Scalability can also refer to text (which are vector graphics), clip art (which needs to fit in many circumstances), and even other types of graphics that need to have special printing needs (fewer colors to manage cost overruns or for specialized presses, such as screen printing).

Answers to Workshop Foundations Activities

Page 294

Eye on Ethics

A company that manufactures health products is likely to be providing information that will sell its products. Even though it might be accurate, it could still be very one-sided.

ASSESS

Reading Check

1. Scalable graphics are important for graphics that will need to be resized, such as logos. Company logos are on business cards, letterhead, envelopes, advertisements and billboards. In these situations, using the same logo is more convenient and cost efficient than recreating the logo for each instance.

2. The only sure way to tell if a graphic is a vector image or a raster image is to look at the file format details. If the image has not been saved in a vector graphic file format, it has become a raster image and loses its scalability.

CLOSE

Choose the Right Tool Ask students to give personal examples of how important it is to choose the right tool for a certain task or job. The examples can extend beyond the scope of choosing the right software application for desktop publishing. Remind students that the ability to use the right tool is an important skill. Point out that it takes time to learn know how to use certain tools effectively, but it is time well spent. Remind students that Illustrator is a complex piece of software and takes some time to master, but it will be very impressive to have on their résumés.

Workshop Toolbox Pages 295–296

The Illustrator Interface

FOCUS

Focus Activity

Introduce the Illustrator Interface Help students recognize the similarities between the Illustrator interface and the Photoshop interface. Then point out the unique features of Illustrator's Control palette. Show students how the options displayed in the Control palette change, depending on the tool that is open and the object that is selected. Because it changes according to the tasks you are performing, the Control palette displays the exact tools you need, just when you need them. This reduces the number of palettes that need to be open on the screen when you are working on a drawing.

> **You Will Learn To:**
> - Identify Illustrator's interface
> - Identify toolbar drawing tools
> - Identify Illustrator palettes

Page 295

Key Term Activity

Compare Palettes to Windows Demonstrate for students how easy it is to use palettes by comparing palettes to Windows. Remind them that palettes can be moved, sized, and closed just like any Windows screen. Have students practice opening palettes under various tabs to make a palette appear at the front of its group, which is similar to using Windows dialog box tabs.

> ### Key Term Definitions
>
> **palette** A set of tools, located in a separate floating toolbar, that relates to a particular action, such as adding color or working with layers. (page 295)

TEACH

Teach Activity

Make Predictions To illustrate the similarities and differences in the Illustrator and Photoshop toolboxes, organize the students in two groups. Using the illustrations on pages 295–296 and 201–202, ask each group to predict the function of as many tools as possible in the Illustrator toolbox.

Answers to Workshop Toolbox Activities

Page 296

Sidebar

Responses will vary. Ask for volunteers to read their descriptions out loud. Follow up with a demonstration of the various Illustrator selection tools.

Customize Your Illustrator Screen Open Adobe Illustrator and have students demonstrate how to display hidden tools, make floating toolbars, change views, and hide the Toolbox and palettes. Have students use the Window menu to open different palettes. Also, have students reset the default settings using the Window menu. Becoming comfortable with the Window menu will help students develop confidence using Illustrator. Students will use the Windows menu often in the projects in this unit.

Practice Shortcuts One of the most useful shortcuts in Illustrator is Shift + Tab which displays or hides all of the palettes at once. Have students practice this shortcut a number of times. It will save them a lot of mouse clicks when they are working on the projects.

ASSESS

Evaluate Assign Reading Check questions and any Sidebar and Eye on Ethics features to assess students' understanding of the chapter Toolbox.

Reading Check

1. Responses will vary depending upon the tool and the applications being compared. Some possibilities might be the Magic Wand, the Pen tool, the Type tool, the Hand, and Zoom. Check to make sure that the tool descriptions are accurate and that the comparison is logical.

2. The Control palette options vary depending on the type of object you select. For example, when you select a text object, the Control palette displays the text formatting options as well as options for changing the color, placement, and dimensions of objects.

CLOSE

Compare Interfaces Programs with complex interfaces discourage certain kinds of users, and programs with user-friendly interfaces, though simpler in nature, may have fewer powerful tools and features. Have students list on the board elements of the Illustrator interface. The list should include the workspace, scratch area, toolbox, and menus. Discuss how this interface compares to Word's or Publisher's. Which do they prefer and why?

Chapter 7 Projects

Pages 297–329

FOCUS

Focus Activity

Differentiate Among Selection Tools One of the more confusing things about Illustrator is that there are two main selection tools that look and work very similarly: the Direct Selection tool (white arrow) and the Selection tool (black arrow). The main difference between the two is that the black arrow (the Selection tool) is used to select an entire object, while the Direct Selection tool (the white arrow) is used to select individual pieces of an object.

The Direct Selection tool can be used to select one point on an object and drag it along a "path." Ask students to look at the illustration on page 297 and locate the parts of a line. They should notice three dots with lines extending from them. Explain that these dots and lines are used by the computer to describe the curve. The concept was invented by a man named Pierre Bezier. Bezier curves will be discussed in Chapter 8.

Projects

Project 7-1
Use Illustrator Tools

Project 7-2
Create an Illustration

Project 7-3
Set Colors

Project 7-4
Apply Gradient Fills

Project 7-5
Apply Blending Modes

Project 7-6
Create a Drawing with the
Blend Tool Project 1-7

Project 7-7
Add Distort Effects

Skills Studio

Project 7-8
Create a Text Illustration

Project 7-9
Enhance Your Text Illustration

 Go Online **PREVIEW**

Before You Begin Students can use the chapter **PowerPoint** presentations and **rubrics** at the Online Learning Center to determine what is expected *before* they complete a project. Students can view the PowerPoint slides on their own computers, or you can project them to preview chapter concepts and show examples of the finished projects. You might also display project solutions so students can easily refer to them while they work. (Presentations and rubrics are also provided on the Teacher Resource DVD for your convenience).

glencoe.com

Key Term Activity

Predict the Definition Write the key terms on separate sheets of paper. Hand each term to a student. Have the students write what they think the definition is, then pass the paper to the next person in the row, who should add to the definition, correct it, or confirm it. Do this at least two more times, then have the last person use the textbook's glossary to write the correct definition. Read the results, and address any questions students may have.

Key Term Definitions

marquee A dotted outline around sections you want to select. (p.297)

object An individual shape, image, or text that can be moved, edited, or manipulated. (p. 297)

path The line that is created when an object is drawn or traced. (p.297)

anchor point The spot where you begin or end a line segment. (p. 297)

grids The framework upon which you place objects for alignment and sizing. (p. 300)

magnify To enlarge your view of an image to see close details. (p. 301)

grayscale A color system that ranges from white to black with shades of gray in between. (p. 306)

RGB Red, Green, and Blue, the primary colors of light. When mixed in different proportions, these three colors can create a large range of colors that can be displayed on a monitor. (p. 306)

CYMK Cyan, Magenta, Yellow, Black. This mode is used for printed documents and is not meant for graphics on a monitor. (p. 307)

HSB Hue, Saturation, Brightness. A method of describing color to a computer. (p. 307)

gradient A gradual change from one color to another. (p. 311)

spectrum The entire range of color from white to black. (p. 311)

radial A circular effect. (p. 311)

gradient stop The beginning or end colors used in a gradient. (p. 311)

transparent A quality which lets you see through an object, making the objects underneath visible. (p. 315)

opaque A quality which makes an object too dark to see through. (p. 315)

morph To gradually blend two images together in such a manner that the first image appears to be transforming into the other image. (p. 317)

warp To bend or distort. (p. 321)

TEACH

Teach Activity

Know How to Select Of all the Illustrator concepts offered in this chapter, the one the students may have the most trouble understanding is how to select objects. The concept is not quite as intuitive in Illustrator as in Word or Publisher, or even Photoshop.

If your students have done much drawing in Word or Publisher, they will recall that they usually had to ungroup an object before they could edit it. In Illustrator, one can use the Direct Selection tool to select a single object within a group. Emphasize how helpful and how much time this Direct Selection tool will save students once they learn how to use it.

In Word and Publisher, students did not have the capability of selecting a single point and making changes either. In Illustrator, points on a drawing object can be moved or removed at the graphic designer's discretion.

Reinforce the advantages of Illustrator's multiple selection tools. Create a circle. Select an individual point on the circle by dragging a marquee around it using the Direct Selection tool. Then, click and drag the point around in the workspace to demonstrate how this feature works.

Teaching Tips ✍ and Troubleshooting Tips ⚠ for Projects

Pages 297–300

🅁
Rubric

Project 7-1 → **Use Illustrator Tools** Students will use the Illustrator Toolbox to create simple objects, and then practice using the Selection and Direct Selection tools. They will also learn how to move objects and fill them with color. **(Solution File 7-1, Rubric 7-1)**

 Encourage Individual Creativity Some students may struggle and become frustrated when working in Illustrator because they think their illustrations must be "picture perfect" or look exactly like the figures in the textbook. Remind the class that no two people would sketch a flower or a house in exactly the same way on paper. The same is true when they use an illustration program like Illustrator. Everyone's design will be unique, and that is a good thing.

⚠ **Restore Default Workspace Preferences** Have students read the Instant Message box on page 300. As a class activity, choose **Window>Workspace>Default** to restore the screen to its default settings.

⚠ **Select Objects** Make sure that students see and understand the difference between the two selection tools. While they look similar and have similar names, they both perform quite different functions. Some students may need individual attention to grasp this concept. Pair advanced students with students who need extra help.

Pages 301–305

Rubric

Project 7-2 **Create an Illustration** In this project, students will use a number of tools and simple shapes to draw a more complex image, a crayon. They will continue the drawing in Project 7-3. **(Solution File 7-2, Rubric 7-2)**

Page 302

Answer to Sidebar The Undo command goes back to your last entered command. The Edit>Revert command goes back to the last saved version of the file.

Draw a Face Ask students how they would draw a human face. Allow students to demonstrate at the board. While those who draw well are likely to volunteer or be prodded by the class, also encourage students who do not feel they draw well to also demonstrate. It is likely that students who can draw well will draw complex outlines, and the ones who do not draw as well will more likely use simple shapes to create the shape such as an oval, two circles, a rectangle, and a triangle. Emphasize to the class that neither way is right or wrong. Even though the more advanced student uses more advanced shapes, you will notice that the shape is still drawn in pieces. Ask the student who is good at drawing if they started this way, or if they started with simpler shapes. The point is that all objects can be drawn through the use of simpler, primitive, shapes such as circles, rectangles, and triangles.

Identify Simple Shapes Have students look at Figure 7.10 on page 304. Ask them to identify the shapes used to create the figure. Students should be able to identify lines, a rectangle, an oval, and a trapezoid.

Apply the Zoom Tool Demonstrate how to create a marquee with the Zoom tool to select part of an image. Then have students practice changing magnification levels. It is important that students understand how to use the Zoom tools and the Navigator palette to create fine details in their illustrations.

Group Objects Students must group all the parts of the crayon label before they drag it onto the crayon shape. Then they must group the object in the completed crayon so they can work with it in Project 7-3.

Pages 306–309

Rubric

Project 7-3 **Set Colors** Students add colors to their crayon illustrations and use the Rectangle tool to create a box for the crayons. Students learn how to use the Color Picker to set colors within the color spectrum by keying specific values. They work with four new palettes: the Color palette, the Swatches palette, the Align palette, and the Control palette. In the Spotlight on Skills, students are also introduced to four color modes: grayscale, RGB, CMYK, and HSB. **(Solution File 7-3, Rubric 7-3)**

Page 307

Answer to Sidebar The shortcut for the Rectangle tool is the letter M, and the shortcut for Gradient palette is Ctrl + F9.

Work with the Color Picker Demonstrate how colors are set using HSB, RGB, and CYMK color modes in the Color Picker. Ask students to suggest specific values as you demonstrate to see the relationship when they increase and decrease values of the color modes.

Explore RGB Young children recognize the primary colors of red, green, and blue at an early age because they are the primary colors of light. Remind students that when the computer combines these three colors together, it can simulate a wide range of other colors. Certain colors (like a florescent green) cannot be printed, but they can be displayed on screen. The RGB model is useful for creating graphics that will be displayed on the computer monitor.

Use CMYK to Print See if students know the four ink colors on printer cartridges. They will be interested to learn that Cyan, Magenta, Yellow and Black (the K stands for "Key," which is printer talk for black) are the colors used by most printers, except for inexpensive printers. If possible, show students a color printer cartridge for each of the color names (Not all students will be familiar with the names cyan and magenta).

Explain that some RGB colors cannot be printed (though they can be viewed on monitors), so the CMYK color model best reflects what can actually be printed. Since most printers use these four inks as primary colors and mix these colors together to create a wide range of other colors, this color model best simulates these results. For additional information, you may wish to review Appendix A Color Theory with students.

Keyboard Shortcuts Remind students that shortcuts for tools in the Toolbox appear in parenthesis next to the right of the tool's name. Many palettes also have keyboard shortcuts. The shortcuts appear to the right of the palette name in the Window menu.

Web-Safe RGB Start students thinking about the Only Web Colors check box. Ask them why the check box is necessary. Explain that the color model is then limited to the 216 colors that are common to all Web browsers. You may wish to introduce students to the term *dithering*. Dithering occurs when a graphic uses a color that is NOT one of the 216 acceptable colors. The computer receiving the information substitutes a different color. The results are not predictable, and this can cause problems with your design.

To ensure that graphics look similar regardless of the receiving computer, it is best to use Web-safe RGB colors when creating graphics that will appear on the Internet. See Appendix A Color Theory and Design for more information about Web-safe colors.

Pages 311–314

Rubric

Project 7-4 ▷ **Apply Gradient Fills** Students use the Gradient palette with a radial option to create an illustration of an eye. They will use the Star tool to add a realistic layered effect on the illustration before grouping the objects. They will continue the drawing in Project 7-4. **(Solution File 7-4, Rubric 7-4)**

✍ **Illustrate Gradients** Some students may not understand what a gradient is. Show students several examples of publications that have used gradients in the design. Ask students to compare Figure 7.25 on page 314 to Figure 7.19 on page 310. How do they look different? Students will notice that the eye illustration color is not a "flat" color. The highlights and textures add dimension to the shape.

⚠ **Demonstrate Gradient Stops** Learning how to set gradient stops is a little tricky and perhaps a little frustrating at first. Guide students with a demonstration at the board on how to use the diamond sliders in the Gradient palette. Explain that the left gradient stop is the starting color of the gradient, and the right gradient stop is the end color of a gradient. Consider using colored chalk to create a gradient on the board. Or, as a class, pick a color and adjust gradients to see if the class can achieve the same gradient effect. Show students how to remove and add gradient stops. Tell students that a gradient's effects can be adjusted by using either the Gradient palette or the Gradient tool.

Pages 315–316

Rubric

Apply Blending Modes In this project, students use blending modes to add additional effects to the eye illustration created in Project 7-4. They use the Transparency palette to change opacity and use the Ellipse tool to add realistic highlights. **(Solution File 7-5, Rubric 7-5)**

✍ **Define Blend** Ask your students to write a description of what it means to "blend." Students are likely to compare blending to drawing with pencils or markers and smearing colors together. Explain that this is what Illustrator does, although these blending modes are more sophisticated and based on darkroom techniques developed by photographers while developing negatives.

✍ **Compare Transparency and Opacity** In Illustrator, you can adjust transparency by lowering the opacity. The lower the opacity, the more transparent a layer or object will be. Opacity and transparency can be adjusted using the Transparency palette.

Have students look at Figures 7.27 and 7.28 on page 316. Ask your students to compare the light effects caused by the different opacities, and explain why those two settings were chosen.

Encourage Blend Experimenting Point out that blending modes are used to make layers interact with each other. These modes are useful for creating shadows, highlights, reflections, and special effects. Because they are based on real darkroom techniques, many of them have unusual names like "multiply." The best way to predict how these modes will act is to experiment with them. Encourage students to practice and experiment in each project, and soon they will be able to predict what kind of effect a blending mode will create.

Pages 327–318]

R
Rubric

Project 7-6 **Create a Drawing with the Blend Tool** Student will use the Blend tool to create the American flag's thirteen stripes and fifty stars. Use the illustration on pages 317 to stimulate interest in the concept of morphing. Students will be eager to learn how to blend images together to transform from one image into the other. **(Solution File 7-6, Rubric 7-6)**

Evaluate Blend Tool Techniques Ask students how much more time it would likely have taken to make the flag by hand. What type of problems did they avoid by using the Blend tool? Remind students that creating blended objects can help them make copies easily and be able to do repetitive tasks (such as making the stars) much more quickly and precisely than by creating each start by hand. It would have been much harder to make sure that every star was the same size and that they were all spaced apart equally.

Design With the Blend Tool As a class, practice the following techniques for using the Blend tool. Point out that the Blend tool can get a bit confusing, but it can be used at least three different ways:

1) The Blend tool can be used to make copies of an object. Draw a simple circle. Hold the Alt key and drag a copy of the circle, placing it elsewhere in the workspace. Double-click the Blend tool in the Toolbox, and choose *Specified Steps 3*. With the Blend tool (notice the cursor has changed), click the first circle and then click on the second. Three more copies appear evenly spaced between the first two instances!

2) The Blend tool can be used to create shades of color. Create two circles again, but this time make the circles different colors. With the Blend tool still set to Specified Steps 3, click the first and then the second circle. Three more shapes with different colors will appear in between!

3) The Blend tool can be used to create blended shapes. Create two shapes that are different, such as a circle and a star. Use the Blend tool to click on the first and then the second shape. Three more shapes will appear, giving a morphed appearance. Tell your students that they can even use this trick with clip art for some dramatic results.

Blend Multiple Shapes You are not just limited to blending two shapes. Demonstrate to students what happens when you blend multiple shapes— they will be impressed with the effects!

Expand Blended Objects After using the Blend tool, students will find that the objects in the middle (the new, blended objects) cannot be selected or altered. Finalize the action by selecting the blended objects and choosing **Object>Blend>Expand**. Now the objects can be selected and altered, but they are still grouped. Remind students that they can now use **Object>Ungroup** to move or delete instances.

Differentiate Between Blending Mode and the Blend Tool Until they have completed Project 7-6, students may wonder what the difference is between the blending modes and the Blend tool. Ask students to summarize how the blending modes were used in Project 7-5, reminding them that the blending modes determine the way that layers interact with each other. Tell them that they will use the Blend tool to make drawn objects interact with each other.

Start Over If students made a mistake blending, they can select the blended object and use **Object>Blend>Release** to start over.

Pages 321–323

Rubric

Project 7-7 ➤ **Add Distort Effects** Students will use the Distort Envelope feature on the American flag that they created in Project 7-6. The effect will make the flag look like it is waving in the breeze. Students will also use the Effect menu to add a drop shadow to the illustration. **(Solution File 7-7, Rubric 7-7)**

Page 321

Answer to Sidebar It is important to see the envelope when editing because once the envelope is applied, it is not easy to make changes to the object, and it helps to see the distort shape.

Understanding Warp and Envelope Be sure that students understand why the somewhat unusual name Envelope Distort is appropriate for the Illustrator tool used to warp an image. Show students how an envelope can be bent to give it a warped appearance. Explain that Illustrator places an invisible "envelope" over objects so that they can be designed with a warped effect.

Apply Three Kinds of Envelope Distort Effects As a class, practice using Envelope Distort features. Use the Horizontal Type tool to create a text box, and key a simple paragraph. Experiment with **Object>Envelope Distort>Make with Warp**. These works similar to WordArt, but show students how they have a lot more control.

Select the example, and choose **Object>Envelope Distort>Release** and delete the envelope that appears. Demonstrate **Object>Envelope Distort>Make with Mesh**. With the Direct Selection tool, select a point and click and drag to distort the text. Notice that each anchor point has a control handle to adjust the angle of distortion.

Again, select the example, choose **Object>Envelope Distort>Release** and delete the envelope that appears. Ceate a trapezoid over the text box, and choose **Object>Envelope Distort>Make with Top Object**. This is a great way to make text appear to be on a book or a road sign.

✍ **Review Envelope Distort** Conduct a quick review of the three types of Envelope Distort effects. Ask students to compare and contrast this feature with Microsoft's WordArt feature. Students are likely to say that this feature is much more powerful, though a bit more complicated to learn.

⚠ **Activate the Grid** Students may have trouble with **Object>Envelope Distort>Make with Mesh**. They must use the Direct Selection tool (the white arrow), and then click and drag around one anchor point, then activate the grid.

Skills Studio

Page 324–329

Design with Text Illustrations

It is important that students understand that it does not matter how effective graphics and layout are if the message does not get read. Sometimes graphics are overdone, and a message is lost. One way to create a dynamic effect is to create text itself as a graphic.

Students may think that making illustrations with text is unexciting and boring. Before students begin the Skills Studio, have them look at Figure 7.44 on page 329. Can they define what a text illustration is based on that picture? Students should be able to see that the text itself becomes part of a graphic, much as it does in a logo.

Ask students what the message is of the flyer shown in the figure. They should see that *Desktop Publishing: Powered by the Imagination* is the main idea, meaning that to create effective publications, you need creative ideas. Discuss with the class how the text illustration adds to that message. They should realize that a light bulb is often used to represent ideas, and that the words *Radiated Outward* are designed to make it look as though light (or ideas) is radiating from the light bulb.

Pages 325–327

Rubric

Project 7-8 **Create a Text Illustration** Students will create a flyer promoting enrollment in a desktop publishing class. They will use the Paragraph and Pathfinder palettes. Students use simple shapes to create a light bulb illustration. Your advanced students can be instructed to create an original illustration. (**Solution File 7-8, Rubric 7-8**)

✍ **Explore the Pathfinder Palette** The Pathfinder palette includes a powerful feature that allows simple shapes to be added together or subtracted from one another. This feature can be a little difficult to comprehend. Tell students that, unlike grouping, these objects are physically melded together, and they lose their individual identity.

Help students grasp the concept with a class activity. Create three simple ovals, all overlapping into a cloud-like shape. Select all three shapes. Use **Window>Pathfinder** to open the Pathfinder palette. Hold the Alt key and click **Add to Shape**. The individual circles are eliminated, and a more complex cloud shape remains.

⚠ **Expand Effects** Students may have trouble with the light bulb if the pieces do not overlap. Additionally, when using the Pathfinder palette, it is a good idea to Expand the effect. Students should either use the Expand button, or they should hold the Alt key while adding or subtracting shapes

Pages 328–329

Rubric

▷ **Project 7-9** **Enhance Your Text Illustration** Students add the finishing details to their light bulb illustration flyer. The goal is to focus on a radiating theme. **(Solution File 7-9, Rubric 7-9)**

✎ **Type on a Path** Ask students to describe what it would mean if they took the path home. Students are likely to answer that the path was some sort of small roadway that they would walk upon to reach a destination. Today, students will be setting text on a path. Using this feature, text can follow any angle and even change angles mid word.

To demonstrate the point, use the Paintbrush tool and draw a wavy line. Then, select the Horizontal Type on a Path tool, and click on the line. The line will become invisible, but an insertion point will be placed above the line. Begin keying, and the characters you key will follow the path at any angle, up and down, in a circle and back again! This feature works well for special effects or for creating maps.

⚠ **Stay on a Path** When keying on a path, make sure that students have Align Left selected. Students should use the Tab key to separate instances of *Radiated Outward* and use copy/paste to repeat the phrase instead of re-keying it over and over.

⚠ **Maintain Proportions** After creating the spiral effect, have students move it behind the light bulb. Then tell them to select all the elements, and choose **Object>Expand Appearance.** This forces the objects to maintain proportions relatively, even if the object is resized later.

ASSESS

Evaluate Encourage students to use the project rubrics and the Review and Revise checklists to be sure that they have completed the key steps to their projects. Encourage students to proofread and assist each other. Students learn best when they are teaching each other. Consider giving bonus points for well-designed projects for both the student and the student who evaluated his/her work.

Lots of positive reinforcement is important. The learning curve is greater for Illustrator than Microsoft Word, Microsoft Publisher, and Adobe Photoshop. Students are often too critical of their drawings when they are learning Adobe Illustrator because they want their drawings to appear professional. Remind students often that the more they practice, the faster they will develop their illustration skills.

CLOSE

Tools Summary Draw a Cause-Effect graphic organizer on the board (See Part 3 of this manual, Graphic Organizers 12 and 13). Write the word *Tools* for the heading of the boxes on the left side, and the word *Effects* for the right side. As a class, list the tools that have been used in the Illustrator projects and the effects that can be created using the tools. Ask students to copy the summary into their class notebooks.

Additional Projects Remind students that additional projects are available at the Online Learning Center at **glencoe.com**. You may choose to assign the projects to the class or offer extra credit to students who complete the projects.

IN THE WORKPLACE

ILLUSTRATORS

Career Activity

Illustrators need to have a solid understanding of design in order to help create attractive illustrations that help convey the message of the document. They must understand the client's need, and they must fulfill that need. While many illustrators can create their drawings digitally, it is still helpful for illustrators to be able to create graphics by hand so they have a wider variety of skills and express a wider variety of moods.

Salaries vary because skill levels and types of jobs differ significantly. For example, an illustrator who creates video games for a large company would probably earn considerably more than one who illustrates ads for local businesses.

Use the following Reading Check and Critical Thinking answers as a guide to help evaluate student understanding of the core concepts. Requiring that your students write in complete sentences will help you grade faster and promote good writing skills. You can have students write answers in their desktop publishing journals, or students can answer these questions at the computer by accessing the Reading Check and Critical Thinking activities on the Online Learning Center at **glencoe.com**.

Page 331

Reading Check

1. Vector graphics are graphics stored as mathematical formulas on the computer. The image is recreated mathematically. This allows the images to be scalable without distortion.

2. In addition to Adobe Illustrator's AI format, the following are the most commonly used vector graphic formats: EPS (Encapsulated Post Script), EMF (Enhanced MetaFile) or a WMF (Windows MetaFile).

3. The Selection tool is used to select an entire object, while the Direct Selection tool is used to select part of an object or group.

4. Palettes are useful because they group related tools together, and you only need to display the palettes related to the specific tools you need.

5. Scalability is one of the main advantages of vector graphics. It allows the same image to be used on a postage stamp or a billboard, recreating the image for different purposes.

Critical Thinking

6. Answers should include four of the following palettes: Pathfinder palette, Layers palette, Colors palette, Swatches palette, Stroke palette, and the Align palette.

7. By using the Pathfinder palette, simple shapes can be combined to create more complex ones.

8. When planning which kind of graphic you need to use in a project, you need to consider the amount of time you have to create the graphic, your proficiency with the software, and the function for the graphic, especially if the image will need to be scalable.

9. Illustrator is used to create drawings, which can then be placed in a document that is created in Publisher, a layout program. Illustrator itself cannot be used to create difficult layouts, and it can only use text for limited purposes.

10. Text illustrations and logos are similar in that they both treat text as art and must graphically convey a publication's message primarily through the use of text.

Assessment activities allow students to demonstrate their understanding of concepts and skills learned throughout this project. Because of time constraints, students may not be able to complete every activity suggested. Match assignments to student ability levels using the leveled projects (★ Easy, ★★ Medium, and ★★★ Challenging). Rubrics are available to evaluate projects on the Teacher Resource DVD and the Online Learning Center at **glencoe.com**.

Page 331

Rubric

1. Independent Practice ★

Prepare an Illustration for a Publication Student should continue working with the box of crayons they created in Project 7-3. Bring in copies of advertisements from toy stores to help students research advertisements aimed at a younger audience. Require that students conduct a thoughtful evaluation of several advertisements.

Assign points for the evaluation and planning stages of the design process. Ask students to conduct peer evaluations (in writing) that consider PARC principles for the design and include this in the grade. Projects should follow the guidelines as described on page 331, but students should be encouraged to add their own ideas. **(Rubric IP 7-1)**

Page 332

Rubric

2. Independent Practice ★★

Create Food Illustrations Provide colorful cookbooks or food magazines to give students ideas on food presentations that look appealing and delicious. Varied colors, textures, and backgrounds are important in food illustrations. Make sure students keep their food choices simple. The purpose of this project is practicing with Illustrator's tools, not trying to create a gourmet meal. However, since students will be working as a team, they should include a variety of breakfast items. **(Rubric IP 7-2)**

Page 332

Rubric

3. Independent Practice ★★★

Create a Technology Illustration Encourage students to be imaginative. To spark the imagination, brainstorm ideas on features they would add to current technology such as cell phones, cars, cameras, etc. Ask students to bring in pictures from advertisements in magazines or advertisements of what they intend to illustrate. They will use the pictures for reference only. Remind students to first consider the simple shapes that will be required to create their new technology. Students should first create sketches, using these shapes, of the technology they intend to create.

Extend the activity by encouraging students to use multiple software applications for this project: For example, they can use Illustrator to draw the illustrations and logo effects, Photoshop to create the background and lighting effects, and then do an overall layout in Publisher. **(Rubric IP 7-3)**

Reteaching Activities

Review Key Skills Illustrator is a difficult program. Encourage students often. It is expected that students will have to repeat some tasks. For students who are struggling, ask them to repeat projects that were difficult. They should follow the same basic steps, but change elements such as colors, patterns, and clip art. For example, they may want to create a new flag for another country, which uses different shapes, and colors.

Finish Worksheets Have students complete Worksheets 8A and 8B, which can be found in Part 3 or this TRM, on the Teacher Resource DVD, or at the Online Learning Center at **glencoe.com**.

Enrichment Activities

Electronic Portfolios Have students create an electronic portfolio of their best work. Portfolios are used by graphic designers to show others how capable they are at creating good designs. Many designers host their work on Web pages or create PowerPoint presentations.

Since Microsoft Word creates document files, not picture files, students will need to use the Print Screen button on the keyboard to take a "picture" of the computer screen. They can then paste it in another Word document or in another application, such as PowerPoint slides or a Publisher document. Students should save their best work and add it to this electronic portfolio to track their progress.

Enrichment If students need an additional challenge, have them complete the activities in the Online Learning Center at **glencoe.com**.

Notes

Chapter 8

Integrating Publisher and Illustrator

Skills You Will Learn

Workshop Foundations: Assess Project Needs

- Compare desktop publishing applications and tools
- Evaluate client needs
- Compare file formats

Workshop Toolbox: Layers Palette in Illustrator

- Identify palettes used to create complex shapes
- Apply the Layers palette

Project 8-1 Create Shapes with Tools

- Apply Pathfinder palette tools
- Create custom colors
- Work with the Layers palette
- Draw with the Pen tool

Project 8-2 Design Vector Images

- Apply the Pathfinder palette
- Add Word clip art
- Apply text outlines
- Apply Expand Appearance
- Customize print output

Project 8-3 Create a Tent Card

- Lay out a tent card
- Insert an Illustrator file
- Format text boxes
- Apply a master page
- Add border art
- Create a custom color

Project 8-4 Apply Live Trace

- Copy and paste clip art
- Apply Live Trace

Project 8-5 Create Shattered Text

- Apply text outlines
- Apply Pathfinder Divide
- Apply three-dimensional (3D) effects

Project 8-6 Lay Out a Poster

- Set poster layout
- Apply gradient transparency
- Set print specifications

Skills Studio

Design a 3D Product

Project 8-7 Create a 3D Cylinder

- Apply 3D effects

Project 8-8 Design a Product Logo

- Create a logo

Project 8-9 Design a Product Label

- Add clip art to a logo
- Apply text outlines
- Add symbols

Project 8-10 Add Symbols to a Label

- Create a map
- Affix a map

Page 333

Start-Up Skills

Integrate Graphic and Layout Software This chapter is intended to teach students how to use Adobe Illustrator and Microsoft Publisher together to create publications. As in Chapter 6, students need to understand the limits of each type of software and the power of combining them. Have students preview the chapter to see the skills they will learn. They should review the objectives Skills You Will Learn and You Will Learn To, titles and headers, and illustrations. See if they can identify the skills that are specific to Illustrator and how these will be combined with Publisher.

Page 333

Design Process: Logos

Create Logos as Vector Images Students created simple logos using Microsoft Word in Chapter 2. In Chapter 8, they will see how much more powerful Adobe Illustrator is for designing logos. Besides having a large selection of drawing tools, Illustrator produces vector graphics, which students should know is the desired format for a logo. Review with students why it is important for logos to be created as vector graphics. They should remember that logos must be scalable in order to be used in everything from business cards to billboards.

Quick Write Activity

Evaluate Logos Students have evaluated logos before this chapter, but by now they should be able to do more sophisticated design analyses. Bring in examples of logos (or have students do this for homework). They should be designed for a wide variety of businesses, organizations, audiences, and media. Ask students to use the chart on page 333 to evaluate at least two distinctly different designs. They should be sure to explain in what type of publication the logo is most likely to be used and how that affects its design. Use students' examples and evaluations as the basis for a class discussion.

LEARNING LINK

This chapter continues to teach new Illustrator skills, while showing students how these skills are applied in the real world. By now, students should realize that Illustrator is a complex and powerful program and that they will learn to use only a small portion of its features and capabilities. However, when they see it combined with the layout capabilities of Publisher, they should have a much better understanding of how it is used commercially. Show them examples of product packaging (e.g., cereal boxes, product labels, drink cans) that are most likely created with a graphics program like Illustrator.

Workshop Foundations
Pages 334–335

Assess Project Needs

FOCUS

Focus Activity

Compare Software Adobe Illustrator is the fourth type of software that students will learn about in this course. Illustrator is a graphics program that plays an important role in the design of desktop publishing. Have students copy the chart on page 334 into their notebooks. Then, as a class, go through the list of desktop publishing tasks in the chart, and discuss why each particular software is best for each.

You Will Learn To:
- Find resources for photographs
- Determine the legal use of a photograph

Page 334

Before You Read Activity

Check Your Understanding Explain to students that being able to summarize what they have just read will help them 1) remember the material better and 2) determine what skills they have mastered and what skills are still unclear. Rather than taking notes as they read, students should stop every now and then and jot down key points they remember. They should use arrows or short comments to show how the concepts are connected. If students prefer to use graphic organizers to do this, briefly discuss how they might use the different chart options that are available in Part 3 of this book and online at **glencoe.com**.

Page 334

Key Term Activity

The Design Process On the board, create a four-column chart. In the first column write each key term. Ask for student volunteers to define each. If the definition is not quite right, ask other students for more specifics until it is accurate. Write the definition in the second column next to the term. For the third column, have students determine what part of the design process is affected by the client, medium, or service bureau. Finally, for the fourth column, ask students for examples of how each of these factors influences the design.

Key Term Definitions

client The person or group of people who commission a publication. (page 334)

medium A delivery method of publications, such as print, CDs or DVDs, Internet publishing, television or radio broadcasts, etc. (page 335)

service bureau A company that provides publishing services, such as scanning and high-resolution printing. (page 335)

TEACH

Teach Activity

Review Vector Graphic Qualities Discuss with students the situations where it is best to use vector-based graphics rather than raster graphics. Some factors for choosing vectors are when the graphic will need to be scalable (especially logos and text graphics), when it is clip art (which needs to fit in many circumstances), and even when there are special printing needs (fewer colors in order to manage costs for specialized presses, such as screen printing).

● Answers to Workshop Foundations Activities

Page 335

Eye on Ethics

Content (information), pictures, artwork, sound, and video are all intellectual property and are protected by copyright laws.

ASSESS

Page 335

 Reading Check

1. Before beginning to work on a project, the designer should be familiar with the project requirements and expectations. This helps to establish the software requirements, resolution needs, file formats, and establishes clear expectations. By understanding the project requirements, workload is reduced.

2. Some file formats work best with different methods of delivery. For instance, when creating something to be professionally printed, one would not want to create graphics in a GIF format.

CLOSE

Communicate with the Client Ask students to explain how the proper tools can help get a job done right. Students may find it surprising that the client should be one of the tools necessary for completing an effective design. Designers need to have open communication with the client throughout the design process. Clear expectations for the project need to be established, and the designer should communicate with the client often to ensure that the project is meeting the client's goals. Nobody would want to finish a project only to find out that the client does not like it.

Workshop Toolbox Page 336

Layers Palette in Illustrator

FOCUS

Focus Activity

Compare Layers Palettes Ask students to look at the illustration on page 336 and compare Illustrator's Layers palette with Adobe Photoshop's Layers palette. Which sort of things are similar? How are the two palettes different? Students are likely to notice that the layout and icons in the Illustrator palette are similar to Photoshop's, but that Illustrator's palette has sublayers that group effects together.

> **You Will Learn To:**
> - Identify palettes used to create complex shapes
> - Apply the Layers palette

Page 336

Key Term Activity

Visualize Layering See if students can come up with some examples of layering in everyday life that have nothing to do with graphics. For example, clothes are often layered to get a particular "look," are pastries are often created in layers to create a certain taste or texture. Ask students how these kinds of layering relate to the layering used when creating images in Illustrator or Photoshop.

> **Key Term Definitions**
>
> **layering** The process of precisely positioning and aligning objects and effects within one design; also called stacking. (page 336)

TEACH

Teach Activity

Analyze the Layers Palette Have students use the figure on page 336 and the figures in Project 8-1 to identify the information that can be determined from the Layers palette. Students are likely to note that the palette tells them which objects are above or below other objects, which ones are visible or locked, which objects are grouped or make up part of a larger object. Point out that when using the command Object>Arrange>Send to Back (or Front), the object order is changed only in relation to the objects on the same layer.

Answers to Workshop Toolbox Activities

Page 336

Sidebar

The keyboard shortcut for *gradient* is G.

ASSESS

Evaluate Learning Assign Reading Check questions to assess students' understanding of the chapter Toolbox.

Reading Check

1. Layering lets you manipulate and edit effects and objects within a design, without affecting the entire design. It also lets you precisely add effects one by one, so you can see how the effect looks and remove it if necessary.

2. You can avoid accidentally changing a layer by locking layers when they are finished and hiding layers when they begin to become obtrusive.

CLOSE

Manage Layers Illustrator's Layers palette has a few valuable tools that can help students design more easily. Students should also understand how they can use the palette to make their design more effective. The following tips might be useful when working with Illustrator.

- Hide layers when you need to see under them.
- Lock layers so you can see them or use them for reference, but keep them from getting accidentally selected.
- Create layer groups to help manage the large number of layers.
- Create sub layers.
- Move layers higher to give them a sense of depth.
- Troubleshoot problems by using the layer descriptions to see if you missed something (for example, envelope distortions that have not been expanded).

Chapter 8 Projects
Pages 337–370

FOCUS

Focus Activity

Review Illustrator Skills Make sure that students are comfortable using the tools they learned about in Chapter 7. As homework before beginning Chapter 8, assign a tool—from Illustrator's toolbox, palettes, or toolbars—to each student. Have students give a brief report on the tool, including a demonstration of how it works and an explanation of how and when to use it.

 Go Online PREVIEW

Before You Begin Students can use the chapter **PowerPoint** presentations and **rubrics** at the Online Learning Center to determine what is expected *before* they complete a project. Students can view the PowerPoint slides on their own computers, or you can project them to preview chapter concepts and show examples of the finished projects. You might also display project solutions so students can easily refer to them while they work. (Presentations and rubrics are also provided on the Teacher Resource DVD for your convenience).

glencoe.com

Projects

Project 8-1
Create Shapes with Tools

Project 8-2
Design Vector Images

Project 8-3
Create a Tent Card

Project 8-4
Apply Live Trace

Project 8-5
Create Shattered Text

Project 8-6
Lay Out a Poster

Skills Studio

Project 8-7
Create a 3D Cylinder

Project 8-8
Design a Product Logo

Project 8-9
Design a Product Label

Project 8-10
Add Symbols to a Label

Key Term Activity

Test Prior Knowledge Have students copy the key terms into their notebooks or key term journals. Ask them to try to define the terms from their previous knowledge. As the students read through the project, instruct them to revise their definitions if necessary.

Key Term Definitions

Bézier curve A precise method of drawing curves that uses anchor points on a path and control points that describe the direction of the path. (page 337)

anchor point The spot where you begin or end a line segment. (page 337)

control points A drawing point defining the angle of a path to its next anchor point. (page 337)

mask A feature that hides areas of an image, so that the data in the image cannot be edited. (page 342)

native format A file format created specifically for a single software program. (page 346)

pixelated Describes when individual pixels are visible in an image. (page 349)

extrude To give an object visual depth. (page 351)

bevel Refers to the angled edges of an object. (page 351)

tile printing A method of printing an image that is larger than what the printer could normally print. The image is separated onto different pages that are later assembled into the complete image. (page 354)

freeware A software program that is downloadable at no charge. (page 354)

3D modeling The process of using a computer to virtually create an object. (page 359)

three-dimensional (3D) The illusion that a drawn object displays depth, width, and height. (page 359)

tracking An adjustment of the horizontal spacing between a series of characters. (page 361)

map An illustration that is wrapped around the outside of an object, as wallpaper is attached to a wall. (page 366)

TEACH

Teach Activity

Create Compatible Images When two types of software are used in a project, any files that are shared must be in a compatible file format. As students will see, to save Illustrator projects in an interchangeable format, they must use the Export command. Have students open a new Illustrator document, and choose File>Export to open the Export box. At the bottom of the box, have them open the *Save as file type* drop-down menu and write down the choices of file formats.

Solution files are provided in native format. Follow directions to resave the files for use with Publisher.

Teaching Tips and Troubleshooting Tips for Projects

Pages 337–341

Rubric

Project 8-1 → **Create Shapes with Tools** Students will use the pen tool and the Layers and Pathfinder palettes to create a coat-of-arms illustration. They will finish the illustration in Project 8-2 and, in Project 8-3, insert the image into a document created in Publisher. (**Solution File 8-1, Rubric 8-1**)

Explain a Coat of Arms If your school permits, have students go online to **www.yourchildlearns.com/her_act.htm** to learn some more about the ancient art of heraldry. The colors, shapes and icons on the shield all have particular meaning. As an enrichment project, have students design their own coat of arms using modern symbols.

Preview the Project Have students look at the final coat-of-arms illustration on page 345. Ask them to predict areas where they expect to have some difficulty. Students are likely to mention the dragon, though this is clip art and easy to use. Astute students will notice that creating the castle shape on the shield is the most challenging aspect of this project. Explain to students that learning how to use the tools to create these effects is valuable and worth learning. Warn them, though, that it may take several tries to become comfortable with the tools, so they should not give up.

Introduce the Pathfinder Palette Trying to precisely draw the castle on the shield for today's project would be pretty challenging. Illustrator's Pathfinder palette has many tools that make this task much easier. To show students one of the palette options, try the following activity:

1. Create a star, and color it green.
2. Create a circle that is larger than the star, and color it red.
3. Hold ALT and drag out a second copy of the circle.
4. Place the circle on top of the star, and position the circle so that part of the star is outside the circle's edge.
5. Select both objects and open the Pathfinder palette, using **Window>Pathfinder.**
6. Choose the Crop tool. Cropping cuts away the top layer from the bottom layer. The circle should disappear, but its shape should cut away parts of the star.
7. Move the second circle on top of the star, and choose **Object>Arrange>Send to back.** The star should look like it is wrapping around the curve of the circle.

Apply the Expand Command Point out the Instant Message on page 338 to students. They will learn more about the Expand command in Project 8-2, but they must apply it in Step 9 by pressing the Alt key when they Subtract from shape. The Expand command makes the change permanent. If students miss this step, there could be problems later.

Working with the Pathfinder Palette Students will have trouble with the project if they do not join the shield halves together (Steps 23-24). If they simply group the two parts, it will not work. The Pathfinder palette can only merge simple shapes, not grouped objects. Also, beginning students often create accidental layers. If the Pathfinder palette does not seem to be working, have students open the Layers palette and delete unnecessary layers that may be causing trouble.

Pages 342–345

Rubric

Student Data File

Project 8-2 ▶ **Design Vector Images** Students finish the coat of arms they started in Project 8-1. They will continue to use both the Layers and Pathfinder palettes, as well as the Type tool and Envelope Distort. To prepare the image for publication in Project 8-3, they will save it in the compatible format WMF. **(Data File 8-2, Solution File 8-2, Rubric 8-2)**

✍ **Demonstrate Pathfinder Tools** Have students look at the illustration on page 342. The shapes were created using the Pathfinder palette. Demonstrate how this was done as described below.

- To create the cloud, use Illustrator to draw three overlapping ellipses. Use the Selection tool to select all the ellipses. In the Pathfinder palette, choose **Add to shape area**. All the ellipses will become a single cloud shape.
- To create the moon, draw two overlapping circles. Select both, then choose **Subtract from shape area** in the Pathfinder palette. The crescent shape should be left.

Have students combine simple objects to create more complex shapes like a chef's hat or a house.

✍ **Expand Shapes** The individual shapes used to draw the cloud in the previous tip can still be selected and moved until the effect is expanded. You can immediately expand the Pathfinder tools by holding ALT while clicking the button in the palette. You can also expand by clicking the Expand button in the Pathfinder palette or by choosing Object>Expand.

✍ **Save in a Compatible Format** Remind students that they will be using this image in a Publisher document, so it must be saved in an interchangeable format (Step 20), rather than Illustrator's native format AI. Since the Publisher document will not need to be printed at a very high resolution, WMF format should be sufficient.

⚠ **Troubleshoot Cropping Problems** It may take several tries to crop the shield. Students may have difficulty if they unintentionally create stray layers. This is a common mistake. If a student's shield is not cropping, open the Layers palette (Windows>Layers) to view the layers in the illustration. Delete any unnecessary layers and try to crop again. Also, make sure that students expanded the castle shape in Project 8-1, Step 9, and did not group the shield halves.

Pages 346–348

Rubric

Project 8-3 ▷ **Create a Tent Cart** Students will use the illustration they created in Projects 8-1 and 8-2 for an invitation to a family reunion. They will use Publisher to create the invitation in tent card layout. **(Solution File 8-3, Rubric 8-3)**

✍ **Identify Compatible File Formats** Have students use Illustrator's Help feature to find file formats for exporting artwork. Have them use the information to create their own chart showing which software can be used with each file format. They should include columns describing the advantages and disadvantages of each format, as well as the best medium for that particular format (i.e., monitor display, Mac computers only, print, and so on). The charts on pages 259 and 294 of the textbook might also help.

✍ **Review Layout Guides** Have students access the Layout Guides dialog box (Arrange>Layout Guides). Ask them to change the settings under Margin Guides and Grid Guides while observing the Preview box. Knowing how to use the Preview box helps students design their own publications.

⚠ **Insert the Image** Students may try to copy and paste the image from Illustrator to Publisher. While this will probably work, they should follow the instructions instead. Copy/paste will result in a white background behind the object that cannot be removed. While that is not a problem with this project, it could be problematic in other ones. Additionally, the resolution will be reduced by using the copy and paste commands.

Pages 349–350

Rubric

Student
Data File

> Project 8-4

Apply Live Trace Students use the Live Trace tool to convert a raster graphic into a scalable vector image. The image will be enlarged to use in a poster that students create in Project 8-6. **(Data File 8-4, Solution File 8-4, Rubric 8-4)**

✍ **Evaluate Graphic Needs** Students have, by this point, had experience with both vector and raster graphics. Ask students which kind of graphic is best. Students might respond that raster graphics using Adobe Photoshop were much easier to create and to edit. The correct answer, however, is that both types of graphics are good, and the usefulness of the graphic depends upon the type of product needed. Realism, file size, and scalability all play a part in determining which graphic is "best." Ask students to copy the chart comparing vector and raster graphics on page 349 into their journals.

✍ **Introduce Live Trace** Adobe Illustrator CS2 has a feature called Live Trace that converts images from raster to vector. Ask students why someone might want to convert a raster image into a vector image. Lead students to conclude that this feature is used when items need to be scalable, so they do not pixelate when enlarged to a size greater than 110% of the original. It can also create an interesting artistic effect and visual interest.

✍ **Demonstrate Live Trace** In Adobe Illustrator, copy and paste a raster picture from Microsoft Word's clip art gallery. With the picture selected, choose **Object>Live Trace>Make**. The original image is converted to a vector image. The effect can be customized by changing the settings on the Options toolbar at the top of the screen. Open the Preset menu to experiment with some options. Once the effect has been edited to your satisfaction, use **Object>Expand** to make the effect permanent. The image can then be scaled more easily.

⚠ **Choose a File Format** In Step 7, students are asked to choose an interchangeable file format using the Export feature. Students can find different compatible formats using File>Save As or File>Export. File>Export has WMF and EMF, which are widely accepted. File>Save As has PDF and EPS, which are also widely accepted and are good quality formats. (Note: To create an EPS document that can be used in Microsoft products, change the version of Illustrator to Illustrator 8 when the EPS dialog box pops up.) Determine which format students should use by testing these commands in advance on a sample document using your available software.

⚠ **Older Versions of Illustrator** If your version of Illustrator is Illustrator CS or older, the Live Trace feature is not available. Have students use the solution file for this project (Solution File 8-4) in the poster they create in Project 8-6.

Pages 351-353

Rubric

Project 8-5 **Create Shattered Text** Students continue creating graphics for the poster they will design in Project 8-6. In this project, they will add 3D and other effects to text so that it appears to be shattered. **(Solution File 8-5, Rubric 8-5)**

Demonstrate the Steps To avoid potential problems, demonstrate the following procedure for your students.

1. Use the Type tool to key a letter O. Zoom in so it is large enough to see well, and fill it with a light color.

2. Select the O, and choose **Type>Create Outlines**.

3. Draw a line through the O and select all objects. In the Pathfinder palette, choose the **Divide** command.

4. Select the object, and choose **Object>Ungroup**.

5. Use the Direct Selection tool to select the two semicircles on the inside of the O. Press Delete. (See the Troubleshooting Tip below for deleting unnecessary shapes.)

6. Use the Selection tool to select half of the O, then move it away from the other half and rotate it slightly.

7. Select both halves and choose **Object>Group**.

8. Select the O group, then choose **Effect>3D>Extrude and Bevel**. Check the Preview box, and experiment with the different settings to demonstrate the features.

Select Unnecessary Shapes It may be difficult for students to find and delete the unnecessary shapes created by overlapping lines and the Divide command. The more intersecting lines they draw, the more shapes they will find. Students should use the Direct Selection tool and move it over the bowls and counters of the letters. As they move the pointer over the letterforms, they will see that a small rectangle sometimes appears next to the arrow. When they see that, they should click to select the shape. They should delete all shapes except the letterform itself.

Preview 3D Options Some older computers may not be able to use the 3D options in Illustrator. Test the lesson in your computer lab before assigning these lessons to your students.

Pages 354–357

Rubric

Student Data File

Project 8-6 **Lay Out a Poster** Students lay out a poster in Publisher and insert the images they created in Projects 8-4 and 8-5. They then use tile printing to print the oversized document. **(Data File 8-6, Solution File 8-6, Rubric 8-6)**

Evaluate Design Have students look at the final design as shown on page 357. In their notebooks, have them create a thumbnail sketch and identify the uses of PARC principles. If you wish, ask students to create two other thumbnails of alternate designs they could use for this poster.

Demonstrate Tile Printing Show students an example of a poster that has been tile printed. Point out that the design has been printed twice along the edges on some pages to allow for overlapping and hiding the seams. When trimming their designs to create the poster, students will need to actually cut into the ink of one of the duplicate edges— they should not simply trim off the white areas. Demonstrate the process of trimming and taping the design together. Place invisible tape on the back of the design.

Sometimes the pages simply will not line up exactly because the rollers in the printer slip. This slipping is called *being out of register*. This even happens with high-end printing devices, though less frequently than with inexpensive printers.

Apply Laminate If possible, display good student work in science labs around the school to increase awareness of desktop publishing and to give students bragging rights for a job well done. Posters that are displayed should be laminated. Given the class budget, you may choose to apply self stick laminate or to use a thermal laminator. Smaller thermal laminators can still laminate something this large by folding and laminating the poster a second time.

Pages 354–357

Save Ink Printing a full-sized, full-color poster like this can use a lot of ink in the classroom. One solution is to use a large white rectangle behind the text, leaving only a small border of the fire background to print.

Skills Studio

Pages 358–370

Design a 3D Product

Ask students if they have seen the latest computer animated movies or *Toy Story* or *Shrek*. Explain that this type of animation is created using 3D modeling software. With this software, images are built up on screen, and their properties are defined (wood, glass, and so on). The computer then calculates the way that light from a light source would behave when the light strikes the object. This process is called ray tracing, and it can create extremely lifelike results. Adobe Illustrator is not a 3D modeling program; it is illustration software. However, it can still create effects that look realistic, if not lifelike. (For further interest, the Shrek DVD has an excellent "making of" section that describes the process of creating this kind of movie.)

Pages 359–360

Rubric

Project 8-7 **Create a 3D Cylinder** Students begin to design a can for a fruit drink. In this project, they create the can shape using the 3D Revolve tool. Explain that 3D illustrations can be used to test product designs on boxes, books, cans, and other simple objects. **(Solution File 6-7, Rubric 6-7)**

Preview Skills Ask students to look at page 359 and identify the shapes used to create the figure. The figure uses only rectangles and lines for highlights. Ask students how long they think that something like this will take. Responses will vary, but tell students that after learning the skills in this Skills Studio, students should be able to create this graphic in less than ten minutes.

Demonstrate 3D Effects Create a 3D apple to demonstrate some of the skills students will learn.

1. Create a circle with a white fill and a thick red outside stroke.
2. Choose the Warp tool and click and drag the shape until it looks like an apple.
3. Choose the Scissors tool. Click an anchor point at the top of the apple in the center, then click an anchor point at the bottom center of the apple.
4. Use the Selection tool to select half the apple (to the points selected with the Scissors tool). Delete the section.
5. Select the remaining half of the apple, and choose **Effects>3D>Revolve**.
6. In the Revolve Options box, check the Preview box.
7. Under Revolve, change the Angle settings. You will see that, depending on the angle, it will look like a whole apple, an apple with a slice removed, or even just a slice.

3D Options Students used the Revolve tool to create their can, but the same effect could have been created by using the Extrude and Bevel tool. Ask students to describe how the same effect could have been created and ask them to predict if it is a better method than revolving. (*Answer: Create a circle and change the extrude depth. Though both methods are good, the revolve option leaves a small imperfection at the top due to the rounded rectangle's rounded corner.*)

Expand 3D Images The 3D Revolve effect can be customized until the final image's appearance is expanded by using Object>Expand.

Encourage Experimentation Students are likely to complete this project quickly and have enough time to do the next project. Since students will probably enjoy using this effect, give them time to create other objects like the puzzle cube, buildings, etc. Students should try revolving simple shapes.

Pages 361–362

Rubric

Project 8-8 **Design a Product Logo** Students continue working on the fruit drink can they started in project 8-7. They will use Illustrator to create a logo, which will be added to a label in Project 8-9. **(Solution File 8-8, Rubric 8-8)**

Identify Types of Logos Have students look at the logo examples on page 71. Ask students to identify how the three logos shown on the page illustrate three different kinds of logos. They should see that the designs illustrate logos that are text based, text with accents, and text with pictures.

✍ **Kern in Illustrator** See if students remember how they kerned text in Word (Project 1-7) and Publisher (Project 3-7). In Illustrator, spacing is adjusted by using the Tracking option in the Character palette. Open the palette for students and demonstrate the options. Ask why it is particularly important to get the spacing right between letters in a logo. (*Possible answers: Logos must be easy to read so people can see a company's name clearly. If they are enlarged, spacing issues will become more obvious.*)

⚠ **Expand the Logo** Remind students that Adobe Illustrator's strength lies in the creation and editing of clip art and logos, such as this one. The last step is to expand the object. Once the logo has been expanded, it can be resized and the stroke thickness will also resize accordingly.

Pages 363–365

Rubric

Project 8-9 ▷ **Design a Product Label** Students use the Align palette to ensure that elements of the Fruit Smoothy label are correctly positioned. They also add their final label design to the Symbols palette, which they will use when they complete the drink can in project 8-10. **(Data Files 8-9a and 8-9b, Solution File 8-9, Rubric 8-9)**

✍ **Identify Label Elements** Before beginning the project, have students look at the finished label in Figure 8.39 (page 365). See if they can identify the different elements that are on food labels. Explain that certain information is required on a product label, depending upon the product. Products will typically have a UPC (Universal Product Code) label, a list of ingredients, nutritional information, information about size and weight, as well as information about the product and its manufacturer.

✍ **Demonstrate the Align Palette** Show students the different options available in the Align palette. In Illustrator, draw three simple shapes and use the Selection tool to select all the shapes. In the Align palette, choose each option to show the results, then undo the last action and see what the next option will do. Repeat until most options have been investigated. Note that the Distribute options will change the middle shape in relation to the two outside shapes.

Click on the Options button in the palette and point out that the Options menu allows you to Align the objects in relationship to the workspace, and not each other. Demonstrate this option too.

⚠ **Align Objects** When placing objects into the label, its helpful to align them using the Align palette. Students should select multiple objects that they want to align in relation to each other, then choose an alignment choice on the palette. Objects can also be aligned in relation to the workspace, instead of each other. (See the Teaching Tip above.)

⚠ **Insert the Logo** Students will move the logo that they created in Project 8-9 into the label illustration. To move files from one Illustrator document to another, students should copy and paste the image, or click and drag the image from one window to another. When resizing illustrations, students should make sure that they Expand the object, or the stroke thickness will not resize in relationship to the image.

Pages 366–370

Rubric

> **Project 8-10**   **Add Symbols to a Label** Students add the label that they designed to the 3D can shape they created in Project 8-7. They will use Illustrator's map feature to add the image to the shape. **(Solution File 8-10, Rubric 8-10)**

Add Symbols to Maps You can only map 2D artwork that is stored in the Symbols palette to a 3D object. Symbols can be any Illustrator art object, including paths, compound paths, text, raster images, mesh objects, and groups of objects. Like wallpaper, the map places a graphic over the surface of the object so that it rotates along with the object. This can be used to add texture or, in this case, create a label for a product.

Discuss 3D Design Ask students what it means when an image is 3D. Encourage students to guess, if they do not know, but 3D is short for *three-dimensional*, which means that an object has three different measurements: height, width, and depth. A two-dimensional image does not have depth, only height and width. The 3D graphics that students create in Illustrator—like the drink can—only have an *illusion* of depth, unlike a real drink can, which is truly three dimensional.

Design in 3D Have students look at the graphic on page 366. Explain to students that this is a graphic created in Illustrator that uses a *map* to place a label on the toothpaste tube and the cap. In this illustration, a seafood theme is carried throughout the design: the graphics, the text, the shape of the bottle, and even the cap itself. However, even a good design will not fix a bad product. Who would want seafood-flavored toothpaste?

Create an Advertisement The Fruit Smoothy image that students create in the Skills Studio uses only Illustrator skills. Encourage students who are faster or more advanced to create a Publisher publication with the image, as suggested in Step 19. They can create an advertisement or packaging for a box that holds a dozen Fruit Smoothy cans.

Edit 3D Objects Students cannot use Object>3D to change the appearance of a 3D object. If they do, Illustrator will give a warning. Tell students that if they want to change the way a 3D object looks, they must select the object and choose Window>Appearance and double-click the Effects button for the effect they want to change. With Illustrator, you seldom have to start from scratch if you want to make adjustments.

Choose a Side Depending upon the 3D object, it may be confusing to determine upon which side the image map will be placed. Encourage students to look at the workspace to see which side is highlighted. If they make a mistake, encourage them to experiment and remind them that the image is digital and can be changed if something strange happens. *Undo* is a great feature.

ASSESS

Evaluate Encourage students to use the project rubrics and the Review and Revise checklists to be sure that they have completed the key steps to their projects. Encourage students to proofread and assist each other. Students learn best when they are teaching each other. Consider giving bonus points for well-designed projects for both the student and the student who evaluated his or her work.

Evaluate students both on their Illustrator work and on how well they combined the Illustrator and Publisher elements of their projects. You can grade the Illustrator elements separately or assess them as part of the finished integrated project.

CLOSE

Class Discussion Bring in several kinds of cereal boxes, some with high fiber, some with high sugar, some expensive, and some store brands. Ask students to identify the audience for each of the cereal boxes and identify the cereal that they would find the most appealing. Most likely students will choose the boxes with the best graphics and expensive printing techniques on the box. Ask them what it is that makes that box look like the contents are the best to them, and how do the images sell the particular product? Point out that quite often the store brand will have a similar product, but will spend less on packaging. How much of a role does packaging play in their purchasing habits? Product design is big business.

IN THE WORKPLACE

BRAND IDENTITY DESIGNERS
Career Activity
By applying psychology to brand identity, Brand Identity Designers can more effectively market their product to their audience, appealing directly to the subconscious wants and desires of their audience.

Use the following Reading Check and Critical Thinking answers as a guide to help evaluate student understanding of the core concepts. Requiring that your students write in complete sentences will help you grade faster and promote good writing skills. You can have students write answers in their desktop publishing journals, or students can answer these questions at the computer by accessing the Reading Check on the Online Learning Center at **glencoe.com**.

Chapter **8** Assessment Answers

Page 372

Reading Check

1. A publication medium can include the Internet, books, magazines, newspapers, radio, television, CDs or DVDs, billboards, packaging, and so on. It is the method in which the message is delivered to an audience.

2. Layering refers to the act of precisely positioning and aligning graphic objects in a design; also called stacking.

3. The Subtract command will take two shapes and "cut" one shape from the other, like a cookie cutter. The Expand command will make the effect permanent, rather than a temporary mask. Both commands can be found in the Pathfinder palette and they are both used to modify the shape of an object.

4. Service bureaus can print copies of publications, but they can also provide a wealth of experience and knowledge about the creation of designs. Before creating a design that will be professionally printed, talk with a printer for tips on the most effective ways to create documents for their machines and which kinds of file formats are best.

5. The medium of delivery greatly affects the type of files and effects that can be used. For example, designs for publication on the Internet need a fast download time and, therefore, large files (like TIFFS) should be avoided. Similar graphics can be created as JPEGs.

Critical Thinking

6. By understanding a client's needs before you begin creating a design, you will not waste as much time creating effects that cannot be used because they are not what the client had in mind, or because the effects will not work in the formats necessary for publication in the client's chosen medium.

7. Converting a raster graphic into a vector graphic is useful for creative effect and for scalability. Any image that must be rescaled to be used in different-sized publications (like a logo), should be converted to vector format.

8. Layers are helpful for creating documents because they can be easily edited.

9. Vector images should be used when the effect needs to be playful, or the graphics need to be able to be scaled, or when a small file size is desirable though quality must be good. Raster images should be used when a realistic appearance is necessary, or when the graphic does not need to be dramatically resized.

10. Some ways that the Layers palette in Illustrator is similar to the Layers palette in Photoshop are: you can rename layers, you can drag layers to change the order, you can click the Hide icon to hide or display a layer, you can lock layers, you can add or remove layers with the buttons at the bottom of the palette.

Assessment activities allow students to demonstrate their understanding of concepts and skills learned throughout this project. Because of time constraints, students may not be able to complete every activity suggested. Match assignments to student ability levels using the leveled projects (★ Easy, ★★ Medium, and ★★★ Challenging). Rubrics are available to evaluate projects on the Teacher Resources DVD and the Online Learning Center at **glencoe.com**.

Page 372

Rubric

1. Independent Practice ★

Create a Language Arts Poster If possible, have students interview their Language Arts teachers as if they were clients, or else bring a Language Arts teacher to the classroom to act as the client for this project. Require that students create interview questions for the client in order to establish the project expectations and limitations. Assign real value to thumbnail sketches and research of the topic. Students should create a design based on PARC principles, and they should include proper citation of research sources and all elements that the student did not personally create. Choose the top designs and show them to the client. Have the client's favorite design or two published and prominently displayed in classrooms. **(Rubric IP 8-1)**

Page 373

Rubric

2. Independent Practice ★★

Create a Proverb Banner Students may want to use proverbs of their own creation, but encourage students to use their research skills to locate an actual proverb that they like that is appropriate for a school audience. Students should find a way to illustrate the meaning, the tone, and the origin of the proverb, including period elements from the country of origin. Be sure that students properly cite research information and graphics. Students can find a wealth of proverbs and popular sayings online at **www.bartleby.com/100** or at **www.quoteland.com** (for quotes of a more modern origin). They should search for specific phrases, popular people, or by topics such as bravery, courage, or hard work. **(Rubric IP 8-2)**

Page 373

Rubric

3. Independent Practice ★★★

Design Cereal Box Packaging Help students form teams for this project. Groups can be 2–4 students and each team member should be assigned specific responsibilities. Have the team brainstorm ideas for a theme and ways to build upon the theme. Students should also do research to get ideas for the packaging, as well as nutritional information. (Visit the Web Resources in the Online Learning Center at **glencoe.com** to find Web sites with additional information that you might be useful to students.)

Below are some suggestions for elements that students might want to include on their boxes. Students might want to assign each member of the group to one or two sides of the box.

- **Front:** logo, a cereal box character, size and weight, cereal, a callout, a colorful background, thematic elements
- **Back:** logo, games, an order form, thematic elements
- **Side1:** logo, nutrition information, packaging information, thematic elements
- **Side 2:** logo, satisfaction guarantee, cereal pictures and descriptions, bar code, thematic elements
- **Top:** logo, callout, opening instructions, graphics of tab
- **Bottom:** logo, instructions for opening other end, bar code, graphics of flaps **(Rubric IP 8-3)**

Reteaching Activities

Review Key Skills Illustrator is a difficult program, and students should try not to get frustrated if they have to repeat a task to get it right. For students who are struggling, have them repeat projects where they had trouble. They should follow the same basic steps, but change elements such as colors, patterns, and clip art. For example, they may want to create a new coat of arms, but they can change the shape of the shield, use triangles for the castle design, and insert different clip art.

Finish Worksheets Have students complete Worksheet 8A and Worksheet 8B, which can be found in Part 3 or this TRM, on the Teacher Resource DVD, or at the Online Learning Center at **glencoe.com**.

Enrichment Activities

Create 3D Images Advanced students may be interested in experimenting more with the 3D images. Have them use Illustrator Help to find more information about creating these images, and then ask them to create at least three different 3D shapes with images and textures.

Enrichment If students need an additional challenge, have them complete the enrichment activities on the Online Learning Center at **glencoe.com**.

Projects Across the Curriculum

Project 1 Create a Food Product ★

Bring in examples of commercial food advertisements from magazines or newspapers for students to look at. Often, local supermarket flyers have food ads. Students may be able to find images online to use in the ad, though they should create a logo for the product using Illustrator. Layout and non-illustrative text should be created using Publisher. Encourage students to write descriptions of their new food product and use a theme and visuals that complement the description and appeal to a particular audience. The Web Resources listed in the Online Learning Center might be a good source of information for students. **(Rubric PAC 4-1)**

Project 2 Create a Graph ★★

Show students how graphs are used in publications such as *USA Today* or *BusinessWeek*. Direct students to find education-related research at **www.census.gov**, the US Government's site for census survey results. Surveys are being done and compiled almost constantly, though the Constitution requires that they be done once every 10 years. Have students use Illustrator's Help feature to create a graph using Illustrator. They should use Publisher to design an attractive page explaining the information in the graph. Students should include real research with proper documentation of both the research data and graphic elements that they did not personally create. Evaluate designs based on productive research, the accuracy and clarity of the graph and descriptive content, and proper documentation of reliable sources. **(Rubric PAC 4-2)**

Project 3 Create a Board Game Review ★★★

Allow students to work together in groups and choose a science topic, or a topic from some other core subject that they can review. Student groups should brainstorm the layout and design of the game's board, what type of information they want to include in game cards, and how players will move on the board. Perhaps they want to create a game similar to Life, Monopoly, Trivial Pursuit, Chutes and Ladders, and so on. Students should research topics, questions, and answers related to information for that subject matter. **(Rubric PAC 4-3)**

Project 4 Create a Pottery Design ★★★

Pottery shape and design helps to indicate the pottery's usefulness and the priorities and resources of ancient cultures. Ask students to research pottery found from an ancient society and note the typical picture pattern, and the shape of the pottery. Using their research, have students design and write a description of their design on paper before beginning their creation. They should use Illustrator's 3D Revolve and Mapping features to create a virtual model of their image. It may be desirable to use the Direct Selection tool to find and delete slight imperfections, though some imperfections should be acceptable. Assign real value to research, properly citing and evaluating the reliability of sources, planning the project's shape and images and the execution of the product. **(Rubric PAC 4-4)**

Design as a Team

Getting Started

About the Unit

In this unit, students will get a real-world lesson on how a team might work together to design materials for a client. The client in this case is Light Travel, a travel agency from the not-too-distant future that specializes in interplanetary vacations. Students will be part of the agency's marketing department, and they are putting together marketing materials for an adventure travel package to Mars. This unit is intended to teach students the fundamentals of working well in groups, an important skill in today's workplace. It will also give students the opportunity to create a consistent design that is used in a variety of publications.

In **Chapter 9**, students learn the basic tools of effective teamwork, including communication skills, workload and deadline strategies, budgeting, and conflict resolution skills. They will use Microsoft Publisher to create a calendar and a flowchart, and Microsoft Excel to create a basic spreadsheet. Once students have reviewed essential teamwork skills, they are ready to develop a logo and business package for Light Travel.

In **Chapter 10**, students will gain more practice working as a team to create marketing materials. They will incorporate some of the design elements they created in Chapter 9 into publications such as brochures, booklets, and Web pages. They will need to use style sheets to give the publications a consistent design that is unique to Light Travel. After students have finished creating their publications, they will have a chance to explain the marketing campaign to the client. Students will learn how to use PowerPoint to create a presentation that will showcase each product.

Quick Write Activity

Learning to work as part of a team is a vital and necessary skill to prepare for the real world. Ask students to write a short paragraph about why it might be important to learn how to work together in groups. When a team works well, its output can sometimes be better than work created independently, and more work can be done in a shorter time period. Nobody works alone in the workplace. Even teachers have state lawmakers who set guidelines, district managers, school administrators, teaching departments, counselors, parents, and students working together to create an effective curriculum.

Assessments

Workshop Foundations Reading Check, pg. 380
Workshop Toolbox Reading Check, pg. 381

End of Chapter 9 Assessment
Reading Check, pg. 404
Critical Thinking, pg. 404

Ⓡ **1.** Independent Practice: Create a New Product, pg. 404

Ⓡ **2.** Independent Practice: Plan a Children's Book, pg. 405

Ⓡ **3.** Independent Practice: Plan a Fund-Raising Campaign, pg. 405

⊙ **Additional Assessments You May Wish to Use**
ExamView Assessment Suite Testbank, Chapter 9

Workshop Foundations Reading Check, pg. 408
Workshop Toolbox Reading Check, pg. 409

End of Chapter 10 Assessment
Reading Check, pg. 443
Critical Thinking, pg. 443

Ⓡ **1.** Independent Practice: Promote a Rock Band, pg. 443

Ⓡ **2.** Independent Practice: Market a Movie, pg. 444

Ⓡ **3.** Independent Practice: Promote a Fund Raiser, pg. 444

⊙ **Additional Assessments You May Wish to Use**
ExamView Assessment Suite Testbank, Chapter 10

ⓘ **Go Online e-Review Self Checks** Chapter 9 and Chapter 10

Estimated Time to Complete Unit

9 Week Course = 5–7 days
18 Week Course = 7–8 days
36 Week Course = 13–15 days

To help customize lesson plans, use the Pacing Guide on pages 29–30 and the Standards Charts on pages 230–283.

Key to Recommended Materials

ⓘ Internet access required

Ⓡ Scoring Rubrics

ⅅⅎ Data Files

⊙ *ExamView Assessment Suite* CD

Ⓣ TechSIM (Technology Simulations available on CD and the Online Learning Center)

The Teacher Resource DVD contains Data Files, Solution Files, Rubrics, Reproducible Worksheets, and PowerPoint Presentations.

Data Files for Unit 5 provided on the Teacher Resource DVD and Online Learning Center

Chapter 9
9-8

Chapter 10
10-2
10-3a to 10-3f
10-4a to 10-4i
10-5a to 10-5b
10-7a to 10-7c
10-8a to 10-8d

Inclusion Strategies
For **Differentiated Instruction Strategies** refer to the **Inclusion in the Computer Technology Classroom** booklet.

ISTE NETS Foundation Standards

1. Basic operations and concepts	4. Technology communications tools
2. Social, ethical, and human issues	5. Technology research tools
3. Technology productivity tools	6. Technology problem-solving and decision-making

Performance Indicators	Textbook Correlation
1. Identify capabilities and limitations of contemporary and emerging technology resources and assess the potential of these systems and services to address personal, lifelong learning, and workplace needs. (NETS 2)	381, 387, 398, 400, 403, 407–408, 409–410, 418, 423, 426, 430, 436, 442
2. Make informed choices among technology systems, resources, and services. (NETS 1, 2)	381, 387, 398, 400, 404–405, 408, 410–412, 423, 426, 432, 436, 443–446
3. Analyze advantages and disadvantages of widespread use and reliance on technology in the workplace and in society as a whole. (NETS 2)	381, 395, 398, 400, 406, 413, 426, 442
4. Demonstrate and advocate for legal and ethical behaviors among peers, family, and community regarding the use of technology and information. (NETS 2)	379, 409
5. Use technology tools and resources for managing and communicating personal/professional information (e.g. finances, schedules, addresses, purchases, correspondence). (NETS 3, 4)	381, 382–384, 385–386, 387–390, 393–394, 395–402, 409, 413–415, 416–417, 418–421, 423–425, 426–429, 431–435, 436–438
6. Evaluate technology-based options, including distance and distributed education, for lifelong learning. (NETS 5)	395, 403, 405, 430, 442, 444
7. Routinely and efficiently use online information resources to meet needs for collaboration, research, publications, communications, and productivity. (NETS 4, 5, 6)	382, 395, 403, 404, 405, 410, 416, 419, 423–425, 426–429, 430, 442, 443–447
8. Select and apply technology tools for research, information analysis, problem-solving, and decision-making in content learning. (NETS 4, 5)	381, 382–384, 385–386, 387–390, 404–405, 409, 413–415, 416–417, 418–422, 423–425, 426–429, 433–435, 437–438
9. Investigate and apply expert systems, intelligent agents, and simulations in real-world situations. (NETS 3, 5, 6)	382–402, 410–441
10. Collaborate with peers, experts, and others to contribute to content-related knowledge base by using technology to compile, synthesize, produce, and disseminate information, models, and other creative works. (NETS 4, 5, 6)	377, 378–381, 382–384, 385–386, 387–390, 391–392, 404–405, 406, 410–412, 413–417, 418–422, 423–429, 430–441

21st Century Skills

Core Subjects Language arts, math, science, social studies	378, 380, 381, 387–390, 398–399, 404–405, 407, 408, 409, 415, 416–417, 419–422, 427–429, 437, 443–446
Learning Skills Information and media literacy; communication skills; critical thinking and systems thinking; problem identification, formulation, and solution; self-direction; accountability	377, 378, 379, 380, 381, 386, 387–390, 391, 392, 397, 403, 404–405, 406, 407, 408, 409, 415, 416–417, 419–422, 423, 427–429, 437, 442, 443–446
21st Century Tools Communication, information processing and research tools; problem-solving tools, personal development and productivity tools	377–380, 381, 382–384, 385–386, 406, 407–409, 423–425, 426–429, 430–435, 436–438, 445–446

Foundation Skills

Basic Skills Reading, writing, math, listening, and Speaking	378, 380, 381, 387–390, 398–399, 404–405, 407, 408, 409, 415, 416–417, 419–422, 427–429, 437, 443–446
Thinking Skills Creative thinking, decision making, problem solving, reasoning	377, 379, 380, 381, 386, 391, 392, 397, 403, 404–405, 406, 408, 409, 416–417, 419–422, 423, 427–429, 442, 443–446
Personal Qualities Self-esteem, responsibility, self-management, and integrity/honesty	377, 378–380, 381, 382, 384, 385–386, 399, 403, 404–405

Workplace Competencies

Resources Allocate time, money, materials, facilities, and human resources	378–381, 382–384, 385–386, 387–390, 404–405, 443–446
Interpersonal Participate on teams, teach others, serve clients and customers, exercise leadership, negotiate to arrive at decisions, and work with cultural diversity	377–381, 382–384, 385–386, 387–390, 391–392, 404–405, 406, 413–441, 443–446
Information Acquire, evaluate, organize, maintain, interpret, communicate, and use computers to process information	404–405, 423, 436, 445–446
Systems Understand, monitor, correct, improve, and design systems	377, 378–380, 381–384, 385–386, 387–390, 395–398, 406, 407–408, 409
Technology Select, apply, maintain, and troubleshoot technology	381, 387–389, 404–405, 443–446, 423, 432, 436

Focus on Teamwork

Skills You Will Learn

Workshop Foundations: Work with Groups
- Work as part of a team
- Resolve conflicts

Workshop Toolbox: Tools for Teams
- Identify software for teamwork
- Compare software features

Project 9-1 Assign Team Roles
- Create a flowchart
- Add connectors

Project 9-2 Create a Timeline
- Modify a calendar template

Project 9-3 Create a Budget
- Create a spreadsheet
- Apply the Sum function
- Enter formulas
- Copy formulas

Project 9-4 Design a Logo
- Brainstorm ideas
- Create a design

Project 9-5 Design a Business Card
- Lay out a business card
- Insert a logo

Skills Studio

Design Business Stationery
Project 9-6 Design Business Letterhead
- Lay out a letterhead
- Insert a logo

Project 9-7 Design Business Envelopes
- Lay out a business envelope
- Add a return address

Project 9-8 Perform a Mail Merge
- Import a data source file
- Merge the data and envelopes

Page 377

Start-Up Skills

Organize Work Groups Point out to students that they have studied word processing, page layout, photo editing, and drawing. Ask students to list their favorite three units of study, in order. Use these lists to divide students into groups so that each group includes students who enjoyed different areas of study.

Design Process: Business Packages

Brand a Product In Chapters 9 and 10, students will create a business package and marketing materials. Ask students to bring in examples of company materials or advertisements that are instantly recognizable. These might include letters or brochures from organizations like banks, airlines, or non-profit groups; the subtle Nike ads that are identified only by the Nike "swoosh;" or the distinctive iPod advertisements. Ask students to analyze how these materials express the identity of the company and the product or service they represent. Ask them to consider how and why the materials communicate effectively to the intended audience.

Quick Write Activity

Evaluate Corporate Branding Students probably do not make a connection between the clean, high-tech look of Apple products and Apple marketing materials. They might think that all coporate stationery or business cards look the same.

If students have brought in examples of company materials, use those for this Quick Write Activity. If not, have examples of your own. Try to use companies with products or services that students will recognize. Give each student his or her own example of a corporate letter, business card, or other type of branded material. Then have students use the Design Process chart on page 377 to evaluate the reasoning behind the design choices. They should write at least two sentences for each element in the chart, explaining how it relates to their specific example.

LEARNING LINK

Many students have come to dislike working in groups because their groups do not work well. Perhaps there are people who do not contribute, and the student feels like they have to do the entire project. Perhaps they find themselves confused, lost, or left out. Another typical reason for disliking groups is that conflict and disagreement are inevitable. In this unit, students gain experience working in groups and acquire important organizational and interpersonal tools. Among other skills, they will learn to establish clear expectations and deal with conflicts. Students will need these skills in all areas of their lives.

Workshop Foundations
Pages 378–380

Work with Groups

FOCUS

Focus Activity

Create Flowcharts Groups fail to work because expectations are not made clear. Have students look at the flowchart on page 378. Ask students to identify the role of each individual. Ask what happens to articles that Adam writes, or to photographs that he takes. In addition to helping each member of the team understand his or her role, what other information can the flowchart provide? The flowchart not only shows who does what, it also maps the sequence of the work.

> **You Will Learn To:**
> - Work as part of a team
> - Resolve conflicts

Page 378

Before You Read Activity

Organize Information To illustrate this point, see if students can easily memorize a phone number that has not been broken up into smaller number groups. Write the number 5796239182 on the board and give students fifteen seconds to memorize it. Cover it up and see how many can remember it. Then write the same number as 579-623-9182, and try again. Ask students if this was easier and why. Encourage students to use index cards or graphic organizers to help them group topics as they read.

Page 378

Key Term Activity

Write Sentences Ask students to write a quick memo introducing themselves to the other members of their group. They must use all four of the key terms in their memo. For example, a student could write: As a project manager, I believe that, to inspire effective teamwork, we should take the time to create a solid flowchart and timeline.

Key Term Definitions

teamwork Working as a group in a way that encourages close cooperation between group members. (page 378)

flowchart A chart showing the parts of a larger procedure, illustrated by using a set of standard symbols. (page 379)

timeline A visual representation, often a chart, that shows when each stage of the project will be completed. (page 379)

project manager The person leading or supervising a team. (page 379)

TEACH

Teach Activity

Create Rules To prevent conflicts before they start, groups should agree upon some rules in advance. How often will the group meet? Who in the group will help to resolve conflicts? What sort of language will be permissible? Have students create ground rules for dealing with conflicts in their current groups. Encourage all students in the group to contribute to creating these ground rules and secure a commitment from each to abide by the rules the group set in place. Look on page 380 for more help.

Answers to Workshop Foundations Activities

Page 379

Eye on Ethics

Answers will vary. Students should mention the consequences of using technology in an unethical manner: regulations to limit the technology, legal fines or jail time, or even fewer original materials due to decreased sales.

ASSESS

Reading Check

1. Teams can work more effectively if: jobs are divided to meet each student's strengths, expectations for each group member are clearly defined, a timeline of work is established, and a conflict-resolution plan are utilized.

2. Ideally, the best solution is the win-win. In the case of two siblings fighting to watch a television show, one can record the show while the other does something else. In the event that the win-win resolution is not possible, the siblings may choose to do something else that they would both enjoy, or choose a show they both can agree upon.

CLOSE

Discuss Organization Ask students how spending time organizing a group will help in the long run. Reinforce the idea that, although group members will have to invest time in the beginning of a project, that time will likely be made up later on. Ultimately, time will be saved because all members of the group will know their responsibilities, thereby avoiding unnecessary work. Quality will be improved because effort will be better targeted. Deadlines will be met because group members will know when projects are on time or behind and will be able to budget their time accordingly.

Workshop Toolbox
Pages 378–380

Tools for Teams

FOCUS

Focus Activity

Identify Leadership Characteristics Ask students to list seven personal characteristics needed to be a good leader. Discuss the results as a class. Among other things, students should mention that a good leader is a good communicator, a good listener, well organized, knowledgeable about the subject matter, patient, calm, and well respected.

You Will Learn To:
- Identify software for teamwork
- Compare software features

Page 381

Key Term Activity

Establish Milestones Ask students to list three activities for which it would be helpful to create a schedule using milestones. Have them describe what those milestones might consist of. Examples of activities might include preparing an academic paper (milestones: identifying the topic, completing research, outline, draft, completing paper), making a short film (milestones: writing the script, choosing actors and locations, filming, editing), or any other activity that can be broken down into smaller tasks.

Key Term Definitions

milestone A critical point in a project. (page 381)

TEACH

Teach Activity

Plan Projects Carefully Besides getting the right person for the right job, groups must also plan a project carefully. While it may seem to take a lot of time to work out the details of a major project, it is time well spent. With a careful plan, group members will know what aspects of the project they are responsible for and what exactly needs to be done. Group members will not spend time working on something that is not useful.

The Workshop Toolbox on page 381 describes the tools that will help teams get organized and keep track of the members' progress. Have a class discussion or ask students to write a brief explanation of how the software that is described might help their projects. If the particular software described in the Toolbox is not available, come up with other strategies for team members to keep in touch and stay on schedule.

Page 381 **Team Communication** It is very important for group members to be able to communicate with each other. If they need to reach each other outside the classroom, provide them with a variety of options. Make sure they exchange phone numbers or e-mail addresses. If that is not possible, try to set up class time when they can meet as a group before beginning their individual tasks.

ASSESS

✓ Reading Check

1. To create a chart that compares the costs of each part of a project, it would be easiest to use Microsoft Excel, or another spreadsheet program.

2. A project manager is responsible for checking on the team's progress. While other group members focus solely upon individual aspects of the project, it is the project manager who looks at the big picture. Spreadsheets can be used to create a schedule to help the project manager make sure that each person on the team is completing his or her part of the project on time. A budget spreadsheet can be used to keep track of expenses.

CLOSE

Divide the Workload Often, in groups, somebody is assigned a job they are not qualified to perform, or interested in doing. Discuss with students the need to divide the workload by skill set, not by the project. They also need to understand how clear communication between team members and understanding of each person's job responsibilities will lead to more productive involvement and a better outcome.

Chapter 9 Projects

Pages 382–402

FOCUS

Focus Activity

Clarify Ideas In this chapter, students will create a business package for a fictitious company. Before they begin designing, encourage students to think about the ideas they want the design to express. To get them thinking about how a letterhead can send a message, ask students to imagine the personal letterhead they would design for themselves. Then have them write a short paragraph describing how they would express their own personality through the design of the letterhead. Have them describe the colors they would use, the style of the font and logo, and the image of themselves they would want to convey.

 **Go Online** PREVIEW

Before You Begin Students can use the chapter **PowerPoint** presentations and **rubrics** at the Online Learning Center to determine what is expected *before* they complete a project. Students can view the PowerPoint slides on their own computers, or you can project them to preview chapter concepts and show examples of the finished projects. You might also display project solutions so students can easily refer to them while they work. (Presentations and rubrics are also provided on the Teacher Resource DVD for your convenience).

glencoe.com

Projects

Project 9-1
Assign Team Roles

Project 9-2
Create a Timeline

Project 9-3
Create a Budget

Project 9-4
Design a Logo

Project 9-5
Design a Business Card

Skills Studio

Project 9-6
Design Business Letterhead

Project 9-7
Design Business Envelopes

Project 9-8
Perform a Mail Merge

Key Term Activity

Make Crossword Puzzles Write the key terms on the board with their definitions. Have a class discussion to see what previous knowledge your students may have about these concepts, then ask them to create a crossword puzzle out of the key terms. Instruct students to write a definition for each key term under the puzzle as clues. Then have them exchange their blank puzzles with another student and correctly fill in the missing key terms. Use graph paper to create the puzzles.

Key Term Definitions

connector A line that stays attached to a shape regardless of where the shape is moved. (page 382)

deadline A time goal. (page 385)

spreadsheet A grid or table that arranges numbers or text so that it is easy to manage and manipulate information. (page 387)

Pantone A color system used by professional print shops that matches computer data with specialized inks. (391)

tagline Slogan. (page 393)

letterhead The heading at the top of stationery, usually containing a name and address and sometimes a company logo. (page 396)

mailing list A large list of people who are intended to receive a copy of a letter or publication in a mass mailing. (page 400)

mail merge A process for producing mass mailings with personalized addresses on form letters, envelopes, and labels. (page 400)

data source A database of names, addresses, and other useful information used in a mail merge. (page 400)

main publication The document in a mail merge (such as a form letter or envelope) that does not change text, punctuation, spacing, or graphics when it is merged with the data source. (page 400)

import To bring in a file or product. (page 400)

TEACH

Teach Activity

Create a Strong Team Ask students to read the introductory paragraphs on page 382. Have them identify all the projects that will be created for Light Travel. Students should see that they will work on a logo, business card, letterhead, envelope, brochure, Web page, PowerPoint presentation, and a budget in the next two projects.

Tell students that the projects they are creating are too big for any one student to accomplish in the time available. This is when group work is much more efficient than working alone. Students will need to divide the tasks to work with one another's strengths so that a good product is created. Project 9-1 will provide the foundations they need to create an effective team that will take them through all the projects in Chapters 9 and 10.

Teaching Tips ✍ and Troubleshooting Tips ⚠ for Projects

Pages 382–385

Rubric

Project 9-1

Assign Team Roles Students use Microsoft Publisher to create a flowchart that divides the work and assigns responsibilities to group members based on their abilities and interests. Students can use the example in the book, but it would be best for them to create a flowchart using their own group members and assigned tasks. **(Solution File 9-1, Rubric 9-1)**

Organize the Teams Before students begin their flowcharts, have them read through the Workshop Foundations and Toolbox on pages 378–381. Review the team skills and tools with them so that they know what is expected. Students should also look at the projects in Chapters 9 and 10. This will give them a sense of what they will need to accomplish. Have them create a list of skills that will be needed to complete these projects. Then have team members decide who is responsible for each of the specific tasks, based on their interests and skill levels.

Determine Which Projects to Use The teams that students form in this project will continue working together to complete the projects in Chapter 10. Before you assign this unit, carefully read through the projects in Chapter 10 and decide whether you want students to complete all the projects or just some of them. Although data files are provided, it would be best if students could create most of the elements on their own. These projects are quite complex, requiring students to use many different skills that they have learned in the course. If you have limited time, you will not be able to complete them all.

Identify Skills To save time, you may choose to list the projects you will be doing in this unit and list the tasks. The brochure, for instance, will require a team to research Mars and the technologies needed to live on Mars, brainstorm content for the brochure, create the brochure layout, research usable pictures, write and edit articles for the brochure, and edit real photographs so that the images appear to be on Mars. Be sure to encourage students to keep track of the resources they used in order to give proper credit for the project.

Pages 385–386

Rubric

Project 9-2 **Create a Timeline** Groups use Microsoft Publisher to create a timeline. The timeline used as an example in this project shows deadlines for each part of the Mars project, which must be completed in two weeks. If possible, have students use an upcoming project to create their timeline, showing which team members are responsible for finishing specific tasks. **(Solution File 9-2 , Rubric 9-2)**

Review Milestones Review the concepts of a milestone and of breaking a longer project into smaller, attainable goals. Timelines can work as a checklist. Ask students to list three benefits of creating a timeline and establishing deadlines for project milestones. They might say that work can be prioritized, time can be managed, and progress can be assessed throughout the entire project. By dividing a long project into several milestones, group members can easily see what they are responsible for working on, and in which order these things should be created.

Use Calendars Remind students that the calendars are in two different places in Microsoft Publisher: the Design Gallery Objects button and the Blank Publications Task Pane. While the instructions call for the Design Gallery Objects calendar feature to be used, students can actually use any calendar feature that they want.

Notice, though, that this is one of Publisher's Smart Objects. When a column or row is deleted, the calendar dates are still accurate. Students can key notes in for each date, or they can create text boxes to have notes span more than one day.

Use Default Settings If students change the font or font size, the information that they key in the calendar will most likely need to be resized. Using the default settings for the calendar feature will save time. Since this is more for organization than for publishing, using the templates should be encouraged.

Pages 387–390

Rubric

Project 9-3 > **Create a Budget** Students consider the printing cost of publishing a set of marketing materials including the business package, brochure, and pamphlet. The amounts used in this project do not cover all the costs of publication. Unlike a real-world business, you will not have to consider costs such as salaries and equipment. **(Solution File 9-3, Rubric 9-3)**

Estimate Costs Using an electronic spreadsheet program such as Microsoft Excel is an essential skill. In this project, students will look at some real numbers related to the classroom production of the upcoming project. They will create formulas to help do the calculations. Emphasize that creating a budget is an important step for deciding if a project is worth the time that it takes to make. Businesses have a special term for this: cost analysis. Freelancers will find this a vital part of their work, for without setting a budget for time and money, a project could very easily become unprofitable.

Calculate Salaries One budget item that is not figured into this spreadsheet is salaries. If time permits, it might be fun to have students include an hourly wage for themselves and for the project manager of the group (who would tend to make more). With realistic numbers, students should see that salaries make up the majority of expenses.

Pages 391–392

Rubric

Project 9-4 > **Design a Logo** Student groups will use Adobe Illustrator to create a logo for their companies. They can create the logo used to illustrate this project or create a design of their own. **(Solution File 9-4, Rubric 9-4)**

Page 391

Answer to Sidebar Set time limits for brainstorming sessions so that the group stays focused. Setting limits encourages brainstorming as a short burst of creativity.

Discuss Color Matching Systems Get different colored red and blue pens from different manufacturers. Ask students which one is the right color blue (or red). While students may have a favorite shade, they are all shades of blue (or red) and students should recognize that inks come in different shades and tints. Remind students that there are over 16.7 million colors in their computer "crayon box." On top of that, there are impurities and different ways to mix the physical ink itself. The only reliable way to get a specific color is to use a color matching system, such as Pantone, where each color has its own pre-mixed ink.

Create Successful Logos Have students use the Web Diagram Graphic Organizer (Graphic Organizer 3 in Part 3 of this TRM) to copy the logo advice given on page 391. Review the four key ingredients for a successful logo: clever but simple, scalable, uses standard colors, and is unique.

Edit Fonts Remind students that fonts are created using vectors. When converted to outlines, they can be edited like drawing objects. Encourage students to use the warp, crystallize, wrinkle, pucker, bloat, or scallop tools to create interesting effects for future logos.

Review Illustrator Skills If students have trouble using the options in the Pathfinder palette, such as *Add to shape* or *Subtract from shape*, have them review the skills taught in Project 8-1.

Pages 393–394

Rubric

Project 9-5 **Design a Business Card** Students create a design for a business card for the Director of Marketing of Light Travel, using the logo they created in Project 9-4. If students have created their own logo and company, they can use the steps in this project to design their own business card. **(Solution File 9-5, Rubric 9-5)**

Analyze Business Card Design Have students look at Figure 9.17 on page 394. Ask students how many alignments are being used in the design. What is the focus of the design? What features make it easily readable? Answers: There are two alignments: both left. The focus is the company logo. Information is easy to read because there is a lot of white space, and different fonts are used to emphasize different types of information.

Use Layout Guides Review the use of Arrange>Layout Guides to divide the workspace into even sections to help keep designs consistent.

Skills Studio

Pages 395–402

Design Business Stationery

In the following Skills Studio, students will design business stationery based on their logo and business card design from Projects 9-4 and 9-5. They will also have a chance to use Publisher's mail merge feature. If possible, bring in examples of form letters that you have received from companies, where your name and other information specific to you is filled in. Use your example to explain to students what a mail merge is, and how it is used. Ask students what the advantages and disadvantages of using a mail merge might be. They might see that, while it makes it easy to do mass mailings with a personal touch, it is still not at all personal. Also, the database could require a lot of oversight to make sure that it is kept up to date.

Pages 396–397

Rubric

Project 9-6 **Design Business Letterhead** Students create business letterhead for a fictitious company. They will incorporate some of the design elements that they used on their business card. Students can use the example in the book, or create their own letterhead design. **(Solution File 9-6, Rubric 9-6)**

Use Consistent Design Elements To send a recognizable, professional message, the design elements of a company's business card, letterhead, and envelope should be consistent and unified. To help students understand consistent branding, have them compare the figures on pages 392, 394, and 395. What elements in these figures show that the designs all represent the same company? The placement of an oversized logo, left aligned Oldstyle text, and the decorative bar are all clearly repeated elements that serve to tie the designs together.

Place the Letterhead Effectively Company letterhead is left mostly blank so that there is enough room for a letter to be written upon it. Although it can look more distinct and exciting to use large designs or place the letterhead in unusual positions, make sure that students leave enough blank space for a standard one-page letter.

Pages 398–399

Rubric

Project 9-7 **Design Business Envelopes** Students complete their business package. The business envelope will include the logo and design elements used on the business card and business letterhead. Students will use the layout grid to help them set up usable space for the envelope. **(Solution File 9-7, Rubric 9-7)**

Design Consistent Elements Ask students if they have ever seen a family and noticed a resemblance. Although each person is an individual, they often share similar traits. The same is true for a business package. While each design should be unique, each design should also echo the others so that there is a "family resemblance." This helps create a unified message and a sense of professionalism.

⚠ **Observe Post Office Guidelines** Remind students that design must follow function. The envelope design is a perfect example. While there is plenty of room for creativity, there are also limitations. With envelopes, we must also pay attention to the standards set by the United States Post Office. Mail in the United States passes through electronic sorting machinery that is capable of sorting 11 pieces of mail per second, for a total of 40,000 pieces of mail an hour. By following certain guidelines, we can ensure smoother passage through the postal system and possibly even get a lower price. A company that mails a lot of items can save a significant amount of money over time.

Pages 400–402

Rubric

Student Data File

Project 9-8 ➤ **Perform a Mail Merge** Students use an Access database table as the data source to perform a mail merge. The mail merge will generate individualized envelopes to mail a publication or other communication. **(Data File 9-8, Solution File 9-8, Rubric 9-8)**

✍ **Use Mail Merge for Personal Correspondence** Encourage students to think about ways they could use mail merge to send correspondence to friends, classmates, or family. They can either import the data from other applications, or create it within Publisher. They can use mail merge to send holiday greeting cards, invitations, or any other customized mass mailing.

⚠ **Review Mail Merge** Students might be confused about how a database is used. Show students Figure 9.23 on page 401, the database they are using for this project. Have them look at the categories that are defined in the database, and then show them Figure 9.25 on page 402. Can they see how each category is automatically added into the address? What other categories might be used in a database that sends letters to customers to see if they are satisfied with a specific item they ordered in a catalog? (*Possible answers: The order number, the item number, a description of the item, the quantity ordered*)

ASSESS

Evaluate Encourage students to use the Review and Revise checklists to be sure that they have completed the key steps to this project. These guidelines will apply whether students use the examples in the book or create their own designs. Encourage students to proofread and assist each other. Students learn best when they are teaching each other. Consider giving bonus points for well-designed projects for both the student and the student who evaluated his/her work.

CLOSE

Assign Additional Activities You have a number of options for students who finish projects early or need more challenges. The Online Learning Center has additional activities, including more projects. Students also can choose from the projects in the Chapter Assessment. See the Enrichment Activities for this chapter on page 300.

IN THE WORKPLACE

TEAM PROJECT MANAGERS

Career Activity

Project managers ensure that a company's image is consistent by establishing and supervising the creative direction for an entire project and communicating effectively with team members and clients.

Evaluate Use the following Reading Check and Critical Thinking answers as a guide to help evaluate student understanding of the core concepts. Requiring that your students write in complete sentences will help you grade faster and promote good writing skills. You can have students write answers in their desktop publishing journals, or students can answer these questions at the computer by accessing the Reading Check and Critical Thinking activities on the Online Learning Center at **glencoe.com**.

Chapter **9** Assessment Answers

Page 404

Reading Check

1. A timeline is a graphic that shows milestones for a project, the related deadlines, and the amount of time spent on each part of a project.

2. To avoid conflicts between team members, members should: avoid getting personal, provide constructive feedback rather than criticism, not dwell on past mistakes, try to understand teammates' needs and feelings, use nonverbal communication such as smiling, and remind group members that you have a common goal.

3. Conflicts among team members can be resolved through one side "winning," through a compromise, or by finding a different approach to the problem.

4. A flowchart clearly illustrates the responsibilities of each member for all to see and follow.

5. A project manager must communicate expectations clearly to team members, managers, and clients. They must understand the nature of the work, be highly organized, and be able to prioritize work to meet deadlines.

Critical Thinking

6. By establishing project milestones, it is easier to monitor whether tasks are being completed in a timely way in order to meet the final deadline.

7. With an I-win strategy, only one side's concerns are met. With a win-win situation, the needs of both sides of a conflict are met to a satisfactory degree.

8. When a team member is falling behind schedule, other members may choose to help a team member, or the team may agree to limit the scope of the assignment to meet project deadlines.

9. Project managers might use e-mail software such as Microsoft Outlook to make sure everyone on the team communicates effectively, they might use Microsoft Excel to create spreadsheets for budgets, and they can use Microsoft Project, or Excel, to create timelines and schedules.

10. If team members do not work well together, project goals and deadlines may not be fulfilled, and clients (and jobs) may be lost.

Evaluate Assessment activities allow students to demonstrate their understanding of concepts and skills learned throughout this project. Because of time constraints, students may not be able to complete every activity suggested. Match assignments to student ability levels using the leveled projects (★ Easy, ★★ Medium, and ★★★ Challenging). Rubrics are available to evaluate projects on the Teacher Resources DVD and the Online Learning Center at **glencoe.com**.

Page 404

Rubric

1. Independent Practice ★

Create a New Product Help students form groups with a diverse set of team members. Be sure to encourage students to have fun and be creative with this project. The new product may be as small as a candy bar, or it may be a new type of toy, a shampoo, or even an online business. Make sure that the team, as a group, determines the kind of audience they expect to sell the product to, and what kind of image and message they want to send to the audience.

Once the group understands its goal, it can assign tasks to each team member and create a timeline. Students should be graded on how well the group works together, and for creating a logo, business card, and letterhead stationery that are consistent with the image of the students' fictional company. **(Rubric IP 9-1)**

Page 405

Rubric

2. Independent Practice ★ ★

Plan a Children's Book Help students form groups with team members who have a diverse set of skills. Be sure to allow students time to look for patterns in children's books targeted for a particular age group. They may notice that many books use large illustrations and large fonts, with bold colors. Children's books often have animals or mechanical objects for characters, are told in the third person, and may use rhymes.

After students know the scope of their project, have them create a timeline and budget. Although the timeline should be just for time needed to complete this assignment, it would be interesting for students to find out what the budget is for an actual book. Have them research the budget for a children's book that contains many colors and illustrations and is published in hard cover.

Grade students on how well the team meets its goals, and whether the two pages the team creates are appropriate for the audience and follow design principles. **(Rubric IP 9-2)**

Page 405

Rubric

3. Independent Practice ★★★

Plan a Fund-Raising Campaign Students can base this project on a fictional fund-raiser. If possible, however, allow students time to research local community charities and other fund-raising ideas. Students may choose to sell items they design, such as shirts, calendars, or stationery to benefit local area shelters, parks, or libraries. There are opportunities for service in every community.

Be sure to consider all three aspects of a fund-raiser: marketing, producing, and delivering. Both the budget and the timeline should be based on the actual amount of time and money that students have to complete this project. If students need help designing a promotional document, have them look at Projects 10-2 through 10-6 for ideas. Grade student projects based on how well the team meets its goals and the design and effectiveness of the promotional materials. **(Rubric IP 9-3)**

Reteaching Activities

Review Team Tools If students have used the examples in Projects 9-1 and 9-2 to create a flowchart and timeline, have them create an original flowchart and timeline for an important goal in their lives. They do not have to be part of a team to still employ these important tools. For example, if they have a big research paper in another class they can use a flowchart to show what needs to be done for each part of the process. They can create a timeline with milestones for each stage of the project: the research, the outline, the rough draft, the final draft.

Complete Worksheets Have students complete Worksheets 9A, 9B, or 9C, which can be found in Part 3 or this TRM, on the Teacher Resource DVD and at the Online learning Center at **glencoe.com**.

Enrichment Activities

Extend Projects The Independent Projects in the Chapter Assessment cover only a small portion of the tasks set up by the scenarios. Interested students should use the projects as a starting point to create more marketing materials. For example, in Independent Project 1, students can create an image of the product itself and design an advertisement with it. In Independent Project 2, students may want to create a book cover, marketing posters, or magazine advertisements.

⚡ **Enrichment** If students need an additional challenge, have them complete the activities in the Online Learning Center at **glencoe.com**.

Creating Marketing Materials

Skills You Will Learn

Workshop Foundations: Maintain Consistency

- Recognize consistent design elements
- Evaluate effective use of color

Workshop Toolbox: Transfer Style Sheets

- Maintain consistency between documents

Project 10-1 Import and Export Style Sheets

- Transfer style sheets in Microsoft Word
- Transfer style sheets in Microsoft Publisher
- Transfer style sheets in Adobe Illustrator

Project 10-2 Create a Brochure

- Design the front panel
- Create the address panel
- Add styles to the back panel

Project 10-3 Create the Brochure Interior

- Add text and graphics
- Apply a style sheet

Project 10-4 Design a Booklet

- Lay out a booklet
- Apply a master page
- Create a cover image
- Add a table of contents
- Import style sheets
- Cite sources

Project 10-5 Design Web Pages

- Create an image in Photoshop
- Format a Web page in Publisher
- Add pages to a publication

Project 10-6 Add Hyperlinks

- Ignore the master page
- Create hyperlinks

Skills Studio

Design PowerPoint Presentations

Project 10-7 Create a PowerPoint Presentation

- Import an outline
- Set up a Slide Master
- Add a Title Master
- Apply the master slides

Project 10-8 Create Images for a Presentation

- Add text to slides
- Take screen captures of documents

Project 10-9 Add Effects to a Presentation

- Add custom animation
- Adjust timing

Page 406

Start-Up Skills

Integrating Desktop Publishing Skills As students have learned throughout this book, desktop publishing is a process that requires more than design skills and technical skills. It also requires an ability to understand people's needs and to be able to communicate those needs to an audience. This chapter continues the marketing campaign that students began in Chapter 9. It provides students with an opportunity to design different marketing materials for different audiences and intentions. Brochures, booklets, and Web pages are created for customers. Students will also be creating a PowerPoint presentation that is meant for the client. Both the images and content will differ from the other products they design in the chapter.

Page 406

Design Process: Marketing Materials

Discuss Advertising Costs Ask students to name specific places where they might see advertisements for a nationally known company, like The Gap, Barnes and Noble, Staples, Target, Wal-Mart, etc. (Choose one company to discuss.) Some of the response might include TV shows, national magazines like Newsweek or Time, Web sites like Yahoo, and local newspapers. Try to get answers that are as specific as possible, like the name of the TV show where students saw an ad, or the name of a Web site where there was a pop-up for that particular business.

Ask students which of those examples would cost the most (*TV*), and which the least (*Web sites or local newspapers*). Why would a company choose one particular publication medium over another, or one particular Web site or TV show over another? What does it say about their audience and their budget? (Answer: *Certain TV shows and Web sites appeal to audiences with different incomes or from different age groups or interests. The same is true of magazines. A company which has a national product might advertise nationally, though it might also want to advertise local stores and promotions through the local paper.*)

Quick Write Activity

Evaluate Advertisements Bring in examples of advertisements from a variety of magazines, newspapers, and even yellow pages. Have students write a paragraph describing the type of publication and explaining why the advertisement might have been published in that publication, whether the budget is high or low, and who they think the target audience is.

LEARNING LINK

In this chapter, students will learn how to use Microsoft PowerPoint, a tool that they will find useful in many of their high school classes and in the working world. Although PowerPoint is not desktop publishing software, students will still used their design skills to create an effective presentation.

Workshop Foundations
Pages 407–408

Maintain Consistency

FOCUS

Focus Activity

Review PARC Principles Discuss the four PARC principles: proximity, alignment, repetition, and contrast. Which principle do students think is the most important when an organization wants its customers to immediately recognize that a publication is from that organization? Students should be able to determine that *repetition* of elements like logos, colors, or other design elements creates a professional identity in publications.

You Will Learn To:
- Recognize consistent design elements
- Evaluate effective use of color

Page 407

Before You Read Activity

How Can You Improve? Conduct a class discussion with students about successful study techniques they use. Write their responses on the board. As a class, come up with strategies for the best way to understand and review the desktop publishing material they have been learning. Since this is the last chapter of the course, use this opportunity to prepare students for any final exam or assessment.

Page 408

Key Term Activity

Define Colors Pantone is a type of spot color, which is always the same and is not created by mixing cyan, magenta, yellow, and black. So if any service bureau is asked to use a Pantone color with a certain code number, the color will always be the same. Have students read Appendix A color theory to learn more about creating specific colors.

Key Term Definitions

Pantone A premixed, custom-color system used by professional print shops. (page 408)

TEACH

Teach Activity

Create Consistent Colors There are so many shades of each color, you simply cannot "eyeball" the design to see if it "looks right." Keep in mind that the color you are seeing is a product of the monitor using red, green, and blue pixels in various intensities to display the color. This display is also affected by the ambient light in your room. On top of all that, monitor settings can be adjusted and monitors do not display the same colors the same way.

That is why, when sharing color data with other group members, it is best to stick to specific numbers. Use the CMYK, the RGB, the Hexadecimal, or Pantone numbers to communicate with group members. CMYK will probably coordinate best with the printer. Pantone (spot) colors are best when matching colors with a professional print shop, though spot colors greatly increase the cost of printing. Use the following techniques to match a color in a design.

- In Microsoft Word and Publisher, select an object that has the color you are trying to match. With the graphic selected, click the Fill Color button and choose More Fill Colors, then click on Custom. This dialog box will give the settings for the current object. Neither Word nor Publisher has ways of matching colors in a photograph; use Photoshop instead.

- In Adobe Photoshop, use the Eyedropper tool to sample a color. Then, double-click the Foreground color icon to display the Color Picker. The color settings for the selected color should be displayed.

- In Adobe Illustrator, use the Direct Selection tool to select the object with the specific color. (If the object is in a photograph, use the Eyedropper tool to set the Foreground color.) Double-click the Foreground color at the bottom of the Toolbox and the Color Picker will display the color settings for the selected color.

ASSESS

 Reading Check

1. Students charts will vary. Students should show the color, the RGB and CMYK settings for the color. After the chart is printed, they should add an explanation that compares how the colors look on screen versus the printed version.

2. Repetition can be created in a design by using repeated graphic elements, layout guides, and style sheets to keep page layout, font schemes, and other design elements consistent. Without repetition, long documents look more like a collection of pages, rather than a complete work. This is equally important for books.

CLOSE

Homework Assignment Have each student locate and bring in at least two examples of publications showing the branding of one organization: business cards, letterheads, newsletters, advertisements, brochures, pamphlets, textbooks—any publication that is recognizable as being from that particular organization. It can be from non-profit organizations, well-known retail stores, or manufacturers of a popular product. See if students can identify any elements that show design repetition from one type of publication to another.

Workshop Toolbox Page 409

Transfer Style Sheets

FOCUS

Focus Activity

Review Style Sheets Create a simple document with a title, a header, and some body text. Have students make notes about the important characteristics of the font. Students would be missing something important if they did not include: typeface name, font size, font style, font color, the location of tab stops, and leading. Remind students that style sheets keep track of all this information—and they can be transferred to other users to ensure consistency throughout a design.

You Will Learn To:
- Maintain consistency between documents

Page 409

Key Term Activity

Associate Words Students might not be familiar with the concept of importing and exporting. Discuss what it means in the world of commerce. Have students do some quick research to see what goods America exports and what types of products we import. Then have them write sentences using the results of their research to illustrate and define what both words mean.

Key Term Definitions

import To bring in a file or product. (page 409)

export To send out a file or product to be used in another location. (page 409)

TEACH

Teach Activity

Compare Designs If you assigned the homework assignment of the Close section on the previous page, have the class discuss some of the examples that students brought in. If they could not find at least two examples of publications from the same organization, see if there are any design similarities between companies in the same categories. For example, do manufacturers of software tend to use similar types of fonts and graphics? Do clothing stores that cater to teenagers lay out their advertisements the same way? Do the brochures from one bank look similar to the brochures from another bank?

If you did not have students bring in examples, show them a few different textbooks from the same publisher—perhaps a history and science textbook from the same grade. See if students can identify common design elements that "brand" the books.

Answers to Workshop Toolbox Activities

Page 409

Eye on Ethics

Students should realize that the friend used someone else's intellectual property to create her graphic novel, which is a violation of copyright laws. Perhaps if she had gotten permission from the creators, she might have been able to use the material on the nonprofit fan site without paying a fee. However, upon publishing her book, she would be making money from someone else's original concept, without the copyright owner's permission or paying any sort of compensation. That is definitely against the law.

ASSESS

Reading Check

1. Style sheets are advantageous because they help keep a design consistent, they make formatting easier, and they can be transferred so designs can be consistent from designer to designer.

2. When group members work with the same software, they can share files, style sheets, and even (sometimes) share workspace. Files could be saved in one format, without the need for interchangeable file versions. With the proper workflow, work can benefit from multiple points of view, more creativity and faster completion.

CLOSE

Apply Style Sheets Across Documents Although students have used style sheets before within one document, this is the first time they will be applying the same styles to a number of different documents. Explain that in the first project, they will learn how to import and export style sheets between different software applications, as well as documents.

Chapter 10 Projects

FOCUS

Focus Activity

Class Discussion Have students look at the figure on page 410. Ask students, if there were no English text, would they be able to tell what company created the Web site? How can students tell? Clearly, this Web site is from Apple Computer. Students can tell mostly from the logo, but also the way the page is designed— with lots of white space.

Corporate branding helps to influence customer habits. Customers are familiar with a company's products, services, and quality. If another company uses a nearly identical design for branding, customers may be mislead and purchase an item that does not have the quality they expect.

 Go Online PREVIEW

Before You Begin Students can use the chapter **PowerPoint** presentations and **rubrics** at the Online Learning Center to determine what is expected *before* they complete a project. Students can view the PowerPoint slides on their own computers, or you can project them to preview chapter concepts and show examples of the finished projects. You might also display project solutions so students can easily refer to them while they work. (Presentations and rubrics are also provided on the Teacher Resource DVD for your convenience).

glencoe.com

Projects

Project 10-1
Import and Export Style Sheets

Project 10-2
Create a Brochure

Project 10-3
Create the Brochure Interior

Project 10-4
Design a Booklet

Project 10-5
Design Web Pages

Project 10-6
Add Hyperlinks

Skills Studio

Project 10-7
Create a PowerPoint Presentation

Project 10-8
Create Images for a Presentation

Project 10-9
Add Effects to a Presentation

Key Term Activity

Write a Short Essay Many of the key terms in the projects are related to marketing. Have students choose at least six of the words on the next page to use in a short essay about a marketing campaign for a new brand of running shoe.

Key Term Definitions

marketing A process that a company uses to promote and distribute its products or services. (page 410)

advertising Using or paying a magazine, television station, Web site, or other medium to promote a company's products or services. (page 410)

brand Words, symbols, designs, or even sounds that identify a product or service, and that customers immediately associate with that particular product or service. (page 410)

channel of distribution The path from producer to consumer. (page 413)

direct channel When a company distributes goods and services directly to a consumer. (page 413)

indirect channel When a company uses a third party to distribute goods and services to a consumer. (page 413)

economy of scale Achieving a lower cost per item by producing large volumes of the item. (page 416)

booklet A publication with multiple pages printed front and back that is smaller or shorter than a book. (page 418)

Web site A collection of files or documents located on the World Wide Web, generally containing hyperlinks for interactivity. (page 423)

promotion A special offer used to persuade people to buy products or services. (page 423)

Web page One file or document within a Web site. (page 423)

splash page The page where users enter a Web site. (page 426)

Rule of Six A presentation principle of using no more than six words per line and no more than six lines per slide(or six short bullet points) in a presentation. (page 431)

PDF (Portable Document Format) A format developed by Adobe that creates an image of a document that can be viewed on any computer. (page 436)

screen capture A feature that allows the images on the computer monitor to be stored as a picture. (page 436)

animation An effect where elements on the screen appear to move. (page 439)

transition An animation or other device that occurs between slides in a presentation. (page 439)

TEACH

Preview the Chapter Remind students that style sheets are useful for setting consistency throughout an entire design…not just for the designer himself, but also for teams of graphic designers. Style sheets help with consistency, with editing, and allow designers to maintain a specific "look" within one publication or throughout a variety of publications.

Have students preview the projects in the chapter. They should notice that the publications they will be creating all have design elements in common, and each publication has consistent design elements within the document itself. Have students identify some of the design elements that they will be carrying through between designs. Then have them find design elements that are specific to a particular publication.

Teaching Tips ✍ and Troubleshooting Tips ⚠ for Projects

Pages 410–412

Project 10-1 ▷ **Import and Export Style Sheets** Students learn how to transfer style sheets in Microsoft Word, Microsoft Publisher, and Adobe Illustrator. (There are no solution files or rubrics for this project.)

✍ **Apply Skills** You might choose to have students practice these skills in preparation for the team projects in this chapter, and then have students use these pages as reference.

✍ **Introduce the Global Template** Show students the Organizer dialog box shown in Figures 10.1 and 10.2 on page 411. Under *Styles available in*, they should see that there are options for Normal.dot (the Normal global template) and a specific file. Explain that styles imported into the global template can be used in any Word document and will be included in the default Style menu. Styles imported into a new document, are only available when working in that file.

⚠ **Transfer Between Applications** Although this project describes how to transfer style sheets within an application, explain to students that style sheets usually cannot be transferred from one application to a different application.

Pages 413–415

Rubric

Student Data File

Project 10-2 ▷ **Create a Brochure** Student teams create the exterior of a tri-fold brochure describing Light Travel's Mars Quest adventure. They will create a space image in Photoshop, and then import it into the Publisher document. They will also use the logo that they created in Chapter 9. Students will complete the brochure in Project 10-3. **(Data File 10-2, Solution File 10-2, Rubric 10-2)**

✍ **Review Team Member Roles** Before beginning any projects in this chapter, have students carefully evaluate the requirements of the projects. They should assign specific parts of the project to each team member, and create a flowchart or timeline to make sure that each member understands his or her responsibilities. If they work outside class time, students should determine how they will exchange work or communicate with each other.

✍ **Create Original Work** Data files are provided, but if your students have the time and motivation, it is highly recommended that they create these brochures from scratch, using their own research and creating their own content. If possible, have a science teacher lead a presentation about Mars to help students get started.

✍ **Create a Space Illustration** If students in your class have different ability levels, have more advanced students create the space illustration in Photoshop, and let other students use it as a data file in their own brochures. You can also have students adapt the images they created themselves in Project 5-8.

⚠️ **Consider Time Limitations** The projects in this chapter require a lot of class time. Before you assign the projects, make sure you review all the projects carefully. Choose the projects that you think students will be able to accomplish in the time you have allotted. Make sure that student groups divide the work in a way that allows different parts of the project to be completed simultaneously.

⚠️ **Encourage Collaboration** Students might be concerned because the steps in these projects are very general. Remind students that they have learned these skills in previous chapters. Encourage students to work with team members to devise their own solutions to problems. They can also review previous projects or use the Help feature of an application.

Pages 416–417

Rubric

Student Data File

> **Project 10-3** **Create the Brochure Interior** Students complete the brochure they started in Project 10-2, applying the style sheet and inserting graphics. **(Data Files 10-3a to 10-3f, Solution File 10-3, Rubric 10-3)**

✍ **Review Economy of Scale** Ask students to consider how giant supermarket chains such as Wal-Mart, Sam's, or Costco are able to keep prices generally lower than local supermarkets. Students have probably heard of the idea that buying in bulk can save money. In order to encourage sales, many suppliers offer discounts to those who buy a lot of product. Explain that this is an example of economy of scale.

✍ **Compare Printing Options** Have students read pages 501–502 of Appendix B. The printing process. Ask students when they would print from their own local printer and when it pays to go to a professional printer. Students may say that using the computer printer is much more convenient. They may think that professional printing costs a lot more because the shop has high set-up costs.

Help students come to the conclusion that for a few copies, the local printer is the least expensive option. However, for hundreds (or thousands) of printouts, the professional print shop becomes the cheaper alternative per page. For example, a single page document from their own printer would cost 8¢. The same page from an imagesetter at a print shop might cost $10.00. Print 1,000 copies of the page and the local printer costs $80. The costs of the professional print shop might be $55 because set-up costs and other expenses are spread over a large printing.

Pages 418–422

Rubric

Student Data File

> **Project 10-4** **Design a Booklet** Students create an eight-page Mars Quest Travel Guide booklet that includes a Table of Contents. They will apply a master page and style sheets to maintain a consistent design. **(Data Files 10-4a to 10-4i, Solution File 10-4, Rubric 10-4)**

✍ **Create Mock-ups** Have students create a quick mock-up of the booklet layout. They should create a blank booklet by assembling four sheets of paper and folding them in half. They can then number the pages: cover, 1, 2, 3, 4, 5, 6, and back cover. Have students then separate the sheets and see how the pages in the booklet are organized. Confusing? Good thing that layout software will arrange complex page layouts automatically!

Preview the Project Have students look at pages 420–422. Student groups will be creating their own original booklets or recreating this exact booklet depending on your instructions. After previewing the project expectations, how could students divide the labor? Will students choose to divide the work page by page? This is best if all students are equally skilled. What would probably be a better way to divide the work? Some students may be better at researching facts and writing content, others might prefer to create and edit the illustrations, and some may be best at working on the design and layout. Encourage students to divide the work creatively, allowing for each person's strengths and weaknesses. This is how teams work best.

Edit Photographs Although data files are provided with photographs that have Mars backgrounds added, students might enjoy altering photos on their own. If there are time constraints, try to have an assortment of photographs ready for students showing interiors and exteriors. They can then add their own special effects, such as the red landscapes and blue sunsets of Mars.

Before You Begin Review the Teaching Tips and Troubleshooting Tips for Project 10-2. They will provide valuable information that can be related to this project.

Pages 423–425

Rubric

Student Data File

Project 10-5 **Design Web Pages** Students begin to create a Mars Quest Web site. They will design a background and navigation bar using Photoshop, and then use it to create a master page in Publisher. They will finish the Web site and add hyperlinks in Project 10-6. **(Data Files 10-5a and 10-5b, Solution File 10-5, Rubric 10-5)**

Discuss Web Sites Ask students if they can explain the difference between a Web site and a Web page. While both are closely related, they do refer to different things. Web pages are like a flyer or one-page document. Although a Web page can be very long and contain interactive elements, it is still an independent document.

A Web site can be one Web page or many. When there is more than one page on a Web site, the pages are usually all related to the subject of the Web site. For example, a Web site for a hotel might have individual pages describing the hotel and its facilities, the different rooms, and the local attractions. There might be other pages where you can book reservations or link to other hotel properties. Web sites usually connect the individual pages through a home page and a menu bar that is displayed on all pages.

Compare Web Hosting Services If you and your school policy allow, have students compare www.bluehost.com, www.geocities.yahoo.com, and http://smallbusiness.yahoo.com/webhosting. Which services would be best for a student? Which ones would work for a company? Ask students if any of them have a Web site. If any do, have these students discuss how they got the site and what they do with it.

Publish on the Web Ask students what it means to publish a document. They should understand that publishing is the distribution of a document to the intended audience. If brochures and booklets are printed, how are Web pages published? They have to be accessible to their audience through the Internet via a *server*. See if any students can explain what a server is. Lead students to understand that a server is another computer that "serves" information to many other computers. When students are surfing the Internet, they are going through a server, which distributes information from their computer to other computers.

Before You Begin Review the Teaching Tips and Troubleshooting Tips for Project 10-2. They will provide valuable information that can be related to this project.

Pages 426–429

Rubric

Project 10-6 **Add Hyperlinks** Students continue the Web site they started in Project 10-5, adding a splash page, content pages, and adding hyperlinks. **(Solution File 10-6, Rubric 10-6)**

Diagram a Web Site Show students a Web site and see if they can diagram the navigation structure. For example, the home page might link to four other pages. Each of those pages might have sub-pages. Every page may link back to the home page. Web designers often use diagrams to ensure that they do not have dead links or dead-end pages. Students may want to use Publisher's flowchart tools (See Project 9-1) to map out the Web site they are creating in Projects 10-5 and 10-6.

Add Hyperlinks to Reports Explain to students that they can easily add hyperlinks in a Word document that is viewed online. Hyperlinks not only add interactivity to the page, they also are a wonderful way to make it come alive. Hyperlinks can make it easier to jump to different topics within the report itself. For example, if there is a table of contents, clicking one item can take you to that section.

Hyperlinks can also be used to link the report to Web sites or other files. Imagine writing a report about Martin Luther King that allows the reader to open videos about him or audio versions of his famous speeches. The Works Cited page can also be linked directly to any online sources.

Traditional hyperlinks are easy to create. Select a word, phrase, or select a graphic and choose Insert>Hyperlink. In the resulting dialog box, choose *Link to: Existing File or Web Page*. Select the file or key the URL for the Web page that you want to link, then click OK. The words you selected to be the "hot spot" will be a different color. To open the Web page, you may have to press CTRL and then click on the hot spot.

Skills Studio

Pages 430–441

Design PowerPoint Presentations

Most students have seen and probably created PowerPoint presentations. Ask students to imagine what presentations must have been like before presentation programs like PowerPoint. Speakers had to use film strip projectors, slide projectors, or overhead projectors. Adding animation or sound was difficult or impossible. PowerPoint has made it easy to create engaging presentations. However, it is easy to overuse effects like animation and sound. As with the other publications that students have studied in this course, presentations also need to be designed with care, and the same PARC design principles still apply.

Pages 431–435

Rubric

Student Data File

Project 10-7 → **Create a PowerPoint Presentation** Students are introduced to PowerPoint and begin creating a presentation to highlight their Mars Quest marketing campaign. They will use the Slide Master to create a Master Title slide and a New Title Master. They will continue working on the presentation in the next two projects. **(Data Files 10-7a to 10-7c, Solution File 10-7, Rubric 10-7)**

Preview the Presentation Have students look at the figures on pages 437 and 438. Ask them how the PowerPoint presentation is different from the other marketing materials they have created in this chapter. Who is the audience? They should notice that rather than describing the Mars Quest vacation, the slides discuss the marketing materials themselves. From this observation, they should conclude that the audience for the presentation could be the marketing team, the company's management, or even other travel agencies who will be marketing the trip. Unlike the other projects, the presentation is not aimed at customers who would be taking the trip.

Format Text in a Presentation Write the following two columns on the board. Ask students to match the type of text on the left with the font on the right.

Title	Oldstyle
Header	Sans Serif
Body Text	Slab Serif

Based on what they have learned about print documents, students should match the body text with the Oldstyle font, the title with slab serif, and the header with sans serif.

Ask them how those general guidelines change when creating a Web page. By now, students should realize that an Oldstyle text would not work for body text in any document that is viewed on a monitor, because the serifs make letters harder to read. Presentations, which are viewed on a low resolution screen or projected at a distance, should follow similar design rules to Web pages. They would use a simpler, bolder font, like a sans serif font, for body text. Titles could still be in a slab serif for contrast.

Pages 436–438

Rubric / Student Data File

Project 10-8 **Create Images for a Presentation** Students continue working on their presentations, adding text and images to slides. They also learn how to create images of documents that they have created in previous projects. Students should be encouraged to create their own images using the instructions on page 436. However, if you have time restrictions, you may prefer they use the data files that are provided. **(Data Files 10-8a to 10-8d, Solution File 10-8, Rubric 10-8)**

Demonstrate Print Screen Students might be surprised that when they press the Print Screen button on their keyboards, nothing seems to happen. Explain that after they press Print Screen, the image is saved to the clipboard. It must then be pasted into a new document in order to see it. Show students how it works, by printing and pasting a screen capture into a new document. Students should see that everything that was visible on the screen is captured in the image.

Determine Resolutions When creating any kind of presentation, whether displayed on a monitor or presented using a projector, students should remember that image quality is no longer important. PC computers can display only 72 ppi, and Macintosh computers can display 96 ppi. Images with better resolution than these settings will only serve to slow down the presentation and will not add to the quality of the presentation whatsoever.

Preview Saving Methods Before you teach this project, check your software to see which methods are best for saving images of documents. If you have the latest version of Publisher, you should find it easy to save documents in graphic formats such as JPEG or GIF. These formats should be suitable to use in a PowerPoint presentation.

Work with Print Screen Captures When using Print Screen for a screen capture, students will capture the document as well as the everything else on the screen. Show students that they can crop out unwanted parts of the image by using the Crop tool on the Picture toolbar. They can also change how the screen looks before taking the screen capture. Toolbars and rulers can be removed from the screen or moved around, and the bottom taskbar can be dragged off the screen. The document should be sized to capture as much as possible. Students should also be aware that Print Screen images are low resolution and, therefore, may not be suitable for printed documents.

Pages 439–441

Rubric

Project 10-9 **Add Effects to a Presentation** Students finish the PowerPoint presentation that they started in Project 10-8. They add animation and prepare to give a presentation. **(Solution File 10-9, Rubric 10-9)**

Present a PowerPoint Presentation If time permits, have each team present its PowerPoint slides. The teams can choose one person to be the presenter, or they can have members take turns. Make sure they follow steps 9–14 to prepare for the presentation.

Relate to Previous Knowledge In the movie, *Star Wars: A New Hope*, George Lucas uses a technique called "wipes" to move to a new scene. If possible, show students a brief clip from *Star Wars* or another movie that uses this technique. Explain to students, that PowerPoint uses similar effects called "transitions." Ask them how this technique can be used effectively, and what might happen if it were overused.

Compare Presentations Show students two PowerPoint presentations that are identical except that one has transitions, and one does not. Ask students to choose the one they prefer. Students are likely to point out that the presentation with transitions seems more complete and seems more interesting and professional.

Show the students another version of the presentation, this time with even more animation and sound effects, to the point where it is annoying. Ask if students prefer this to the previous examples. Students should see that adding too many effects can be distracting and unprofessional.

Add Transitions Quickly When limited on time, use the effects under Slide Show>Slide Transition. You can also access these options from the toolbar in the Slide Sorter view. Random transitions can be added to all slides with a few short clicks. When thoughtfully added, these transitions can be used to help support the message.

ASSESS

Evaluate Encourage students to use the project rubrics and the Review and Revise checklists to be sure that they have completed the key steps to their projects. Encourage students to proofread and assist each other.

The projects in this chapter have many options that can be considered for grading. Teams can be graded on how well team members worked together, how effectively the work was divided, and whether the project was completed in the allotted time. Students who created original projects, rather than following the examples in the book, should be evaluated on how well they followed the entire design process, as well as on their final designs.

CLOSE

Present a Course Overview When students complete this unit, they should have a strong sense of how the skills they have learned in this textbook relate to both the creative world of design and the practical world of business and commerce. They should be able to make judgments that will help them make day-to-day decisions and give them a head start when they enter the job market. Wrap up the course by discussing with students how they benefited from learning about desktop publishing.

IN THE WORKPLACE

WEB DESIGNER

Career Activity

Although Web designers need a broad range of skills, they still need to create Web sites that are attractive and readable to viewers. Even if the designer is part of a team that includes graphic artists, Web designers should have an understanding of design principles, graphics, and resolution to make their work effective.

Notes

Use the following Reading Check and Critical Thinking answers as a guide to help evaluate student understanding of the core concepts. Requiring that your students write in complete sentences will help you grade faster and promote good writing skills. You scan have students write answers in their desktop publishing journals, or students can answer these questions at the computer by accessing the Reading Check and Critical Thinking activities on the Online Learning Center at **glencoe.com**.

Chapter 10 Assessment Answers

Page 443

Reading Check

1. Business packages generally include business cards, letterhead stationery, and envelopes.

2. The use of repetition adds consistency throughout designs and gives a sense of professionalism. It is a common hallmark of an amateur to use as many fonts and alignments as possible, while the professional maintains visual consistency. The use of consistent design elements also creates a specific style or branding that people associate with one company.

3. Importing a style sheet means bringing font settings into your document for use, while exporting style sheets means making font settings available for other users.

4. Style sheets can keep track of font typefaces, font sizes, font colors, font styles, alignments, tab settings, margins, and sometimes even borders and shading settings.

5. Branding sends a consistent, easily recognizable message to the audience to help promote a company and influence buying habits.

Critical Thinking

6. Style sheets help keep designs consistent throughout a design and even across projects. This technique is especially helpful when working in groups, since style sheets can be transferred and used by different designers, thus ensuring a consistent look no matter how many people work on a publication.

7. When incorporating repetition into designs, designers must be careful not to create a boring design. Contrast is also needed in a good design.

8. When transferring style sheets in Microsoft Word, one must select a file with style sheets and choose specific styles to import. In Microsoft Publisher, one selects a document with a style sheet and then imports all styles from that document. Styles may then be selected and deleted as needed.

9. Design elements such as logos, borders, fonts, and colors are often used to create a consistent look in each component of a business package.

10. To control costs, companies should consider how they distribute their marketing materials and how many they need to print. They can keep the Cost per Page down by carefully choosing where they place their advertisements. They can avoid the cost of a middle man by using direct channels of distribution. They should also create marketing materials that will not be outdated quickly so that they can print enough copies to take advantage of lower printing costs.

Assessment activities allow students to demonstrate their understanding of concepts and skills learned throughout this project. Because of time constraints, students may not be able to complete every activity suggested. Match assignments to student ability levels using the leveled projects (★ Easy, ★★ Medium, and ★★★ Challenging). Rubrics are available to evaluate projects on the Teacher Resources DVD and the Online Learning Center at **glencoe.com**.

Page 443

1. Independent Practice ★

Promote a Rock Band Students should enjoy this project. Have students form groups. Then as a group they should choose a type of music, brainstorm a name for their band, develop a logo and a poster. As an extension activity, students might want to create a CD cover (or a CD label), a bumper sticker, or flyers for posting.

To encourage variety, you might choose to randomly assign specific music genres or audiences. Have students develop a band for seniors, for pets, for children, or for teens/young adults. How do the graphics change based on audience? Encourage student creativity and develop a rubric that rewards all aspects of the project, from brainstorming, to sketching out ideas, to the development of ideas. Use the bullet points on page 443 as a guide. **(Rubric IP 10-1)**

Page 444

2. Independent Practice ★★

Market a Movie Students will enjoy this project, as well. Have students research actual movie posters in a particular genre and create thumbnail sketches based on those layouts. Afterwards, students should brainstorm possibilities for their posters and sketch ideas. Students are likely to want to use Illustrator for the logos, Photoshop for photo editing and creating collages, and Publisher for the layouts.

Students will need to develop content for their movie's Web site. They might choose to create a page about the movie's plotline (is it based on a book?), the actors and director, behind the scenes of the movie, links to pages related to the movie's content, downloads for movie wallpaper, etc.

Encourage students to create original material, though they may have to rely upon photos from stock imaging sites or Internet sites. Remember to monitor students carefully when using stock imaging sites since there can be offensive/inappropriate content that can easily bypass filtering systems. Encourage student creativity and develop a rubric that rewards all aspects of the project, from brainstorming, to sketching out ideas, to developing the ideas. Use the bullet points on page 444 as a guide. **(Rubric IP 10-2)**

Page 444

3. Independent Practice ★★★

Promote a Fund Raiser Chances are, your school really does have some student organization that needs to raise community awareness and raise funds for donations. It may be a foreign language club, the debate team, theater arts, the choir, or the band. You might want student groups themselves to develop contacts with these organizations and meet with the client. Encourage students to consider the audience that is likely to help the organization in question and to create materials targeted for that specific audience.

In addition to the brochure and PowerPoint presentation, students may choose to develop flyers, a newsletter, or a mailer to help the club or organization. Be sure to encourage student creativity and develop a rubric that rewards all aspects of the project, from brainstorming, to sketching out ideas, to the development of ideas. Use the bullet points on page 444 as a guide. **(Rubric IP 10-3)**

Reteaching Activities

Review Key Skills In these projects, students have many tasks to complete, requiring many of the skills that they learned throughout the book. If a student is having problems with a particular part of a project, have them review the original chapter and project where they first learned the skill. Pair struggling students with more advanced students so that they can review information that they might have forgotten or missed the first time.

Complete Worksheets Have students complete Worksheets 10A to 10D, which can be found in Part 3 or this TRM, on the Teacher Resource DVD, or at the Online Learning Center at **glencoe.com**.

Enrichment Activities

Create Electronic Portfolios Have students create electronic portfolios of their best work, as a way of tracking their progress and also as examples for college or employment. Professional designers often host their work on Web sites or create PowerPoint presentations. If these are not an option for students, have them insert images of their design into a Word or Publisher document, where they can also add descriptive text.

To create images of their Word documents, students will need to use the Print Screen button to capture the document as it appears on their monitor. They can then paste it into another application such as a PowerPoint slide or a Publisher document. They should crop the image, as necessary, and then write an explanation of the document's purpose and why specific design decisions were made.

⊘ **Enrichment** If students need an additional challenge, have them complete the enrichment activities on the Online Learning Center at **glencoe.com**.

Projects Across the Curriculum

Page 445

Rubric

Project 1 Create a Marketing Brochure ★

Students will be creating a logo and a brochure. Students will need to research the content, consider the audience, brainstorm ideas and develop the designs. Encourage students to research other professional designs and to work together to create theirs. Have students set style sheets that each team member will use.

Consider assigning students particular kinds of restaurants or audiences. You might decide to invite actual restaurant owners from the local area to come listen to student presentations and choose a specific design based on those presentations. Be sure to encourage student creativity and develop a rubric that rewards all aspects of the project, from brainstorming, to sketching out ideas, to the development of ideas. Use the bullet points on page 445 as a guide. **(Rubric PAC 5-1)**

Page 445

Rubric

Project 2 Create a Math Study Guide ★★

If students cannot meet with teachers, have students research the state standards for math for a particular grade level. They can use those as guidelines for what should be included in a math study guide. Students should choose specific standards that they want to include, and develop graphics to help illustrate the point.

Students should plan the book, the content for each page, and a unifying theme that can be carried throughout the book. Will they have a cartoon character, sidebars and callouts, or other features? Will they have a "cute" appearance, or a sophisticated look? For variety, you may choose to limit the number of colors in this design to two or three.

You may also have students design full-color, front and back covers to be printed on card. Students should then create, trim, and assemble their booklet. Create a rubric that rewards students for the entire process from brainstorming, to sketching out ideas, to the development of ideas. Use the bullet points on page 445 as a guide. Give top booklets to math teachers to check for accuracy, or to use to help struggling students. **(Rubric PAC 5-2)**

Page 446

Rubric

Project 3 Market a Political Campaign ★★

Have students research popular images and layouts of political campaign advertisements. Students will notice a similarity in layout, fonts, colors and symbolism—regardless of the candidate's political party. You may choose to extend this activity by having students research popular issues and create a position flyer comparing candidates and their positions. Students might also choose to create a bumper sticker or magazine advertisement for their candidate.

You might choose to have students research a particular candidate, create a hypothetical candidate, research a historical candidate, or assign students a candidate randomly. For variation, you might choose a historical year for students to work, or provide a fact sheet for a futuristic campaign. Create a rubric that rewards students for research and the entire design process. Encourage student creativity and develop a rubric that rewards all aspects of the project, from brainstorming, to sketching out ideas, to the development of ideas. Use the bullet points on page 446 as a guide. **(Rubric PAC 5-3)**

Page 446

Rubric

Project 4 Create a Healthy Lifestyle Campaign ★★★

Give students time to brainstorm the content they might include in a health newsletter. They should then research those possibilities and choose the best topics. They can use the same content and images in the newsletter and Web site. Encourage students to consider their audience and to choose healthy lifestyles that are appropriate for a school environment. You might want to send home a letter of intent to parents if students choose topics that are of questionable nature.

If students want to extend the activity, they can create posters, flyers, bumper stickers, or buttons raising student awareness of healthy lifestyle choices. Create a rubric that rewards students for research and the entire design process. Encourage student creativity and develop a rubric that rewards all aspects of the project, from brainstorming, to sketching out ideas, to the development of ideas. Use the bullet points on page 446 as a guide. **(Rubric PAC 5-4)**

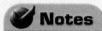

Notes

Reproducible Worksheets

HOW TO USE THE WORKSHEETS

Worksheets are provided as additional activities to accompany each chapter in the student textbook. Look for suggestions of when to use each worksheet throughout Part 2: Lesson Plans and Answer Keys in this manual. Worksheets are also available at the Online Learning Center.

- Students can complete worksheets independently as a review of material covered in the chapter.

- Worksheets can be assigned as extension activities if students complete a project early.

- Students can be paired up to complete the worksheets in class and then check each other's work.

Encourage struggling students to refer to their textbooks or software applications as they complete the worksheets. Advanced students can be asked to complete the worksheets without consulting their books or software.

ANSWER KEYS

Complete answer keys are included in this manual following the worksheets and on the Online Learning Center Web site. Answer keys are located on the password protected portion of the site so that only teachers have access. Visit the Teacher Online Learning Center at **glencoe.com** for user name and password information (registration is *not* required).

Chapter 1: Worksheet 1A

Rate Your Computer Skills

Directions This survey will help evaluate how much you know about what will soon be taught. Later you can use it to determine how much you have learned. Answer each question fairly and to your best ability.

> Rate your response 1–5, based on the following statements:
>
> 1 = I do not know anything about this.
>
> 2 = I recognize some of these terms.
>
> 3 = I know how to do about half of these things.
>
> 4 = I do not know everything, but I can probably figure this out on my own.
>
> 5 = I know how to do this, and I have done it before.

Basic Computer Skills

_____ **1.** I know the difference between RAM and ROM.

_____ **2.** I can start up and shut down a computer system and its peripherals.

_____ **3.** I can use the following terms appropriately: CPU, monitor, hard disk, floppy disk, flash drive, megahertz, megabyte, bit, software, and hardware.

_____ **4.** I can point, click, double-click, and click and drag with a mouse.

_____ **5.** I can select, open, move, resize, and close a window.

_____ **6.** I can scroll up/down, left/right within a window.

_____ **7.** I can start an application and create a document.

_____ **8.** I can name, save, retrieve, revise, and rename a document.

_____ **9.** I can find lost files.

_____ **10.** I can preview a document before printing it to see how it will look.

_____ **11.** I can format, name, and rename a floppy disk.

_____ **12.** I can copy a document from the hard disk to a floppy disk and vice versa.

_____ **13.** I can create and name/rename folders, directories, and subdirectories.

_____ **14.** I know some strategies for guarding against computer viruses.

_____ **15.** I know some of my rights and responsibilities under copyright law.

_____ **16.** I can copy files and save them to another location without first opening them.

_____ **17.** I can use the following terms appropriately: WYSIWYG, interface, icon, window, document, application, kilobytes (KB), file system, and save as.

(continued)

Chapter 1: Worksheet 1A (continued)
Word Processing

_____ **18.** I can select text.

_____ **19.** I can copy and move blocks of text.

_____ **20.** I can change font size and font style.

_____ **21.** I can change text alignment.

_____ **22.** I can categorize fonts into six different families, and I know when to use them.

_____ **23.** I can change text margins and line spacing.

_____ **24.** I know how to switch between portrait and landscape orientation.

_____ **25.** I can set and use tab stops and add leaders to the tab stop locations.

_____ **26.** I can create a table and format the table to make it more readable.

_____ **27.** I use writing tools like the spell checker, the thesaurus, and the grammar checker.

_____ **28.** I can create a header and footer within a document.

_____ **29.** I can instruct the computer to insert the date, time, and page number into a document.

_____ **30.** I can insert symbols not found on the keyboard like: ¿, é, ÷, π, ¢, and $^{1}/_{3}$.

_____ **31.** I know how to make letters appear superscripted, subscripted, embossed, and shadowed.

_____ **32.** I can insert clip art into a document.

_____ **33.** I can insert and edit WordArt.

_____ **34.** I can insert, move, and resize text boxes.

_____ **35.** I can change text direction.

_____ **36.** I can change the text wrapping around a drawing object.

_____ **37.** I can have the computer place drawing objects in the exact center of a page.

_____ **38.** I can add a decorative page border without using clip art.

_____ **39.** I can adjust the leading in a paragraph.

_____ **40.** I can kern text.

_____ **41.** I can create a drop cap.

_____ **42.** I can use the following terms appropriately: tab stop, kerning, leading, drop cap, format, layout, header and footer.

Chapter 1: Worksheet 1B
Review Desktop Publishing Skills

Directions Match each font in the box below with the correct description.

a. **Font**	c. *Font*	e. Font
b. *Font*	d. Font	f. *Font*

_____ **1.** decorative

_____ **2.** modern

_____ **3.** Oldstyle

_____ **4.** sans serif

_____ **5.** script

_____ **6.** slab serif

Directions Circle **T** for true or **F** for false for each statement below. For each false statement, write the correct answer on the lines below.

7. The dash is correct in the following example: The festival will be held June 26-July 8. **T F**

_____

_____

8. Use the space bar to align text. **T F**

_____

_____

9. Leading should be 120 percent–150 percent of the font size, depending on font, audience, and purpose. **T F**

_____

_____

10. Paragraphs are more readable when you use an Oldstyle serif font like Garamond. **T F**

_____

_____

11. Arial is a serif font. **T F**

_____

_____

12. When you use the Cut command, you delete the selected item. **T F**

_____

_____

Chapter 2: Worksheet 2A

Review Microsoft Word Skills

Directions Fill in the answers below.

1. How do you display the Drawing toolbar on your screen?

_____

_____

2. What button can you use to "nudge" an object when moving it using the arrow keys?

_____

_____

3. What should you do to combine simple objects so they can be moved or resized together?

_____

_____

4. What keyboard buttons can you use to select more than one item?

_____

_____

5. When would a piece of clip art have square black handles instead of circular white handles?

_____

_____

6. What two methods can you use to position text so it is sideways?

_____

_____

7. Why use a style sheet to format a newsletter?

_____

_____

8. How does the Show/Hide button on the Standard toolbar help you format a document?

_____

_____

9. Look at the diagram. How would you bring the circle between the triangle and the rectangle?

_____

_____

_____

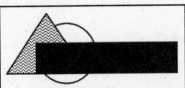

Chapter 2: Worksheet 2B

Identify Microsoft Word Drawing Tools

Directions Match each button labeled in the Drawing toolbar below to its name.

_____ **1.** Line Style

_____ **2.** Text Box

_____ **3.** Fill Color

_____ **4.** Shadow Style

_____ **5.** Line

_____ **6.** Insert Clip Art

_____ **7.** Line Color

_____ **8.** Insert WordArt

Directions Use the illustration above to help you fill in the answers below.

9. The _____ button lets you remove lines or change their color.

10. You can find the Group command by using the _____ button.

11. To place text anywhere on the page, you would use the _____ button.

12. The _____ button has a menu that lets use choose different callouts.

13. You can color a shape with the _____ button.

14. Create perfect squares by pressing the Shift key and using the _____ button.

15. To draw a triangle shape, you would first click the _____ button.

16. If you wanted to place an image behind text, you would use the _____ button.

17. To insert a picture from a file, use the _____ button.

18. The _____ button is used to create dashed borders.

Chapter 3: Worksheet 3A

Review Microsoft Publisher Skills

Directions Use the figure to determine if the statements that follow are true or false. Circle **T** for true of **F** for false. For each false statement, write the correct answer.

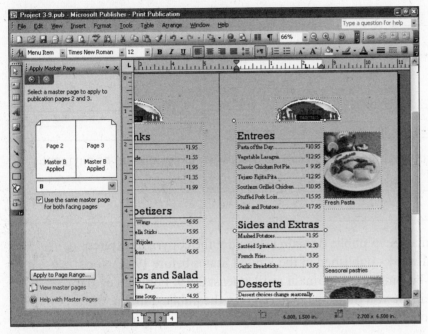

1. The current document is two pages long.   T   F

_____

2. The Task Pane is displayed.   T   F

_____

3. The magnification level is set at 100 percent.   T   F

_____

4. The full page spread is visible on the screen.   T   F

_____

5. The format displayed for the style sheet is Caption style.   T   F

_____

6. The page is laid out as a booklet.   T   F

_____

7. Different Master Pages are applied to pages 2 and 3.   T   F

_____

8. The prices are aligned with a tab and use leaders.   T   F

_____

Chapter 3: Worksheet 3B

Evaluate Ethical Use of Materials

Directions Answer the following questions.

1. Define *copyright*.

   _____

   _____

2. Define *fair use*.

   _____

   _____

3. Describe a situation when copyrighted material can be used without permission or payment.

   _____

   _____

Directions One reason a work may be in public domain is because the copyright expired. The copyright has expired for all works published in the United States before 1923. No works published after 1923 will become public domain until at least 2019. For each of the following, circle **Public Domain** if the you think the material is in the public domain, or circle **Copyright** if the material could still be copyrighted.

4. William Shakespeare's *Romeo and Juliet* (1597)	**Public Domain**	**Copyright**
5. Maya Angelou's *I Know Why the Caged Bird Sings* (1969)	**Public Domain**	**Copyright**
6. Disney's *Finding Nemo* (2003)	**Public Domain**	**Copyright**
7. Francis Scott Key's "The Star Spangled Banner" (1814)	**Public Domain**	**Copyright**
8. Emily Bronte's *Wuthering Heights* (1847)	**Public Domain**	**Copyright**
9. The Brothers Grimm's *Hansel and Gretel* (1812–1814)	**Public Domain**	**Copyright**
10. Stevie Wonder's "You Are the Sunshine of My Life" (1973)	**Public Domain**	**Copyright**
11. Isabel Allende's *The House of the Spirits* (1985)	**Public Domain**	**Copyright**
12. John Newton's "Amazing Grace" (1800)	**Public Domain**	**Copyright**
13. Homer's *Iliad* (800 BC)	**Public Domain**	**Copyright**
14. President John F. Kennedy's *Profiles in Courage* (1956)	**Public Domain**	**Copyright**

Chapter 4: Worksheet 4A

Review PARC Principles and the Design Process

Directions Answer each of the following questions.

1. Break down the design process into six steps.

    a. _____

    b. _____

    c. _____

    d. _____

    e. _____

    f. _____

2. Why should design planning be done on paper rather than the computer?

    _____

    _____

3. What is proximity, and how is it created in a document?

    _____

    _____

4. What are some ways to ensure alignment?

    _____

    _____

5. What is repetition, and why is it important?

    _____

    _____

6. How is a focal point created by using contrast?

    _____

    _____

7. How should white space be used in a document?

    _____

    _____

8. What is a disadvantage of using center-aligned text for an entire document?

    _____

    _____

Chapter 4: Worksheet 4B

Evaluate a Design

Directions Identify problems with the following design.

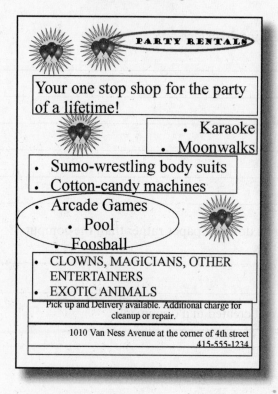

Proximity

_____

_____

Alignment

_____

_____

Repetition

_____

_____

Contrast

_____

_____

Grammar and Punctuation

_____

_____

Chapter 5: Worksheet 5A

Review Adobe Photoshop Vocabulary

Directions Match the definitions to the key terms on the right. Write the letter of the correct key term next to the definition.

_____ **1.** Uses lenses in a digital camera to magnify an image and create very little image distortion

_____ **2.** A tool that creates distortions, textures, blurs, and more

_____ **3.** The intensity of the color

_____ **4.** A graph that shows the number of pixels for each color in an image

_____ **5.** A dotted line that shows the area that is selected

_____ **6.** The letters displayed after a file name used to indicate the type of file format, such as .jpg, .exe, and .doc

_____ **7.** The beginning of a new line segment

_____ **8.** A floating toolbar with a set of tools related to a particular action, such as adding color or working with layers

_____ **9.** The clarity of an image, measured in terms of pixels per inch (ppi) on the monitor, or dots per inch (dpi) on the printer

_____ **10.** A tool that allows layers to interact with each other

_____ **11.** Resizable without any loss of image clarity or resolution

_____ **12.** To fix an image

_____ **13.** A feature that allows the photographer to look through the camera's viewfinder and actually see the image through the camera lens

_____ **14.** To copy a range of pixels for placement elsewhere in an image

_____ **15.** A lighter area of an object caused by a light source

_____ **16.** An enclosed figure with straight sides

_____ **17.** To merge all layers in Photoshop into a single layer

_____ **18.** A feature that hides areas of an image and does not delete the data

_____ **19.** A picture-element, the smallest square of color in an image

_____ **20.** Graphics made up of tiny colored squares (pixels) that work together to form an image

a. anchor point
b. blending modes
c. clone
d. file name extension
e. filter
f. flatten
g. highlight
h. histogram
i. marquee
j. mask
k. optical zoom
l. palette
m. pixel
n. polygon
o. raster graphic
p. resolution
q. retouch
r. saturation
s. scalable
t. single lens reflex

Chapter 5: Worksheet 5B
Review Adobe Photoshop Tools

Directions Circle the letter of the word or phrase that best answers each question.

1. Which tool would you use to select an object that is one solid color on a solid background?
   a. Polygonal Lasso
   b. Magnetic Lasso
   c. Magic Wand
   d. None of the above

2. Which tool would you use to select an irregularly shaped object that has curves and straight lines?
   a. Polygonal Lasso
   b. Lasso
   c. Magnetic Lasso
   d. None of the above

3. To resize an image, choose the _____ tool and click Show Transform Controls.
   a. Move
   b. Hand
   c. Lasso
   d. Crop

4. If you wish to undo a mistake you just made three steps earlier, you could
   a. Press CTRL + Z on the keyboard.
   b. Click an earlier action in the History palette.
   c. Click Edit>Undo.
   d. All of the above

5. How can the Tolerance setting affect the Magic Wand's selection range?
   a. It can make the Selection tool choose a wider range of colors.
   b. It can make the Selection tool choose a wider range of image properties.
   c. It can make the Selection tool choose a wider range of image shapes.
   d. It has no effect.

6. What is the advantage of using layers?
   a. File sizes are much smaller.
   b. Images are less confusing to work with.
   c. Fewer windows are on your screen.
   d. Layers can be edited independently.

7. How do you hide or show individual layers?
   a. Minimize or enlarge a layer's window.
   b. Choose File>Hide Layer or File>Reveal Layer.
   c. In the Layers palette, click on the eye icon to toggle on/off.
   d. All of the above

8. How can you make one layer appear in front of another layer?
   a. In the Layers palette, click and drag the layer up toward the top.
   b. In the Layers palette, click and drag the layer down to the bottom.
   c. Right-click on an image in the workspace, and choose "Bring to Front."
   d. Right-click on the layer in the Layers palette, and choose "Bring to Front."

Chapter 6: Worksheet 6A

Review Adobe Photoshop Terms

Directions On each line, write the term that best matches the definition.

PSD	**bitmap**	**JPEG**
Paint Bucket	**Clone Stamp**	**gradient**
marquee	**bevel**	**vector**
tile	**resolution**	**TIFF**
crop	**Magnetic Lasso**	**Sponge**
Magic Wand	**saturation**	**Color Picker**

1. Fills an entire enclosed area with a color _____

2. A gradual transformation from one color to another _____

3. Duplicates the pixels of a selection and pastes them in another area _____

4. Selects an area by automatically "snapping" to its edges _____

5. Selects a range of contiguous colors _____

6. Photoshop's native file format _____

7. Saturates or desaturates a color _____

8. A printing method for creating oversized documents _____

9. File format that is compatible with many programs and good for
   general purposes _____

10. An image that is created and stored using mathematical formulas _____

11. Format used most for printing _____

12. Angled sides that give a three-dimensional appearance _____

13. Lets you create a specific color _____

14. An image that is created and stored using pixel values _____

15. Selects a specified area _____

16. Purity of a color _____

17. Deletes all of the image except the selected area _____

18. Measurement of image quality, measured in pixels-per-inch (ppi) _____

Chapter 6: Worksheet 6B

Review Integration Skills

Directions Circle the letter of the phrase that best answers each question.

1. What is GIF?
   a. A format for saving a picture file
   b. A tool that allows for files to be saved automatically, allowing for the space available
   c. It refers to the three colors that can be used to create Web pages.
   d. A mnemonic device that determines a 3:44 relationship between image size and resolution

2. How does a TIFF compare with a JPEG?
   a. A TIFF is much smaller than a JPEG.
   b. A TIFF is a good format for the Internet.
   c. A TIFF has better image quality.
   d. Answers **a** and **b**

3. What happens to a bitmapped image when it is enlarged?
   a. It changes size and keeps its image quality.
   b. It changes size and loses image quality.
   c. If resized using the same proportions, it keeps its image quality.
   d. It cannot be resized.

4. When images are stored at a lower resolution,
   a. they take longer to send through the Internet.
   b. the computer must keep track of a lot more data.
   c. they can usually be displayed clearly on a monitor.
   d. they can be used for professionally printed documents.

5. What is the difference between bitmap images and vector images?
   a. Bitmap images can be photographic quality, but cannot be resized easily.
   b. Vector images can be photographic quality, but cannot be resized easily.
   c. Bitmap images can be photographic quality, and can be resized easily.
   d. Vector images can be photographic quality, and can be resized easily.

6. Which of the following formats can be used in both Photoshop and Publisher?
   a. PSD and JPEG
   b. PSD and TIFF
   c. TIFF and JPEG
   d. All of the above

7. In order to tile print an oversized document, you must
   a. print it as a Publisher document.
   b. print it as a Photoshop document.
   c. print it on an imagesetter.
   d. use special oversized paper.

Chapter 7: Worksheet 7A

Identify Adobe Illustrator Tools

Directions Write the name for each tool that is called out in the Illustrator toolbox shown below.

A. _____

B. _____

C. _____

D. _____

E. _____

F. _____

G. _____

H. _____

I. _____

J. _____

K. _____

L. _____

M. _____

N. _____

Chapter 7: Worksheet 7B

Review Adobe Illustrator Vocabulary

Directions Fill in each blank with one of the words in the box below.

Stroke	Path	RGB	Direct Selection
Tab	Zoom Out	Warp	Blend
AI	Zoom In	Hand	Control
Extension	Opacity	Selection	Triangle

1. The _____ tool selects a specific object within a group.

2. You can identify a vector image by checking the file name _____.

3. The _____ tool will move the workspace.

4. When words follow a selected shape, you are keying on a _____.

5. You can temporarily hide the toolbox and pallets with the _____ key.

6. To make copies between two objects, use the _____ tool.

7. You can tell there are hidden tools on the toolbox when a tool has a small

 _____ in the corner.

8. Use _____ to magnify an object.

9. To change the weight of a line, use the _____ palette.

10. Use _____ colors to create illustrations for Web sites.

11. The _____ palette changes options depending on the tool you are using.

12. Adobe Illustrator's native format is _____.

13. To see your entire document, you should _____.

14. Objects that block out the layers below have a high _____.

15. Envelope Distort allows you to _____ an image.

16. You can move an object with a bounding box by using the _____ tool.

Chapter 8: Worksheet 8A

Review Adobe Illustrator Skills

Directions Answer each of the following questions. There may be more than one way to perform some of these skills.

1. How do you change an object's order within an illustration?

_____

_____

2. How do you flip an object?

_____

_____

3. How do you change the selected object to No Fill?

_____

_____

4. How do you distort a circle?

_____

_____

5. How do you turn on Smart Guides?

_____

_____

6. How do you display the Pathfinder palette?

_____

_____

7. How do you find the answer to a question about Illustrator?

_____

_____

8. How do you change a font typeface?

_____

_____

9. How do you add an envelope distortion effect?

_____

_____

Chapter 8: Worksheet 8B

Review Adobe Illustrator Key Terms

Directions Match each definition to the key term on the right. Write the letter of the correct key term next to the definition.

_____ 1. Hue, Saturation, Brightness, a method of describing color to a computer.

_____ 2. The framework upon which you place objects.

_____ 3. A property which allows an object to be seen through, making visible the objects underneath

_____ 4. The ability of a graphic to be resized without losing image quality.

_____ 5. An object that cannot be seen through.

_____ 6. Ranges from white to black with shades of gray in between.

_____ 7. The primary colors of light used to create images displayed on monitors.

_____ 8. A gradual change from one color to another.

_____ 9. Indicates the type of file format, such as .jpg, .exe, .doc.

_____ 10. The color system primarily used for printing.

_____ 11. To give an object visual depth.

_____ 12. The line that is created when an object is drawn.

_____ 13. The beginning of a new line segment.

_____ 14. To gradually blend two images together in such a manner that the first image appears to be transforming into the other image.

_____ 15. The delivery method of publications, such as print, CDs, disks, television and radio broadcasts, and Internet publishing.

_____ 16. A circular effect.

_____ 17. An illustration that is wrapped around the outside of an object, as wallpaper is attached to a wall.

_____ 18. The entire range of color.

_____ 19. Refers to the angled edges of an object.

_____ 20. The process used to precisely position and align graphic objects in a design, also called stacking.

a. anchor point
b. bevel
c. CMYK
d. extrude
e. file name extension
f. gradient
g. grayscale
h. grids
i. HSB
j. layering
k. map
l. medium
m. morph
n. opaque
o. path
p. radial
q. RGB
r. scalable
s. spectrum
t. transparent

Chapter 9: Worksheet 9A

Review Conflict Resolution Skills: Scenario 1

Directions Read the scenario in the table below. Consider each type of conflict resolution strategy. Complete the chart to consider possible solutions to the problem.

Scenario Two groups of teens want to use the local area basketball court to play ball at the same time. Complete the chart below to consider possible solutions to the problem.		
Resolution Strategy	**Definition**	**Solution**
I Win		
You Win		
Win Win		
Abandonment		

Chapter 9: Worksheet 9B
Review Conflict Resolution Skills: Scenario 2

Directions Read the scenario in the table below. Consider each type of conflict resolution strategy. Complete the chart to consider possible solutions to the problem.

Scenario Two group members both want to be the Photoshop expert in the group.		
Resolution Strategy	**Resolution**	**Solution**
I Win		
You Win		
Win Win		
Abandonment		

Name _____ Date _____ Class _____

Chapter 9: Worksheet 9C

Review Spreadsheet Elements

Directions Use the Excel spreadsheet below to answer the following questions.

	Microsoft Excel - Bake Sale Workbook.xls					
	File Edit View Insert Format Tools Data Window Help			Type a question for help		
	Arial ▾ 10 ▾ **B** *I* U ≡ ≡ ≡ $ % ,					
	A4 ▾ *fx* Brownies					

	A	B	C	D	E	F
1		Bake Sale Profits				
2	**Treats**	**Number Sold**	**Cost per Item**	**Total Sales**		
3	Chocolate Chip Cookies	60	$ 1.00	$ 60.00		
4	Brownies	150	$ 2.00	$ 300.00		
5	Caramels	300	$ 0.25	$ 75.00		
6	Sponge Cake	60	$ 3.00	$ 180.00		
7	Orange Juice	50	$ 1.00	$ 50.00		
8	Coffee	100	$ 1.00	$ 100.00		
9	Tea	50	$ 1.00	$ 50.00		
10			**Grand Total**	$ 815.00		
11						
12						

Treats / Calendar / Profits /

Ready   Sum=452   NUM

1. How many rows have numbers? _____

2. How many columns have numbers? _____

3. What is the text from cell A5? _____

4. Which column(s) use(s) currency? _____

5. Which row is currently selected? _____

6. What are the names of the three worksheets? _____

7. What is the name of the workbook? _____

8. What is the font and font size? _____

9. Which row(s) has (have) merged cells? _____

10. Which cell has text that wraps? _____

Chapter 10: Worksheet 10A
Review Desktop Publishing Skills

Directions Match the following descriptions with the terms shown below. Write the letter of the correct description in the space provided.

_____ 1. desktop publishing

_____ 2. WYSIWYG

_____ 3. word processor

_____ 4. resolution

_____ 5. layout

_____ 6. sans serif

a. Refers to the clarity of an image

b. Means the computer screen displays what the final printed document looks like

c. The arrangement of elements on the page

d. Typeface without small cross strokes at the top and bottom

e. A software application that allows the user to enter and edit text

f. The ability to design and develop publications on a personal computer by combining text and graphics

Directions Read each question below. Then fill in the circle next to the word or phrase that best answers the question.

7. How many times should you press the space bar after a question mark?
- ○ none
- ○ one
- ○ two
- ○ three

8. In terms of readability, what kind of font should generally be used for a paragraph?
- ○ sans serif
- ○ serif
- ○ decorative
- ○ bold

9. Which of the following alignments should generally not be used together?
- ○ left and right
- ○ left and center
- ○ center and justified
- ○ right and right

10. What is a drop cap?
- ○ a capital letter that is smaller than the font's x-height
- ○ a capital letter that is larger than a single line of text
- ○ a command that allows the user to eliminate capitalized words easily
- ○ an exception to the rule about using all-caps

11. Why should elements be repeated on every page?
- ○ They give a summary explanation of the story.
- ○ They capture the reader's attention.
- ○ They increase white space.
- ○ They visually tie different pages together.

Chapter 10: Worksheet 10B

Review Adobe Photoshop Skills

Directions Read each question below. Then fill in the circle next to the phrase that best answers the question.

1. After you have used the marquee, what area of the image can be edited?
   - ○ The area to which you are applying the tool
   - ○ Only the area outside the selection
   - ○ Only the area inside the selection
   - ○ Only the area rasterized by the vector image

2. How does the Magic Wand tool determine which areas of an image to select?
   - ○ It determines hard edges of an object and selects that form.
   - ○ It selects areas based solely through the similarity of pixel colors.
   - ○ It selects areas based on image properties such as shadows.
   - ○ It selects areas based upon the history palette and computerized intuition.

3. What is an advantage to using layers?
   - ○ File sizes are much smaller.
   - ○ Images are less confusing to work with.
   - ○ Fewer windows are on your screen.
   - ○ Layers can be edited independently.

4. What is one way that a TIFF file format compares to JPEG file format?
   - ○ A TIFF is much smaller than a JPEG.
   - ○ A TIFF is used for Internet publishing.
   - ○ A TIFF has greater image quality.
   - ○ A TIFF file format is not different from a JPEG file format.

5. What happens to a bitmapped image when it is enlarged?
   - ○ It changes size and keeps its image quality.
   - ○ It changes size and loses image quality.
   - ○ If resized using the same proportions, it keeps its image quality.
   - ○ Bitmapped images cannot be resized.

6. What is a pixel?
   - ○ It refers to a square in an image that displays a single color.
   - ○ It is a tool that smoothes image quality.
   - ○ It is a tool that automatically reduces red-eye problems in pictures.
   - ○ It is a tool use to make corrections in photographs.

7. Which statement is accurate?
   - ○ Bitmap images can be photographic quality, but they have large file sizes.
   - ○ Vector images can be photographic quality, but they have large file sizes.
   - ○ Bitmap images can be photographic quality, but they have small file sizes.
   - ○ Bitmap images are never photographic quality.

Chapter 10: Worksheet 10C
Review Adobe Illustrator Skills

Directions Match the following descriptions with the Illustrator tools shown below. Write the letter of the correct tool in the space provided.

_____ 1. Selects a specific object within a group

_____ 2. Sets anchor points and draws lines between those points

_____ 3. Selects an entire grouped object

_____ 4. Makes copies

_____ 5. Moves the workspace

a. Hand tool

b. Selection tool

c. Direct Selection tool

d. Blend tool

e. Pen tool

Directions Read each question below. Then fill in the circle next to the word or phrase that best answers the question.

6. Which file format below is the native format created specifically for Illustrator?
   ○ JPEG
   ○ PNG
   ○ GIF
   ○ AI

7. Why is there a triangle shape on the bottom corner of some of the tools in the toolbox?
   ○ Some areas in the toolbox have hidden tools underneath.
   ○ These are the tools recommended by the Adobe staff.
   ○ These tools can be customized.
   ○ The Delta is merely part of interface design.

8. What does it mean to "type on a path?"
   ○ Begin to key text at an anchor point.
   ○ Text follows the shape of a line.
   ○ Text will assume the shape of selected artwork.
   ○ Text is keyed in a text box.

Directions Write the name of the Illustrator palette described in the question on the blank line.

9. Which palette adds, subtracts, merges, and crops shapes?

_____

10. Which palette shows the layers so they may be viewed, deleted, locked, or reordered?

_____

11. Which palette changes the thickness of the lines?

_____

12. Which palette serves as Illustrator's "clip art"?

_____

Chapter 10: Worksheet 10D

Review Presentation Skills

Directions Answer the following questions about preparing for a PowerPoint presentation.

Know the Audience

1. Why is it important to make sure your presentation is age-appropriate?

_____

_____

2. Why is it important to know how much knowledge your audience has about the information you will present?

_____

_____

_____

Practice

3. Why is it important to make sure you know how to explain and pronounce everything in your presentation?

_____

_____

4. Why is it important to practice giving the presentation?

_____

_____

Timing

5. Why is it important to know if your audience might be hungry?

_____

_____

6. Why is it important to know exactly how much time you have to complete your presentation?

_____

_____

Prepare Yourself

7. Why is it important to make sure your appearance and clothes look professional?

_____

_____

Worksheet 1A Rate Your Computer Skills (p. 334)

Students' answers will vary. Use this worksheet to evaluate students' skill-levels before beginning the course. Have students fill out the worksheet later in the course to assess what they have learned and what still needs to be taught.

Worksheet 1B Review Desktop Publishing Skills (p. 336)

1. f
2. d
3. e
4. b
5. c
6. a
7. F, Use an en-dash in a range: The festival will be held June 26–July 8.
8. F, Use tabs or tables to align text.
9. T
10. T
11. F, Arial is a sans serif font.
12. F, Cut saves the item to the clipboard so it can be pasted elsewhere.

Worksheet 2A Review Microsoft Word Skills (p. 337)

1. Press **View>Toolbars>Drawing**.
2. Select the object, then hold the Control key and move the object with the arrows.
3. Group objects to combine them into one image that can be moved or resized.
4. Shift or Control will select more than one object.
5. Square black handles means that the clip art is set to *In line with text* and cannot be moved.
6. You can rotate WordArt or use a text box and choose **Format>Text Direction**, and choose the sideways option.
7. Style sheets make it easy to apply consistent formatting to all headers, bylines, and text in a newsletter.

8. The Show/Hide button shows spacing and hard returns, which makes it easier to know where to place your cursor or select items for formatting.
9. Select the circle, click the Draw button on the Drawing toolbar, and choose **Order>Bring Forward**.

Worksheet 2B Identify Microsoft Word Drawing Tools (p. 338)

1. E
2. B
3. D
4. H
5. A
6. C
7. G
8. F
9. Line Color
10. Draw
11. Text Box
12. AutoShapes
13. Fill Color
14. Rectangle
15. AutoShapes
16. Draw
17. Insert Picture
18. Dash Style

Worksheet 3A Review Microsoft Publisher Skills (p. 339)

1. F, The Page Navigation buttons at the bottom of the screen show that there are 4 pages.
2. T
3. F, The magnification level is set at 66%.
4. F, We only see a portion of the open page spread on the screen.
5. F, The style window on the Formatting toolbar shows Menu Item style.
6. T
7. F, Both pages use Master Page B.
8. T

Worksheet 3B Evaluate Ethical Use of Materials *(p. 340)*

1. *Copyright* is the legal right of an individual or company to protect his or her creation from being used without permission.
2. *Fair use* is an exception to copyright law that allows copyrighted material to be used for certain educational purposes wthout requiring permission or royalty payments.
3. Under fair use, a copyrighted work might be used for educational purposes. For example, a copyrighted image can be included in a student report without having to get permission or pay royalties.
4. Public domain
5. Copyright
6. Copyright
7. Public Domain
8. Public Domain
9. Public Domain
10. Copyright
11. Copyright
12. Public Domain
13. Public Domain
14. Copyright

Worksheet 4A Review PARC Principles and the Design Process *(p. 341)*

1. a) Get specific instructions from the client
   b) draw thumbnail sketches
   c) modify the design
   d) revise based on feedback
   e) try the design in the medium in which it will be published
   f) make final adjustments.
2. It takes too long to create and revise a design on the computer to meet a client's needs.
3. Proximity is how elements are grouped together on a page. It can be created using white space, lines, boxes, or similar fonts and colors.

4. Objects can be aligned using tabs, margin guides, layout guides, ruler guides, and the Align or Distribute tool in the Arrange menu.
5. Repetition is when important design elements are repeated throughout a design. It creates harmony in a design.
6. Contrast creates a focal point by using a different color, alignment, font, or design feature to draw the eye into the document.
7. White space should be active and flow through the document to allow the eyes to rest and make a document more readable.
8. Center-aligned text is safe, but boring, and it would probably not attract as much attention as a document created with more interesting alignment.

Worksheet 4B Evaluate a Design *(p. 342)*

Proximity: There are too many boxes. Hard to tell what goes with what.

Alignment: Haphazard use of center, left, and right alignment. Bullet points do not align.

Repetition: Too many balloons.

Contrast: No real contrast between the titles, contact information, and the rest of the text. No focal point to enter the document.

Grammar and Punctuation: In the top box, "one stop" should be hyphenated. At the bottom, change to: "Pick up and delivery are available. Additional charge added for cleanup or repair." The word "street" should be capitalized in the bottom box.

Worksheet 5A
Review Adobe Photoshop
Vocabulary (p. 343)

1. k) optical zoom
2. e filter
3. r) saturation
4. h) histogram
5. i) marquee
6. d) file name extension
7. a) anchor point
8. l) palette
9. p) resolution
10. b) blending modes
11. s) scalable
12. q) retouch
13. t) single lens reflex
14. c) clone
15. g) highlight
16. f) polygon
17. g) flatten
18. j) mask
19. m) pixel
20. o) raster

Worksheet 5B Review
Adobe Photoshop Tools (p. 344)

1. c
2. c
3. a
4. b
5. a
6. d
7. c
8. a

Worksheet 6A Review
Adobe Photoshop Terms (p. 345)

1. Paint Bucket
2. Gradient
3. Clone Stamp
4. Magnetic Lasso
5. Magic Wand
6. PSD
7. Sponge
8. Tile
9. JPEG
10. Vector
11. TIFF
12. Bevel
13. Color Picker
14. Bitmap
15. Marquee
16. Saturation
17. Crop
18. Resolution

Worksheet 6B
Review Integration Skills (p. 346)

1. a
2. c
3. b
4. c
5. a
6. c
7. a

Worksheet 7A Identify
Adobe Illustrator Tools (p. 347)

A. Selection
B. Direct Selection
C. Magic Wand
D. Lasso
E. Type on a Path
F. Line
G. Rounded Rectangle
H. Gradient
I. Blend
J. Hand
K. Zoom
L. Fill Color
M. Stroke Color
N. No Fill (None)

Worksheet 7B
Review Adobe Illustrator
Vocabulary (p. 348)

1. Direct Selection
2. extension
3. Hand
4. path
5. Tab
6. Blend
7. triangle
8. Zoom In
9. Stroke
10. RGB
11. Control
12. AI
13. Zoom Out
14. opacity
15. warp
16. Selection

Worksheet 8A
Review Adobe Illustrator
Skills (p. 349)

1. Choose Object>Arrange>Bring to Front/ Back, or change the order of the layers.
2. Choose Object>Transform>Reflect.
3. Select the object and click No Fill in the toolbox, Colors pallet, or Color Picker.
4. Effects>Distort and Transform, or use the Direct Selection tool and click/drag an anchor point
5. View>Smart Guides
6. Choose Window>Pathfinder.
7. Choose Help>Illustrator Help.
8. Choose Type>Font, or Window>Type> Character.
9. Choose Object>Envelope Distort.

Worksheet 8B
Review Adobe Illustrator
Key Terms (p. 350)

1. i) HSB
2. h) grids
3. t) transparent
4. r) scalable
5. n) opaque
6. g) grayscale
7. q) RGB
8. f) gradient
9. e) file name extensions
10. c) CMYK
11. d) extrude
12. o) path
13. a) anchor point
14. m) morph
15. l) medium
16. p) radial
17. k) map
18. s) spectrum
19. b) bevel
20. j) layering

Worksheet 9A
Review Conflict Resolution Skills:
Scenario 1 (p. 351)

Scenario Two groups of teens want to use the local area basketball court to play ball at the same time. Complete the chart below to consider possible solutions to the problem.

Resolution Strategy	Strategy	Solution
I Win	Insists on own solution without regard to other possibilities.	The first group to arrive gets to play.
You Win	Allows the other point of view to dominate without regard to own preferences.	The first group lets the second group play.
Win Win	Creates a compromise that fulfills most of the requirements for all sides of the conflict.	Everybody plays together, or play half-court basketball.
Abandonment	Devises a more acceptable substitute situation or way of choosing.	Go to a different court, or choose a different activity.

ANSWER KEY

Worksheet 9B
Review Conflict Resolution Skills:
Scenario 2 (p. 352)

Scenario	Two group members both want to be the Photoshop expert in the groud.	
Resolution Strategy	**Strategy**	**Solution**
I Win	Insists on own solution without regard to other possibilities.	The first person who "called it" gets to be the Photoshop expert, or the person with the highest Photoshop grades gets to be the Photoshop expert.
You Win	Allows the other point of view to dominate without regard to own preferences.	One person lets the other be the Photoshop expert.
Win Win	Creates a compromise that fulfills most of the requirements for all sides of the conflict.	Divide the workload to accommodate two experts.
Abandonment	Devises a more acceptable substitute situation or way of choosing.	Stage a contest, draw straws, allow the group to vote, or choose somebody else to be the Photoshop expert.

Worksheet 9C Review
Spreadsheet Elements (p. 353)

1. 8
2. 3
3. Caramels
4. C, D
5. 4
6. Treats, Calendar, Profits
7. Bake Sale Workbook
8. Arial 10
9. 1, 10
10. A3

Worksheet 10A Review
Desktop Publishing Skills (p. 354)

1. f
2. b
3. e
4. a
5. c
6. d
7. one
8. serif
9. left and center
10. a capital letter that is larger than a single line of text
11. They visually tie different pages together.

Worksheet 10B Review
Adobe Photoshop Skills (p. 355)

1. Only the area outside the selection
2. It selects areas based solely through the similarity of pixel colors.
3. Layers can be edited independently.
4. A TIFF has greater image quality.
5. It changes size and loses image quality.
6. It refers to a square in an image that displays a single color.
7. Bitmap images can be photographic quality, but they have large file sizes.

Worksheet 10C Review
Adobe Illustrator Skills *(p. 356)*

1. c
2. e
3. b
4. d
5. a
6. AI
7. Some areas in the toolbox have hidden tools underneath.
8. Text follows the shape of a line.
9. Pathfinder palette
10. Layers palette
11. Stroke palette
12. Symbols palette

Worksheet 10D Review
Presentation Skills *(p. 357)*

Students answers will vary, but should be similar to the following:

1. The material should not be over the heads of a younger or less-informed audience, or too simple for an older audience who might be bored.
2. If the audience is less-informed or more-informed than expected, the audience could lose interest because they do not understand the information or because it is too simple.
3. Presenters should practice the presentation and find any weaknesses so they do not get caught off guard in front of an audience. Mispronouncing words or being unable to explain a topic can make the presenter look foolish and unprepared.
4. Practicing the presentation will allow the presenter to be confident, which will make the presentation more effective. It allows the presenter to fix any mistakes, predict questions, fix holes in the slides, and time him or herself.
5. Is the presentation during or close to a usual meal time? Sometimes food, snacks, or beverages will keep an audience satisfied and less distracted.

6. Sometimes it takes practicing a presentation out loud to be sure it will fill up, but not go over, the time allotted for the presentation.
7. Appropriate, pressed clothing gives off a professional appearance. A sloppy, uncombed, or unclean presenter will be distracting. Attitude, body language, and confidence can help the speaker look more informed and knowledgeable.

What Are Graphic Organizers?

Graphic organizers are visual ways to organize written material. Charts, graphs, diagrams, and maps are all examples of graphic organizers. The use of graphic organizers promotes critical reading and thinking. In addition, writing information in a visual or an illustrated way helps students clarify and categorize data for easier recall. Using graphic organizers also helps students see connections among parallel or related facts. Finally, many teachers believe that having students list information in a graphic organizer makes learning more fun than just taking notes in the traditional way.

Why Use Graphic Organizers?

Use graphic organizers like the one shown below to:

◆ Set a purpose for student reading.

◆ Help students organize and understand important material as they read.

◆ Provide a visual way for students to reinforce what they read.

◆ Prepare students for tests or quizzes.

◆ Help students brainstorm and organize ideas for projects.

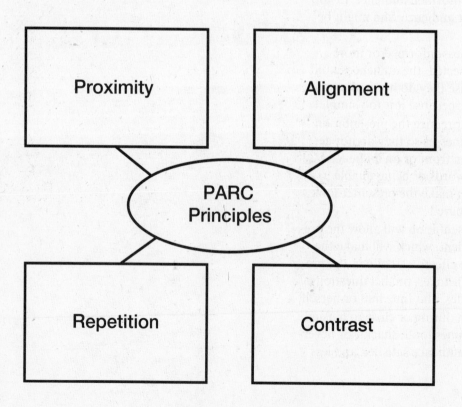

Using the Graphic Organizers in the Classroom

◆ Copy the graphic organizer you want from pages 363–376 of this manual.

◆ Print the Graphic Organizer PDF files. These are available on:

  • The Teacher Resource DVD.

  • The Online Learning Center Web site at **www.glencoe.com**.

◆ Alternately, students can hand draw each organizer on a separate sheet of paper, or they can create organizers on the computer, using the tools in Microsoft Word or Microsoft Publisher.

◆ Give a copy to each student when you assign a section of a chapter.

◆ Have students follow your directions in order to fill in the information.

◆ You may need to complete the first few organizers with students if they are not familiar with using graphic organizers.

Once students are comfortable filling in the organizers on their own, you may wish to use the different types of organizers provided on the following pages to help students focus their reading, take notes, and reinforce new knowledge.

Using Graphic Organizers Effectively

The graphic organizers provided in this section are intended to help students take notes and organize information from their textbooks. Students can also use them as a way to organize ideas when brainstorming for a project.

◆ Before requiring students to complete an activity, describe the purpose of the particular graphic organizer.

◆ Demonstrate how to use the textbook and prior knowledge to fill in information for the various parts of the graphic organizer.

◆ Provide opportunities for students to work in groups as well as individually when completing the graphic organizers, which will teach students to analyze the text more closely.

◆ After students have completed an activity, discuss the responses as a class. This will help students learn to revise their thought processes and better clarify the strategies for using the graphic organizers.

Graphic Organizer Library Overview

There are 14 reproducible graphic organizers provided in this section. Each type of organizer is best suited for a specific kind or purpose of presentation. For example, one type of organizer may be better suited to categorize information sequentially; another to compare or contrast; a third to describe, support, or exemplify a main idea; and so on. The following information will explain for what purpose each of the graphic organizers is best suited.

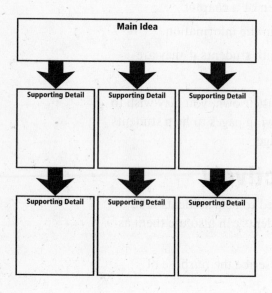

Graphic Organizer 1: Main Idea Chart

This type of graphic organizer is helpful when you want students to find the main idea of a paragraph or section, and then to analyze the reading further for more information that exemplifies or supports that main idea.

Graphic Organizer 2: K-W-L-H Chart

The K-W-L-H chart is used to activate students' prior knowledge and interest before they read as well as to set a purpose for reading. This chart asks for student feedback on what they Know already, what they Want to find out, what they Learned, and How they can learn more.

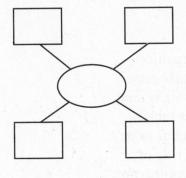

Graphic Organizer 3:
Web Diagram

Web diagrams are often used to help students identify one central idea and organize related information around it. Students must determine the broad categories that should be listed in the outer parts of the web. Then students must determine what is relevant factual material and group this data into the appropriate related categories.

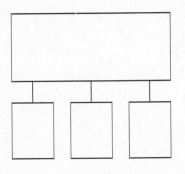

Graphic Organizer 4:
Tree Diagram

A tree diagram is based upon the traditional "family tree" organizational graphic. Students are required to record how subordinate facts or statements are related to one another and to a larger, unifying statement. Tree diagrams may also be utilized as a main idea/supporting details type of graphic organizer.

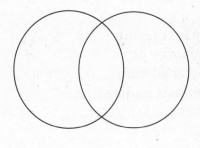

Graphic Organizer 5:
Venn Diagram

Venn diagrams are used to compare and contrast information or to show similarities and differences among various objects or subjects. The Venn diagram consists of two or more overlapping circles. Differences are listed in the outer parts of the circles. Similarities are described where the circles overlap. Venn diagrams are especially helpful in displaying similarities and differences at a glance.

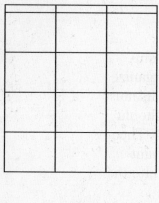

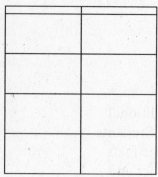

Graphic Organizers 6 and 7: Matrix and Table

Matrices and tables are used to organize or categorize information or to make comparisons among categories. A matrix is used to compare multiple items, while a table is used to compare two items. The items to be compared are listed along the left side of the table's rows, and the general features are listed across the top of the table before filling in the cells with facts or supporting information. Graphic Organizer 7 may also be used as a storyboard.

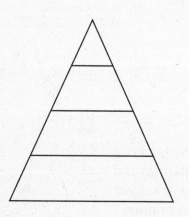

Graphic Organizer 8: Pyramid Table

A pyramid table is very effective for organizing information in a majority/minority or general-to-specific manner. A pyramid table can also be used to list details or facts leading up to a climax or culminating event.

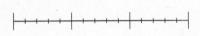

Graphic Organizer 9: Fishbone Diagram

The purpose of a fishbone diagram is very similar to that of a main idea/supporting details chart. A main idea statement or category is written on the single line to the left. Supporting facts, examples, or subcategories are written on the lines to the right. In many cases, a third set of lines can be generated and attached to the subcategories with additional information or facts.

Graphic Organizer 10: Horizontal Time Line

Time lines are used to list important dates in chronological order. Horizontal time lines require students to analyze information by sequencing events. Time lines also require students to determine baseline dates and to be cognizant of the "backward" nature of B.C. chronology.

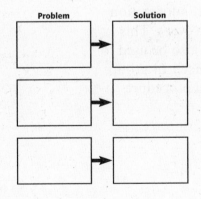

Graphic Organizer 11: Problem-Solution Chart

The purpose of this type of graphic organizer is to help students streamline the steps involved in recognizing a problem and utilizing problem-solving skills. The problem-solution chart may be best suited for group discussion after the teacher has explained an event or action. Students may then describe or predict the problem, after which they may brainstorm multiple solutions and possible results of those solutions.

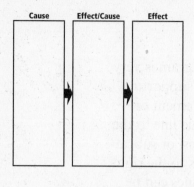

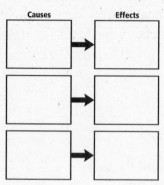

Graphic Organizers 12 and 13: Cause-Effect Charts

This type of organizer helps students analyze information by identifying cause-and-effect relationships. In some cases, students may be required to identify a sequence of a cause and its effect, which becomes the cause of yet another effect. In other cases, students will identify separate causes and their effects (see Graphic Organizer 13).

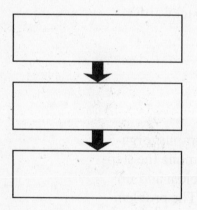

Graphic Organizer 14: Chain-of-Events or Flowchart

A chain-of-events, or flowchart, asks students to organize and interpret information by sequencing the stages of an event. This type of graphic organizer can also be used to describe the actions of a character or group, or the steps to be followed in a procedure.

Graphic Organizer 1: Main Idea Chart

Main Idea

Supporting Detail

Supporting Detail

Supporting Detail

Supporting Detail

Supporting Detail

Supporting Detail

Graphic Organizer 2: K-W-L-H Chart

What I Know	What I Want to Find Out	What I Learned	How Can I Learn More

Graphic Organizer 3: Web Diagram

Graphic Organizer 4: Tree Diagram

Name _____ Date _____ Class _____

Graphic Organizer 5: Venn Diagram

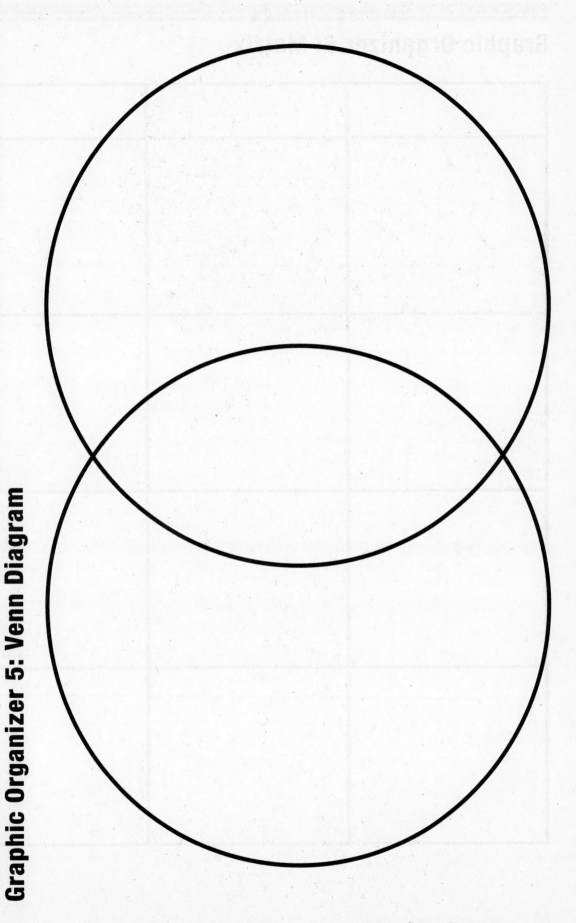

Graphic Organizer 6: Matrix

Graphic Organizer 7: Table

Graphic Organizer 8: Pyramid Table

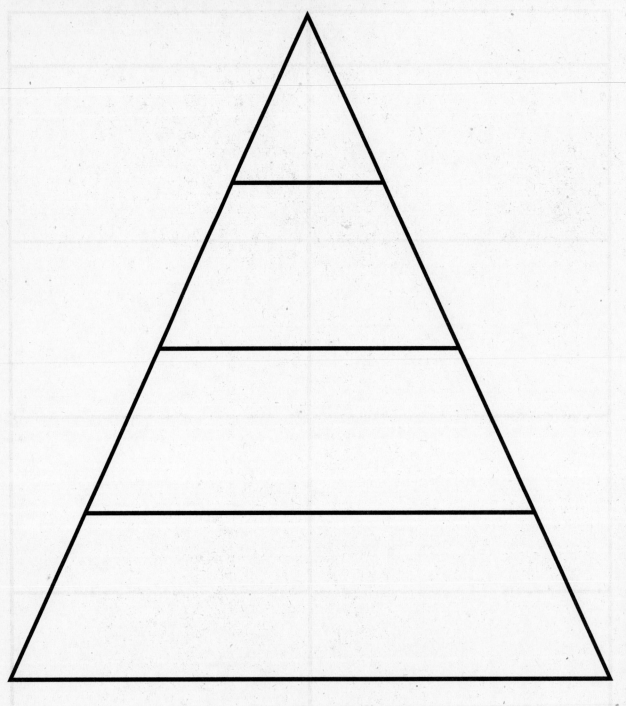

Graphic Organizer 9: Fishbone Diagram

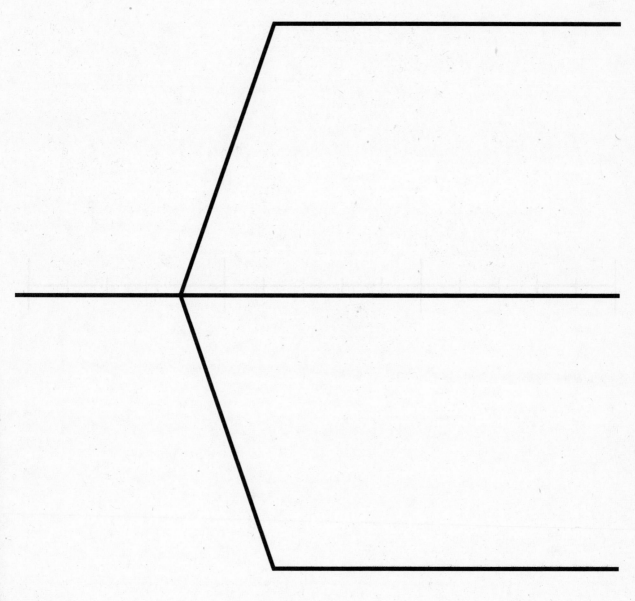

Graphic Organizer 10: Horizontal Time Line

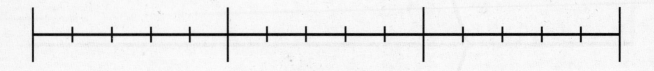

Graphic Organizer 11: Problem–Solution Chart

Problem

Solution

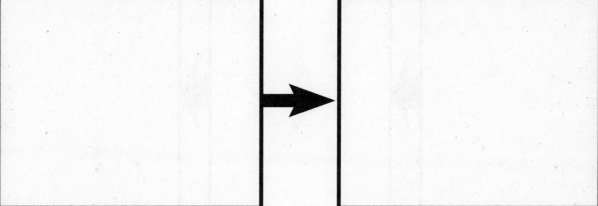

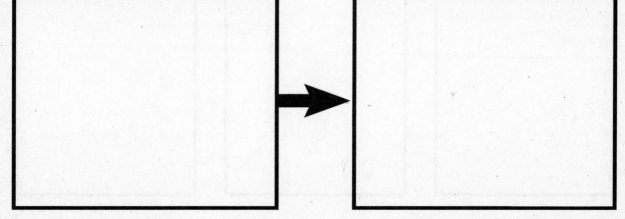

Graphic Organizer 12: Cause–Effect Chart A

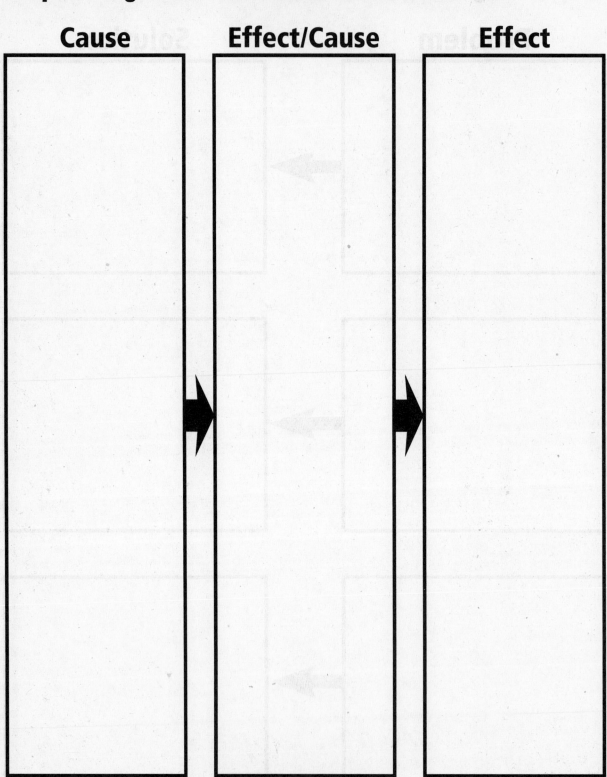

Cause   **Effect/Cause**   **Effect**

Graphic Organizer 13: Cause–Effect Chart B

Causes

Effects

Graphic Organizer 14: Chain-of-Events or Flowchart

PART 4

PowerPoint® Presentations, *ExamView® Assessment Suite*, and TechSIM™ Interactive Tutorials

POWERPOINT PRESENTATION INFORMATION

The Teacher Resource DVD contains ten PowerPoint presentations, one presentation for every chapter of *Introduction to Desktop Publishing With Digital Graphics*. Each presentation includes important headings, figures, and key terms that students will encounter while using the textbook.

Using Presentations in the Classroom

The following suggestions may help you use the PowerPoint Presentations in the classroom.

◆ Use the PowerPoint Presentations to introduce chapter content, or use them to review material.

◆ You may wish to show students only part of the presentations at a time. For example, view the Project information just before they begin each project.

◆ When students are creating a specific project, you may want to display the solution and leave it displayed during the class period so students can refer to it as they work.

◆ Students may also use the presentations on their own for independent study.

◆ If your school has a wireless mouse for your computer (or another means of advancing slides in PowerPoint Presentations), you can circulate around the classroom as you teach. This will allow you to focus on an individual student's work and deal with problems before a student falls too far behind.

◆ Even if your class does not have a wireless mouse, you will only need to return to your computer to advance the presentation one slide at a time with one keystroke. You will not be tied to the computer as you review material in front of the class.

◆ The PowerPoint Presentations are intended to supplement your presentation of the material in the textbook. They are not designed as a substitute for the text or for your guided classroom teaching.

Ultimately, these PowerPoint Presentations can make your job easier, accelerate learning, and allow for more individualized teaching.

INSTALLATION AND STARTUP INSTRUCTIONS

Setting Up Your Equipment

Before you begin using PowerPoint presentations, check your equipment connections. To use PowerPoint presentations, you will need a computer (see System Requirements below), PowerPoint software or PowerPoint Viewer software, and a projector or large screen monitor capable of displaying high-color images. Make sure your monitor is set to high-color mode.

System Requirements

Verify that your computer meets or exceeds the hardware and software requirements listed below. Check your PowerPoint user manual or **www.microsoft.com** to check the system requirements for your version of PowerPoint.

WINDOWS

- Intel Pentuim 233 MHz or faster
- 128 MB of RAM or greater
- DVD drive
- Super VGA (800 x 600) or higher-resolution video monitor
- Mouse
- Printer *(optional, but recommended)*
- Microsoft PowerPoint 97 or later, or PowerPoint Viewer
- Microsoft Windows 2000 with Service Pack 3 (SP3), Windows XP, or later

MACINTOSH

- Any PowerPC processor-based, Mac OS-compatible system
- 120 MHz processor recommended
- 32 MB of RAM
- DVD drive
- VGA or higher-resolution video monitor, supporting 256 colors and 640x400 or greater resolution
- Mouse
- Printer *(optional, but recommended)*
- Microsoft PowerPoint 98 or later, or PowerPoint Viewer
- Apple System 8.5 or later

Loading the Presentations

The PowerPoint presentation files have not been compressed; therefore, they can be run directly from the DVD or Online Learning Center. In most cases, the PowerPoint presentations will run faster if saved to your hard drive. If you save the presentations to your hard drive, you may wish to organize them in a separate folder.

Running a Presentation with PowerPoint

The best way to run a PowerPoint presentation is with PowerPoint software. The following instructions assume that PowerPoint is located on your hard disk, and that the extension ".ppt" is recognized by your computer as a PowerPoint presentation.

1. Insert the Teacher Resource DVD into your DVD drive. If the DVD does not start automatically:
   ◆ (For Windows) double-click on the **My Computer** icon on your desktop, and then on the icon for your DVD drive. Next, double-click on the **StartUp** file.
   ◆ (For Macintosh) double-click on the DVD icon on your desktop. Then, double-click on the **StartUp** file.

2. Click the **PowerPoint Presentations** link.

3. Click the PowerPoint presentation you wish to view. (This should automatically start the presentation.) Depending on your software configuration, you may need to change the **View** option to **Slide Show** to run the presentation as a slide show.

Navigating Between Slides	
Next Slide	**Previous Slide**
◆ Right arrow key	◆ Left arrow key
◆ Down arrow key	◆ Up arrow key
◆ Page Up key	◆ Page Down key
◆ Right arrow button on screen	◆ Left arrow button on screen
◆ Space bar	
◆ Click left mouse	

Running a Presentation with PowerPoint Viewer

If you do not have PowerPoint, you can go to the Microsoft Web site to download a free PowerPoint Viewer. Visit **www.microsoft.com**, or if you are a Mac user, visit **www.microsoft.com/mac**. Once this Viewer has been installed, follow these directions:

1. Start the PowerPoint Viewer program.

2. In the pop-up menu, navigate to the Teacher Resource DVD or saved presentation.

3. Choose the PowerPoint Presentations folder and then the presentation you wish to view.

4. When you start a presentation, you will see an opening slide. Click the mouse or press the right arrow key to proceed to the next slide.

5. To access the PowerPoint Viewer resources, use your mouse to right-click on the screen. From the pop-up menu, you can select next, previous, or specific slides. You can also access Help and printing from this menu.

6. To end the presentation, press the Esc (Escape) key.

Customizing a Presentation

The PowerPoint presentations were created using Microsoft PowerPoint 2003 (Windows). If you wish, you can customize any of the presentations using PowerPoint 97, or a later version. Follow the steps provided in your PowerPoint user manual or in the online Help system that is part of the PowerPoint program.

Troubleshooting Tips

If you experience problems using PowerPoint presentations, refer to the troubleshooting tips in the Help system. A comprehensive list of potential problems is provided along with suggested solutions. To access this information, start a presentation and click on the **Help** button. Select **Microsoft PowerPoint Help** and key in your question.

ExamView Assessment Suite
SOFTWARE INFORMATION

ExamView Assessment Suite software allows you to generate ready-made and customized objective tests using multiple choice, true/false, fill-in-the-blank, and essay questions. The questions cover all chapters in the text.

Components of the *ExamView Assessment Suite* Software include:

◆ *ExamView Assessment Suite* Software User's Manual (Windows/Macintosh)

◆ *ExamView Assessment Suite* Software (Windows/Macintosh)

The CD software contains the testbank generator program that lets you retrieve the questions you want from the chapter testbanks. Answers to all questions are provided in the testbanks. The software also lets you edit and add questions as needed.

Site License

Your adoption of this textbook entitles you to site-license duplication rights for all components of the *ExamView Assessment Suite* Software with the restriction that all copies must be used within the adopting schools. This license shall run for the life of the adoption of the accompanying text.

Using the Testbank

Before you begin, follow the directions in the *User's Manual* on the CD to make backup copies of the software. Then, set up your computer and printer and configure the software, following the instructions. The *User's Manual* contains all the instructions on how to use the software. Refer to this manual as needed to preview and select questions for your tests.

Software Support Hotline

Should you encounter any difficulty when setting up or running the programs, contact the Software Support Center at Glencoe Publishing between 8:30 A.M. and 6:00 P.M. Eastern Time. The toll-free number is **1-800-437-3715**. Customers with specific questions can contact us via the Internet at the following e-mail address: **epgtech@mcgraw-hill.com.**

ExamView Assessment Suite COMPONENTS

ExamView Assessment Suite is a test generator program that enables you to quickly create printed tests, online tests, and computer (LAN-based) tests. The program includes three components: Test Builder, Question Bank Editor, and Test Player. The **Test Builder** includes options to create, edit, print, and save tests. The **Question Bank Editor** lets you create or edit question banks. The **Test Player** is a separate program that your students can use to take online (LAN-based) tests or access study guides.

Test Builder

The Test Builder allows you to create tests using the QuickTest Wizard or to create a new test on your own. Use the Test Builder to prepare both printed and online tests or study guides.

◆ *If you want ExamView to select questions randomly from one or more question banks,* choose the **QuickTest Wizard** option to create a new test. Then, follow the step-by-step instructions to (1) enter a test title, (2) choose one or more question banks from which to select questions, and (3) identify how many questions you want on the test. The QuickTest Wizard will automatically create a new test and use the Test Builder to display the test on screen. You can print the test as is, remove questions, add new questions, or edit any question.

◆ *If you want to create a new test on your own,* choose the option to create a new test. Then identify a question bank from which to choose questions by using the **Question Bank** option in the **Select** menu. You may then add questions to the test by using one or more of the following selection options: *Randomly, From a List, While Viewing, By Criteria,* or *All Questions.*

Question Bank Editor

The Question Bank Editor allows you to edit questions in an existing publisher-supplied question bank or to create your own new question banks. Always use the Question Bank Editor if you want to change a question permanently in an existing question bank. If you want to make a change that applies only to a particular test, create a new question or edit that question in the Test Builder.

A question bank may include up to 250 questions in a variety of formats, including multiple choice, true/false, modified true/false, completion, yes/no, matching, problem, essay, short answer, case, and numeric response. You can include the following information for each question: difficulty code, reference, text objective, state objectives, topic, and notes.

Online Testing (LAN-based versus Internet)

The *ExamView Assessment Suite* software allows you to create paper tests and online tests. *ExamView* includes many features that let you customize an online test. You can create a test for a specific class, or you can prepare a study guide for anyone to use. Using the Online Test Wizard, you can schedule a test or allow it to be taken anytime. As your students work on a test, *ExamView* will scramble the question order, provide feedback for incorrect responses, and display a timer if you selected any of these options.

The program provides two distinct online testing options: **LAN-based** testing and **Internet** testing. The option you choose depends on your particular testing needs. You can choose either option to administer online tests and study guides.

The **LAN-based** testing option is designed to work on a local area network server. To take a LAN-based test, students must have access to the Test Player program included with the *ExamView* software. The Test Player is a separate program that lets your students take a test or access a study guide at a computer. You can copy the test or study guide along with the Test Player software onto your local area network. Then students can take the test at computers connected to your server.

The **Internet** testing option provides a computerized testing solution for delivering tests via the Internet or an intranet. This option is great for making sample tests and study guides available to students at home. Students do not need any other program (unlike the LAN-based option). When your students take a test, the results are automatically sent to you via e-mail.

You can publish an online test to your own Web site, or you can use the *ExamView* Internet test-hosting service. If you subscribe to the *ExamView* test-hosting service,[1] you can publish a test directly to the Internet with just a few simple steps. Students will have immediate access to the tests that you publish and you can get detailed reports. For more information on the Internet test-hosting service, visit the **www.examview.com** Web site.

As you work with the *ExamView* test generator, you may use the following features:

◆ An interview mode or "wizard" to guide you through the steps to create a test in less than five minutes

◆ Five methods to select test questions

  – Random selection

  – From a list

  – While viewing questions

  – By criteria (difficulty code, objective, topic, and others–if available)

  – All questions

◆ The capability to edit questions or to add an unlimited number of questions

◆ Online (Internet-based) testing

  – Create a test that students can take on the Internet using a browser

  – Receive instant feedback via e-mail

  – Create online study guides with student feedback for incorrect responses

  – Include any of the twelve question types

◆ Internet test-hosting[1]

  – Instantly publish a test to the *ExamView* Web site

  – Manage tests online

  – Allow students to access tests from one convenient location

  – Receive detailed reports

  – Download results to your gradebook or spreadsheet

◆ Online (LAN-based) testing

  – Allow anyone or selected students to take a test on your local area network

  – Schedule tests

  – Create online study guides with student feedback for incorrect responses

  – Incorporate multimedia links (movies and audio)

  – Export student results to a gradebook or spreadsheet

---

1. The Internet test-hosting service must be purchased separately. Visit www.examview.com to learn more.

- A sophisticated word processor
  - Streamlined question entry with spell checker
  - Tabs, fonts, symbols, foreign characters, and text styles
  - Tables with borders and shading
  - Full-featured equation editor
  - Pictures or other graphics within a question, answer, or narrative
- Numerous test layout and printing options
  - Scramble the choices in multiple choice questions
  - Print multiple versions of the same test with corresponding answer keys
  - Print an answer key strip for easier test grading
- Link groups of questions to common narratives

INSTALLATION AND STARTUP INSTRUCTIONS

The *ExamView Assessment Suite* is provided on CD. The CD includes the program and all of the questions for the corresponding textbook. The *ExamView* Player, which can be used by your students to take online (LAN-based or Internet) tests, is also included.

Before you can use the test generator, you must install it on your hard drive. The system requirements, installation instructions, and startup procedures are provided below.

System Requirements

To use the *ExamView Assessment Suite* or the online test player, your computer must meet or exceed the following minimum hardware requirements:

WINDOWS
- 120 MHz Pentium II or compatible processor
- Windows 98, Windows 2000, Windows XP (or a more recent version)
- Color monitor capable of displaying 16-bit color with 800 x 600 resolution
- CD-ROM drive
- Hard drive with at least 24 MB space available
- 32 MB available memory
- A mouse (or a compatible pointing device)

MACINTOSH
- 120 MHz or faster Power Macintosh
- OS X (10.2 or later)
- Color monitor capable of displaying 16-bit color with 800 x 600 resolution
- CD-ROM drive
- Hard drive with at least 24 MB space available
- 32 MB available memory
- A mouse (or a compatible pointing device)

> For PCs and MACs, Netscape 4.0/Explorer 4.0 (or a more recent version) and an Internet connection are required to take or publish an Internet test. OSX (10.2 or later) is also required for MAC users.

Installation Instructions

Follow these steps to install the *ExamView Assessment Suite* software. The setup program will automatically install everything you need to use *ExamView*.

WINDOWS

Step 1
Turn on your computer.

Step 2
Insert the *ExamView* disc into your CD-ROM drive.

Step 3
Click the **Start** button and click **Run**.

Step 4
Click the drive letter that corresponds to the CD-ROM drive on your computer and double-click the file titled **setup.exe** (e.g., d:\setup.exe).

Step 5
Follow the prompts on the screen to complete the installation process.

View or print the *ExamView Assessment Suite* User Guide by clicking the drive letter that corresponds to the CD-ROM drive on your computer (e.g., d:). Double-click to open the file titled **Manual**.

MACINTOSH

Step 1
Turn on your computer.

Step 2
Insert the *ExamView* disc into your CD-ROM drive

Step 3
Open the installer window, if necessary. It may open automatically.

Step 4
Double-click the installation icon to start the program.

Step 5
Follow the prompts on the screen to complete the installation process.

View or print the *ExamView Assessment Suite* User Guide by double-clicking the CD icon on the desktop. Double-click the file titled **Manual.**

The Getting Started section explains the options used to create a test and edit a question bank.

Startup Instructions

After you complete the installation process, follow these instructions to start the *ExamView* test generator software.

Step 1

WINDOWS: Click the **Start** button on the Taskbar. Click the **Programs** menu and locate the *ExamView* **Test Generator** folder. Click the *ExamView* option to start the software.

MACINTOSH: Locate and open the *ExamView* folder. Double-click the *ExamView* program icon.

Step 2

The first time you run the software, you will be prompted to enter your name, school/institution name, and city/state. You are now ready to begin using the *ExamView* software.

Step 3

Each time you start *ExamView*, the Startup menu appears. Choose one of the options shown.

Step 4

Use *ExamView Assessment Suite* to create a test, or to edit questions in a question bank.

Using the Help System

Whenever you need assistance using *ExamView*, access the extensive Help system. Click the **Help** button or choose the **Help Topics** option from the Help menu to access step-by-step instructions from more than 150 Help topics. If you experience any difficulties while you are working with the software, you may want to review the troubleshooting tips in the user-friendly Help system.

The Glencoe TechSIM™ Interactive Tutorials can help students learn more about file management, e-mail, system settings, and the Control Panel. The tutorials allow a safe, self-contained environment for students to explore the Windows desktop and Explorer, Microsoft Outlook, and the Windows Control Panel.

USING THE TechSIM™ INTERACTIVE TUTORIALS

The interactive tutorials can be used to further students' understanding of the selected topics while allowing them to gain hands-on practice. For example:

◆ **TechSIM A: File Management** If the computers in your classroom or lab use different versions of operating systems, then use the TechSIM to allow all students to practice using Microsoft Windows. The skills taught in this series of tutorials can easily be applied when students use other operating systems, including Macintosh systems or even future versions of Windows.

◆ **TechSIM B: E-mail** Students can also learn how to use Microsoft Outlook to send e-mail without having Outlook software installed on their machines.

◆ **TechSIM C: System Settings and the Control Panel** Students can learn how to change settings in the Control Panel tutorials without actually changing any settings on their own computers.

INSTALLATION INSTRUCTIONS

TechSIM tutorials can be used on a PC or a Mac. They can be accessed directly from the *Introduction to Desktop Publishing With Digital Graphics* Online Learning Center at **www.glencoe.com**, or they can be installed from the optional TechSIM™ Interactive Tutorials CD. (Note: If you install the tutorials from the CD, Internet access is *not* required.)

In order to view and run the TechSIM tutorials (online or once installed from CD), you will need to have the **Macromedia Flash Player** installed on each computer using the tutorials. The Flash Player is available at no charge from the Adobe Web site at **www.adobe.com**.

SOFTWARE SUPPORT

For specific information about how to install the tutorials from the CD-ROM, refer to the instructions provided with the CD. If you have lost your CD or it is not working properly, contact Glencoe Software Support Center at Glencoe/McGraw-Hill between 8:30 A.M. and 6:00 P.M. Eastern Time. The toll-free number is **1-800-437-3715**. Customers with specific questions can also contact us at the following e-mail address **epgtech@mcgraw-hill.com**.

USING THE TechSIM™ INTERACTIVE TUTORIALS WITH THE STUDENT TEXTBOOK

You can use the TechSIM tutorials to reinforce student textbook topics or assign them as stand-alone activities. The tutorials can be used alongside or in place of projects from the student textbook, or as enrichment activities.

TechSIM A: File Management
A-1 Get to Know Windows Explorer
A-2 Work with Folders
A-3 Work with Files
A-4 Open and Save a File
A-5 Work on the Desktop
A-6 Search for Files
A-7 Assessment—File Management

TechSIM B: E-mail
B-1 Get to Know Microsoft Outlook
B-2 Create and Send an E-mail Message
B-3 Attach a File to an E-mail Message
B-4 Save a Draft and Reply to an E-mail Message
B-5 Forward an E-mail Message
B-6 Manage E-mail
B-7 Work with the Address Book
B-8 E-mail Settings
B-9 Assessment—E-mail

TechSIM C: System Settings and the Control Panel
C-1 Get to Know the Control Panel
C-2 Change the Date and Time
C-3 Modify the Display
C-4 Adjust the Audio
C-5 Customize the Mouse and Keyboard
C-6 Add a Printer
C-7 Internet Options
C-8 Assessment—System Settings and Control Panel

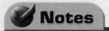

PART 5

Standards and Correlations

Every chapter in the student textbook has been correlated to ISTE's NETS·S standards and performance indicators for students. Unit correlations appear in each Unit Lesson Plan in Part 2 of this Resource Manual. For your convenience, the following pages provide comprehensive correlation charts so you can quickly see where each performance indicator and standard is met throughout the textbook.

NATIONAL EDUCATIONAL TECHNOLOGY STANDARDS FOR STUDENTS (NETS·S)

The NETS·S are divided into six broad categories:

1. Basic operations and concepts

2. Social, ethical, and human issues

3. Technology productivity tools

4. Technology communications tools

5. Technology research tools

6. Technology problem-solving and decision-making tools

Each of the six categories listed above is aligned to the performance indicators. Textbook correlations for all of the performance indicators are supplied on the following pages. The related NETS·S standard is given in parentheses after the performance indicator. For a full list of the NETS·S and performance indicators, see pages 6–11 in Part 1 of this Manual. To find out more about ISTE and the NETS·S, please visit **www.iste.org**.

NETS Performance Indicator

1. Identify capabilities and limitations of contemporary and emerging technology resources and assess the potential of these systems and services to address personal, lifelong learning, and work-place needs. (NETS·S)

Textbook Correlation

Chapter 1	3, 15–16, 20–21, 46–47, 48, 52, 53
Chapter 2	56–57, 58, 88, 96
Chapter 3	103, 104–105, 106, 110, 125, 130, 133, 136, 145, 147
Chapter 4	158, 162, 170, 172, 180, 185, 191, 193
Chapter 5	197–200, 201–202, 203, 224, 239–240, 247, 249
Chapter 6	251–252, 253, 254, 258–259, 266, 277, 283, 286, 289–290
Chapter 7	293–294, 295-296, 297, 301-302, 306-307, 324, 330
Chapter 8	333, 334–335, 346, 349, 351, 354, 359, 366, 371
Chapter 9	381, 387, 398, 400, 403
Chapter 10	407–408, 409–410, 418, 423, 426, 430, 436, 442
Appendix	497–500, 501–502, 505–506, 507
Technology Handbook	448–490

NETS Performance Indicator

2. Make informed choices among technology systems, resources, and services. (NETS·S 1, 2)

Textbook Correlation

Chapter 1	4, 15–16, 20–24, 25–29, 36–40, 46
Chapter 2	56, 59, 75, 89, 93, 96
Chapter 3	103, 105, 106, 115, 120, 125, 130, 133, 145, 147
Chapter 4	150, 152–153, 158, 172, 173, 180, 193, 194
Chapter 5	197–200, 203, 211, 240
Chapter 6	251–252, 253, 258–259, 266, 287–288, 289–290
Chapter 7	292, 293–294, 297, 321, 331, 332
Chapter 8	333, 334–335, 346, 349, 359, 372, 373, 374, 375
Chapter 9	381, 387, 398, 400, 404–405
Chapter 10	408, 410–412, 423, 426, 432, 436, 443–446
Appendix	497–500, 501–502, 507, 509–512
Technology Handbook	448–462

NETS Performance Indicator

3. Analyze advantages and disadvantages of widespread use and reliance on technology in the workplace and in society as a whole. (NETS·S 2)

Textbook Correlation

Chapter 1	3, 4, 5, 13, 16, 21, 22, 52
Chapter 2	79, 96, 97
Chapter 3	129, 130, 145, 146, 147
Chapter 4	191, 192, 193
Chapter 5	202, 224, 239, 247, 248
Chapter 6	252, 266, 269, 273, 286, 287
Chapter 7	292, 330, 331–332
Chapter 8	333, 355, 358–359, 361, 363, 366, 370, 371, 372–373
Chapter 9	381, 395, 398, 400, 403
Chapter 10	406, 413, 426, 442
Appendix	
Technology Handbook	448, 477–481, 485

NETS Performance Indicator

4. Demonstrate and advocate for legal and ethical behaviors among peers, family, and community regarding the use of technology and information. (NETS·S 2)

Textbook Correlation

Chapter 1	4, 36, 41, 43
Chapter 2	59
Chapter 3	105, 130, 147
Chapter 4	152, 153
Chapter 5	202
Chapter 6	251–252, 273, 287, 289
Chapter 7	292, 295, 330, 331–332
Chapter 8	333, 355, 358–359, 361, 363, 366, 370, 371, 372–373
Chapter 9	379
Chapter 10	409
Appendix	
Technology Handbook	480–482

NETS Performance Indicator	
5. Use technology tools and resources for managing and communicating personal/professional information (e.g., finances, schedules, addresses, purchases, correspondence). (NETS·S 3, 4)	
Textbook Correlation	
Chapter 1	7–9, 10–12, 15–19, 20–24, 25–29, 30–35, 46–47, 52, 53
Chapter 2	55, 56–57, 58–60, 61, 75–78, 88–92, 93–95, 96
Chapter 3	106–109, 110–114, 115–119, 130–132, 133–135, 145, 146–147
Chapter 4	148, 185–186, 187–188, 189–190, 191, 192–193, 194
Chapter 5	197, 224–228, 229–233, 239, 240–243, 244–246 247, 248–249
Chapter 6	251–252, 254–257, 258–260, 266–268, 273, 277–278, 286, 287–288, 289–290
Chapter 7	292, 294, 301–302, 307, 330, 331–332
Chapter 8	334–335, 346–348, 354, 358, 359–360, 361–362, 363–365, 366–370, 371, 373, 374–375
Chapter 9	381, 382–384, 385–386, 387–390, 393–394, 395–402
Chapter 10	409, 413–415, 416–417, 418–421, 423–425, 426–429, 431–435, 436–438
Appendix	507
Technology Handbook	487–490

NETS Performance Indicator

6. Evaluate technology-based options, including distance and distributed education, for lifelong learning. (NETS·S 5)

Textbook Correlation

Chapter 1	4, 5, 6, 10, 13, 15, 16, 21, 26, 30, 31, 37, 48, 49, 52, 54
Chapter 2	57, 71, 88, 89, 96, 98
Chapter 3	136, 145, 147
Chapter 4	162, 185, 191
Chapter 5	247, 249
Chapter 6	277, 286, 288
Chapter 7	324, 330, 332
Chapter 8	358, 371, 373
Chapter 9	395, 403, 405
Chapter 10	430, 442, 444
Appendix	
Tecchnology Handbook	477–486, 487–490

NETS Performance Indicator

7. Routinely and efficiently use online information resources to meet needs for collaboration, research, publications, communications, and productivity. (NETS·S 4, 5, 6)

Textbook Correlation

Chapter 1	7, 52, 53, 54
Chapter 2	61, 88, 96, 97, 98, 99, 100
Chapter 3	106, 136, 145, 146, 147
Chapter 4	154, 162, 185, 191, 192, 193, 194–195
Chapter 5	203, 239, 247, 248–249
Chapter 6	254, 277, 286, 287, 288, 289, 290
Chapter 7	297, 324, 330, 331–332
Chapter 8	337, 358, 370, 371, 372–375
Chapter 9	382, 395, 403, 404, 405
Chapter 10	410, 416, 419, 423–425, 426–429, 430, 442, 443–447
Appendix	507
Technology Handbook	483–484, 487–489

NETS Performance Indicator

8. Select and apply technology tools for research, information analysis, problem-solving, and decision-making in content learning. (NETS·S 4, 5)

Textbook Correlation

Chapter 1	31, 37, 41–45, 43–55
Chapter 2	98, 99–100
Chapter 3	126–129, 145, 146–147
Chapter 4	149–150, 150,154–158, 162–166, 167–171, 172–175, 177–179, 180–184, 186–190, 191, 192–193, 194–195
Chapter 5	234–238, 240–243, 247, 248–249
Chapter 6	250, 269–272, 273–276, 286, 287–288, 289–290
Chapter 7	317–320, 321–323, 330, 331–332
Chapter 8	337–341, 342–345, 351–353, 354–367, 370, 372–373, 374–375
Chapter 9	381, 382–384, 385–386, 387–390, 404–405
Chapter 10	409, 413–415, 416–417, 418–422, 423–425, 426–429, 433–435, 437–438
Appendix	499–500, 503–505
Technology Handbook	477–486, 487–490

NETS Performance Indicator

9. Investigate and apply expert systems, intelligent agents, and simulations in real-world situations. (NETS·S 3, 5, 6)

Textbook Correlation

Chapter 1	52, 53–54
Chapter 2	71, 79–87, 88–95, 96, 97–100
Chapter 3	110–114, 115–119, 120–124, 125–129, 130–135, 136–144, 145, 146–147
Chapter 4	151–153, 154–161, 162–171, 172–179, 180–184, 185–190, 191, 192–195
Chapter 5	211–219, 220–223, 224–228, 229–234, 239–246, 247, 248–249
Chapter 6	254–260, 261–268, 269–276, 277–285, 286, 287–290
Chapter 7	325–329, 330, 331–332
Chapter 8	334–335, 354–357, 358–359, 361, 363, 366, 370, 371, 372–375
Chapter 9	382–402, 403
Chapter 10	410–441, 442
Appendix	505
Technology Handbook	448, 477–490

NETS Performance Indicator

10. Collaborate with peers, experts, and others to contribute to content-related knowledge base by using technology to compile, synthesize, produce, and disseminate information, models, and other creative works. (NETS·S 4, 5, 6)

Textbook Correlation

Chapter 1	49–51, 54
Chapter 2	79–87, 88–95, 97–100
Chapter 3	102, 125–129, 130–135, 147
Chapter 4	148, 186–190, 193, 194–195
Chapter 5	197, 240–246–248–249
Chapter 6	250, 278–282, 288, 290
Chapter 7	292, 331–332
Chapter 8	333, 354–357, 372–373, 374–375
Chapter 9	377, 378–381, 382–384, 385–386, 387–390, 391–392, 404–405
Chapter 10	406, 410–412, 413–417, 418–422, 423–429, 430–441, 443–446
Appendix	503–513
Technology Handbook	477–486, 487–490

Every unit in the student textbook has also been correlated to the Partnership for 21st Century Skills framework. This framework updated the concepts of workplace skills based on SCANS (Secretary's Commission on Achieving Necessary Skills). Correlations for each unit appear in the Unit Lesson Plans in Part 2 of the Resource Manual. For your convenience, the following pages provide comprehensive correlation charts so you can see where each performance indicator and standard is met throughout the textbook.

21ST CENTURY SKILLS

Core Subjects

◆ Language arts

◆ Math

◆ Science

◆ Social studies

Learning Skills

◆ Information and media literacy skills

◆ Communication skills

◆ Critical thinking and systems thinking

◆ Problem identification, formulation, and solution

◆ Creativity and intellectual curiosity

◆ Interpersonal and collaborative skills

◆ Self-direction

◆ Accountability and adaptability

◆ Social responsibility

21st Century Tools

◆ Communication, information processing, and research tools

◆ Problem-solving tools

◆ Personal development and productivity tools

To find out more about The Partnership for 21st Century Skills, please visit **www.21stcenturyskills.org**.

Foundation Skills and Workplace Competencies

Today's business environment is highly competitive and demands skilled employees. Successful employees are able to deal with the varied demands of the fast-paced world of business, which requires insightful decision making, creative problem solving, and skill at interacting with diverse groups—employees, management, investors, customers, or clients.

What skills do your students need in order to prosper in the competitive workplace? In 1991, the U. S. Department of Labor released a report that identified five competencies that, in conjunction, with a three-part foundation of skills and personal qualities, lies at the heart of job performance. These Foundation Skills and Workplace Competencies were deemed essential for all workers in the rapidly changing workplace.

Foundation Skills

Basic Skills

- Reading
- Writing
- Math
- Speaking
- Listening

Personal Qualities

- Responsibility
- Self-management
- Self-esteem
- Integrity/honesty

Thinking Skills

- Creative thinking
- Decision making
- Problem solving
- Reasoning

Workplace Competencies

Resources: Identifies, organizes, plans, and allocates resources

- Allocating time
- Allocating money
- Allocating material and facility resources
- Allocating human resources

Interpersonal Skills: Works with others

- Participating as a member of a team
- Teaching others
- Serving clients/others
- Exercising leadership
- Negotiating to arrive at a decision
- Working with cultural diversity

Information: Acquires and uses information

- Acquiring information and evaluating information
- Organizing and maintaining information
- Interpreting and communicating information
- Using computers to process information

Systems: Understands complex relationships

- Understanding systems
- Monitoring and correcting performance
- Correcting systems

Technology: Works with a variety of technologies

- Selecting technology
- Applying technology to a task
- Maintaining and troubleshooting technology

Integrate 21st Century Skills

The activities and projects in Introduction to Desktop Publishing With Digital Graphics provide important real-world skills that will help students apply the skills they learn in the classroom to their lives outside of schools.

The framework provided by The Partnership for 21st Century Skills encompass crucial 21st century skills. The skills that were defined as 21st century skills encompass:

◆ **Critical Thinking/Problem-solving** Frame, analyze, and solve problems; make complex choices; understand the connections between systems; be open to new ideas; develop, implement, and communicate new ideas.

◆ **Information/Communication** Understand and create various types of oral, written, and multimedia communication; evaluate, create, and integrate information and media.

◆ **Interpersonal/Self-direction skills** Demonstrate effective teamwork and leadership; work productively with others; exercise personal responsibility; meet standards and goals; monitor one's own understanding; demonstrate ethical behavior

Skills	Technology	How Technology Reinforces Skills
Critical Thinking/ Problem-solving	Problem-solving tools (design tools, layout software)	Organizes complex information to find creative, analytical solutions
Information/ Communication	Communication, information processing, and research tools (design publications, Web page development, presentations, integrated applications)	Allows users to access, manage, evaluate, create, and communicate information
Interpersonal/ Self-direction	Personal development and productivity tools (collaboration, team projects)	Provides increased productivity for individuals and team members

At the beginning of each unit in this Teacher Resource Manual is a Planning Guide, which includes a 21st Century Skills correlation chart. This chart specifies which activities in the unit can be used to reinforce these skills.

Skills, School, and Careers

A variety of student text features provide opportunities for your students to improve foundation and workplace skills identified by the The Partnership for 21st Century Skills. The Partnership's fundamental purpose is to encourage a high-performance economy characterized by high-skill, high-wage employment.

These skills and competencies help students use the knowledge they have learned in school and apply it to all facets of their lives, including education, work, and community. Connecting education and skills development supports students in their career pursuits.

Connections Between Skills, School, and Careers

Skills	School	Career
Basic skills	Foundation for schoolwork	Foundation for work tasks
Motivation	Motivated to attend classes	Motivated to excel at work
Thinking skills	Solve case studies, equations	Solve work problems
Creativity	Creative experiments	Creative work solutions
Control of time	Homework first	Work priorities in order
Control of money	Personal budget	Departmental budgets
Writing	Writing papers	Writing reports, memos
Speeches	Oral reports	Presentations
Test taking	Tests in class	Performance reviews
Information	Selecting class information	Selecting work information
Learning	Learning for class	Learning job skills
Systems	Learning school systems	Learning organization systems
Resources	Using school resources	Using work resources
Technology	Using computers for papers or assignments	Using computers for work

21st Century Skills	
Core Subjects: Language arts, math, science, and social studies	
Textbook Correlation	
Chapter 1	3, 4, 6, 10, 15, 20, 30, 36–38, 41–46, 53–54
Chapter 2	56, 57, 60, 68–70, 75, 79, 89, 93–94, 98–100
Chapter 3	103, 105, 110–112, 117, 125–129, 130–132, 136–144, 146–147
Chapter 4	149, 150, 153, 155–157, 162–166, 167, 169–171, 186–190, 192, 193, 194–195
Chapter 5	198, 199, 202, 203–206, 211–214, 220–223, 224–228, 234–238, 240–246, 248–249
Chapter 6	251, 252, 253, 254–257, 269–272, 274–276, 287–288, 289–290
Chapter 7	293, 294, 296, 297–300, 311–314, 315–316, 318–320, 322–323, 331–332
Chapter 8	334, 335, 336, 337–341, 344–345, 349–350, 355–357, 366–370, 372–373, 374–375
Chapter 9	378, 380, 381, 387–390, 398–399, 404–405
Chapter 10	407, 408, 409, 415, 416–417, 419–422, 427–429, 437, 443–446
Appendix	491–493, 501–502
Technology Handbook	448, 477–479

21st Century Skills	
Learning Skills: Information and media literacy; communication skills; critical thinking and systems thinking; problem identification, formulation, and solution; self-direction; accountability	
Textbook Correlation	
Chapter 1	2, 3, 4, 6, 30, 36–38, 52, 53–54
Chapter 2	56, 57, 59, 60, 68–70, 93–94, 96, 97, 98–100
Chapter 3	102, 103, 104–105, 130–135, 136–144, 146–147
Chapter 4	162–166, 180–184 185–190, 192–193, 194–195
Chapter 5	197, 198, 199, 200, 202, 203–206, 211–214, 224–228, 240–246, 274, 248–249
Chapter 6	250, 251, 252, 253, 266, 278–282, 286, 287–288, 289–290
Chapter 7	292, 293, 294, 296, 297–300, 302, 311–314, 315–316, 321, 325, 330, 331–332
Chapter 8	333, 334, 335, 336, 337–341, 344–345, 349–350, 355–357, 366–370, 371, 372–373, 374–375
Chapter 9	377, 378, 379, 380, 381, 386, 387–390, 391, 392, 397, 403, 404–405
Chapter 10	406, 407, 408, 409, 415, 416–417, 419–422, 423, 427–429, 437, 442, 443–446
Appendix	491–500
Technology Handbook	447–490

21st Century Skills

21st Century Tools: Communication, information processing and research tools; problem-solving tools, personal development and productivity tools

Textbook Correlation

Chapter 1	5–6, 7, 10, 13, 15, 16, 20, 36, 46, 52, 53–54
Chapter 2	58–60, 61, 93, 96, 97–100
Chapter 3	104–105, 106–109, 115–119, 130–135, 136–139, 145
Chapter 4	151–153, 180–184, 191, 194–195
Chapter 5	198–200, 201–202, 239–243, 247, 248
Chapter 6	251–252, 253, 258–259, 266–268, 286
Chapter 7	293–294, 295–296, 297, 306, 325, 330, 332
Chapter 8	334–335, 336, 337, 359, 371
Chapter 9	377–380, 381, 382–384, 385–386
Chapter 10	406, 407–409, 423–425, 426–429, 430–435, 436–438, 445–446
Appendix	
Technology Handbook	477–486, 487–490

Foundation Skills

Basic Skills: Reading, writing, math, listening, and speaking

Textbook Correlation

Chapter 1	3, 4, 6, 30, 36–38, 53–54
Chapter 2	56, 57, 60, 68–70, 93–94, 97, 98–100
Chapter 3	103, 105, 110–112, 117, 146–147
Chapter 4	149, 150, 153, 162–166, 167, 169–171, 192–193, 194–195
Chapter 5	198, 202, 203–206, 211–214, 224–228, 240–246, 248–249
Chapter 6	251, 252, 253, 287–288, 289–290
Chapter 7	293, 294, 296, 297–300, 311–314, 315–316, 331–332
Chapter 8	334, 335, 336, 337–341, 344–345, 349–350, 355–357, 366–370, 372–373, 374–375
Chapter 9	378, 380, 381, 387–390, 398–399, 404–405
Chapter 10	407, 408, 409, 415, 416–417, 419–422, 427–429, 437, 443–446
Appendix	501–512
Technology Handbook	

Foundation Skills
Thinking Skills: Creative thinking, decision making, problem solving, and reasoning

Textbook Correlation	
Chapter 1	2, 3, 4, 6, 52, 53–54
Chapter 2	55, 56, 57, 59, 96, 97–100
Chapter 3	103, 105, 120, 130, 140, 145, 146–147
Chapter 4	148, 149, 150, 151–153, 154, 163, 167, 172–173, 181, 191, 192–193, 194–195
Chapter 5	187, 197, 199, 200, 202, 247, 248–249
Chapter 6	250, 252, 253, 266, 278–282, 286, 287–288, 289–290
Chapter 7	292, 294, 296, 302, 321, 325, 330, 331–332
Chapter 8	333, 334–335, 336, 349, 371, 372–373, 374–375
Chapter 9	377, 379, 380, 381, 386, 391, 392, 397, 403, 404–405
Chapter 10	406, 408, 409, 416–417, 419–422, 423, 427–429, 442, 443–446
Appendix	
Technology Handbook	

Foundation Skills

Personal Qualities: Self-esteem, responsibility, self-management, and integrity/honesty

Textbook Correlation

Chapter 1	4, 36, 52
Chapter 2	59, 96, 97
Chapter 3	105, 116–119, 145, 147
Chapter 4	152, 153, 191, 193
Chapter 5	198–202, 247, 248
Chapter 6	251–252, 273, 286
Chapter 7	293, 330, 331–332
Chapter 8	334, 335, 352–353, 355–357, 371, 372–373, 374–375
Chapter 9	377, 378–380, 381, 382, 384, 385–386, 399, 403, 404–405
Chapter 10	407, 409, 410-441, 443-444, 445-446
Appendix	
Technology Handbook	480, 481, 482, 483-486

Workplace Competencies

Resources: Allocate time, money, materials, facilities, and human resources

Textbook Correlation

Chapter 1	2, 4, 53, 54
Chapter 2	55, 97, 98, 99–100
Chapter 3	146–147
Chapter 4	192–193, 194–195
Chapter 5	248–249
Chapter 6	287–290
Chapter 7	331–332
Chapter 8	372–373, 374–375
Chapter 9	378–381, 382–384, 385–386, 387–390, 404–405
Chapter 10	443–446
Appendix	501–512
Technology Handbook	

Workplace Competencies	
Interpersonal: Work on teams, teach others	
Textbook Correlation	
Chapter 1	2, 52
Chapter 2	55, 96, 97, 98
Chapter 3	102, 146–147
Chapter 4	148, 192–193
Chapter 5	197, 247, 248–249
Chapter 6	250, 286, 289
Chapter 7	292, 331–332
Chapter 8	333, 372–373, 374–375
Chapter 9	377–381, 382–384, 385–386, 387–390, 391–392, 404–405
Chapter 10	406, 413–446, 443–446
Appendix	503–512
Technology Handbook	

Workplace Competencies

Information: Acquire, evaluate, organize, maintain, interpret, communicate, and use computers to process information

This standard is addressed throughout the textbook as students must use a computer to complete almost all projects in this course. However, we have provided specific references below to help highlight examples of where these skills are taught.

Textbook Correlation

Chapter 1	2–6, 53–54
Chapter 2	58–60, 97–100
Chapter 3	102–105
Chapter 4	154–189
Chapter 5	200, 240–243, 248–249
Chapter 6	252, 253, 258–259, 266, 278–282
Chapter 7	294–296, 302
Chapter 8	335–336
Chapter 9	404–405
Chapter 10	423, 436, 445–446
Appendix	495–500, 503–506, 507–508, 509–512
Technology Handbook	447–490

Workplace Competencies

Systems: Understand, monitor, correct, improve, and design systems

Textbook Correlation

Chapter 1	2, 3, 4, 52
Chapter 2	55, 96
Chapter 3	103, 104–105
Chapter 4	149–150, 151–153, 162–166, 174–176, 177–179
Chapter 5	197, 198–200, 240
Chapter 6	258–259, 266–268, 278, 293–294
Chapter 7	293–294
Chapter 8	333, 334–335, 358, 359–360, 361–362, 363–365, 366–370
Chapter 9	377, 378–380, 381–384, 385–386, 387–390, 395–398
Chapter 10	406, 407–408, 409
Appendix	497–500, 501–502
Technology Handbook	447–490

Workplace Competencies

Technology: Select, apply, maintain, and troubleshoot technology
This standard is addressed throughout the textbook as students must use a computer to complete almost all projects in this course. However, we have provided specific references below to help highlight examples of where these skills are taught.

Textbook Correlation

Chapter 1	5–6, 16, 49, 53–54
Chapter 2	58–60, 97–100
Chapter 3	103, 107, 109, 110, 112, 114, 116, 130–135, 140, 146–147
Chapter 4	173, 180, 189, 192–193, 194–195
Chapter 5	199, 200, 205, 207, 208, 211, 220, 224–228, 240–243
Chapter 6	253, 254, 258–259, 266–268, 269, 287–290
Chapter 7	294, 296, 300, 301, 302, 307, 322, 331–332
Chapter 8	334, 335, 336, 338, 342, 346, 349, 354, 372–374
Chapter 9	381, 387–389, 404–405
Chapter 10	443–446, 423, 432, 436
Appendix	500, 501–502, 507
Technology Handbook	447–490

Notes

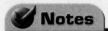
Notes

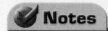
Notes

Notes

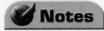
Notes

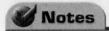